American Culture in the 1930s

Twentieth-Century American Culture
Series editor: Martin Halliwell, University of Leicester

This series provides accessible but challenging studies of American culture in the twentieth century. Each title covers a specific decade and offers a clear overview of its dominant cultural forms and influential texts, discussing their historical impact and cultural legacy. Collectively the series reframes the notion of 'decade studies' through the prism of cultural production and rethinks the ways in which decades are usually periodized. Broad contextual approaches to the particular decade are combined with focused case studies, dealing with themes of modernity, commerce, freedom, power, resistance, community, race, class, gender, sexuality, internationalism, technology, war and popular culture.

American Culture in the 1910s
Mark Whalan

American Culture in the 1920s
Susan Currell

American Culture in the 1930s
David Eldridge

American Culture in the 1940s
Jacqueline Foertsch

American Culture in the 1950s
Martin Halliwell

American Culture in the 1960s
Sharon Monteith

American Culture in the 1970s
Will Kaufman

American Culture in the 1980s
Graham Thompson

American Culture in the 1990s
Colin Harrison

American Culture in the 1930s

David Eldridge

Edinburgh University Press

© David Eldridge, 2008

Edinburgh University Press Ltd
22 George Square, Edinburgh

Typeset in 11/13 pt Stempel Garamond by
Servis Filmsetting Ltd, Stockport, Cheshire, and
printed and bound in Great Britain by
CPI Antony Rowe Ltd, Chippenham, Wilts

A CIP record for this book is available from the British Library

ISBN 978 0 7486 2258 0 (hardback)
ISBN 978 0 7486 2259 7 (paperback)

The right of David Eldridge to be identified as author of this work
has been asserted in accordance with the Copyright, Designs and Patents Act 1988.

Published with the support of the Edinburgh University Scholarly Publishing Initiatives Fund.

Contents

Figures

Case Studies

Acknowledgements

I wish to thank all those who have helped me to construct this project, including Steve Leiken, Edward Gottlieb, Jordan Karney at the Mary Ryan Gallery, Joy and Ned Norris at RUSC.com, Jeff Mennel and my parents, Martin and Lesley Eldridge. I am grateful to the University of Hull for allowing me leave to develop the manuscript, and to my colleagues John Osborne, Laura Rattray, Ed Abramson, Sylvia Tynan and especially Jenel Virden for supporting and encouraging me. Thanks also to Nicola Ramsey at Edinburgh University Press and Series Editor, Martin Halliwell; without Martin's advice, aid and patience this book may never have made it. I dedicate this book to my partner, Richard McBain, who more than anyone will be glad to see it in print.

Chronology of 1930s American Culture

Date	Events	Criticism	Literature	Performance
1930	Worldwide economic depression deepens. Unemployment rate climbs from 3.2 per cent to 8.7 per cent. Chrysler Building opened (27 May). Smoot-Hawley Tariff raises duties prompting sharp decline in international trade (17 June). Last Allied troops leave the Rhineland (30 June). New York police battle Communists in Union Square riot (1 August). Hitler's Nazi Party emerges as majority party in German national elections (September). 1,300 banks close, including New York City's Bank of the United States (December).	John Dewey, *Individualism Old and New* The Twelve Southerners, *I'll Take My Stand* Mike Gold, 'Wilder: The Genteel Christ', *New Republic* (22 October)	Sinclair Lewis first American to win Nobel Prize for Literature (November) US customs officials seize James Joyce's *Ulysses* as obscene Edward Dahlberg, *The Bottom Dogs* John Dos Passos, *The 42nd Parallel* William Faulkner, *As I Lay Dying* Mike Gold, *Jews Without Money* Dashiell Hammett, *The Maltese Falcon*	Maxwell Anderson, *Elizabeth the Queen* Marc Connelly, *Green Pastures* George and Ira Gershwin score *Girl Crazy* (272 performances)
1931	Unemployment rises to 16 per cent. 'Scottsboro Boys' convicted and sentenced to death (April). Empire State Building opened (1 May). Japanese troops invade China and seize Manchuria (September). US Steel announces 10 per cent cut in wages (October). Al Capone sentenced to 11 years for income tax evasion (17 October).	Constance Rourke, *American Humor: A Study of the National Character* Theodore Dreiser, *Tragic America* James Truslow Adams, *The Epic of America* Frederick Lewis Allen, *Only Yesterday: An Informal History of the 1920s* Edmund Wilson, *Axel's Castle*	Pearl Buck, *The Good Earth* William Faulkner, *Sanctuary* Ogden Nash, *Hard Lines* Willa Cather, *Shadows on the Rock* Stephen Vincent Benet, *Ballads and Poems* Laura Ingalls Wilder, *Little House on the Prairie* First appearance of *Dick Tracy* comic strip by Chester Gould	Group Theatre founded Eugene O'Neill, *Mourning Becomes Electra*

Film	Radio	Music	Art and Design
Production Code adopted (31 March) Workers Film and Photography League founded *All Quiet on the Western Front* (Lewis Milestone) *Anna Christie* (Clarence Brown) *Hell's Angels* (Howard Hawks) *The Big Trail* (Raoul Walsh) *Whoopee!* (Samuel Goldwyn)	David Sarnoff becomes RCA president (3 January) *Amos 'n' Andy* reaches an audience of 40 million CBS begin broadcasts of New York Philharmonic, conducted by Toscanini *Little Orphan Annie* (1930–6) *The Shadow* (1930–54) *American School of the Air* (1930–48)	Cab Calloway, *Minnie the Moocher* Hoagy Carmichael and Stuart Gorrell, *Georgia on My Mind* Lorentz Hart and Richard Rogers, *Ten Cents a Dance* Bing Crosby releases *An Album of Cowboy Songs*	Edward Hopper, *House by the Railroad,* first painting to enter MoMA's permanent art collection Grant Wood, *American Gothic,* exhibited at Art Institute of Chicago Thomas Hart Benton, *America Today* murals installed at New School for Social Research Aaron Douglas paints murals for Fiske University Plans submitted for Rockefeller Center (15 June)
Cimarron (Wesley Ruggles) *City Lights* (Charlie Chaplin) *Dracula* (Tod Browning) *Frankenstein* (James Whale) *Little Caesar* (Mervyn LeRoy) *Monkey Business* (Marx Bros/Norman McLeod) *The Public Enemy* (William Wellman)	Educators campaign for Fess Bill, to reserve channels for education *March of Time* begins on CBS *Pittsburgh Courier* launches campaign against *Amos 'n' Andy* CBS ends sponsorship of Father Coughlin's broadcasts Bing Crosby makes solo radio debut on CBS	Hoover signs Act making *The Star-Spangled Banner* official national anthem (March) Duke Ellington has hit with *Mood Indigo* Rudy Vallee records *Life is Just a Bowl of Cherries* Howard Dietz and Arthur Schwartz, *Dancing in the Dark*	Georgia O'Keefe, *Cow's Skull: Red, White and Blue* Grant Wood, *The Midnight Ride of Paul Revere* Whitney Museum of American Art opens in New York First *Annual of American Design*

Date	Events	Criticism	Literature	Performance
1932	Unemployment at thirteen million; monthly wages for those in work are at 60 per cent of 1929 levels. Reconstruction Finance Corporation established (22 January). Baby son of Charles Lindbergh abducted (1 March). Wisconsin passes first unemployment insurance law in US. Bonus Army of First World War veterans march on Congress (May–July). Amelia Earhart is first woman to fly solo across the Atlantic (20 May). New York Mayor, Jimmy Walker, resigns following corruption investigations (1 September). American Communist Party nominates William Foster for president. Frankie Lane and Ruthie Smith set dance marathon record of 3,501 hours (19 October). Franklin D. Roosevelt elected president pledging a 'new deal for the American people' (8 November).	League of Professional Groups for Foster and Ford, *Culture and the Crisis* Stuart Chase, *A New Deal* Charles Beard (ed.), *America Faces the Future* Edmund Wilson, *The America Jitters* Reinhold Neibuhr, *Moral Man and Immoral Society*	James Farrell, *Young Lonigan* John Dos Passos, *1919* Ernest Hemingway, *Death in the Afternoon* Dashiell Hammett, *The Third Man* Damon Runyon, *Guys and Dolls* Erskine Caldwell, *Tobacco Road*	Radio City Musical Hall opens in New York (27 December) Lynn Riggs, *The Cherokee Night* Langston Hughes, *Scottboro Limited*

Film	Radio	Music	Art and Design
A Farewell to Arms (Frank Borzage) *American Madness* (Frank Capra) *Freaks* (Tod Browning) *Grand Hotel* (Edmund Goulding) *I am a Fugitive From a Chain Gang* (Mervyn LeRoy) *Scarface* (Howard Hawks) *Tarzan, the Ape Man* (W. S. Van Dyke) Walt Disney awarded special Oscar for Mickey Mouse	*The Jack Benny Show* (1932–55) *Lum and Abner* (1932–54) *Vic and Sade* (1932–57) *The Al Jolson Show* (1932–49) *Ed Sullivan Show* begins on CBS Walter Winchell goes on air for NBC RCA demonstrates electronic TV using cathode-ray picture tube receiver	Jack Yellen, *Happy Days Are Here Again,* adopted by Democratic Party *Americana* revue features 'Brother, Can You Spare a Dime?' Cole Porter scores *The Gay Divorce,* including song 'Night and Day' Duke Ellington, *It Don't Mean a Thing If It Ain't Got That Swing* Louis Armstrong has hit with *All of Me*	Ben Shahn, *The Passion of Sacco and Vanzetti* Grant Wood, *Daughters of the American Revolution* John Steuart Curry, *The Tornado* Stuart Davis, *Men Without Women* Group f/64 founded in San Francisco Lewis Hines publishes *Men at Work* Norman Bel Geddes publishes *Horizons* Frank Lloyd Wright publishes *Autobiography* and *Disappearing City* Philadelphia Savings Fund Society skyscraper (George Howe and William Lescaze)

Date	Events	Criticism	Literature	Performance
1933	Adolf Hitler appointed as Chancellor of Germany (30 January). Nazis burn the Reichstag building and accuse Communists of setting the fire (27 February). Inauguration of President Roosevelt (4 March). FDR declares national bank holiday, restoring public confidence in banks. New Deal launched with 'First Hundred Days' of intensive legislative activity, including the Emergency Banking Relief Act, Federal Emergency Relief Administration, Agricultural Adjustment Act, the Tennessee Valley Authority, the National Recovery Administration and the Public Works Administration. Frances Perkins, Secretary of Labor, becomes first woman cabinet member. Chicago World's Fair opens (May). Arts projects sponsored by Civil Works Administration. Prohibition is repealed (5 December).	Gilbert Seldes, *The Years of the Locust* Granville Hicks, *The Great Tradition* Rexford Tugwell, *The Industrial Discipline and the Governmental Arts* Sidney Hook, *Toward the Understanding of Karl Marx* Seward Collins, 'Monarch as Alternative', *The American Review* Max Eastman, 'Artists in Uniform,' *Modern Quarterly*	Hervey Allen, *Anthony Adverse* Erskine Caldwell, *God's Little Acre* Josephine Herbst, *Pity Is Not Enough* Gertrude Stein, *The Autobiography of Alice B. Toklas* Jack Conroy, *The Disinherited*	Lincoln Kirstein and George Balanchine found School of American Ballet Eugene O'Neill, *Ah Wilderness* Irving Berlin scores *As Thousands Cheer* (400 performances)

Film	Radio	Music	Art and Design
RKO declares itself bankrupt	Roosevelt's first 'fireside chat'	Jimmie Rodgers dies (26 May)	Hopper receives solo exhibition at MoMA
42nd Street, Gold Diggers of 1933 and *Footlight Parade*, choreographed by Busby Berkeley and released by Warner Bros.	Alexander Woollcott, *Town Crier* (1933–8) *The Lone Ranger* (1933–54) *Ma Perkins* (1933–49) *National Barn Dance* (1933–50)	Roy Harris, *Symphony: 1933* Irving Berlin, *Easter Parade* Duke Ellington, *Sophisticated Lady*	John Reed Club exhibition, *The Social Viewpoint in Art* (February) Work halted on Diego Rivera's Rockefeller Center mural (22 May)
Baby Face (Alfred Green)	*The Romance of Helen Trent* (1933–60)	Ethel Waters records *Stormy Weather*	Margaret Bourke-White creates
Duck Soup (Marx Brothers/Leo McCarey)	Newspapers Associated Press to cut news service to radio	Jimmy and Tommy Dorsey form jazz orchestra	photomurals for NBC studios
King Kong (Merian C. Cooper)	Edwin Armstrong patents frequency	Frank Churchill composes *Who's Afraid of the Big Bad Wolf* for	Dorothea Lange, *The White Angel Breadline* Unveiling of
Little Women (George Cukor)	modulation (FM) broadcasting	Disney Gene Autry records	streamlined Burlington *Zephyr* and Union-
Mae West stars in *She Done Him Wrong*		*The Last Round-Up*	Pacific M-100,000 at Chicago World's Fair
State Fair (Henry King)			Public Works of Art Project created
Three Little Pigs (Walt Disney)			(December)

Date	Events	Criticism	Literature	Performance
1934	New Deal continues with Federal Housing Administration, Federal Farm Mortgage Corporation and Securities and Exchange Commission. Roosevelt initiates 'Good Neighbor Policy' with Latin American nations (March). General strike in San Francisco in support of 12,000 striking dock workers (May). 'Public Enemy No. 1', John Dillinger shot and killed by FBI (22 July). Hitler becomes Fuhrer of Germany (19 August). Mao Tse-tung begins 'Long March' (October).	Ruth Benedict, *Patterns of Culture* Lewis Corey, *The Decline of American Capitalism* Malcolm Cowley, *Exile's Return* John Dewey, *Art as Experience* John Dewey, 'Why I am Not a Communist' in *Modern Quarterly* James Rorty, *Our Master's Voice* George Soule, *The Coming American Revolution* Henry Wallace, *New Frontiers* *Partisan Review* published through New York John Reed Club	Henry Miller, *Tropic of Cancer*, banned in the US, published in Paris James Cain, *The Postman Always Rings Twice* James Farrell, *The Young Manhood of Studs Lonigan* F. Scott Fitzgerald, *Tender is the Night* Langston Hughes, *The Ways of White Folk* Zora Neale Hurston, *Mules and Men* Henry Roth, *Call It Sleep* William Saroyan, *The Daring Young Man on the Flying Trapeze* Daniel Fuchs, *Summer in Williamsburg*	Theatre Union founded Lillian Hellman, *The Children's Hour* Maxwell Anderson, *Valley Forge* Samuel Raphaelson, *Accent on Youth* Virgil Thomson and Gertrude Stein, *Four Saints in Three Acts* Cole Porter scores *Anything Goes* (420 performances)

Film	Radio	Music	Art and Design
Paramount faces bankruptcy Joseph Breen appointed to run Production Code Administration (6 July) Legion of Decency orchestrated *Cleopatra* (Cecil B. DeMille) *It Happened One Night* (Frank Capra) *Little Women* (George Cukor) *Our Daily Bread* (King Vidor) *The Thin Man* (W. S. Van Dyke) Shirley Temple sings 'On the Good Ship Lollipop' in *Bright Eyes* Louis de Rochemont begins *March of Time* newsreels	Communications Act establishes regulatory Federal Communications Commission (June) Mutual Broadcasting System creates new network (15 September) Father Charles Coughlin, a rising force in radio, forms National Union for Social Justice (11 November) Arch Oboler, *Light's Out* (1934–47) *Lux Radio Theatre* (1934–55) *Ford Sunday Evening Hour* (1934–46)	Benny Goodman organizes swing band, recording *Moon Glow* John Lomax publishes *American Ballads and Folk Songs* Aaron Copland, *El Salon Mexico* George Gershwin, *Variations on 'I Got Rhythm'* Richard Rodgers and Lorenz Hart, *Blue Moon* Guy Lombardo records *Winter Wonderland* The Carter Family record *Can the Circle Be Unbroken*	Paul Cadmus, *The Fleets In!* removed from Corcoran Gallery (April) Controversy over PWAP murals for Coit Tower, San Francisco (July–August) Paul Manship sculpts Prometheus Fountain in Rockefeller Center Associated American Artists formed Artists Union publishes *Art Front* (1934–7) Joe Jones, *Social Protest in Old St Louis* Aaron Douglas, *Aspects of Negro Life* Raphael Soyer, *In the City Park* *Time* devotes cover story to 'The American Scene' (December)

Date	Events	Criticism	Literature	Performance
1935	Unemployment falls to 20 per cent. Harlem Race Riot (March). Hitler renounces Versailles Treaty (March). Soil Conservation Service established to solve the problem of soil erosion in the Dust Bowl (April). Works Progress Administration established (6 May). Supreme Court rules the National Recovery Act unconstitutional (27 May). National Labor Relations Board established (5 July). Congress passes Social Security Act providing unemployment compensation and old-age retirement insurance (15 August). Comintern calls for a Popular Front of democracies to combat Fascism (20 August). Huey Long assassinated (10 September). German Jews stripped of rights by Nuremberg race laws (September). Italian forces invade Ethiopia (October).	Rexford Tugwell, *The Battle for Democracy* Grant Wood, 'Revolt Against the City' Hadley Cantril and Gordon Allport, *The Psychology of Radio* Sherwood Anderson, *Puzzled America*	Federal Writers' Project (FWP) established, directed by Henry Alsberg (27 July) Granville Hicks and Mike Gold, *Proletarian Literature in the United States* James Farrell, *Judgment*, concludes the Studs Lonigan trilogy Horace McCoy, *They Shoot Horses, Don't They?* John O'Hara, *Butterfield 8* John Steinbeck, *Tortilla Flat*	Federal Theatre Project (FTP) established, directed by Hallie Flanagan (27 August) Maxwell Anderson, *Winterset*, poetic drama based on Sacco and Vanzetti case Clifford Odets publishes *Waiting for Lefty* and *Awake and Sing* Robert Sherwood, *The Petrified Forest* George Gershwin and Dubose Heyward, *Porgy and Bess* opens in New York (10 October, 124 performances)

Film	Radio	Music	Art and Design
Twentieth Century-Fox formed through merger (31 May)	Hauptman trial verdict broadcast from New Jersey (13 February)	Federal Music Project (FMP) established, directed by Nikolai Solokoff	John Reed Clubs and NAACP sponsor 'anti-lynching' art exhibitions (February–March)
Nykino documentary film group formed	Federal Radio Education Committee formed (December)	FMP Composer-Forum Laboratories begin	Roy Stryker establishes photographic project of the Resettlement Administration's Historical Section (July)
A Night at the Opera (Sam Wood)	*Backstage Wife* (1935–59)	Roy Harris, *A Farewell to Pioneers*	
Black Fury (Michael Curtiz)	*Cavalcade of America* (1935–53)	Woody Guthrie writes *Dusty, Old Dust (So Long, It's Been Good to Know Ya)*	Federal Art Project (FAP) established, directed by Holger Cahill (29 August)
The Bride of Frankenstein (James Whale)	Fred Allen, *Town Hall Tonight* (1935–40)	Fred Astaire and Ginger Rogers record *Cheek to Cheek* by Irving Berlin	Treasure Relief Art Project established
David Copperfield (George Cukor)	*Fibber McGee and Molly* (1935–56)		
The Informer (John Ford)	*Your Hit Parade* (1935–59)	Cole Porter records *You're the Top*	Harry Sternberg, *Southern Holiday*
G-Men (William Keighley)			Frank Lloyd Wright designs Fallingwater
Mutiny on the Bounty (Frank Lloyd Wright)			John Reed Clubs disbanded (December)
Top Hat (Mark Sandrich)			

Date	Events	Criticism	Literature	Performance
1936	Government expenditures push national debt to $34 billion. Boulder Dam is completed (1 March). German troops reoccupy the Rhineland (7 March). Spanish Civil War begins (17 July). First of Stalin's 'purge' trials of counter-revolutionaries opens (19 August). Roosevelt elected for second term in landslide victory (4 November). Edward VIII abdicates as king of England (10 December). Outbreak of sit-down strikes (winter 1936–7).	Lewis Corey, *The Crisis of the Middle Class* Lawrence Dennis, *The Coming American Fascism* Sidney Hook, *From Hegel to Marx* Howard Kershner, *The Menace of Roosevelt and His Policies* Henry Luce publishes *Life* magazine James Farrell, *A Note on Literary Criticism* Gilbert Seldes, *Mainland* Joseph Freeman, *An American Testament* Herbert Agar and Allen Tate (eds), *Who Owns America?* Walter Benjamin, 'The Work of Art in the Age of Mechanical Production', published in German Theodor Adorno, 'On Jazz', published in German	John Dos Passos, *The Big Money*, completes his *U.S.A.* trilogy Robert Frost, *A Further Range* wins him the Pulitzer Prize Walter Edmonds, *Drums Along the Mohawk* William Faulkner, *Absalom, Absalom!* Margaret Mitchell, *Gone With the Wind* John Steinbeck, *In Dubious Battle*	Eugene O'Neill, first American playwright to win Nobel Prize for Literature FTP premieres Sinclair Lewis *It Can't Happen Here* and US premier of T. S. Eliot's *Murder in the Cathedral* *Triple-A Plowed Under* is FTP's first Living Newspaper Orson Welles directs all-black cast in *Macbeth* for FTP George Kaufman and Moss Hart, *You Can't Take It With You* Robert Sherwood, *Idiot's Delight* Clare Boothe Luce, *The Women*

Film	Radio	Music	Art and Design
Irving Thalberg dies of pneumonia (14 September) *Charge of the Light Brigade* (Michael Curtiz) *Modern Times* (Charlie Chaplin) *Mr Deeds Goes to Town* (Frank Capra) *San Francisco* (W. S. Van Dyke) *Swing Time* (George Stevens) *The Plow That Broke the Plains* (Pare Lorentz, scored by Virgil Thomson) Frontier Films established	Republican Party produces *Liberty at the Crossroads* *Columbia Workshop* begins H. V. Kaltenborn describes battle of Irun *Rise of the Goldbergs* moves to CBS *The Green Hornet* (1936–52) *Raymond Gram Swing* (1936–51) Camel Caravan features Benny Goodman, 'Swing School' (1936–9)	*Billboard* publishes first Hit Parade (4 January) Benny Goodman first leader to racially integrate his band when he hires Teddy Wilson and Lionel Hampton Bing Crosby records *Pennies From Heaven* Billie Holiday records *Summertime* Tommy Dorsey records *The Music Goes Round and Round* Jerome Kern and, Dorothy Fields publish *A Fine Romance*	First American Artists' Congress meets in New York American Abstract Artists formed (November) MoMA stages *Fantastic Art: Dada and Surrealism* (December) Dorothea Lange, *Migrant Mother* Margaret Bourke-White, *Fort Peck Dam* Thomas Hart Benton, *The Social History of Missouri* Reginald Marsh, *Twenty Cent Movie* Ben Shahn creates New Jersey Homestead mural Frank Lloyd Wright designs Johnson Wax Headquarters

Date	Events	Criticism	Literature	Performance
1937	Unemployment falls to 14 per cent. Roosevelt's plans to enlarge the Supreme Court are opposed by Congress. Flint, Michigan sit-down strike settled (14 February). General Franco declares Spain a totalitarian state (20 April). 'Memorial Day Massacre' at Republic Steel in Chicago (30 May). Dirigible *Hindenburg* explodes at Lakehurst, NJ (6 May). Neville Chamberlain becomes British Prime Minister (28 May). Farm Security Administration created when Resettlement Administration is moved to Department of Agriculture.	Walter Lippmann, *The Good Society* Robert and Helen Lynd, *Middletown in Transition* Erskine Caldwell and Margaret Bourke-White, *You Have Seen Their Faces* Philip Rahv and William Philips relaunch *Partisan Review* Thomas Hart Benton, *The Artist in America* Dale Carnegie, *How to Win Friends and Influence People* Karen Horney, *The Neurotic Personality of Our Times*	Zora Neale Hurston, *Their Eyes Were Watching God* John Steinbeck, *Of Mice and Men* Richard Wright, *Uncle Tom's Children* FWP publishes *American Stuff*	Clifford Odets, *Golden Boy* Paul Green, *The Lost Colony* *Pins and Needles* revue staged by International Ladies Garment Workers Union (1,108 performances) Richard Rodgers and Lorentz Hart, *Babes in Arms* (289 performances) Orson Welles, anti-fascist production of *Julius Caesar* Marc Blitzstein, *The Cradle Will Rock* Power, FTP Living Newspaper FTP sponsors Helen Tamiris, *How Long Brethren*

Film	Radio	Music	Art and Design
Snow White and the Seven Dwarfs (Walt Disney) *The Awful Truth* (Leo McCarey) *Way Out West* (Laurel and Hardy/ James Horne) *The Life of Emile Zola* (William Dieterle) *The Good Earth* (Sidney Franklin) *Dead End* (William Wyler) *A Star is Born* (William Wellman) *The Spanish Earth* (Joris Ivens)	NBC Symphony Orchestra formed with Arturo Toscanini as conductor (1937–54) Archibald MacLeish, *The Fall of the City* (April) Aaron Copland, *Music for Radio* premieres on CBS *Edgar Bergen and Charlie McCarthy* (1937–56), Mae West's 'Adam and Eve' sketch creates scandal *Mary Margaret McBride* (1937–54) *The Tommy Dorsey Show* (1937–47) Woody Guthrie broadcasts on Los Angeles KFVD (1937–9)	Artie Shaw forms swing band featuring Billie Holiday as vocalist Count Basie records *One O'Clock Jump* Richard Rodgers and Lorenz Hart, *The Lady is a Tramp*	Solomon R. Guggenheim Museum founded in New York (21 October), with Frank Lloyd Wright commissioned as architect Sponsored by FAP, Berenice Abbott, *Changing New York* is exhibited (October) Philip Evergood, *American Tragedy* Philip Guston, *Bombardment* Isaac Soyer, *Employment Agency* New Bauhaus School of Design founded in Chicago

Date	Events	Criticism	Literature	Performance
1938	Congress of Industrial Organizations breaks from American Federation of Labor. Germany announces *Anschluss* with Austria (March). House Committee Un-American Activities established by Congress (May). Temporary National Economic Committee established to investigate monopolies and price fixing (16 June). Congress passes Fair Labor Standards Act (23 June). Munich Agreement permits German occupation of the Sudetenland (30 September). Racehorse 'Seabiscuit' beats 'War Admiral' (1 November). Republicans gain seats in Congress during elections for first time since 1928.	Thurman Arnold, *The Folklore of Capitalism* Max Lerner, *It's Later Than You Think* Cleanth Brooks and Robert Penn Warren, *Understanding Poetry* Howard Odum and Harry Estill Moore, *American Regionalism* Constance Rourke, *Charles Sheeler: Artist in the American Tradition*	Pearl Buck receives Nobel Prize for Literature Ernest Hemingway, 'The Snows of Kilimanjaro' Muriel Rukeyser, *The Book of the Dead* Archibald MacLeish, *Land of the Free* Edith Wharton, *The Buccaneers* Kenneth Roberts, *Northwest Passage* Superman appears in *Action Comics*, No. 1	Playwrights' Producing Company formed Thornton Wilder, *Our Town* Robert Sherwood, *Abe Lincoln in Illinois* *Hellzapoppin'* revue opens (22 September, 1,404 performances) FTP presents *One-Third of a Nation*

Film	Radio	Music	Art and Design
Pare Lorentz, *The River* released *Bringing Up Baby* (Howard Hawks) *My Man Godfrey* (Gregory La Cava) *In Old Chicago* (Henry King) *The Adventures of Robin Hood* (Michael Curtiz) *Blockade* (William Dieterle) *Jezebel* (William Wyler) *The City* (Willard Van Dyke and Ralph Steiner) United States Film Service created	Ed Murrow describes annexation of Austria (March) Joe Louis's defeat of Max Schmeling broadcast by NBC (22 June) Munich Crisis covered by H. V. Kaltenborn (September) Orson Welles, *War of the Worlds* broadcast causes panic (31 October) CBS buys Columbia Records *The Bob Hope Show* (1938–58) *Stella Dallas* (1938–55) Norman Corwin, *Words Without Music* (1938–41)	Benny Goodman's Carnegie Hall concert (16 January) Glenn Miller Orchestra formed (March) John Hammond presents *From Spirituals to Swing* at Carnegie Hall (December) Aaron Copland composes *Billy the Kid* Roy Harris composes *Symphony No. 3* Ella Fitzgerald achieves fame with *A-Tisket A-Tasket* Artie Shaw records Cole Porter's *Begin the Beguine* Roy Rogers records *Hi-Yo Silver*	Walker Evans, *American Photographs* retrospective at MoMA Stuart Davis, *Swing Landscape* Museum of Modern Art completed

Date	Events	Criticism	Literature	Performance
1939	FDR asks Congress for $535 million defence appropriation (12 January). Golden Gate International Exposition in San Francisco opens (25 February). Supreme Court rules sit-down strikes illegal (27 February). Nazi troops take Czechoslovakia (March). New York World's Fair opens (20 April). Nazi–Soviet Non-Aggression Pact (23 August). Hitler invades Poland, bringing about the start of the Second World War in Europe (1–3 September).	John Dewey, *Freedom and Culture* Clement Greenberg, 'Avant-Garde and Kitsch' Perry Miller, *The New England Mind* Raymond Moley, *After Seven Years* Robert Lynd, *Knowledge for What?* Margaret Thorp, *America at the Movies* Lewis Jacobs, *The Rise of the American Film* Dorothea Lange and Paul Schuster, *An American Exodus: A Record of Human Erosion*	John Dos Passos, *Adventures of a Young Man* Carl Sandburg, *Abraham Lincoln: The War Years* John Steinbeck, *The Grapes of Wrath* James Thurber, 'The Secret Life of Walter Mitty' Nathanael West, *The Day of the Locust* Katharine Anne Porter, *Pale Horse, Pale Rider* Robert Frost, *Collected Poems*	FTP abolished by Congress (30 June) Philip Barry, *The Philadelphia Story* William Saroyan, *The Time of Your Life* Lillian Hellman, *The Little Foxes* Eugene O'Neill, *The Iceman Cometh* Maxwell Anderson, *Key Largo* Joseph Kesselring, *Arsenic and Old Lace* George Kaufmann and Moss Hart, *The Man Who Came to Dinner*

Film	Radio	Music	Art and Design
David O. Selznick's premiere of *Gone With the Wind* *The Wizard of Oz* (Mervyn LeRoy) *You Can't Take It With You* (Frank Capra) *Mr Smith Goes to Washington* (Frank Capra) *Ninotchka* (Ernst Lubitsch) *Stagecoach* (John Ford) *The Roaring Twenties* (Raoul Walsh) *Confessions of a Nazi Spy* (Anatole Litvak) *Young Mr Lincoln* (John Ford) MoMA retrospective on 'The Non-Fiction Film'	RCA television demonstration at New York World's Fair (April) Armstrong completes FM station at Alpine, New Jersey Roosevelt delivers 'fireside chat' on the German invasion of Poland (3 September) National Association of Broadcasters introduced new rules to end Coughlin's access to airwaves (15 October) *Ballad for Americans* sung by Paul Robeson on CBS (5 November) *The Adventures of Ellery Queen* (1939–48) *The Milton Berle Show* (1939–48) *I Love a Mystery* (1939–52)	Kate Smith records *God Bless America* by Irving Berlin Elie Seigmeister forms American Ballad Singers Billie Holiday, *Strange Fruit* Judy Garland, *Over the Rainbow* Glenn Miller, *Moonlight Serenade* Harry James hires Frank Sinatra as lead vocalist Leadbelly records *The Bourgeois Blues*	Metropolitan Museum presents *Three Hundred Years of American Painting* Edward Hopper, *Cape Cod Evening* and *New York Movie* Treasury Section stages '48 States Competition' for post office murals Face of Theodore Roosevelt dedicated on Mount Rushmore, sculpted by Gutzon Borglum Norman Bel Geddes designs *Futurama* exhibit for New York World's Fair

The Intellectual Context

With the Wall Street Crash in late October 1929 and the Japanese attack on Pearl Harbor in December 1941, most accounts of American history present 'the thirties' as a decade with ready-made 'bookends': two shocking events which underscore the unremittingly traumatic nature of the intervening years. As a financial event, the Crash serves as a symbolic watershed, ending the prosperity of the 'Roaring Twenties' and putting economic history at the very centre of ensuing narratives (even if the stock market collapse did not cause the Depression itself). On this account Pearl Harbor marks the resolution of the crisis, in the sense that the war economy restored prosperity to the United States. It also denotes a new age of international engagement after a decade focused on domestic problems, and the end of a period of social reform as President Franklin Delano Roosevelt went from being 'Dr New Deal' to 'Dr Win-the-War'. Like any decade, of course, the very notion of 'the thirties' is a *post facto* construct, an abstraction of more symbolic freight and critical convenience than a reflection of genuine historical experience. The effort to categorize that decade with a central theme is likewise only ever an effort to impose an 'orienting sense of cohesion and unity' on the 'inconsistencies, tensions and cacophony of voices' that constitute the complexity of any given moment in time.[1] Yet despite awareness of how simplistic and problematic the construct is, the fundamental narrative of the United States in the 1930s remains that of the Great Depression.

Never before had Americans encountered such a widespread economic failure. Of course, the Depression did not become 'Great' until 1931 or so; what began in the summer of 1929 was at first regarded as an ordinary recession. Unemployment may have risen to 4.3 million by 1930, but this still seemed less significant than the previous recession of 1921 when the jobless had numbered 4.9 million and gross national product (GNP) had fallen by 24 per cent. The stock market crash had been a major shock: from 23 October to the middle of November, some $26 billion in paper values evaporated, with the $16.4 million loss on 'Black Thursday' (29 October) setting a record that lasted for almost forty years. Nevertheless, many commentators at the time saw even this as an unalarming correction to an abnormal bubble of giddy speculation and, contrary to the popular image, relatively few individual investors were affected directly, with only 2.5 per cent of the population owning stock. Indeed, it was not until late 1930 that the crisis really became apparent, when mobs of depositors descended on banks in Kentucky, Illinois and Missouri to withdraw their savings in cash and gold, leading 600 banks to collapse in just sixty days. The cause of this great loss of confidence has never been entirely certain, though many commercial banks had been blighted by the Crash having financed loans for stock speculation at the height of the 1920s boom. Whatever the reason though, 1,000 banks had failed by the end of the year, and a series of further panics practically shut down the American banking system by 1933.

The consequences were tumultuous. The failure of 5,000 banks cost thousands of people their life savings, wiping out $7 billion in deposits. Struggling to preserve liquidity, other banks sold off stocks (further depressing the market), called in loans and accelerated foreclosures on anyone who did not keep up with their mortgage payments. One hundred and fifty thousand homeowners lost their properties in 1930, followed by 200,000 more in 1931 and 250,000 in 1932. Business investment plummeted as well, from $24 billion in 1929 to just $3 billion in 1933, exacerbated by the fact that some major corporations had unwisely invested in stocks rather than plant and machinery during the 1920s. With no demand for housing or corporate development, construction contracted by 80 per cent, impacting on the lumber and steel industries, carpenters, plumbers, roofers, architects and so forth. Thirteen million people were out of work by 1933 – a quarter of the American workforce. Some industrial cities like Detroit saw unemployment rates reach 50 per cent. An estimated one-third of those who remained in work only held on to jobs by working part-time and for lower wages. This hit tax revenues as well. As the burden on city and state governments increased, several were forced into so much debt that they too defaulted on their obligations or cut into social service budgets at a time when demand had never been so great. That 100,000 Americans applied for jobs in Soviet Russia seemed symbolic of the 'American Dream' having ground to an abrupt halt.

This was 'the thirties' of shuttered factories, breadlines and 'Hoovervilles' (the shelters made by the homeless from salvaged wood and tin). Natural disaster added to the ravages when the worst drought in modern American history struck the Great Plains in 1934, and windstorms stripped the topsoil from millions of acres, destroying crops and livestock. Some 2.5 million people left the states of Oklahoma, Texas and Kansas, most heading to California – the Dust Bowl 'Okies' taking to the road form another indelible image of 1930s. The agricultural depression had already made farming untenable for many, affecting communities all through the 1920s, not just after 1929. Even before the 'Dust Bowl', the average per capita income of a farm household in 1933 was just $167 per year; and having borrowed money to mechanize their operations, indebted farmers faced banks foreclosing on them at the rate of 20,000 per month.

President Herbert Hoover, inaugurated in March 1929, had tried to bolster the banks, persuade industrialists to maintain wage rates, stabilize the farm crisis and generally prevent the 'shock waves' of the stock market collapse 'from blasting through the economy as a whole'.[2] However, the situation had overwhelmed the government by 1932 and, as the Hooverville appellation suggests, responsibility for the situation was laid at the Republican President's door, however unfairly. The action taken by Franklin Roosevelt and his administration's New Deal, did help restore confidence – especially in the banking system, following an emergency bank holiday in March 1933. Yet the New Deal never effected a full recovery. Industrial output did grow, with GNP rising from a low of $73 billion in 1933 to $100 billion in 1936, but it remained below the 1929 high of $104 billion. Unemployment shrank, but never dropped much below nine million, prompting economists to suggest that full employment might never again be achievable. Then came a 'depression within a depression' in the economic nose-dive of 1937–8. Different schools of thought attribute this recession to cuts in the government budget following five years of New Deal investment, to labour conflict discouraging industrial investment, or to the unwillingness of businesses to commit to new enterprises when government policy toward corporations was uncertain.[3] In any event, another crash in the stock market, a 40 per cent decline in industrial output and the laying-off of more than two million workers again meant that the Depression continued throughout the decade.

The notion of the 'Depression decade' does need some qualification, if only because the contrast between an ebullient 1920s and a despairing 1930s distracts attention from the fact that some sectors of the economy were depressed long before 1929. Even in the 'good years' of the 1920s, forty million Americans lived on an income below the level of subsistence, including not only rural farmers and poorly-paid workers like miners, but also ten million non-whites and a majority of the elderly.[4] From this perspective, writes David Kennedy, 'the Depression was not just a passing crisis but an episode that revealed deeply-rooted structural inequalities in American society', clearly not a moment that can be seen as an anomalous interlude between eras of uncomplicated economic progress.[5] It also needs to be acknowledged that different people experienced the consequences of the Depression with different intensity, and that economic difficulties did not entirely define their existence. However, it remains true that almost every other narrative conceptualization of the years in question – whether the 'Red Decade', the 'New Deal era', the 'Fervent Years', the 'age of Roosevelt', or the 'age of the CIO' – is rooted in the immediate context of the Depression, drawing 'defining characteristics' from the intellectual, political and cultural responses to the crisis.

The Angry Decade

Epithets such as the 'Fervent Years', the 'Angry Decade' and the 'Years of Protest' consistently accrue around the 1930s, emphasizing narratives of conflict. Certainly there were times when social struggle seemed to be endemic. On the eve of the 1932 election, General Douglas MacArthur led troops against 15,000 First World War veterans, evicting them and their families from makeshift camps around Washington DC. Unemployed and destitute, most of the men in this 'Bonus Expeditionary Force' had come to the capital to demand early payment of a bonus that they were due to receive in 1945; instead they met obstruction in Congress and forceful dispersal by the army they had once served. Gassed, shot at or bayoneted, two protestors were killed and two children died of asphyxiation. To many observers, it seemed an omen of civil war or revolution, especially when movements across the country erupted in similar violence. Race riots broke out in Harlem in 1935, a reaction to rumours that an African American shoplifter had been beaten to death by white police. The Midwest saw the rise of the Farmers' Holiday Movement, beginning with events such as the near-lynching of a judge in Le Mars, Iowa, who had presided over the evictions of indebted farmers. In October 1933, firebrand Milo Reno called for a farm strike until government put an end to foreclosures and provided relief. Road and railways were barricaded to prevent goods from reaching market, milk and other produce was destroyed and property auctions saw many violent clashes between farmers and authorities. Labour unrest also escalated repeatedly into violence. Battles between strikers and the National Guard occurred in Toledo, Ohio, when the American Workers Party sought to make the Electric Auto-Lite Company recognize a newly-formed union. In San Francisco, Harry Bridges led his longshoremen's union to shut down the ports for almost two months. Two workers were killed when local business interests decided to use force to break the strike, prompting Bridges to call for a general strike in July 1934, which brought the entire city to a standstill. Corporate leaders, however, were not deterred elsewhere. Mill owners in the South, the Growers Associations in California, and opponents of the Teamsters in Minneapolis, all formed private vigilante armies and hired toughs to crush labour organizing efforts in murderous confrontations.

In 1935–6, the labour movement itself erupted in internal conflict as John L. Lewis led dissident unionists in a break from the American Federation of Labor to create the Congress of Industrial Organizations (CIO). Its subsequent drive to organize mass-production industries such as steel, automobiles and textiles saw tactics of new militancy: sit-down strikes in which the workers forcibly seized the means of production. One in December 1936 in Flint, Michigan, hit General Motors at its most vulnerable when 'gearing up for the largest production runs' since the Depression began, giving the CIO a great victory and prompting a wave of copy-cat strikes.[6] The subsequent summer of 1937 proved to be the most violent in the history of American labour. Ten steelworkers were killed and dozens more wounded by Republic Steel's private police force in South Chicago in the infamous 'Memorial Day Massacre'. Five more were shot in Youngstown and Massilon, Ohio, but the violence did not budge Republic's president, who announced he would rather shut the plants than capitulate to labour's demands.

This war between unionists and industrialists and the increasing militancy of labour is usually associated with the unprecedented vitality of left-wing radicalism in the United States. The prestige enjoyed in the United States by Marxism, Communism and the Soviet Union was never greater than in the 1930s, and accounts of the 'Red Decade' present it as the defining intellectual thrust of these years. Belief in the supremacy of capitalism was shaken fundamentally by the rapid collapse of the American economy, while the centrally-planned socialist

Figure I.1 'The Memorial Day Massacre: The Republic Steel Strike, Chicago, Illinois (1937: Chicago Daily News Inc., reproduced with the permission of the Chicago History Museum).

economy of the Soviet Union now carried the 'aura of a great idealistic experiment'.[7] Communists throughout the Western world were energized by the sense that Karl Marx's predictions of the collapse of capitalism were coming true, and through the first years of the crisis the American Communist Party (the CPUSA) was determinedly revolutionary, proclaiming that 'nothing less than the reconstruction of American society on the Soviet model would constitute a proper use of the opportunity the Depression presented'.[8] Its dismissal of the Socialist Party as a party of 'mere reformism' devolved into a rhetorical struggle so heated that the two groups even rioted at a Madison Square Garden rally in 1934.

Many intellectuals and artists, as well as professionals such as teachers and lawyers were drawn to the CPUSA. Groups sponsored by the party, such as the literary John Reed Clubs, gave artists and writers the feeling of belonging to a vital community of like-minded souls, part of 'a cause larger than themselves' that made them 'significant actors on the stage of history' (see the 'Culture and the Crisis' case study below).[9] Many plunged into political activity with great zeal, assuming 'leading posts in labor defense, propaganda, and organizational fields', sending 'delegations to Washington protesting the shooting of bonus marchers', and travelling the country in support of strike actions.[10] The party's emphasis on justice for the oppressed also gave them a 'sense of solidarity' with the working classes, mitigating the 'feeling of alienation' that had been so characteristic of American artistic sensibilities in the 1920s.[11] Its stance against racism and colonialism also furthered its appeal, especially when the party took the lead in 1931 in defending the Scottsboro Boys – nine black youths, whose conviction of rape by a highly prejudiced all-white Alabama jury was seen widely as a travesty. Publicly championing such victims of Southern racism, the CPUSA also fought for anti-lynching legislation to be passed by the federal government. Even liberal intellectuals who balked at actually joining the party could praise its apparent humanism. When the Spanish Civil War, beginning in 1936, prompted vigorous efforts by Moscow to build a broad anti-fascist coalition to support the Spanish Republicans against the armies of General Francisco Franco and his Italian and German allies, even more Americans saw the Soviet response as 'the last chance to defeat the fascists and prevent another war'.[12] The Popular Front policy of this period, looking more favourably on collaboration with Socialists and even backing Roosevelt's New Deal in a show of anti-fascist unity, attracted further support.

Yet despite all the apocalyptic rhetoric of the early 1930s and for all that the CPUSA and the Popular Front galvanized the American Left into action for specific causes, the evidence for a broad-based Marxist movement in the United States simply does not exist. The party's presidential candidate in 1932, William Foster, polled only 102,000 votes; and just 80,000 were cast for his successor, Earl Browder, in 1936. Even after five years of the Depression, the CPUSA in 1934 could count only 300,000 members, one-third of whom lived in New York City. Moreover, even among intellectuals sympathetic toward socialism, a growing number distrusted Communist behaviour too much to ever embrace the party. The philosopher John Dewey, for instance, thought the Communist Party 'alien' to the democratic spirit of the American people, lacking in 'respect for individual freedoms', and misguided in pitching its appeal to the proletariat. While quite ready in 1931 to use *Common Sense* magazine to declare that 'Capitalism must be destroyed', Dewey insisted on the need for a new party to achieve this.[13] Moreover, as the decade progressed, Stalin's actions in the Soviet Union only increased concern. As the Russian leader staged show 'trials' and sent former colleagues to Siberian gulags, and as reports circulated of Communists murdering Trotskyites and anarchists behind Republican lines in Spain, so the anti-Stalinist Left grew, with its intellectual expression mediated through the pages of the political-literary journal *Partisan Review*. When Stalin then shocked the world in August 1939 by signing a non-aggression pact with Hitler, few American intellectuals retained any further faith in Communism.

In short, the notion of the years 1930–9 as the 'Red Decade' does not stand up to scrutiny. In fact, it was a perception generated primarily by anti-Communists, with the epithet coined in 1941 as the title of a book by Eugene Lyons. Presenting the CPUSA as 'almost omnipotent' in its ability to 'dictate cultural trends' and 'control US foreign policy', Lyons's polemical *The Red Decade* was widely dismissed at the time of publication. Some years later, however, with the onset of the Cold War, its version of the 'communist infiltration of American institutions' proved useful currency in the atmosphere of McCarthyism and, however much it misrepresented history, 'its title gained currency as a shorthand description of the 1930s as a whole'. As a narrative construct too, the 'Red Decade' suggested that the appeal of Communism had been a short-lived aberration, drained of its appeal by the return of prosperity and the onset of the war. It further served, as Graham Barnfield comments, to blame the villainous 'Reds', rather than the economic slump, for the social turmoil of the 1930s.[14]

It also distracted attention from domestic fascism. Individual right-wing organizations may have had little interest in ideology: the Black Legion, for instance, was little different from the Ku Klux Klan, launching vigilante attacks against unionists alleged to be part of an international conspiracy to subvert 'their' America. Others, like the German American Bund and the Italian Black Shirts really only represented European fascism transplanted to the United States, with the Bund initially formed in 1933 from existing German-American societies. Yet American fascism did possess its own intellectual dimension, as energized as Communism by the disorder created by the apparent collapse of capitalism and equally convinced that 'there is no solution but a revolutionary solution'.[15] For fascists though, it needed to be a revolution 'on behalf of authority, order and justice'. Lawrence Dennis, the author of *The Coming American Fascism* (1936) and editor of *The Awakener*, believed that what stood in the way of 'social order' were the 'prevailing values of liberalism', by which he meant 'the sanctity of individualism, freedom of contract, and democracy'.[16] What was needed instead was an 'authoritarian executive state' or, as the editor of *The American Review*, Seward Bishop Collins argued, a 'New Monarch'.[17] Both Collins and Dennis saw in Hitler the 'raw power' they believed was needed to create order, defeat 'the Communist threat' forever, and compel everyone to work 'in the interests of a national plan . . . to create full employment'.[18] In contrast to Communism, individuals rather than the state would own their property but, reflecting the key concerns of the Depression, redistribution would still be essential to achieve the goals of the fascist state. As Collins put it, 'the rich . . . have done us out of liberty by gobbling up most of the property'.[19]

Collins was particularly impressed with Huey Long, the demagogic senator from Louisiana whose 'Share Our Wealth' platform called for the confiscation of large fortunes and their redistribution to every American in the form of $5,000 to purchase a home and automobile. Long's critics often compared him with Hitler and Mussolini, and in Louisiana itself he indeed exercised near dictatorial power, buying and intimidating public officials and reducing the state legislature to subservience. Intellectually, however, Long's roots were less in fascism than in home-grown populism. Proclaiming himself the 'people's champion', coupled with a 'hillbilly' image that marked him as a political ingénue, he drew on the speeches of the previous generation's populist orator, William Jennings Bryan, to take 'Every man a king, but no one wears a crown' as his slogan. Promises to guarantee every family a minimum annual income of $2,500 and attacks on the 'entrenched economic interests' of plutocrats like the Rockefellers and Morgans, also distilled the 'old populist dream of unchained affluence and radical levelling'. Whatever he might have achieved was cut short by his assassination in September 1935, yet the simplicity of Long's platform attracted millions and offered a powerful demonstration of the 'pent up rancor' among Americans, especially the rural poor, still 'mystified by the Depression'.[20] His appeal too, like that of radio priest Father Charles Coughlin, suggested frustration that Roosevelt's New Deal had not gone far enough. Throughout 1932, Coughlin had used his radio sermons, which reached an audience of over ten million listeners, to hurl invective at Hoover and impress upon his audience that the choice was 'Roosevelt or Ruin!'. Yet when, to Coughlin's way of thinking, the newly-elected president 'failed' to punish Wall Street and listen to the priest's prescriptions for economic reform, FDR came to stand for 'Franklin Double-Crossing Roosevelt'. Coughlin though, went further than Long toward fascism. His thinking mirrored Collins who had also hoped that FDR's bold executive action in handling the banking crisis might serve to 'familiarize opinion with the monarchical conception', but was then bitterly disappointed when it became clear that the president intended to 'save' capitalism.[21] Coughlin used his appeal among immigrant workers, whose economic status was particularly precarious, to convince them that they had 'been betrayed by the New Deal and [were] left with no true spokesman but him'.[22] He also conjured a conspiracy of international bankers, Communists, union agitators and 'Jew Dealers' and built a political organisation on the strength of his following, forming the National Union for Social Justice in 1934 and the Union Party in 1936. Subsequently renamed the Christian Front, this movement came to act as an 'umbrella organization' which became ever more extreme as the decade progressed, to the point where Coughlin held up Hitler's government as a model to be copied and urged his followers to form quasi-military platoons.[23]

However, while dissidents from all over the political spectrum tried to seize on the discontent of the millions of unemployed and the insecurity of those whose jobs were vulnerable, the American Right fared little better than the communists. The Bund peaked with 100,000 members, while groups like the Silver Shirts, formed in North Carolina by admirers of Hitler, never attracted more than 10,000. The appeal of radical rhetoric could itself be very strong: Long's Share Our Wealth societies claimed over five million members nationwide, while Coughlin's grass-roots appeal could be measured in both listening figures and the $5 million he took in each year simply from small donations to his church. Indeed, it was predicted by private polls that if Long had run for president in 1936 he could have drawn four million votes. However, when Coughlin and Long's self-appointed successor, Gerald K. Smith, launched the Union Party in 1936, it polled just a miserable 2 per cent.[24] The politics of anger and resentment was attractive, but most voters realized that there was too much at stake to sanction a revolution in reality. None of the dissidents constituted a 'viable radical alternative to the New Deal', and Roosevelt won re-election in 1936 with what was then the largest share of the popular vote in US history.[25]

Culture and the Crisis (1932)

While the New Deal was eventually to sap the appeal of Marxism among America's liberal intellectuals, prompting them consider whether their predictions of the death of capitalism had been too hasty, many had not been predisposed to vote for Roosevelt in the first instance. Indeed, in 1932, fifty-two prominent writers had instead publicly announced their support for the Communist Party's presidential candidate, William Z. Foster and his African American running mate, James Ford. Calling themselves the League of Professional Groups for Foster and Ford, they published *Culture and the Crisis: An Open Letter to the Writers, Artists, Teachers, Physicians, Engineers, Scientists, and Other Professional Workers* in September of that year. Encompassing a wide variety of disciplines, its signatories included playwright Sherwood Anderson, author John Dos Passos, novelist and social historian Waldo Frank, African American poet Langston Hughes, literary critics Edmund Wilson and Malcolm Cowley, historian Matthew Josephson and philosopher Sidney Hook. Most of it was written, however, by Lewis Corey, a founding member of the US Communist Party in 1919 and a radical economist who had spent much of the late 1920s 'exposing the shallowness' of 'New Era' capitalism, and predicting the coming 'awakening'.[26] Encapsulating themes Corey was to later develop in *The Decline of American Capitalism* (1934), *Culture and the Crisis* asserted that the intelligentsia faced the choice between 'a world that was slowly dying and one that was about to be born'.[27] There was no middle ground; either the United States had to undergo a Soviet-style socialist revolution or slip into fascism. Arguing that the Republicans and Democrats merely wished to patch up the 'decaying house' of capitalism, and that the Socialists (led by Norman Thomas) were more interested in winning elections than in the struggles of the working classes, Corey insisted that only a strong showing for Foster would 'expand Communist influence among the American masses' and 'prepare the country for a genuine socialist transformation'.[28] Moreover, as its title suggests, the statement linked the fate of culture closely to the economic disaster.

The immediate 'cultural crisis' included the unemployment of artists, writers, intellectuals, the 'teachers on the breadlines' and the 'actors and playwrights [who] starve' while theatres close – concerns that later informed the New Deal's Arts Projects. But while lamenting 'all this training and talent thrown away', the League further argued that capitalism was innately hostile to 'genuine culture'.[29] 'The blight of capitalism', wrote Corey, 'is not only an economic question, it is a cultural question too'.[30] Capitalism either regarded artists and intellectuals as 'superfluous', or applied 'false money standards' to creative endeavours. The result, in either case, was 'spiritual degradation' of both the artist and the nation. But whereas America had 'never yet been able to provide its population with a sufficiently large body of trained intellectuals and professionals to satisfy its cultural needs', the outpouring of creative innovative work in Russian painting, film and theatre during the 1920s seemed to 'give substance' to the claim that Communism 'provided freedom and inspiration for the arts'.[31] Only the Communists, asserted *Crisis and the Culture*, were committed to a 'total social and cultural revolution', assuring artists of a 'new cultural renaissance', where professional workers would be 'liberated to perform freely and creatively their particular craft function':

> the architect is released from profit and speciality motives and may express his finest aspirations in buildings of social utility and beauty, the physician becomes the unfettered organizer of social preventive medicine, the teacher, writer, and artist fashion the creative ideology of a new world and a new culture.[32]

Offering such a vision, Corey also sought to awaken America's intellectuals to the sense that they too were 'of the oppressed', making an explicit appeal for them to find common cause with the working classes in the 'struggle for the emancipation of society'.[33] 'Practically everything that is orderly and sane and useful in America', claimed the League, 'was made by two classes of Americans': the lower classes of 'the muscle workers' and 'our class, the class of brain workers'.[34] Critics have justifiably pointed out that 'trying to pass themselves off' as 'intellectual workers' not only patronized the working classes but was also symptomatic of liberals being 'half-ashamed' of their own professions and their middle-class origins.[35] Yet at the time it seemed to be an important statement to make, driven by concern that if the Communist Left failed to appeal to the professional middle classes, then 'this class might turn to fascism'. Intellectuals were needed in this struggle to 'reassert Enlightenment ideals' and challenge the middle classes to align with the working classes, to 'move forward and not backward'.[36] It was an incipient anxiety that was to preoccupy Corey even further in *The Crisis of the Middle Class* (1936).

In the end, plans for magazines and books surveying the state of American culture went unrealized as the 'ad hoc alliance' of the League of Professionals proved to be a brief affair.[37] Sidney Hook, for instance, was to break completely with the international Communist movement just months later, holding Stalin's policies responsible for the triumph of Nazism in Germany. Corey himself became disillusioned too, publishing in 1940 a three-part manifesto in *The Nation* entitled 'Marxism Reconsidered' – suggesting how capitalism could be transformed peacefully rather than overthrown.[38] In later years, especially during the Cold War, it was common for signatories such as John Dos Passos to dismiss their involvement in the League as 'a youthful protest vote'.[39] Yet *Culture and the Crisis* remains an important document: contemporarily, as a precursor to the CPUSA's subsequent Popular Front effort to unite white-collar workers and intellectuals with working-class unionism; and historically, as a corrective to accounts which tend to 'detach the culture of the Left from the economic conditions which gave it new impetus'.[40]

The New Deal Era

There were times when the New Deal itself appeared to be as steeped in radical populism as Coughlin or Long ever were. Accepting the Democratic Party's presidential nomination for the second time in 1936, Roosevelt pledged war against 'organized money' and the 'industrial dictatorship' which had taken 'economic freedom' away from ordinary working men and women.[41] He turned that year's State of the Union address into a blatant political speech as well, relishing the fact that the forces of 'entrenched greed' had become 'unanimous in their hate for me'. Roosevelt presented the enemies he had made among America's 'economic royalists' as evidence that the New Deal policies were working.[42] To continue the fight, he then called for taxes as high as 79 per cent on the largest incomes, stiffer inheritance taxes, and taxes on corporate income and profits. This was the New Deal promising to 'soak the rich'.

As David Kennedy argues, however, this moment of 'radicalism' was more a 'carefully staged performance' than an ideology. FDR had 'little to lose by alienating the right' at this point – America's elites already regarded the patrician president as a 'traitor to his class', and opposition had consolidated in 1934 under the banner of the American Liberty League, sponsored by the DuPonts.[43] What he had to do in 1936 instead was to win back potential supporters of the Union Party and prevent the Democrats' new working-class constituency from being divided. Roosevelt's Secretary of the Treasury, Henry Morgenthau, later admitted that the tax proposal was really a 'campaign document' – a 'hell–raiser, not a revenue raiser'.[44] The 79 per cent tax, for example, sounded harsh, but since it applied only to incomes over $5 million, it affected only one man, John D. Rockefeller. The tax bill as a whole generated only $250 million in new revenue, with little redistributive effect. Rhetoric withstanding, class war was never really the philosophy of the New Deal.

In fact, the opportunism and political manoeuvring engaged in by Roosevelt presented contemporaries and historians alike with a problem in defining what the philosophy of the New Deal actually was. With fifteen major bills passed by Congress within one hundred days, the first surge of New Deal legislation seemed characterized more by its dynamism than its consistency. Some measures sought to 'prop up' capitalism, such as the Emergency Banking Act enacted to halt the panic, or 'rationalize' it, as the National Industrial Recovery Act (NIRA) was intended to do in allowing manufacturers to agree on set prices and end 'excessive' market competition. After the NIRA was declared unconstitutional by the Supreme Court, a National Labor Relations Board was established instead, making government the 'broker' between unions and industry. Others programmes also directly increased the managerial power of the government in certain sectors, such as the Securities Act's regulation of the financial system or, on a bigger scale, the Agricultural Adjustment Act (AAA), by which the government sought to bring down farm production by 30 per cent, artificially creating scarcity in order to inflate market prices and thus farmers' incomes. Even greater centralized planning was evident in the Tennessee Valley Authority (TVA), creating a federally-owned corporation, stretching into seven states to generate hydroelectric power, build dams for flood control, combat soil erosion and oversee the area's economic development. The government also addressed unemployment and under–investment in infrastructure at the same time, first through the Civil Conservation Corps and the Civil Works Administration, putting millions of Americans to work on construction projects. In 1935, a 'Second New Deal' added the Works Progress Administration (WPA) to take 3.5 million off the dole, which had initially been paid to them by the Federal Emergency Relief Administration, by offering them government-created jobs instead. Social Security was also created, instituting both unemployment insurance and old-age pensions, while in 1938 a Fair Labor Standards Act established minimum wages and maximum working hours – measures that were not only reformist but also undertaken with the idea of addressing the continuing Depression by increasing the purchasing power of ordinary Americans.[45]

As Alan Brinkley comments, 'the nation's problems were serious enough, the political possibilities great enough to permit the coexistence of many different prescriptions for government's response'.[46] Roosevelt had proclaimed from the outset of his 1932 campaign that what the country needed most was 'bold, persistent experimentation'. Given the extent of the difficulties, it was, he said, simply 'common sense to take a method and try it. If it fails, admit it frankly and try another. But above all, try something'.[47] Something of a philosophical dimension could be discerned in just this attitude. Arthur Schlesinger Jr, for example, associated FDR's remarks with the pragmatic 'experimentalism' articulated by philosophers John Dewey and William James.[48] Rejecting claims to 'absolute certainty', pragmatism emphasized the testing of ideas and hypotheses in real situations, stressing the need for flexibility and freshness of approach in tackling problems, not confining oneself to 'inherited moral formulations or other forms of idealism'.[49] In this perspective, the New Dealers were not committed to any pre-formed ideology, but tried out ideas and judged them by their results. However, other historians have argued that the New Deal's 'haphazard' programmes lacked the disciplined methods of inquiry and empirical verification of results which marked 'true philosophical pragmatism' and, like Richard Hofstadter, suggest that Roosevelt's experimentalism was less a philosophy than a 'temperament'.[50]

Certain hypotheses, though, did hold more sway than others in informing New Deal policies, all making the broad assumption that 'the nation's greatest problems were rooted in the structure of modern industrial capitalism and that it was the mission of government to deal somehow with the flaws in that structure'.[51] Rexford Tugwell, in the president's 'Brains Trust', and Hugh Johnson of the National Recovery Administration (NRA), for instance, believed the key 'flaw' was to be found in the 'unrestricted individual competition' of the 1920s – or what Johnson characterized as 'dog-eat-dog and devil take the hindmost'.[52] Price gouging in certain industries had slashed profit margins so hard that even the most benevolent of employers had been impelled to cut wages and lay off workers. The NRA itself was a response to this verdict – establishing 'code authorities' in an ill-fated attempt to end this kind of competition, allowing former rivals in industry and manufacturing to collude on common prices and production policies, while also involving organized labour in the negotiation of minimum wages and working conditions. Others, such as Marriner Eccles at the Federal Reserve Board, argued that the central problem was one of 'underconsumption' – an idea presented in Stuart Chase's 1932 text, *A New Deal*.[53] With factories lying idle and the government paying farmers *not* to produce, America was not facing a shortage of 'productive power', but rather a situation in which millions of Americans lacked 'the purchasing power that would enable them to buy the things they desperately need'.[54] Thus, while the NRA sought to address production, other agencies like the WPA sought to create jobs and enable people to spend, while social security legislation ensured that the purchasing power of the unemployed and the retired would be maintained in the long term. Some also argued for the government's support of labour unions in the Wagner Act on the basis that collective bargaining would increase wages; while the AAA's policies were also rationalized in this light, since improving the incomes of farmers would enable rural workers to become part of the consumer economy (even if it simultaneously raised agricultural prices). 'Balance' was a critical component in New Deal thinking. As Roosevelt stated plainly: 'What we seek is balance in our economic system – balance between agriculture and industry, and balance between the wage earner, the employer and the consumer'.[55]

Achieving such a balance, however, meant recasting the government as a powerful 'broker' between competing interests – which involved the New Deal in a redefinition of liberalism. Nineteenth-century liberalism had been an ideology of laissez-faire economics, decentralization and limited government but awareness that industrialization was not creating a 'just society' had already reoriented liberalism toward reformism at the turn of the century. Herbert Croly and Walter Lippmann, for instance, had perceived the negative effects of industrial monopoly on free enterprise, democratic politics and individual liberty and, with the founding of *New Republic* in 1909, had called for dynamic executive leaders like Theodore Roosevelt and Woodrow Wilson to protect citizens from 'excessive corporate power'.[56] The New Deal inherited much of this progressive vision of positive government and the basic assumption that 'liberalism meant a commitment to reform' – though its revulsion of 'cut throat' competition meant that anti-monopoly policies were largely abandoned until 1938.[57] Still, the New Deal was a vehicle for many who possessed a fervent faith in government as 'the agency of justice and progress', and books like *The Administrative Process* (1938) by James Landis and *The Folklore of Capitalism* (1938) by Thurman Arnold argued for even 'more plentiful and more powerful government agencies' that could be charged 'with overseeing and fine-tuning the increasingly complex industrial economy'.[58] Indeed, the scope of federal regulation expanded to embrace agricultural production, labour management, investment institutions, utilities and energy production, radio broadcasting, airline operation and much more besides.

This was a major expansion of the federal state. Severely limited when the Depression began, federal expenditures had accounted for only 3 per cent of the GNP. By 1939 this had more than tripled, and the government's relationship with its citizens was transformed in the process. Some 1.3 million people were directly employed in civilian and military posts, with another 3.3 million on the WPA's work-relief programmes. The government also underwrote unemployment insurance for twenty-six million Americans, and the first federal pensions were paid in 1940. Four million had had their property saved from foreclosure by the government's Home Owners Loan Corporation, while banking reforms had secured the savings of millions more. Thousands of families displaced by the Dust Bowl received shelter in government camps, while the TVA brought electricity to large sections of the depressed South. This won Roosevelt and the Democrats a lot of allies, but it was also the cause for great consternation. A 1936 book called *The Menace of Roosevelt and His Policies* represented the belief

that Roosevelt had transformed a government 'for the most part confined to the essential functions' into 'a highly complex, bungling
agency for throttling business and bedevilling the private lives of free
people'.[59] It was not necessarily a reactionary viewpoint. Lippmann,
the earlier champion of progressive liberalism and 'the positive leadership of a creative statesmanship', became openly hostile toward
Roosevelt's tax plans, relief expenditures and agricultural programme.
Arguing that FDR was not a true liberal, but a 'Tory philanthropist'
who was 'more inclined to help the people than to let them help themselves', Lippmann feared that that 'plans for a collectivist economy'
were emanating from Washington.[60] In 1937 he published *The Good
Society*, a condemnation of collectivism that responded both to the rise
of totalitarianism and his sense that the New Deal had become damaging to individual liberties.

The New Deal did indeed represent a challenge to the ethos of
'rugged individualism'. Yet, as Martin Rubin has documented, the
country's individualist dream had been problematic for many even
before the Crash. According to Robert and Helen Lynd's research in
Middletown (1929), the rise of giant corporations in the 1920s had alienated people from their jobs, subordinating 'individual personality' to
'the assembly line and the large office'.[61] Dewey, too, saw 'the individual bewildered and diminished' by the 'increasing corporateness of
industrial capitalism' and 'the decline of rural community life'.[62] The
Depression merely intensified this critique, with historian Charles
Beard among many claiming that 'the individualist creed of everybody
for himself' was 'principally responsible' for the crisis.[63] With Dewey's
Individualism – Old and New (1930) dismissing the creed as a cultural
myth and not a 'natural' aspect of the human condition, the New Deal's
attempts to redefine 'individuality' on a 'social basis' were part of a
broader intellectual current.[64] As Roosevelt expressed it, the creed of
self-interest was a corrosive 'definition of liberty, under which for many
years a free people were being gradually regimented into the service of
the privileged few'. 'I prefer and I am sure you prefer', he continued,
'that broader definition of liberty under which we are moving toward
greater freedom, to greater security for the average man than he has ever
known before in the history of America'.[65] In fact, 'security' was the
touchstone which obfuscated the tensions between 'individualism' and
'collectivism'. New Deal security, as Kennedy asserts, meant regulation
in the economic realm, planned development in the physical, job security for 'people in all occupations of life and in all parts of the country'
and the 'assurance that they are not going to starve in their old age'.[66]

Attainment of those securities, it was argued, surely could not be in conflict with any individual's 'rational self-interest'.

Despite such appeals, however, considerable momentum had been lost as early as 1937. Opposition among conservative Democrats and Republicans coalesced, and Roosevelt failed to get any new measures passed by the special session of Congress he called in 1937. The 'Roosevelt Recession' of 1937–8 caused significant loss of faith and direction as well, with the Fair Labor Standards Act of June 1938 the last New Deal reform to be inscribed into law. Even in that short time frame, though, it is difficult not to see the substantial energy and activism of the New Deal as the 'defining event' of the 1930s, touching far more people than the Left ever did. Moreover, although they were less committed to restructuring the economy after the Second World War, as Brinkley observes, New Deal liberals still upheld the central responsibilities of government in the economy for years to come.[67]

Other accounts of the decade also demonstrate that the social vision of the New Deal extended well into the Second World War and beyond. Michael Denning's narrative of the 'Age of the CIO' and the Popular

Figure I.2 President Franklin D. Roosevelt signing the Repeal of Prohibition Bill, December 1933 (The Art Archive/Culver Pictures).

Front is one of the most important of recent contributions, emphasizing not the 'radicalism' of industrial unionization but rather the 'social democratic culture' that the movement shared with New Dealers.[68] For all that the sit-down strikes of 1937 sought to seize control of the means of production, the CIO's demands were not communistic. John L. Lewis's principal demand was simply the recognition of the United Auto Workers as the legitimate bargaining agent for General Motors employees. His vision was not one of revolution, but for workers to 'enjoy middle class standards of living' – the guarantee of steady employment, shorter hours and wages 'that will enable them to maintain themselves and their families in health and comfort'.[69] 'The central issue in this life of modern man', asserted union leaders in full accord with Roosevelt's analysis, 'is the quest for security'.[70] With such a vision to the forefront, the CIO energized the American working class in a way that Communism never did, and by August 1937 it could claim over 3.4 million members. Putting this alongside the New Deal as the central narrative, Denning argues that since the principal cultural impulse of the period was not 'Red', the dissipation of the radical Left did not mean the end of the 'working-class' cultures fomented in the 1930s.[71]

Franklin D. Roosevelt

The 'pragmatic' and 'experimental' nature of the New Deal is frequently credited to the mental habits of the thirty-second President himself. If Hoover's 'rigorous analytical mind' rendered him relatively inflexible when it came to the problems of the Depression, Roosevelt, by contrast, was more of an open-minded student.[72] Preferring to learn through conversation and discussion, he accumulated around him a 'Brains Trust' that included professors of government, economics and law (Raymond Moley, Rexford Tugwell and Adolf Berle Jr, respectively), as well as many policy intellectuals and idealistic young lawyers (such as Lauchlin Currie or Thomas Corcoran) who had far more coherent visions of what the New Deal was or ought to be. Roosevelt, though, enjoyed 'listening to everybody and anybody', open to 'all number and manner of impressions, facts, theories, nostrums and personalities'.[73] Aware of his obsession with stamp-collecting, one historian observed acerbically that FDR had a 'collector's mind' – 'quick to grasp and classify bits and pieces of information, but unresponsive to the challenge of the abstract'.[74] Contemporaries certainly did not think it made for intellectual depth or coherence; Hoover harshly dismissed him as 'a chameleon on plaid'.[75] And Justice Oliver Wendell Holmes delivered an assessment that continues to resound in most historical accounts, summing up the President as: 'A second class intellect. But a first-class temperament'.

For Holmes, though, it was the second part of his assessment that mattered most – and historians often hold Roosevelt's character, energy and
empathy to have informed the New Deal's activism and positive engagement with 'the people', as much as his intellect informed its eclecticism.
Roosevelt's temperament, according to most historians, was rooted in his
earlier experiences. Born in 1882, the only child of wealthy landed gentleman, James Roosevelt, and his wife, Sara Delano, Franklin's upbringing on
their country estate at Hyde Park in upstate New York seemed unlikely to
produce a 'man of the people'. Yet, as David Kennedy suggests, much of
the drive of the New Deal could be ascribed to a desire to give 'ordinary
Americans' a 'measure of the security that the patrician Roosevelts
enjoyed as their birthright'.[76] Certainly both his parents and his schooling
at Groton instilled in him the call to 'Christian responsibility through public
service'.[77] Family connections also fueled his enthusiasm for politics, most
notably the example of his distant but legendary cousin, Theodore
Roosevelt. The name certainly opened doors, with local Democratic Party
leaders inviting Franklin to run for the state Senate in 1910. That he then
followed Theodore's career trajectory in accepting the position of Assistant
Secretary of the Navy during the First World War, is generally seen as a sign
of early presidential ambition, charting the same course to the White
House.

That path, however, was almost wrecked in August 1921 when
Roosevelt contracted polio. Within days he lost the use of both his legs
and would never again stand without heavy steel braces. Much of the next
seven years were spent convalescing and in a futile search for a cure. The
experience may not have brought about the 'spiritual transformation' that
some historians suggest, but certainly FDR himself believed he emerged
'a stronger, more resilient person'.[78] The Democratic Party national con-
vention in 1928 witnessed this new 'aura of radiant indomitability' as he
took to the stage to nominate Al Smith, 'walking' with the support of a
cane and his son's arm, using his hips to swing his lifeless legs forward,
'all the while beaming and bantering with onlookers to distract attention
from his ordeal'.[79] Roosevelt's determination not to let paralysis defeat his
ambitions may have exacerbated his deceptiveness, but it also developed
a 'kind of forcefully willed optimism' which, when president, came across
vibrantly in his speeches.[80] This was particularly true of the 'fireside chat'
radio broadcasts that became one of the signatures of his presidency, in
which he exuded confidence and 'refused' to submit to the disaster. His
wife Eleanor, whom he had married in 1905, also claimed that the polio
and its excruciating pain taught her husband 'infinite patience' and
increased his understanding of 'what suffering meant' – awakening in him
qualities of empathy and compassion.[81] Certainly FDR's convalescence
provided an opportunity for Eleanor herself to become his 'social conscience', as she stood in for him at political functions during this time and
became a key conduit for bringing social reform and human rights issues
to his attention.

Indeed, as he resumed his political career, these concerns became the marker of his governorship of New York. Even before the Depression hit, he had a reputation as a 'reform Democrat', instituting the New York Public Service Commission, developing publicly-owned hydroelectric power and providing assistance to the state's farmers. After the Wall Street Crash, he offered direct relief programmes and was the first governor to advocate unemployment insurance. Eager to prove that he was heir to the progressive reform legacy of Woodrow Wilson and Theodore Roosevelt, his 'command, compassion, and understanding of the gravity and extent of Depression conditions' also marked out his distance from Hoover.[82] It may not have been a 'philosophy' but it was a different attitude towards government. As speeches suggested, his conception was simple: having been created by the people 'for their mutual protection and well being', the state had a 'social duty' toward all of its citizens that was 'the duty of the servant to the master'.[83] Yet government was also the 'protector' of its citizens, and if private enterprise could not provide them with work or sustenance, the people had 'a right to call upon the government for aid'.[84] And 'in the final analysis', he argued, any suitable response had to be built on the understanding that 'the progress of our civilization will be retarded if any large body of citizens falls behind'.[85]

In many biographies, Holmes' comment has effectively become a shorthand representation of the strengths and weaknesses of the New Deal, reducing it down to a reflection of the personality of its leader.[86] Even some of the New Deal's 'failures' are attributed to a politically 'Machiavellian' side of Roosevelt's character – as in his decision not to alienate white Southern Democrats by preventing an anti-lynching bill from being passed, or the fact that his 'duplicity' provided a rallying point for opposition to coalesce against his plans to reform the Supreme Court. Obviously, this is problematic. Roosevelt the man was not synonymous with the New Deal, and the whole administration, intellectuals, senators, congressmen, state politicians, lobbyists, the labour movement, farmers groups and many ordinary citizens all helped define it. Yet the fusion of the personality of Roosevelt with the New Deal is not just a historians' contrivance. It was, indeed, a contemporary phenomenon of such weight that, for many people, FDR himself 'overwhelmed' the limitations and contradictions of the policies and programmes, as ordinary people credited him personally with the changes the New Deal made to their lives – saying 'He saved my home', or 'He gave me a job'.[87] With the imprint of one man so obviously venerated, Arthur Schlesinger Jr, certainly had some justification in referring to this period simply as the 'Age of Roosevelt'.[88]

The New Era of Nationalism

For all the significance and impact of the New Deal, cultural historians have argued that ultimately, like domestic communism and fascism, it was only one manifestation among many of the urge to 'reorder the world' on a more rational basis. Economic certainties were thrown into chaos by the Depression for sure, but so too were cultural concepts – such as the creed of 'rugged individualism' already discussed, the myth of the American Dream, or even belief in progress itself. Gender roles were also complicated as many men lost both their breadwinner status and the self-respect they had invested in it. Prevailing racial assumptions were also disrupted as many impoverished whites found themselves on the same rung of the economic ladder as African Americans. For some sectors of society, these challenges called for the reinforcement of what they saw as 'traditional' ways and values: putting blacks 'in their place' through intimidation and segregation, for example, or discouraging married women from holding jobs in an effort to stem the perceived erosion of 'traditional' masculine authority. For others though, such traditions were thoroughly discredited. People wanted to make sense of where they now stood. This, according to Warren Susman, prompted an intensified and 'self-conscious search for a culture' that could 'make their own world comprehensible' again. This broad impulse, he argues, was responsible for a 'new era of nationalism', in which defining an 'American Way of Life' became the cultural imperative.[89]

Nationalism in the 1930s has often been associated with isolationism, prompted both by the pressing need for Americans to focus on their domestic problems and by fears about being again entangled in a European war. It is also often associated with conservatism, as in the 'uncompromising nationalism' of Collins' brand of fascism. However, the CPUSA's Popular Front slogan, 'Communism is 20th Century Americanism', provides evidence that nationalist appeals ran the breadth of the political spectrum. More generally, at a moment when America 'seemed to be on the precipice of social disintegration', there was an understandable desire to 'forge a stronger, more perfect domestic union' by finding ways of expressing common bonds of national cultural identity.[90]

The belief that this was possible was built on a number of ideas that predated the 1930s. In the nineteenth century, 'culture' was understood typically to refer to the 'high culture' of illustrious arts and letters. However, led by practitioners such as Frank Boas of Columbia University, the emergence of cultural anthropology challenged this, redefining culture more inclusively as all existing patterns of human activity. 'Culture' came to stand for the behaviours and beliefs of identifiable groups of people and the symbolic embodiment of their values in the artefacts they produced. Boas's students, particularly Ruth Benedict and Margaret Mead, popularized this new definition for

American readers, especially when Benedict's *Patterns of Culture* became an unlikely bestseller in 1934, capturing the public imagination with her vivid descriptions of the Dobu culture of New Guinea, the Pueblo culture of the American southwest and the Native Americans of the Great Plains. Her evidence that their values, 'even when they seemed strange', were 'intelligible in terms of their own coherent cultural systems' not only promoted Benedict's belief in cultural relativism but enabled readers to 'think about national and social identity in a basically new way', and consider that they themselves might think and behave 'in the context of a distinctly "American" cultural pattern'.[91]

Many intellectuals were as disquieted as they had been in the past by the particular 'American cultural patterns' they saw developing in the 1930s. The mass communications media of radio, cinema and advertising were certainly forging national bonds. Newsreels, documentaries and photographic journals like *Life* magazine (launched in 1936) made it possible to see and know 'the details of life' in different areas of the country, 'to feel oneself part of some other's experience'. Roosevelt's 'fireside chats' and other radio broadcasts brought 'the figures of power . . . into the immediate experience of most Americans'.[92] Hollywood stars and genres became common currency across the nation. Even the array of seemingly mundane consumer products (Wonder Bread and Birds Eye frozen vegetables being among those introduced in the 1930s) represented aspects of life in which many Americans came to share.[93] But for critics like German émigrés Theodore Adorno, Max Horkeimer and Leo Lowenthal, this mass culture was not one of 'genuine experience'. In their analysis, it could not reveal or reflect the authentic beliefs and values of the people, because it was a commercial product that sought to manipulate consumers and impose external values (those associated with capitalism) upon them. This Marx-influenced observation informed a broader intellectual critique of popular culture as offering only 'standardization, stereotypy, conservatism and mendacity', distracting citizens not only from the immediate woes of Depression, but also from the long-term corrosiveness of modern capitalist society.[94]

Anthropological models, though, offered a retort to this in their relativist presumption that every culture should be studied for what it is, rather than judged against arbitrary standards of what it 'should be'. Gilbert Seldes in *The Seven Lively Arts* (1924) had already advanced the then controversial claim that popular entertainment should be treated as seriously as so-called 'high art', but Constance Rourke in

America Humor (1931) broke further ground in demonstrating how popular plays, minstrel shows and tall stories were of immeasurable significance when it came to revealing the national character (see case study below). Perry Miller's towering history of *The New England Mind* (1939) also derived its analysis of the American Puritans as a distinctive culture from close reading of sermons and sources that had been neglected previously as beneath intellectual consideration.[95] This attitude also converged with another train of intellectual sentiment which believed that the development and appreciation of an indigenous American culture had been smothered by European ideas about art. George Santayana's 1911 lecture, 'The Genteel Tradition in American Philosophy' and Van Wyck Brook in *America's Coming of Age* (1915) had been early expressions of this, prompting many subsequent 'declarations of cultural independence' by writers such as Waldo Frank, Hart Crane and William Carlos Williams, denouncing standards which judged intellectual and artistic achievement in the United States to be second-rate.[96] Although the 1920s still saw many intellectuals perpetuating the belief in America's cultural inferiority by regarding the European cities of London, Paris and Berlin as the only places to learn about art, literature and music, this was turned around in the 1930s when the onset of the Depression and Hitler's rise in Germany forced many of them to return to the United States. As Malcolm Cowley mythologized it in *Exile's Return* (1934), this was a crucial factor in the 'resuscitation of national culture', with a generation of expatriates now intrigued to 'know what home was'.[97] Also, for those already 'sympathetic to the production of indigenous culture', the collapse of Europe left Americans 'finally free' to 'build something new on native grounds'.[98]

For many this meant finding inspiration for 'high culture' from distinctive American materials. Stephen Vincent Benet's poetry in *A Book of Americans* (1933) or Aaron Copland's ballet of *Billy the Kid* (1938) could be considered in this light. Efforts to 'separate out' the American cultural experience from that of Europe also gave rise in academia to a new emphasis on national history and literature, led by scholars such as Miller, Vernon Parrington, Samuel Eliot Morrison and Henry Nash Smith. Indeed, the field of American Studies started to flourish in this decade, including the efforts of universities such as Harvard and Yale 'to find special qualities and unique stories in American history and artefacts'.[99] The impulse to 'forge a stronger domestic union' was also evident in the ways in which that national history was constructed, with Abraham Lincoln, in particular, becoming an historic emblem for the times. From Robert Sherwood's play *Abe Lincoln in Illinois* to John Ford's film *Young Mr Lincoln*, to Carl Sandburg's biography, *The War Years*, the sixteenth president became a human symbol of 'the American democratic tradition' and its 'commitment to free institutions in the face of adversity', as well as an 'example to reinforce the spirit of national unity, challenged by divisions at home and conflict abroad'.[100] Along with spectacular commercial successes like *The Epic of America* (1931) by James Truslow Adams, the decade also saw many highly visible public markers of an historicized national culture – including the construction of the Jefferson Memorial in Washington DC, the completion of Mount Rushmore in the summer of 1939 and the nationwide celebrations of the 150th anniversary of the ratification of the Constitution.

A culture of 'native grounds' was not always synonymous with a national culture. The concept of regionalism was a recurring motif in political and cultural discourse, a central part of the groundswell to establish American culture on native grounds, imbued with the sense that the uniqueness of the country's cultural expression was derived from its spatial qualities and landscape.[101] This could be divisive. The manifesto of *I'll Take My Stand* (1930) was predicated on the assertion that the South was a 'coherent region possessed [of] a culture distinct from that of the rest of the United States'. Published by the so-called Southern Agrarians, who included poets John Crowe Ransom, Allen Tate, and author Robert Penn Warren, *I'll Take My Stand* represented a strand of regionalism that resisted national 'homogenization' as a threat to the region's 'organic' culture. Indeed, it argued that the South had its own 'way of life' that it should be allowed to pursue with regional autonomy. Set against this was the alternative argument of Howard Odum and Harry Estill Moore in *American Regionalism* (1938). While accepting that different areas of the country possessed distinctive cultural qualities that needed to be preserved and, indeed, delineating six major American regions on this basis, Odum and Moore rejected sectionalism and called instead for a pluralist conception of 'unifying regionalism' whereby each made its distinctive contribution to the national whole.[102] Similarly, the great surge of interest in 'folk culture' in the 1930s became a 'multi-accented slogan'. For some proponents it was perceived as an effort to remember and preserve 'older patterns of culture' before they were lost and erased from consciousness by the rising tide of modernity.[103] Others saw in the supposedly 'authentic' and 'unmediated' qualities of folk music and art, a challenge to commercialized culture. Yet the folk revival was also carried out in the spirit of finding 'roots' for American culture that did not derive from European models and refuting the supposed inadequacy of the nation's traditions.

Such folk materials also added to an expanding picture of the diverse make-up of the United States. New Deal projects for writers produced studies of groups such as 'Georgia Coastal Negroes', 'The Italians of New York' and 'The Armenians of Massachusetts', thus opening up ethnic cultures to view for the rest of the population. The federal government also sponsored John Lomax's work in the Archive of American Folk Song, and appointed Constance Rourke to edit the Index of American Design. 'Proletarian novels' revealed to wider audiences the working-class experiences of different immigrant communities, while plays and novels about Native American and African American cultures, and the documentary photography movement all sought to 'introduce America to Americans' in unprecedented diversity.[104] Many of those engaged in this process argued that the evidence of heterogeneity they were documenting was, in itself, revealing the *true* 'American Way of Life'. To them it was a vision of America which could unify precisely because it was more inclusive, drawing attention to the contributions made by those who had previously been excluded from definitions of the nation, such as sharecroppers, African Americans, Native American tribes, immigrant-born communities, and 'forgotten' localities throughout the country.[105] Horace Kallen had first advanced this pluralist conception in 1909, comparing American culture to 'a vast and various symphony orchestra, whose musical richness was enhanced precisely by the tonal distinctiveness of each of its members'. It stood in contrast to the assimilationist idea of a 'melting pot' and the politicized call for immigrants to commit themselves to '100% Americanism', which, Kallen asserted, would 'destroy that symphonic richness and substitute for it a bland and homogeneous unison'.[106]

Not everyone in the 1930s accepted this argument. Its emphasis on the ethnic dimensions of American identity particularly riled some opponents who charged that it falsely suggested 'all of us had been dumped down together at Ellis Island a few short years ago'.[107] It also became politicized through the Popular Front when, as Denning argues, cultural pluralism became a key component of the Left's efforts to mediate 'between Anglo-American culture, the culture of ethnic workers, and African-American culture'. Moreover, presenting pluralism at the heart of 'a new era of nationalism' requires a somewhat paradoxical synthesis of 'pride in ethnic identity' with 'an assertive Americanism'.[108] This 'conceptual tension' between an all-encompassing 'American Way of Life' and the 'smaller cultures' that ethnography, folk studies and regionalist sentiments were unearthing, persisted throughout the 1930s.[109] Terry Cooney's description of the decade as a 'balancing act' is particularly appropriate in this regard.[110]

Yet as the decade progressed, and consciousness of Nazism grew stronger, the tensions tended to be submerged in the assertive belief that the differences inherent in the United States offered a positive contrast to totalitarianism and fascism. Cultural pluralism and heterogeneity were used as evidence of 'America's true richness and its independence from Europe'.[111] Celebrated as strong, alive, varied and changing, rather than tied to the past, it was associated too with a 'culture of democracy' which 'sustained openness and experimentalism' and 'promoted compromise rather than quest for domination'. In John Dewey's analysis, as the nation contemplated war, these were the qualities which made the nation 'worthy of defense'.[112]

Constance Rourke, *American Humor: A Study of the National Character* (1931)

'Grown from an enjoyment of American vagaries, and from the belief that these have woven together a tradition which is various, subtle, sinewy . . . but not poor', Constance Rourke's *American Humor* announced itself from the outset as a refutation of those who dismissed the United States as an artistic wasteland and as an exploration of cultural 'vagaries' that had not yet been subjected to serious analysis. Taking what seemed to be the least serious subject of all as her theme, Rourke redefined humour as 'one of those conceits which give form and flavor to an entire character' and assigned the 'comic folk tradition' a central role in the 'proper appreciation' of national culture.[113]

Born in 1885 in Cleveland, Ohio, Rourke's interest in folk culture was first piqued while travelling in Europe in 1908 – and she returned to the United States to begin a quest for American materials comparable to European folk tales. First teaching and then as a freelance writer, she devoted herself to 'living research', travelling the country in search of all manner of native folklore, arts, crafts and music, and immersing herself in popular mythologies. Subjects like Paul Bunyan, vaudeville, and her study of Victorian-age popular heroes (published in 1927 as *Trumpets of Jubilee*) convinced her that while American culture may not have been artistic in the 'genteel tradition', it was certainly active, lively and exuberant. *American Humor* was written to prove this thesis.

At the heart of *American Humor* is Rourke's identification of three arche-typal figures of popular comedy: the Yankee; the backwoodsman; and the minstrel. The Yankee was a rural New England type, possessed of a sly intelligence that often hid behind a mask of hick-like simplicity – used to good effect in popular satires. The backwoodsman, by contrast, was a frontier force of nature, developed from the legends that grew around indi-viduals like Davy Crockett (who could 'whip his weight in wildcats') and Mike Fink (who, according to one tale, had gone *up* Niagara Falls on the back of an alligator). An exuberant, boastful and rough archetype, it was associated with the humour of outrageous tall tales, and the comic oratory of 'free invention'. The minstrel was more problematic, with Rourke acknowledging that the black-face minstrelsy of white actors such as Jim Crow Rice and Dan Emmett had been 'long considered a travesty'. It could be presented as a distinctively American humour in the extent to which it derived from the fables, spirituals and dances of Southern blacks and their 'genuine' folk culture, as Rourke argued. However, her suggestion that this created a humour of energetic nonsense verse in which 'burlesque was natural to the negro' is rather more difficult to accept today.[114] The point of *American Humor*, though, was to demonstrate that all three archetypes were indigenous, and that they had a long history of representation in popular culture: from frontier theatre plays, joke books, comic almanacs such as *The Rip Snorter*, journals like *The Spirit of the Times*, song books and even political stump speeches. Where other critics had depicted an American culture shaped by a Puritan heritage of repressed emotions, Rourke suggested they had been looking in the wrong places, and revealed instead an America that was a 'nation of mythmakers' and storytellers with 'riotous imagination'.[115]

She then went further, however, to claim that this 'low' culture actually stood as the foundation of great American literature; that it was the 'authentic' and 'unique' soil 'out of which serious literary art' had grown. Walt Whitman, for instance, was credited with using the 'expansive, flam-boyant language of the backwoodsman' to sound his 'barbaric yawp', turning the 'native comic rhapsody' into poetic form. Edgar Allan Poe was, she argued, 'near to those story-tellers of the West who described wild and perverse actions with blank and undisturbed countenances', with hoax stories like *Hans Pfall* descended from the frontier's tall tales. Herman Melville drew on 'those lusty undirected energies which had persistently maintained the sense of legend', with *Moby Dick* containing echoes of New England sea lore and the tall story of 'The Big Bear of Arkansas'. Even Henry James in *The American* utilized the archetypal Yankee in the char-acter of Newman, who confuses others as to whether he is 'very simple or very deep'. Through to contemporary writers such as Willa Cather, Ring Lardner Jr, and Sinclair Lewis, Rourke traced a 'consistent native tradition' with evidence that America's 'high' and 'folk' cultures were built on the same base.[116]

The imprecise nature of some of the links drawn between the comic trio and their literary antecedents is a weakness of the study. Yet for Rourke to proceed with a reevaluation of American culture, it had been necessary to make *American Humor* as forceful as possible, to refute arguments that had earlier been made by her friend Van Wyck Brooks. In *America's Coming of Age* (1915), Brooks had argued that the nation's cultural development had always been impeded by the great divide between 'Highbrows' and 'Lowbrows' and the lack of 'genial middle ground' in which the cultures could nourish one another.[117] Moreover, in *The Ordeal of Mark Twain* (1920), he also claimed that America had 'no folk-music, no folk-art, no folk-poetry, or next to none', and thus had few foundations for an original literary tradition.[118] *American Humor* undercut both claims. In fact, Rourke devoted most of a chapter to Twain, demonstrating at length how stories like *The Jumping Frog of Calaveras* drew on the author's formative years in the region where 'the tall tale had grown in stature'; how his writing possessed the 'garrulity and inconsequence of the earlier comic storytellers of stage and tavern'; and how *Innocents Abroad* reshaped the Yankee fable.[119] Brooks accepted Rourke's correction with grace, revising *The Ordeal* in 1933 to strike out his earlier assertions about the poverty of native culture. He later acknowledged readily how 'my horizon was indefinitely broadened by Constance Rourke's eager and eloquent studies'.[120]

American Humor embodied Rourke's determination to undertake what she called 'the difficult task of discovering and diffusing the materials of the American tradition, many of them still buried'.[121] It was a mission she continued with great energy and output. She produced over one hundred articles and reviews mapping indigenous and contemporary culture, and authored biographies of Davy Crockett and John James Aubudon, exploring the myths constructed around them. In 1934 she organized the National Folk Festival in St Louis, and in 1936 was appointed as editor of the government–sponsored Index of American Design – a vast pictorial survey of the nation's heritage in decorative and folk arts. She also compiled research from all over the country for her planned multi-volume *History of American Culture*, with the ambition of presenting 'evidence of enough native culture to convert a generation of disenchanted artists'.[122] Her sudden death of an embolism in 1941 unfortunately meant the project was never finished. However, the work which was published posthumously in *The Roots of American Culture*, alongside *American Humor*, irrefutably confirmed Rourke's status as a pioneer in American Studies.

Further Considerations

The dominant narratives assigned to a decade can be illuminating, at least when the various ideas about history, life and culture that they serve to represent are explored rather than taken for granted. Some cultural activities in the 1930s did correspond to the prevailing labels, as in the case of proletarian literature in regards to the 'Red Decade' or the Federal Theatre Project's Living Newspapers as a self-conscious component of the 'New Deal Era'. Yet it is also patently true that tensions were rife within the elements of American cultural experience encompassed by such critical constructs. Many different and often competing visions of the New Deal co-existed, coming to the fore in different programmes. Moreover, the fact that seventeen million Americans still voted for the Republican candidate Alf Landon in 1936 cannot be dismissed as a 'reactionary' vote. The effort to rationalize cultural and regional diversity as a vital component of national identity was never completely satisfactory, and often flew in the face of continuing localism and sectionalism. Even Rourke's work was problematic in its use of commercially produced materials (plays, books and almanacs) as evidence of 'folk' culture. And the posturing of left-wing intellectuals as 'brain workers' barely disguised the fact that they were effectively rewriting Marxism to give themselves a role in the 'class struggle'. In fact, the very idea of a proletarian revolution in the United States repeatedly ran up against the social and economic aspirations of the enormous American middle class, prompting a perpetual tension throughout the decade between radicalism and reformism, even within the American Communist Party itself.

It was such tensions, as much as the dominant impulses of the decade, which stimulated the diverse and rich responses that constitute the culture of the 1930s. Despite the selectivity and reductivism inherent in any such study, I have sought to include a measure of the variety of the arts, forms and genres of cultural production, not only those which were direct and easily understandable, but also those which were unusual and more difficult to categorize. Considering some of the key debates over radicalism, nationalism, regionalism and contemporary concerns abut the cultural relativism, subsequent chapters have been organized so as to emphasize the connections between prevalent cultural forms: (1) literature and drama; (2) film and photography; (3) radio and music; and (4) art and design. Chapter 5 is then devoted to the federal government's direct involvement in cultural production, particularly the patronage of the New Deal's arts programmes. Against the necessary segmentation of this book into such distinct chapters, however, the reader should always bear in mind that a great cultural dialogue existed in the 1930s that defies such separation, and that poets, photographers, composers, novelists, dramatists, film-makers and designers all stimulated each other, and often worked together in both their artistic and political commitments.

Chapter 1

Literature and Drama

By 1933 publishing revenues were less than half of what they had been in 1929. The following year only fifteen American authors sold more than 50,000 copies of their books. Several publishing houses declared bankruptcy and few had the money to risk making advances to new, untested authors. Literary magazines either suspended publication or slashed their page counts, reducing the opportunities for poets and short-story writers. Playwrights were hit even harder. Outlets for traditional drama had always been limited but in the Depression touring legitimate theatre virtually ceased to exist, regional and local theatres could rarely afford the rights to popular contemporary works, and by 1932 two-thirds of playhouses on Broadway were closed. Only the investment of Lee Schubert's personal fortune enabled the Schubert theatre organization to escape from receivership. Few but the most prominent authors and dramatists were able to make their living exclusively by writing and, of those who did, most were able to do so only by heading to Hollywood and contributing their often uncredited talents to movie-scripts.

Yet writing itself did not slump. New plays were staged by Eugene O'Neill, Clifford Odets, Maxwell Anderson, Thornton Wilder, Lillian Hellman and William Saroyan – playwrights whose work will always count among the nation's greatest dramatic achievements. Some critics have also ventured to describe the decade as one of the 'great ages' of the novel, encompassing the best works of John Steinbeck, William Faulkner, John Dos Passos and Zora Neale Hurston among others. Langston Hughes, Muriel Rukeyser, Kenneth Fearing and William Carlos Williams were among those making significant contributions to American poetry, while 1938 saw the publication of the textbook *Understanding Poetry* by Cleanth Brooks and Robert Penn Warren which, for decades to come, transformed the way in which literature was analysed and appreciated in classrooms around the country. The literary potential of the South in particular bore remarkable fruit in a celebrated 'Southern Renaissance'. The poetry of Warren, Allen Tate and John Crowe Ransom, the fiction of Faulkner, Ellen Glasgow, Thomas Wolfe, Katherine Anne Porter, Erskine Caldwell, and even the African American perspective of Hurston and Richard Wright's *Uncle Tom's Children* (1937), all used specifically Southern material to explore questions about humanity, history and the needs of the nation. Notwithstanding the economic downturn, new marketing strategies helped maintain a popular market, including the Book-of-the-Month Club which grew to distribute nearly 300,000 copies of the books it recommended, and the advent in 1939 of Pocket Books Inc. which issued paperback reprints of bestsellers and classics for just 25 cents. Detective novels, epic historical romances like *Gone With the Wind*, and 'women's novels' such as *Back Street* by Fannie Hurst and *All This and Heaven Too* by Rachel Field proved to be the most popular fiction of the decade. Radio also provided a new forum for plays and poetry as witnessed by Archibald MacLeish's *Fall of the City* and Orson Welles's Mercury Theatre of the Air.

In explaining the conditions in which literature still flourished, there is truth in the suggestion that an economy of high unemployment left 'writers and readers alike' with 'time for contemplation'.[1] The return to the United States of many of the expatriate generation of the 1920s once 'the checks to Paris stopped', also meant that more American writers contributed to their native culture. Writers were galvanized particularly by the painful collapse of the economy and the threat of national disintegration itself. One explanation given for the Southern Renaissance is that 'when the Crash came, bringing the nation down almost into the dust, it found the South waiting there, already on familiar terms with history's great negative lessons of poverty, failure, defeat and guilt'.[2] More generally the 'desire to explore the disordered nation, celebrate its epic qualities and speak for its troubled populace' lay behind a vast outpouring of words, questioning 'what had America become? What future might it anticipate?'. In answering these questions, 'radicalism was no longer disloyalty'. This in itself brought new vigour to the theatre, with Communist-affiliated groups such the Theatre Union (1934–7), the left-wing Group Theatre (1931–41) and union-organized workers' theatres creating drama that sought to stir audiences to political action.[3] Likewise during its heyday of 1933 and 1934 the 'revolutionary' movement for 'proletarian literature' briefly revitalized the literary world, encouraging new novels by writers such as Jack Conroy, James Farrell, Edward Dahlberg and Clara Weatherwax, along with dozens of experimental magazines publishing new poems, short stories and essays (many anthologized by Granville Hicks and Michael Gold in *Proletarian Literature in the United States*, 1935). For a while, at least, many writers were energized by the thought that they were playing a central role in both a cultural revival and a political revolution.

The limited ability of the commercial sector to provide America's writers with a livelihood also led to alternative efforts to institute a 'safety net'. The Communist movement provided aspiring writers with the support network of John Reed Clubs. With thirty branches and 1,200 members in 1934, the Clubs offered writers' schools, ran small magazines and encouraged 'real-life proletarians' to become novelists, including Richard Wright and Nelson Algren.[4] Although the Marxist orthodoxy could be 'very severe on you', recalled Meridel Le Sueur, 'I don't think any of us would have survived without the Reed Clubs and our bond with each other . . . We wouldn't have tried without them'.[5] Although the Clubs were dissolved by Soviet dictat in 1935, the American Writer's Congress continued the Communist Party's involvement in supporting a left-wing literary community until the end of the decade. By then, however, a greater stimulus was provided by the federal government's projects for writers and dramatists. The Federal Writers Project provided work for over 6,000 people, encouraging such notable authors as Wright, Ralph Ellison, Saul Bellow and John Cheever. The Federal Theatre Project encouraged new dramatists in innovations like the 'Living Newspaper' and premiered plays such as *Prologue to Glory* by E. P. Conkle and *It Can't Happen Here* by Sinclair Lewis. It also spurred new developments such as Welles's Mercury Theatre and the co-operative venture of the Playwrights Producing Company, established in 1938 by Robert Sherwood, Maxwell Anderson and others to ensure the staging of their own works.

Vitality in literature, drama and poetry cannot, however, be related simply to the issues raised by the Depression or the encouragement of outside agencies. The imperatives and impulses which drove Americans to write were as diverse in the 1930s as in any other decade. Focusing on the ways in which matters of radical politics, national identity and 'escapist' culture were examined within contemporary literature, this chapter discusses how authors were pulled in various directions at once: political radicalism vs escapism; literary modernism and theatricalism vs realism; region vs nation; man vs nature; and nostalgia vs hope for the future. The case studies under examination (Steinbeck's *The Grapes of Wrath*, Hurston's *Their Eyes Were Watching God* and Wilder's *Our Town*) are not necessarily representative, but they do remind us not to reduce the literary 1930s to simplistic notions of the 'Depression Era' or the 'Red Decade'.

Literature as a Weapon

One of the more misleading notions about the culture of the 1930s is epitomized by Tom Wolfe's assertion that 'for more than ten years', American writers 'suspended the Modern movement'.[6] The decade is often presented as a lamentable hiatus in which modernism was displaced by Marxist 'social realism' which ruthlessly 'eschewed verbal acrobatics' and aesthetic form 'for the sake of the wider cause'.[7] This perception, however, often owes more to the sharp exchanges between literary critics on the intellectual Left than to the literary and dramatic works themselves.

The so-called 'literary wars' stemmed from the demand for 'proletarian literature' and 'workers' theatre' framed by Mike Gold, Joseph Freeman, Granville Hicks and other Marxist critics. At the moment of capitalism's collapse, these men believed in the need for a socially-engaged literature that could function as a 'weapon' in the presumed imminent revolution. The modernist emphases on aesthetic experimentation and the creation of art as a sufficient end unto itself presented ideological obstacles to their goals. For the written word to be effective in raising class-consciousness, workers needed to be able to comprehend it and relate it to their own experiences. As Gold characterized modernist literature, the 'sickly mental states of idle Bohemians, their subtleties, their sentimentalities, their fine-spun affairs', had 'nothing to do' with 'the real conflicts of men and women who work for a living'.[8] Instead, the call was for frank and accessible material – if possible, written by working-class authors 'toughened by life' – that conveyed the 'revolutionary élan' the proletariat needed to move toward militant organization and insurgency.[9]

The response was substantial, especially from young writers for whom the movement promised both 'a renaissance and a revolution' in which their writing 'was work for a great future'.[10] Much of the resulting literature consisted of narratives of self-discovery in which individuals attained their class awareness. Gold's *Jews Without Money* (1930) fictionalized his own childhood in the slums of the Lower East Side and his family's descent into poverty, ending with his conversion to Marxism and his dedication to the workers' revolution. Similar trajectories shaped other quasi-autobiographical novels, such as Edward Dahlberg, *The Bottom Dogs* (1930), Agnes Smedley, *Daughter of the Earth* (1929) and Jack Conroy, *The Disinherited* (1933). Conroy's own experiences, including the death of his father in a coal mine and his itinerant years of ill-paid work in automobile plants and rubber factories, were relived through the character of Larry Donovan, culminating in Larry leaving to organize poverty-stricken farm workers. The actual process of labour organization was then followed through in stories that depicted strikes in locales and industries as diverse as the lumber mills of the Pacific Northwest in *Land of Plenty* by Robert Cantwell (1934) and the New York department stores of Leanne Zugsmith's *A Time to Remember* (1936).

The most celebrated strike drama of the decade, however, was presented on the stage. When the closing shout of Clifford Odets's *Waiting for Lefty* – 'STRIKE! STRIKE! STRIKE!' – was taken up by the audience as well as the actors, it was labelled 'the birth cry of the thirties'.[11] Through flashbacks, the play depicted the experiences of people from various walks of life, now only able to find work as taxi drivers. One driver argues constantly with his wife about the debasing poverty they have been reduced to; another loses his girlfriend because her family objects to his financial inability to support a wife; a third had his career as a laboratory technician cut short when he objected to the unscrupulous practices of his employers. As these men debate whether or not to strike, a corrupt union racketeer counsels patience, but with each vignette their grievances mount. The final straw comes when they learn that Lefty Costello has been murdered, shot in the head by opponents of the strike.

Workers' theatres further engaged responsive audiences by playing direct to unions and labour councils, especially in industrial centres like Pittsburgh and Detroit. Some unions themselves developed drama groups, such as New York's Local 65 of the United Wholesale and Warehouse Employees which produced the *Wholesale Mikado*, or the International Ladies Garment Workers Union whose *Pins and Needles* revue was such a success that it transferred to Broadway. Other productions addressed particular concerns that the CIO wanted to bring to the attention of workers. *Stevedore* by Paul Peters and George Sklar, and *Let Freedom Ring* by Albert Bein were both designed to encourage white ethnic workers to rethink their prejudices against African American labour. The latter play demonstrated how the owners of textile mills had used racial divisions to their advantage and offered the blunt lesson to white working-class audiences that if they did not 'include African-Americans in your organizing drives', then employers would hire them as strike breakers.[12]

The prominence of ideology in such fiction and drama gave fuel to the 'literary wars'. A debate over the 'mechanical' application of Marxism to art had existed from the outset, as critics such as Philip Rahv and William Philips asserted that the 'zeal to steep literature overnight in the political program of Communism' produced only 'sloganized and inorganic writing'.[13] Hicks himself acknowledged he had 'tolerated' formulaic tales of 'conversion' in order to further encourage writers to 'project revolutionary optimism'.[14] But it was not until serious splits developed in the left-wing consensus that a devotion to 'modernist values' became an explicit political position in itself.[15] With their faith in the Soviet Union betrayed by the brutality of the Moscow trials, Stalin's persecution of Leon Trotksy and eventually the Nazi–Soviet Pact of 1939, politically-committed writers such as James Farrell came to view the whole decade as a time when they had been led down the 'wrong path', accepting the 'ready-made political slogans and programs' of the Party without thinking for themselves, and producing work which was more often 'intellectual suicide' than the 'path of intellectual adventure'.[16] Championed particularly after 1937 in the pages of Rahv and Philips's reconstituted *Partisan Review*, the defence of modernism came to be seen as a marker of a writer's supposed independence, casting the 'Old Left' as having been in thrall to a dogmatic and philistine anti-modernist philosophy.

Such charges might stick to a few works that were naive or blunt, but for the most part it had been critics (rather than the authors or playwrights) who had insisted on judging the worth of a book or play in terms of its 'service to the working class'. The notion of a 'hiatus' in modernism during the 1930s obscures far more than it reveals. Indeed, recent re-evaluations such as Barbara Foley's *Radical Representations* and Robert Schulman's *The Power of Political Art* have done much to demonstrate how authors, poets and dramatists who sought to present a social viewpoint in their art did so in more aesthetically sophisticated ways than the narrow labels of 'proletarian' and 'social realist' literature convey.

Several left-wing poets, for example, followed the modernist approach of incorporating the language of the 'low' media of movies, advertising and photography into their art, but for the purpose of making a radical political statement. Langston Hughes in *Come to the*

Waldorf Astoria (1931), for instance, turned a two-page advertisement he had seen in *Vanity Fair* (where 'the depression did not exist') into a satiric call for the homeless and destitute to 'choose the Waldorf as the background for your rags', inviting them to 'take advantage of the amenities' and dine with some of 'the men and women who got rich off of your labor'.[17] The poem certainly drew on inflammatory Communist slogans, but Hughes used parody and absurd juxtapositions to imbue them with new vigour. Similarly Muriel Rukeyser in *The Book of the Dead* (1938) fuses poetic language and excerpts from the ancient Egyptian Book of the Dead in a radical montage far more powerful and affecting than any 'slogans about workers'.[18] Like many pieces of social fiction, *Book of the Dead* engaged with a particular cause, in this case the workers of Gauley, West Virginia, who had breathed in pure silica while drilling a tunnel for Union Carbide and were subsequently dying of silicosis. Combining high art with left-wing politics and documentary innovations akin to the Federal Theatre's 'Living Newspaper' productions, sections of the poem transcribe the Congressional hearings which exposed how Union Carbide had deliberately diverted the tunnel through a rich vein of silica in order to sell it to the steel industry, chose to save money by not wetting down the drill, and did not warn the men to wear masks because, 'as one foreman said, the black workers were not worth $2.50'.[19] These facts are then juxtaposed with the dramatic monologues of a mother whose sons had died of silicosis, an engineer on the project, doctors who treated the dying and workers who were suing for compensation, all based on letters and Rukeyser's own visit to Gauley. As Schulman argues, 'the subtlety, accuracy and moving power of their speech rendered into poetry' allows language itself to 'celebrate their dignity, importance and humanity' – doing justice to their anguish and pain at the same time as indicting capitalists for their exploitation of men who were 'drilling their death'.[20]

Even in drama that might be formulaically Marxist, modernist techniques were employed with considerable effect. *Waiting for Lefty*, for example, dissolved the boundary between audience and stage, with actors planted in the auditorium as 'voices' of the union. *Winterset* by Maxwell Anderson (1935), however, stands out as one of the most aesthetically challenging of political plays. Through Mio Romagna's quest to prove the innocence of his father, a radical thinker executed for a payroll robbery and murder he did not commit, Anderson presented the tragic consequences of justice perverted by political expediency, prejudice and brute power. A rumination on the American Left's *cause*

celebre of the trial and execution in 1927 of Italian immigrant anarchists Nicola Sacco and Bartolomeo Vanzetti, *Winterset* is a verse play.
While Anderson's earlier verse plays, such as *Elizabeth the Great*
(1930) and *Mary Queen of Scotland* (1933), used a distant historical
locale to provide an 'appropriate aura' for his 'unrealistic' poetic
diction, *Winterset* disturbed audiences by situating blank verse dialogue in modern America, with the effect of presenting the Sacco and
Vanzetti case as a national tragedy of Shakespearean proportions.[21]

Among novels, Josephine Herbst's trilogy of *Pity is Not Enough*
(1933), *The Executioner Waits* (1934) and *Rope of Gold* (1939) offers a
prime example of literature in accord with Marxist theory, yet which is
neither formulaic nor anti-modern. Like *Jews Without Money* and *The
Disinherited*, the work is quasi-autobiographical, drawing on Herbst's
family history with protagonist Victoria Chance as her surrogate. In the
first two volumes, Victoria explores her family's history. First, though
the story of uncle Joe, the narrator examines the corrupt workings of
Gilded Age politics and finance, as the railroad defrauds the state of
Georgia. Then, she compares her own father's business struggles to the
success enjoyed by his brother-in-law, a banker who made his first
money by exploiting miners. As Victoria learns of this, she comes to see
that her family's 'failings' had been due to 'capitalist forces beyond their
control'.[22] Radicalized like Herbst, she marries a Communist writer
and becomes a journalist documenting the struggles of the poor, first in
rural Pennsylvania and then among the peasant revolutionaries of
Cuba. While such a brief description may sound formulaic, Herbst's
novels expand 'radical fiction beyond a narrow insistence on a proletarian setting' by emphasizing a middle-class background, and challenge the masculine emphasis of much proletarian literature by
exploring the impact on women of 'their involvement with men
engaged in the quest' for money and power.[23] Linear chronology is also
disrupted, as Victoria reconstructs her family's past from the vantage
point of the present day, and fragmented by the inclusion of what
Herbst called 'interpretative inserts' which blend journalism and
fiction. In *The Executioner Waits*, for instance, an episode on the
International Workers of the World (IWW) during the First World War
is juxtaposed with two scenes from 1932 of Iowa farm strikes and a
young militant voting for Foster and Ford, establishing the roots of
contemporary radicalism within the United States. *Rope of Gold* also
introduces the narrative of Steve Carson engaged in a sit-in strike at the
Ford automobile plant in Detroit, which has no direct bearing on
Vicky's story but presents the reader with a larger context of 'real' paths

toward radicalism that are just as meaningful as Vicky/Herbst's fictionalized experience. While Herbst leaves the parallels up to the reader
to judge, Vicky's episodes in Cuba and Steve's experiences in the United
States 'mutually reinforce one another', with the threat of dictatorship
abroad and Henry Ford's contempt for workers' rights becoming two
aspects of the same 'worldwide threat'.[24]

The text, that most disrupts the stereotypes of Marxist literature,
however, is undoubtedly John Dos Passos's trilogy of U.S.A.
Throughout *The 42nd Parallel* (1930), *Nineteen Nineteen* (1932) and
The Big Money (1936), Dos Passos embarked on a self-consciously
formal modernist design, juxtaposing different modes of writing,
rhetorical strategies and conventions from a variety of genres to represent the 'sounds' of America's 'many voices'.[25] The lives of twelve
fictional characters are followed from just before the First World War
to the Depression in a conventional style, though their narratives inter-
sect only occasionally. But as 'threads in the American tapestry', they
are set against the biographies of twenty-seven real figures from
American history, such as president Woodrow Wilson, architect Frank
Lloyd Wright and socialist Eugene Debs. Sixty-eight sections present
another mode of address, as collages of headlines, song lyrics and
speeches, often seemingly random, like a 'verbal equivalent of what an
inattentive viewer might gather' from the cinematic newsreels.[26] A
further fifty-one sections present what Dos Passos called 'the Camera
Eye' – his most experimental writing, employing modernist techniques
of stream-of-consciousness commentary, incomplete sentences and
intense subjectivity to form introspective and poetic meditations on
the times. As each mode changes and breaks up the narrative, the frag-
mentation itself conveys anxiety about the state of America.

The overall effect is assertively political, 'collectively enact[ing] the
nation's decline'.[27] A recurring trope among the fictional characters is
of people selling their humanity in pursuit of the 'big money': writer
Dick Savage prostitutes his talents to the demands of advertising, and
actress Margo Dowling chases the 'easy money' by marrying men who
can propel her to stardom. Engineer Charley Anderson initially typi-
fies the American dream of success through creative ingenuity, seeking
only to design better airplanes, but success leads him into ruthless
business practices, associating with corrupt politicians and selling out
his friends. A growing hunger for wealth propels Charley to marry
into the upper classes, but he becomes progressively frustrated and
addicted to drink, dying an emotional wreck. Parallels in Dos Passos's
positive biographical sketches of inventors like Orville and Wilbur

Wright and negative ones of Thomas Edison and Henry Ford, whose energies become misdirected when 'aimed toward amassing wealth for its own sake', underscore a narrative of America's hopes and ideals being compromised, abandoned and destroyed.[28] The novel's form is thus integral to Dos Passos's political perspective.

Yet for all *New Masses* critics claimed Dos Passos as their ideal, *U.S.A.* privileges a native tradition of radicalism over Marxist ideology. *The 42nd Parallel* celebrates the progressivism of Wisconsin's Robert LaFollette, for instance, while *Nineteen Nineteen* aligns the author's sympathies with the IWW martyrs Wesley Everest and Joe Hill. In some ways, this heritage establishes that radicalism is not unAmerican. *The Big Money,* however, displays growing hostility to Communism, as the fictional narrative of party hack Don Stevens demonstrates how dogmatic acceptance of Marxism can be just as dehumanizing as selling your soul to capitalism. Instead, the novel's most positive biography is of American economist Thorstein Veblen, whose own writings on the domination of monopoly capitalism are presented as native alternatives to the Left's reliance on Marx. In an 'unusually direct connection' the biography of Veblen appears shortly before the fictional character of Mary French is radicalized by reading his *The Theory of the Leisure Class* (1889).[29] Dos Passos may have agreed that Marxists were correct in their analysis of the situation, but he did not believe in their solutions, declaring in 1934 that what the country needed most was 'a passionate unMarxian revival of Anglo-Saxon democracy'.[30]

In short, there was a wealth of left-wing literature and drama in the 1930s that was far from formulaic, uniform, inartistic or anti-modern – some of it embodying Marxist ideology, some reconfiguring native radicalism. Recent critical reappraisals have drawn attention to previously overlooked works such as Robert Cantwell's *The Promised Land* (1934) and Edward Newhouse's *You Can't Sleep Here* (1934) and many women writers such as Grace Lumkpin, Myra Page, Josephine Johnson and Tillie Olsen. Alan Filreis's study of poet Wallace Stevens has shown how 'left discourse and poetics significantly influenced even those like Stevens who were not part of the organized left'.[31] Even F. Scott Fitzgerald advocated the reading of Marx, and described *Tender is the Night* protagonist Dick Diver as 'a communist-liberal-idealist' in his draft manuscripts.[32] In seeking to rehabilitate individual writers and works from the anti-Stalinist vision of the 'Red Decade', some critics have in the past sought to strip them of their politics, but arguments such as Schulman's rightly stress the need to respect the political engagements of all this writing without perpetuating restrictive formulations.

John Steinbeck, *The Grapes of Wrath* (1939)

John Steinbeck's political consciousness emerged comparatively late in the decade, in part due to his isolation in northern California from the radical debates of New York's literati. It was also because the suffering of the Depression hit his home state hardest in the years after 1935, when the influx of midwestern migrants from the Dust Bowl reached flood tide. As a million impoverished people entered California in a despairing search for the promised land, Steinbeck found himself increasingly exposed to what he was to call 'the most heart-breaking thing in the world'.[33]

The Grapes of Wrath was the product of his genuine anger and anguish as the state's agricultural companies exploited the 'Okie' migrants, paying the lowest wages they could to those who were starving and desperate to work. Victims of both the natural disasters of drought and dust storms and of the economic collapse, Steinbeck produced a journalistic record of their situation as 'The Harvest Gypsies' for the *San Francisco News*. Witnessing how the landowners sanctioned police brutality to crush efforts among the workers to organize and protect their rights, Steinbeck became determined to 'knock these murderers on their heads'.[34] An early effort resulted in a work of satirical fury, but he destroyed this manuscript (titled *L'Affaire Lettuceberg*), conscious that it was intended 'to cause hatred' rather than help 'people understand each other'.[35] Conceived in a different frame of mind, *Grapes* retained his insights into the tyranny of bankers and California's Growers Associations, but married them to the very human struggles of the fictional Joad family – people who maintain their integrity and dignity, even as nature and capitalist greed conspire against them.

Although Steinbeck asserted that he 'never had much . . . faith nor belief in realism', the novel's detail and veracity was drawn from first-hand research. He made further trips into California's agricultural heartlands in the company of Tom Collins, the manager of a Farm Security Administration camp set up by the government to shelter migrant workers.[36] Witnessing, too, the staggering suffering caused by the floods at Visalia and Nipomo in 1938, in which thousands of families were marooned in the waters, Steinbeck turned *Grapes* into a thorough testament to their woes. But like Josephine Herbst before him, Steinbeck adopted an unconventional structure in which chapters on the Joad family's exodus are juxtaposed with short, factually-oriented interchapters. Often lyrical and stylized, these chapters treat the climatic, social and economic forces besetting other anonymous migrants: banks foreclosing on farmsteads; tractors 'raping' the land; and agribusinesses who spend more money on buying guns to repress the migrants than they do on paying wages. In doing so, Steinbeck put the emotional core of the Joads' particular story into a more universal context.

Of the Joads, Tom's narrative is the most politicized, charting a relatively conventional transformation from self-interested loner to champion of the class struggle, radicalized by the conditions he encounters and the treatment he receives. His consciousness is shaped in particular by the former preacher, Casy, who is eventually murdered by the Growers' Association's thugs when he tries to organize a strike among migrant peach-pickers. Killing one of those vigilantes in self-defence, Tom picks up Casy's mantle, telling his mother that all injustices are now his cause and that wherever people are in trouble or fighting 'so hungry people can eat', 'why, I'll be there'. Yet the politics of this protest were less informed by Marxism than by nature. From his reading of Ralph Waldo Emerson and his observations of marine biology, Steinbeck had already formed a theory of 'group man' or the 'phalanx', holding the basic socio-biological belief that when individuals form groups they become part of some larger 'organism'. This, to Steinbeck, was 'a truer thing than ideologies'.[37] As Casy expresses the idea in the novel, 'maybe all men got one big soul ever'body's a part of'.

Casy's union organizing and Tom's announcement of his activist intent represent this realization of one man's relation to other men and his responsibility to them all. The interchapters prepare the reader for this 'movement from "I" to "we"', narrating the trials of all those others who migrated in search of work. But it is the progressive expansion of 'family' which really presents this concept, first with the Joads joining the Wilsons and the Wainwrights on the road, then at the temporary camps where 'twenty families became one family'. The novel ends by privileging this consciousness over one dictated by class interest. Following the floods, Ma Joad encourages her eldest daughter, Rose of Sharon, to breastfeed a starving old man. Ma's own family has been broken up, and Rose's baby has been stillborn, but this intimate nurturing of a complete stranger, recognizing only his need, reconstitutes a broader humanity. 'It used to be that fam'bly was first', states Ma, but 'it ain't so now. It's anybody'.

An immediate sensation, *The Grapes of Wrath* sold almost half a million copies in the first six months after its publication in March 1939. As a story that could be read both as a call for left–wing action and a conservative paean to agrarianism, a populist epic of human resilience, or a celebration of the New Deal's intervention on behalf of the migrants, Steinbeck's novel could be all things to all people.[38] In fact, reactions were often polarized. Oklahoma's representatives in Congress denounced it as a vulgar lie, but Senate hearings also vindicated it as the truth about California's farm labour conditions. Dozens of libraries banned it, yet others had waiting lists for the novel that were months long. Literary critics such as Leslie Fielder dismissed it as 'sentimental entertainment (hoked up with heavy-handed symbolism)', yet it was also awarded the Pulitzer Prize.[39] Directed by John Ford and starring Henry Fonda as Tom and Jane Darwell as Ma Joad, the 1940 film adaptation also picked up awards, with two Oscars and five other nominations, even though it provided a more optimistic ending at the New Deal camp and omitted the desperate struggle to survive the flood. The quality which comes through the movie, however, is the same epic dimension of heroic endurance that made the novel so popular, manifest in Darwell's final lines: 'We're the people that live. They ain't gonna wipe us out. Why we're the people – we go on'.

Figure 1.1 Frank Darien, Russell Simpson and Henry Fonda as the Joads in John Ford's adaptation of *The Grapes of Wrath* (1940: Twentieth Century-Fox/The Kobal Collection).

Rediscovering America

In his groundbreaking 1973 study, William Stott presented 1930s social fiction as part of a broader culture of 'documentary expression'.[40] *The Book of the Dead* and the 'Newsreel' chapters of *U.S.A.* are cases in point, as are *The Grapes of Wrath*'s roots in Steinbeck's journalistic undertakings. Even while writing the novel, Steinbeck still wondered if the best way to 'put a tag of shame on the greedy bastards who are responsible for this' would be 'through newspapers' rather than fiction.[41] Yet the widespread desire to expose the experiences of America's people went further than just a leftist 'documentary impulse'. Rather it was driven by a broad range of concerns – from regionalist and nationalist, political and journalistic, ethnographic and personal – which together produced a body of work that not only 'documented' the crisis, but reconfigured what was meant by 'America'.

The Depression certainly caused some writers to abandon their earlier work and take up new causes; poet George Oppen, for example, stopped writing temporarily in order to organize the unemployed in

Brooklyn. Others, like Theodore Dreiser, felt that the country's conditions made any effort to write fiction completely 'ridiculous'.
Asking 'How can one more novel mean anything in this catastrophic
period?', Dreiser instead produced a series of journalistic reports
examining the struggles of tobacco farmers and coal miners.[42] His 400-
page *Tragic America* (1931) presented a swathe of raw data assaulting
the corporate, religious and educational organizations that he judged
responsible for this new 'American tragedy'. Numerous writers likewise 'set aside their former genres for the travel report'.[43] Sherwood
Anderson, Louis Adamic, Lorena Hickok and Edmund Wilson, to
name just a few, were driven – often in anger – to try to comprehend a
moment of national disaster that seemed 'so full of confusion that one
could not be certain of events unless he actually witnessed them'.[44]
Especially at the start of the decade when Hoover made blithe assurances that 'no one has starved', writers felt impelled to reveal the reality
of the situation and to personalize the suffering that statistics 'fail to
express'.[45] Nathan Asch was a typical example, spending four months
of 1932 circling the country by bus in 'search' of ordinary people's
responses to the Depression. Reports of firsthand encounters were
often published in magazines such as *New Republic* and then followed
up in book-length studies, such as Asch's *The Road: In Search of
America* (1937), Anderson's *Puzzled America* (1935) or Gilbert
Seldes's *The Years of the Locust* (1933). Sometimes these works suggested that Americans were 'beaten' psychologically, as the failing capitalist system first made them unemployed and then encouraged them
to take responsibility for their own circumstances. Others presented
'the people' as resilient and dignified in the face of adversity. In either
frame, these texts focused on America's dispossessed as middle-class
writers sought to put a human face to the economic collapse and to
'lessen the distance' between themselves and its victims.[46]

    Some commentators have since viewed this turn to reportage as a
symptom of art falling foul of politics, and draw attention to accounts
such as Tillie Olsen's of the 'pressure exerted on her by the Young
Communist League to submerge her "writing self" by turning her
interests from fiction to journalism'.[47] Others depict it as a 'failure of
narrative imagination', as in Walter Lowenfels explaining that he had
'died as a poet' when 'It wasn't that I had no more to say, but that I had
no way to say it'.[48] Yet for some, the documentary impulse either com-
plemented their creative work or became an artistic effort in its own
right. In one instance, Erskine Caldwell embraced documentary
writing to refute critics who questioned the realism of his fiction,

specifically the degenerate Georgia 'crackers' who populated his novels *Tobacco Road* (1932) and *God's Little Acre* (1933). *Some American People* (1935) and the photo-journalism of *You Have Seen Their Faces* (1937) were both produced to document the sad reality that the 'pathetic and depraved' tenant farmers and sharecroppers, the 'grotesques riddled with poverty and disease' of Caldwell's novels, were far from figments of his imagination.[49] In doing so, Caldwell drew attention back to the social criticism implicit behind the bawdy humour of his fiction, namely that cultural and economic deprivation had ground away any semblance of civilization among the poorest of the South, reducing to primitivism the families of dirt farmers such as Ty Ty Walden and Jeeter Lester.

On the other hand, James Agee's text for *Let Us Now Praise Famous Men* (1941) sought to 'see the dispossessed in new ways', creating an original approach to documentary literature that reacted against the decade's 'exposés of suffering' even as Agee wrote one himself.[50] Initially commissioned by *Fortune* magazine to 'do a story' on three sharecropper families in Alabama, Agee confronted the 'presumption' of the privileged world 'pry[ing] intimately into the lives of an undefended and appallingly damaged group of people'.[51] In reflecting his misgivings about 'exploiting' the Ricketts, Gudger and Woods families who hosted him and photographer Walker Evans for eight weeks, Agee strove to forge a style that would be 'as unpalatable to the aesthetes of suffering as he could possibly contrive'.[52] In consequence, the book is full of dense detail, rendering their bleak lives with incredibly close attention to everyday objects which he treats with 'the importance they had for the families'.[53] Social protest is certainly present in this; the dilapidated homes are an 'abomination' to Agee, their meager possessions 'a steady shame and insult' to society. Yet it also remains a 'deeply self-conscious' work meditating on how to represent those 'who cannot represent themselves – cannot speak in their own voices. . . cannot defend their interests or assert their rights'.[54]

This determination to seek out those 'who cannot represent themselves' was integral to the documentary literature, as projects such as Richard Wright's *12 Million Black Voices* and the Federal Writers' Projects publications gave new visibility to African Americans, Native Americans, immigrants and ethnic minorities, sharecroppers, blue-collar workers and the unemployed. Some regionalist publications, particularly *I'll Take My Stand* (1930) and *Who Owns America?* (1936), counted a uniquely 'Southern experience' among the cultures of the United States that had allegedly been 'ignored' and from which the nation as a whole could draw strength and fortitude. For the most part, however, the literature was one of cultural pluralism rather than an argument for any given culture's 'rightness'. Like Agee, the majority of writers adopted an approach that sought to awaken readers to their kinship with a range of Americans about which they may never previously have known. It was a spirit that then extended into fiction, poetry and drama.

Fiction that sought to 'tell the story of the actuality of the American Melting Pot' came into particular focus in the 1930s, nurtured initially by the autobiographical emphasis of the proletarian movement.[55] Stories of the working class were often intrinsically the stories of second-generation immigrants, whether sons of Irish painters in Farrell's *Studs Lonigan* trilogy, Italian bricklayers in Pietro di Donato's *Christ in Concrete* (1939), or Chinese laundrymen in H. T. Tsiang's *And China Has Hands* (1937). In keeping with the mood of the Depression, these immigrant sagas (or 'ghetto pastorals') were often critical of the naive American Dream of the first generation, but their basis in personal experiences 'as lived' rather than imagined, compelled readers to reconsider what it meant to be American.[56] Jewish American literature, in particular, flowered, with new writers including Nelson Algren, Isadore Schneider, Paul Goodman and Daniel Fuchs. *Jews Without Money* (1930) by Michael Gold epitomized a predominantly secular tone which posited radicalism or social reform rather than Judaism as the answer to the degradations of the immigrant slums. In *Call It Sleep* (1934), Henry Roth used a stream-of-consciousness narrative to explore the effect of the ghetto on the impressionable mind of six-year-old David Schearl, and convey his struggle to comprehend a confusing world 'created without thought of him'. Roth's prose style also captures the disorienting multilinguistic soundscape of the 'melting pot', as David encounters characters whose first tongue remains Yiddish, German, Italian or Polish. All these immigrants, alike, are torn between the promises of the American Dream and the realities of urban hunger and fear. Few immigrant writers now soft-peddled ethnic and racial divisions, for if (in the reformist vision) the nation was ever to be reconstituted more inclusively, these problems needed to be acknowledged and addressed.

An emergent Native American literature also took issues of degradation and assimilation as its key themes. First performed in 1932, Lynn Riggs's play *The Cherokee Night* depicted a number of 'mixed-breed' young adults as tragic figures caught between the two worlds of Indian and white culture. Born in the Indian Territory of Claremore,

Oklahoma, to a mother who was one-eighth Cherokee, Riggs projected on to his characters his own conflicted feelings about this inherited identity (a sensibility intensified by a struggle with his homosexuality). Viney Jones, for example, associates 'Indian' life with only the squalor and social collapse of the contemporary reservation, and leaves Claremore to marry a wealthy white man. She hates her origins and denies them, asking what would 'being a part–Indian get me? Do you think I want to be ignorant and hungry and crazy in my head?. John Joseph Mathews and D'Arcy McNickle explored similar feelings in their novels, with both Archilde Leon in McNickle's *The Surrounded* (1936) and Chal Windzer in Mathews's *Sundown* (1934) embarrassed by their tribe's customs and drawn toward pursuing a 'white' life instead. Yet in contrast to Rigg's Viney, these protagonists come to realize that the circumstances they despise have resulted from the efforts of white society to enforce assimilation and break down tribal traditions. Mathews's novel also locates this process not in the distant past but in the 1920s, when oil and natural gas found on the estates of the Osage Indians attracted white opportunists, who both exploited Native society and encouraged newly wealthy Osages to denigrate their own culture. *Sundown* met a particularly receptive audience, alert to the Dust Bowl, who now understood the 'human devastation that was brought about by the unchecked exploitation of natural resources and poor people'.[57]

The drive to dramatize the degenerative effects on personal identity of white values and racist actions was increasingly strong, too, among African American writers. Langston Hughes in *Not Without Laughter* (1930), presents the character of Tempy in the same vein as Riggs's Viney. The daughter of a poor but beloved black washerwoman, Tempy absorbs white middle-class values as her own, rejecting the spirituals of her community as 'too Negro', and asserting that African Americans needed to come 'up to the level of white people, talk like white people, think like white people – and then they would no longer be called niggers'.[58] Books such as Claude McKay's *Banana Bottom* (1933) and Hughes's 1934 collection of short fiction *The Ways of White Folk* went further in exposing the way in which white society constrained black identity within their prejudiced expectations. The harshest dissection was undoubtedly Richard Wright's *Native Son* (1940), wherein Bigger Thomas can only mark out an identity of his own through violence. Born in Chicago's South Side, Bigger takes the chance to escape poverty by working as a chauffeur for a wealthy white family, but his fearful awareness of white prejudice and racial injustice, born of his experiences in the ghetto, conspires against him. Putting the family's daughter Mary to bed after she has drunk herself into oblivion, Bigger is so terrified of being caught in the 'forbidden territory' of a white woman's bedroom that he uses a pillow to stifle her moans and accidentally suffocates her. Realizing he has committed murder, he disposes of Mary's body in the basement furnace and implicates her boyfriend by forging a kidnap note. Rationalizing that whites would never suspect a black man of being intelligent enough to plan such a crime, 'elation' filled Bigger at having broken the ultimate taboo.[59] The act in itself created an identity for him, one that rejects the passivity and stupidity ascribed to him by white society, and for the time Bigger eludes detection, 'never had his will been so free'.

The frankness of Wright's novel confronted white America with the rage and frustration that oppressive racism was incubating. And, despite his political affiliations, Wright included the Communist Party in his indictment. Although the Party supplies Bigger with a sympathetic lawyer, Max sees him more as a 'cause', a representative case of racial injustice in which 'every Negro in America's on trial', rather than as an individual human being. White America – however well–meaning – can only restrain Bigger's existence by limiting it to the dimension of race.[60]

As is the case with much commentary on 1930s literature, political interpretations come to the fore, but the perceived need among writers to identify and promote the racial, ethnic and regional qualities of the national experience was always entwined with an anthropological dimension. Tempy in *Not Without Laughter*, for instance, is only one character among many, with Hughes giving greater attention to the lives of the ordinary 'folk', in a detailed recreation of the 'endurances, humor, love and courage' by which such poverty-stricken black communities existed. For Hughes, only through such awareness of cultural resources could African Americans resist the 'urge within the race to whiteness, the desire to pour racial individuality into the mold of American standardization'.[61] Riggs felt the same way about Native American culture, with all the characters in *Cherokee Night* conflicted and unhappy, except for the pure–blood John Gray-Wolf who remembers 'the way my people lived' and thus retains a 'laconical peace of spirit'.[62] Renditions of dialect, as in Roth's portrayal of language in *Call It Sleep*, similarly reflected a contemporary determination to capture the 'real' way in which under-represented people spoke and behaved. It was even present in works that perpetuated stereotypes, as in Marc Connelly's play, *Green Pastures* (1930), which placed Old

Testament stories in the setting of rural Louisiana with an exclusively African American cast. As a white author, Connelly's notion of setting the Creation at a fish-fry, for instance, appears condescending, but he conceived it as 'an attempt to present certain aspects of a living religion in the terms of its believers' – and he studied rural communities near Baton Rouge firsthand to achieve an authentic representation of dialect when bringing their spirituals to the stage.[63] Indeed, it won an award from the National Association for the Advancement of Colored People (NAACP) in 1931, embraced by W. E. B. DuBois as an 'extraordinarily appealing and beautiful play based on the folk religion of Negroes'.[64] Whatever its limitations, *Green Pastures* fulfilled one of the key functions of the literature of 'the people' that so characterized the 1930s: seeking to give a voice in American culture to those who had not before been heard by the nation.

Zora Neale Hurston, *Their Eyes Were Watching God* (1937)

Matters of representing and gaining a previously quieted cultural voice were central to Zora Neale Hurston in *Their Eyes Were Watching God*. Celebrating the quest of Janie Crawford, an African American woman, to progress toward self-awareness and find her own voice, the novel was also Hurston's vehicle for rendering visible to the rest of the United States the expressive culture of the independent all-black community of Eatonville, Florida.

It opens with Janie returning to Eatonville to tell her story to her friend Phoeby Watson. She traces her life from childhood to middle age, through relationships with three men, the first two of whom deny her an independent identity. Local farmer Logan Killicks is chosen for her by her grandmother, and when Logan treats Janie more like a mule than an intelligent woman, she says nothing but runs away with the ambitious Joe Starks. Yet as Starks becomes mayor of Eatonville, he treats Janie as a trophy wife and forces her to again conform to *his* notions of propriety. Her voice is explicitly denied. When the townspeople elect Joe and ask Janie for a few words, he interrupts, saying that 'mah wife don't know nothin' 'bout no speech-making . . . She's uh woman and her place is in de home'.[65] Abused by Joe, Janie withdraws into herself to discover she 'had a host of thoughts she had never expressed to him, and numerous emotions' which had never been articulated. She also realizes that 'she was saving up emotions for some man she had never seen'.[66] When Joe dies, she finds that man in Tea Cake and, in the passionate and spontaneous love they share, she also finds her 'natural' self. Even when a rabid dog bites Tea Cake and Janie tragically has to kill her lover in self-defence, this process does not end. The very telling of her story to Phoeby demonstrates that Janie has found her voice, and she finishes by pulling 'in her horizon like a great fish-net', no longer needing to seek for meaning and validation outside herself.[67]

The feminist dimensions of Janie's achievement of a sense of self against men who view black women as possessions, account for much of the novel's continued resonance since its 'rediscovery' in the 1970s.[68] Yet in 1937, Hurston was best known as a 'champion of the primacy of black folk culture'.[69] She had known Eatonville from her childhood (her family had moved there shortly after her birth in the 1890s), and when she began studying anthropology in the late 1920s she returned to collect folk tales, spirituals, work songs and blues: material she described as 'the arts of the people before they find out there is any such thing as art'.[70] She travelled further in the South and the Caribbean, recording and analyzing stories and customs, while a Guggenheim Fellowship also enabled Hurston to research the anthropology of voodoo in Jamaica and Haiti, which is where she composed *Their Eyes*. Indeed, throughout the 1930s, Hurston explored a variety of ways in which to bring her ethnographic documentation of African American culture to the widest possible audience. *Mules and Men* (1934) was a book of folk tales collected in Florida and New Orleans, while she used *Jonah's Gourd Vine* (1934) as a fictional vehicle for the sermons of folk preachers. In *The Great Day* (1931), *From Sun to Sun* (1933) and *All De Live Long Day* (1934), Hurston found the performative dimensions of the stage play particularly effective in disseminating the material she had accumulated, authenticated further by casts featuring many of Eatonville's citizens. She conceived *Their Eyes* in this frame, its innovative use of language representing the speech patterns of African American dialect. Suffusing the text with the 'similes, metaphors, and the rhythms that are the poetry of black vernacular expression', Hurston sought to preserve and render the oral culture in a literary form.[71]

In this context, Janie's struggle for voice represents a confluence of folklore, language and black self-determination. The novel is full of long sections of playful exchanges, passages of 'signifying' in which characters try to outdo each other in trading humorous put-downs and insults, which Hurston knew from the storytellers who sat on the porch of Eatonville's store and 'passed around pictures of their thoughts for the others to look at and see'.[72] These displays of verbal prowess and improvization are depicted in the novel as the means by which one becomes a full member of the community – a means denied to Janie by Joe, who deems her participation unladylike. At first Janie 'pressed her teeth together and learned to hush'.[73] But when Joe insults her failing looks in front of the townspeople, speech finally becomes her weapon. She fights back, insulting his manhood by telling all who could hear that 'When you pull down yo' britches, you look lak de change uh life'.[74] Her silence and submission is over, and Joe's dominance is fatally crushed. Later, when Janie hears the men in the Everglades holding 'big arguments like they used to on the store porch', she can now 'listen and laugh and even talk some herself if she wanted to'. Indeed, she 'got so she could tell big stories herself' – the biggest being the story of her life.[75]

If *Their Eyes* originated in Hurston's desire to preserve the expressive vernacular of African American storytelling traditions, her focus on Eatonville suggested how black America had created its own culture, independent and apart from white America. However, the resulting depiction of a self-contained black experience with little evidence of racial conflict invited considerable criticism from Richard Wright. Attacking Hurston's novel for failing to engage with 'either race or the class struggle', in contrast to his own angry, socially-motivated writing, he damned it as carrying 'no theme, no message, no thought'.[76] Critics have since noted that Wright's reading was at the very least blind to the theme of 'patriarchal power' that infuses the novel – which itself embodies an element of racial criticism.[77] Joe Stark's lust for control over both Eatonville and his wife, for instance, is, as Janie recognizes, conceived in emulation of 'rich white folks'. Further, in the aftermath of a hurricane, the evils of racism are apparent when the bodies of the white dead are given individual coffins, while blacks are thrown into a mass grave. Ultimately though, Hurston's response to Wright was that she was simply more interested in probing 'that which the soul lives by', than in documenting oppression. To her, African American fiction that focused exclusively on 'the race problem. . . saturated with our sorrows', was itself a false picture. 'We talk about the race problem a great deal', she wrote, 'but go on living and laughing and striving like everybody else'. [78] Instead, 'I made up my mind to write about my people as they are' – creating the 'sense of black people as complete, complex, undiminished human beings' that readers like novelist Alice Walker have so admired.[79]

Dreams Deferred

Wright's dismissal of *Their Eyes Were Watching God* as devoid of social problems and espousing 'no message' was characteristic of the politicization of literary criticism. The label of 'escapist' was applied frequently, and usually derogatorily, to works that appeared to be apolitical or used fantasy, humour or nostalgia as 'relief' from the miseries of the Depression. Humorists such as James Thurber and S. J. Perelman, for example, were charged by the Left with producing 'triviality' so 'resolutely turned away from anything in life' that they were nothing more than 'court jesters for their decaying betters'.[80] Thornton Wilder, in particular, came under assault for 'turning his back on the ravages of capitalism', as Mike Gold launched a notorious attack on his period-set bestsellers, such as *Woman of Andros* (1930), as prime examples of a 'decadent' and 'genteel' escapism. In a tirade that painted Wilder's writing as 'a daydream of homosexual figures', Gold chastised the author not only for writing for a wealthy minority who wanted nothing in their literature that would disturb their comfortable lives, but also for distracting the middle classes from the serious issues of the times.[81] From the Marxist perspective, literature that failed to engage with contemporary social realities was an act of evasion, guilty of perpetuating a 'false consciousness'.

For some writers, however, escapism was as legitimate a response to contemporary circumstance as proletarian fiction. Thurber's rejoinder to his critics was a great celebration of fantasy, 'The Secret Life of Walter Mitty', published in *The New Yorker* in March 1939. Mitty overcomes the routine drudgery of his life by drifting into fanciful daydreams where, in his imagination of wartime heroics, sensational murder trials and *Dr Kildare*-style soap opera, he can always be 'Walter Mitty the Undefeated', possessing the mastery and respect he lacks in the real world.[82] His is an escape from the mundanity of suburbia and a domineering wife, rather than from economic disaster, but the opposition of his fantasy life to his ineffectual existence struck a universal chord. Not without coincidence, the *Superman* comic strip, launched in 1938, embodied similar masculine/boyhood fantasies with the all-powerful hero hiding behind the Mitty-like disguise of Clark Kent.[83] In reconsidering such 'escapist' elements of popular culture, Lawrence Levine observes that 'even in their "escape", people can be realistic in understanding what it is they need to do to maintain themselves; what kinds of fiction, myths, fantasies they require, not primarily to escape reality but to face it day after day after day'.[84] Given the 'crisis of masculinity' that accompanied the massive unemployment of the Depression, with the loss of 'breadwinner' status undermining traditional male authority, the fantasies of Mitty and *Superman* were hardly less of a 'realistic' response than the cult of the male working-class body and the belligerent masculinism celebrated in proletarian art and literature.

As Robert Escarpit has argued, when evaluating 'escapist' culture, it is essential to 'know what and towards what we are escaping'.[85] The great popular appetite for historical novels certainly suggested a desire to retreat towards the past. Books such as *The Good Earth* (1931), *Anthony Adverse* (1933) and *Northwest Passage* (1937) topped the bestseller lists each year of the decade, with *Gone With the Wind* (1936) reported to have outsold every other book except the Bible. These lengthy behemoths, as the *New York Times* suggested, 'furnished several weeks entertainment for only $3', and offered most readers 'prolonged escape into a more colorful, romantic world than the shabby one about them'.[86] Yet rather than offering the solace of 'simpler times', most authors insisted that their books had contemporary relevance. The Chinese setting of *The Good Earth* by Pearl Buck drew readers into an alien culture, but was also familiar in its story of beleaguered peasants forced to leave their farmstead due to drought and crop failure. Walter Edmonds's account of valley farmers during the War of Independence in *Drums Along the Mohawk* (1936) similarly depicted the poverty, starvation and threat of war early pioneers had faced, as well as their disillusionment with a distant central government that failed to respond effectively to local problems. Edmonds's introduction stressed that this was 'not a bygone picture'.[87] Even Hervey Allen, tracking his hero's adventures from Napoleonic France to the American West, conceived of *Anthony Adverse* as 'the biography of a man struggling to remain a complete human being in the midst of a dying commercial civilization and a rising one of international capitalism, industrialism and competitive nationalism'. Allen confessed, though, that it would 'never do to say that aloud', and readily acceded to publishers who advertised it as romantic, rather than social, fiction.[88]

   Gone With the Wind has long been considered in this light. Margaret Mitchell's depiction of Civil War Georgia presents a world not 'far removed' from America in the 1930s: a world which begins 'bursting with hope and promise' like the America of the 1920s, only to disintegrate suddenly into 'chaos and unreason'.[89] This was not a conscious parallel, for Mitchell began writing in 1926 and had finished by 1930. Rather, Scarlett O'Hara's transformation from southern belle to an opportunistic and ruthlessly acquisitive 'embodiment of self-willed energy' suggests that Mitchell was engaged more immediately with regionalized concerns about the nature of the 'New South'.[90] Rhett Butler's observation that the 'Southern way of living is as antiquated as the feudal system of the Middle Ages . . . It had to go and it's going now', echoes the contemporary argument that the region had to move away from the 'aristocratic' agrarian values of its antebellum society toward a 'Northern' style industrial-political economy.[91] But beyond this subtext, *Gone With the Wind* was always a story of survival, an examination, as Mitchell described it, of 'what makes some people able to come through catastrophes and others, apparently just as able, strong and brave, go under'.[92] In the Depression this clearly had great resonance. Observers like Malcolm Cowley acknowledged that such historical literature flourished not because the past was 'picturesque', but because writers like Mitchell were using it 'to find heroes whose example would assure us about the future'.[93] *Drums Along the Mohawk* affirmed the strength of those like Lana and Gil,

Figure 1.2 Clark Gable reads Margaret Mitchell, *Gone With the Wind* (Hulton Archive/Getty Images).

who find everything they have dreamt of – land, a home and family security – taken from them by war, yet who continue to fight and rebuild their lives. Robert Rogers' resourceful leadership in *Northwest Passage* by Kenneth Roberts offers an heroic idealism that succeeds against French and Indian attackers, the weather, exhaustion and hunger. *Gone With the Wind* tops them all, as Scarlett O'Hara survives the war, the siege of Atlanta, the destruction of the 'Old South' and her reduction to poverty, to take control of her destiny, rebuild her plantation and make good on her vow to 'never go hungry again'. Compounded by David O. Selznick's epic film adaptation in 1939, the story of Scarlett's resilience became a phenomenon of 1930s culture.

The popularity of detective fiction was also phenomenonal, with almost half of the best-selling novels of the 1930s belonging to this genre. Erle Stanley Gardner's Perry Mason stories made him the market leader throughout the decade, but the genre also proved lucrative for John Dickson Carr (with his Dr Fell 'whodunits' like *The Mad Hatter Mystery*, 1933), Rex Stout (whose creation Nero Wolfe first appeared in *Fer-De-Lance* in 1934), and Ellery Queen (the penname of

Frederic Dannay and Manfred Lee). Public taste for detectives crossed over into comic books (Chester Gould's *Dick Tracy* debuted in 1931), radio (*The Shadow* and *I Love a Mystery*, for instance), and film (including *Charlie Chan* and *The Thin Man* series). The decade also witnessed the debut of Nancy Drew with *The Secret of the Clock* (1930) followed by a further seventeen stories by 1941. At a time when a quarter of a million teenage Americans were 'riding the rails' in a desperate search for itinerant work, 'Nancy Drew country' seemed like pure escapism, occurring in 'another time dimension, untouched by the outside world', as the pretty, popular and affluent sixteen-year-old 'supergirl' solved mysteries and righted wrongs.[94] Gardner similarly eschewed any social purpose, claiming he wrote only 'to make money and . . . give the reader sheer fun'.[95] The 'fun' of many of these imaginatively constructed adventures, however, came from enabling readers 'to confront mystery, peril and even death', in a world that was often rotten and crooked, but which yielded ultimately to the courageous detective's efforts to return order to society.[96]

The emergence of a distinctly 'hard-boiled' style of crime fiction complicates this picture. Dashiell Hammett, in particular, is credited with bringing the genre 'back to the real world', and his *Red Harvest* (1929) was more akin to proletarian fiction than *Perry Mason*. Brutal gangsters are hired by a powerful industrialist to suppress a miners' strike, but when the thugs themselves take over the town, the reader is confronted by a world in which 'gangsters masquerade as businessmen, capitalists contract with criminals, and no one can tell the difference between them'.[97] The world in which Hammett set *The Maltese Falcon* (1931) is similarly one of ubiquitous duplicity and murderous anarchy unleashed by competitive greed. Raymond Chandler also developed such cynical visions of contemporary society. In *The Big Sleep* (1939), for instance, the daughters of the wealthy Sternwood family consort with gangsters and pornography racketeers, and behave as if their class and money puts them above the law. Chandler's Philip Marlowe at least possesses some form of moral superiority in this environment, but more often, as in the case of Hammett's Continental Op and Sam Spade, the detective himself was 'half gangster'.[98] Moreover, the 'triumph' in hard-boiled crime fiction was a world apart from the usual affirmation of detective novels, withholding the comfort of the solution to the crime restoring good order to society. Although evil is resisted in *The Big Sleep*, justice remains elusive and the pornographer, blackmailer and 'killer by remote control' goes free.[99] Marlowe's detective work changes little.

In fact, such fiction reflects something of a broader current within American literature that was reacting against 'escapist' elements of Depression era culture. William Faulkner's *Absalom, Absalom!* (1936), for example, could be interpreted as a modernist challenge to the escapist qualities of both detective and historical fiction, when Quentin Compson's investigation into the rise and fall of Thomas Supten exposes the destructive racist insistence on white supremacy at the heart of Supten's story and of Southern history in total.[100] There is no 'escape' or 'solution' for Quentin (or the reader) in this history, unless he comes to terms with its consequences in the present, and even then Faulkner's conclusion sees Quentin anguished and immobilized with disgust for the society that made him. Even aspects of *Gone With the Wind* seem to question the cultural hold awarded to fictive, legendary pasts, critical of Ashley Wilkes's unrealistic, nostalgic attachment to the 'Old South', and characterizing Scarlett as one who instead 'draw[s] her courage from the future'.[101]

For other writers, though, it was Hollywood that perpetuated the most destructive escapist myths and illusions, especially when (to them at least) the Depression rendered belief in the American Dream untenable. In James M. Cain, *The Postman Always Rings Twice* (1934), it was Cora's dream to make it in the movies. The failure and frustration of this dream, having ended up as a waitress in an emotionally and sexually unfulfilling marriage, is what leads inexorably to the murder of her husband. Nathanael West in *Day of the Locust* (1939) likewise focuses on the lives of disenchanted Midwesterners who come to Hollywood to make their fortunes, drawn by fantasies of luxury, power, sex and excitement, but meet only with frustration and failure. Realistic hopes and dreams, in West's analysis, have been displaced in popular culture by fatuous and counterfeit ones – escapist illusions that may keep the film industry functioning, but which only cheat the people who believe in them. Painting his vision of the overthrow and ruin of Los Angeles, Tod Hackett predicts the bitterness and anger that will come when these people realize their dreams are just delusions. As the novel concludes with a frenzied riot at a movie premiere, Tod's vision seems about to be realized. Violence is the inevitable consequence when the pursuit of happiness is displaced by the pursuit of the unattainable.[102] The final stage of this abrasive nihilism was presented by Horace McCoy in *They Shoot Horses, Don't They?* (1935), as two out-of-work film extras, Gloria and Robert, partner each other in a gruelling five-week long dance marathon. Initially subscribing to the American dream – 'an ideological fantasy world where penniless

Hollywood extras can miraculously become wealthy and powerful' – Robert gradually drifts toward his partner's bitter but clear sense of the hypocrisy and exploitation of these fantasies. When the dance ends suddenly and even the last-ditch hope of winning the prize money is taken away, Robert accedes to Gloria's request to shoot her and put her out of her misery.[103]

Yet if writers like West and McCoy, and indeed many of the 'proletarian' writers responded to the times with an anxious sense of fatality, bleak scenes of entrapment and the destruction of hopes and dreams by an unjust society, the American public was not quite ready to share their cynicism. Cain's *Postman* may have been a bestseller because of its frank sexual content, but West was never a commercial success before his death in 1940. *They Shoot Horses* was dismissed unjustly as a 'penny dreadful' at its first appearance, and American publishers rejected McCoy's second novel, *No Pocket in a Shroud*. Louis Adamic's report in 1934 on 'What the Proletarian Reads', demonstrated that workers 'had very little interest in the literature addressed to them by the radicals of the period', with the 1935 American Writers Congress reporting that proletarian novels rarely sold more than one or two thousand copies.[104] It was a miniscule fraction of sales of 50,000 copies a day achieved by *Gone With the Wind*. And as an endorsement of escapism, the popular response to 'The Secret Life of Walter Mitty' was so great that it was dramatized on radio, adapted by Hollywood and made into both a musical comedy and an opera. Nathaniel West's analysis of the power of 'counterfeit' fantasies may have been accurate, since Mitty's daydreams clearly derive from the popular culture of movies, adventure fiction, soap opera and tabloid journalism. However, if the reaction to Mitty is anything to judge by, most Americans were still more inclined to embrace such fantasies than revolt against them.

Thornton Wilder, *Our Town* (1938)

Set at the turn of the twentieth century in the fictional New Hampshire community of Grover's Corner, *Our Town* depicts three days in the lives of Emily Webb, George Gibbs and their respective families. Through those days the common experiences of life are presented. Emily and George grow up, fall in love, get married and start a family. Emily dies in childbirth, yet this is presented not as a great tragedy but as a sad fact of human existence. Nothing unusual happens in Grover's Corner; it is, as one character

notes a 'very ordinary town if you ask me'.[105] Yet for all that *Our Town* tran-
scended political conflict for a 'timeless meditation' on human existence it
was very much a product of its times, conceived by Wilder in reaction to
the Left's criticism of his work.

Mike Gold's assault on Wilder as 'The Prophet of the Genteel Christ', in
an article for the *New Republic* in October 1930, had been a crucial opening
salvo in the decade's 'literary wars', as Gold staked out why Marxists would
no longer tolerate the 'subtleties', 'sentimentalities' and 'fine-spun affairs'
of a 'moribund bourgeois culture'. With a series of novels set in eighteenth–
century Peru (*The Bridge of San Luis Rey*, 1927), Rome (*The Cabala*, 1926)
and pre-Christian Greece (*The Woman of Andros*, 1930), Wilder was vulnerable 'to charges that he was either indifferent' to contemporary social
problems 'or unable to confront them'. Where, asked Gold, was the 'blood
and horror and hope' of breadlines, sweatshops and strikes? In Gold's
assessment, Wilder was writing about a 'museum, not a world', so much in
love with 'the archaic' that he failed even to use history 'as a weapon to
affect the present'.[106] Such work could possess no social function.

Superficially, *Our Town* does little to refute Gold's charges. Grover's
Corner possesses the potential for class conflict. Ten per cent of the
population are illiterate labourers, working in the mill owned by the town's
banker Mr Cartwright, and ethnic groups of Catholic Poles and French-
Canadians are separated by the railway from the white Protestant middle-
class homes of the Gibbs and Webbs. However, these aspects are reported
to us by the Stage Manager simply as facts; they have no bearing on the
narrative, and we never see Cartwright or any of the workers.[107] They are,
however, important in their irrelevance. When actors planted in the audience
are given the opportunity to ask questions of the play's characters, a
'Belligerent Man' asks if anyone in town is 'aware of social injustice and
industrial inequality', and why they don't 'do something about it?'. Editor
Webb's response is one that stresses humanism over dogma. Social justice
is defined as matter of ensuring that 'the diligent and sensible can rise to
the top', while the community tries 'to take care of those that can't help
themselves, and those that can we leave alone'.[108] *Our Town* is escapist,
but self-consciously and defiantly so, acknowledging the divisive issues of
ethnic diversity, economic hardship and social injustice, but then deliberately dismissing them – in pointed rejection of the Left's contention that only
writing about the immediate problems of the day could be significant.

Instead of socio-politics, 'significance' in *Our Town* lies in the erstwhile
trivialities of everyday life. Routine occurrences such as the milkman and
newspaper boy making their daily rounds, choir practice and chatter
between neighbours about chicken incubators constitute *events* in this
play. Grander occasions such as George and Emily's wedding day are also
rendered as 'ordinary', with the minister noting that weddings are 'interesting' only 'once in a thousand times'. Unlike agit-prop drama, no profound conflicts emerge to make life in Grovers' Corner in any way different
to that of anywhere else. Yet as the act of stringing beans or sharing a soda
become the subject matter of a play, these things are imbued implicitly with

cultural freight. Wilder presents the morning of Act I as merely an average day, but because the audience has never before observed a Gibbs family breakfast this simple unpretentious scene acquires its own authority as a novel experience. Indeed, it is suggestive of the contemporary argument of anthropologists such as Ruth Benedict, that the significance of a culture is to be found in the 'pattern of living' followed by its people.

Act III, however, evolves this into a broader philosophy, as the spirit of Emily joins the ranks of the dead in Grovers' Corner cemetery. Given the chance to revisit one day in her life, Emily chooses her twelfth birthday as one of the happiest – and we see a familiar breakfast scene unfold again. But seeing it through the perspective of Emily's dead soul gives it an unanticipated and overwhelming sense of transience. Emily's excitement turns to sorrow when she sees how that day was taken for granted. The tragedy of the play is not Emily's death, but the failure of human beings to feel 'the full intensity of each moment'.[109] In Wilder's analysis the most pressing concern is not, as the Marxists would suggest, people's 'ignorance and blindness' to the social ills of the world, but rather their blindness to the value of life itself. *Our Town* shows instead that the commonplaces of small town America could provide the central, life-affirming idea that simply existing is 'too wonderful for anybody to realize' in its fullness.[110]

Nostalgia certainly plays a large part in this metaphysical sentiment, for the people of Grover's Corner seem to be able to take the time to smell the heliotrope, appreciate the beauty of the moonlight and otherwise cherish their existence, because their life is one of 'simpler times'.[111] The three selected days take place in 1901, 1906 and 1913, isolated from modernity: before boys from the town were killed in the First World War, before mass industry came, and just before the automobile fractured local ties. Yet nostalgia for such an innocent idyll is complicated by the staging of *Our Town*, which is deliberately minimalist, with bare costuming, no scenery and an absence of props requiring the actors to mime their everyday actions. This theatricalism, of course, foregrounds the artificiality of the production, making us aware that both the play and the small town are allegorical constructions. However, the need to imagine objects that do not exist, including the town of Grovers' Corner itself, fully implicates the audience in its nostalgia. It requires each spectator to construct his or her own vision of what turn-of-the-century New England small towns looked like, adapting personal or culturally-mediated memories to Wilder's text. The charge that Wilder presents a 'false consciousness' of the past cannot stick to *Our Town*, because it is the audience whose consciousness is brought into play.[112] On the stage, the idea that she can 'go back' to the past seduces Emily; and it seduces the audience too. Probably the most treasured play of the 1930s, and one of the most performed of the century, *Our Town* constructs nostalgic escapism as a universal desire fundamental to the way in which we come to terms with life. Yet it also simultaneously underscores the lesson that we should savour and cherish every moment of the present instead.

Figure 1.3 Thornton Wilder, *Our Town* (1938: Wisconsin Center for Film and Theater Research).

Further Considerations

This chapter has allowed little space for works such as F. Scott Fitzgerald's *Tender is the Night*, Ernest Hemingway's 'Snows of Kilimanjaro' (1936) and Edith Wharton, *The Buccaneers* (1938), while there is much more to be said about Faulkner's *Absalom, Absalom!* and his other novels and stories. Readers wishing to better understand the decade should also consider poets as diverse as Wallace Stevens and Robert Frost, and plays from John Howard Lawson's *Marching Song* (1937) to Philip Barry's *The Philadelphia Story* (1939). As *Our Town* demonstrates, even as writers were fully aware of the currents of ideological criticism and the political and social traumas of the decade, not all were striving to produce 'timely discussions' of the Depression's social problems. The sensitivity of writers to the human predicaments of life, love and death often took on a politicized dimension during the 1930s, but it was never truly eclipsed by angry or doctrinaire political statements, and individual voices continued to defy categorization.

Chapter 2

Film and Photography

Documentary photographs of extensive human misery allowed for little by way of escape from the Depression. Those like Dorothea Lange, Carl Mydans and Russell Lee, who became documentary photographers during the decade were often personally distressed by the suffering they witnessed in the country at large, and hoped that 'with sympathetic portraits of the downcast they could protest the circumstances of stricken Americans'.[1] Many perceived photography as the perfect medium for 'more direct involvement' with the harsh and confusing realities of the 1930s which writers were trying to make sense of.[2] Their efforts were filled with 'a feeling that if suffering could just be exposed, then surely it would be eased somehow'.[3] The government itself, through the New Deal's Resettlement Administration (RA) and later the Farm Security Administration (FSA), quickly employed these photographers for just such a purpose, using their images as visual arguments in support of specific relief legislation and interventionist programmes, believing that 'the only way to make the public understand' this crisis was to 'take them there with pictures'.[4]

Yet the best known photographs of the 1930s were not the emblematic images of Dorothea Lange's 'Migrant Mother' (1936) or Walker Evans' pictures of the Gudger family in *Let Us All Now Praise Famous Men* (1941). Instead, more than 30 million Americans every year clamoured for copies of the work of George Hurrell, Ernest Bacharach, Lazlo Willinger and Clarence Sinclair Bull. These were the men who took the portraits of Joan Crawford, Norma Shearer, Greta Garbo, Johnny Weismuller and Fred Astaire and many others, developing stylish still images that encapsulated the 'essence' of the movie star. Dramatic lighting, bold styles and extensive retouching of the negatives imbued them with 'glamour' – defined contemporaneously as 'sex appeal plus luxury, plus elegance, plus romance' – and recast

Figure 2.1 Spectres of the Depression: Dorothea Lange, 'Children in Cotton Growers'
Camps' in Eloy District, Arizona (1940: National Archives, Washington DC/The Art Archive).

Hollywood actors as a pantheon of modern gods and goddesses, in a
fantasy that denied the mundane reality.[5] Even President Roosevelt
was sold on the escapist iconography of Hollywood, publicly praising
Shirley Temple's 1934 film *Baby Take a Bow* with the observation that:

> When the spirit of the people is lower than at any time during this
> Depression, it is a splendid thing that for just 15 cents, an American
> can go to a movie and look at the smiling face of a baby and forget his
> troubles.[6]

Figure 2.2 'The Smiling Face of a Baby', Shirley Temple (c. 1935: General Photographic Agency, Getty Images).

Shirley Temple was no mere child star, but *the* superstar of the Depression. She was the top box office attraction every year from 1935 to 1938. Almost 90 per cent of Twentieth Century-Fox's profits for 1936 were attributable to just three of her films. The films themselves may not have always allowed Americans to 'forget' their troubles:

Baby Take a Bow, for instance, saw Temple's character reduced to poverty. But Roosevelt was not wrong about Shirley Temple's appeal. Her 'smiling face' *was* escapist, and quite specifically so. Unlike the generalized glamour of most star images, hers was an image that offered relief from 'the most persistent' and disturbing 'spectre' of the Depression: the image of children in unwarranted distress.[7] In November 1930, the White House Conference on Child Health and Protection had reported that six million children in America were chronically undernourished, and documentary photographers rarely let Americans forget this. Russell Lee pictured starving children in Illinois and Iowa, Margaret Bourke-White in *You Have Seen Their Faces* presented children deformed by illness and disability, and a pale sad-eyed boy haunted Walker Evans's photographs from West Virginia. Ben Shahn's 'Children of Destitute Ozark Mountaineer, Arkansas 1935' caught children with nothing to play with except a broken doll and a wretched-looking cat. Two children lean on the shoulder of Lange's iconic 'Migrant Mother' in need of comfort, but their faces are turned away from the world, their postures slumped in defeat or exhaustion. The baby in her lap is practically hidden from view. Distracted and anxious, the mother seems almost unaware of their presence, as if worrying about how she can protect her children from further suffering. One of Lange's 1936 photographs from Oklahoma was simply entitled 'Damaged Child'.

Evoking direct emotional responses, these images sought to convey how desperately help was needed. Innocents like these should not know such poverty, want and despair. Children who ought to be showing 'the natural exuberance of youth' had become exhausted witnesses to tragedy, and their powerlessness makes the spectator long to be able to protect them.[8] In contrast to photographs of adults, who frequently evidenced quiet dignity and resilience in the face of difficult circumstances, the pictures of children conveyed 'defeat and disaster'.[9] The image of Shirley Temple, then, was an alternative vision – even when she was reduced to poverty herself in films like *Dimples*, servitude in *The Little Princess*, or orphaned in *Captain January*. Whereas Mydan's 1936 portrait of 'Baby Girl near Lexington, Tennessee' captured a 'heart rending' expression that 'suggests circumstances have robbed her of childhood's lightheartedness', no circumstances could ever rob Shirley of hers.[10] She possessed all the qualities the photographed children lacked: effervescence, optimism, vivacity. Temple was more aligned with the FSA pictures of adults, offering a symbol of resilience, pluck and fortitude. Her sunny disposition in the face of desperate odds was clearly at the core of her popular resonance. Indeed, 'Little Miss Sunshine' was the image of an idealized childhood, possessed of confidence, innocence and optimism, constructed by grown-up filmmakers who sought to preserve their hopes for the children of America.[11]

This contrast underscores a common perception of Depression era culture dichotomies – whereby the movies were dominated by escapism and photography by the documentary impulse. There is evidently considerable truth behind this. Photographers such as Willard Van Dyke expressed the then widely-held belief that 'art must be identified with contemporary life' and that the 'Photo-Document is the most logical use of the medium'.[12] On the other side, the head of the film industry, Will Hays, confidently predicted in 1934 that 'historians of the future' would agree that the movies had 'literally laughed the big bad wolf of the depression out of the public mind'.[13] However, for all of the contrast between the images of Shirley Temple and the 'Damaged Child', the fact remains that the actual narratives of Temple's films saw her confront difficult circumstances time and time again. And the fact remains that the sultry, seductive portraits of Norma Shearer produced by George Hurrell were a million miles away from Lange's 'Migrant Mother'. These facts alone should again caution against accepting any reductive readings of 1930s culture.

Making the World a Happier Place to Live In

One particular fallacy is the notion that Hollywood was 'depression proof'. The surge in profits generated by the introduction of sound certainly enabled studios to ride out the first years of the downturn, and record receipts were made in 1930 when weekly attendance reached a high of 80 million people. But decline set in through 1931, hitting cinema chains in major cities especially. Fox's losses in 1931–2 amounted to almost $12 million, and led to a merger with Twentieth-Century Pictures. Paramount, RKO and Universal called in the receivers. Despite having generated extraordinary profits in the late 1920s, Warner Bros. now only avoided bankruptcy by closing half of its theatres, cutting wages and slashing budgets. Only Loews-MGM remained in the black, though even its profits of $10 million in 1930 had fallen to just $1.3 million in 1933.[14] Even the sale of popcorn provides evidence of the slump. During the 1920s, cinema owners who sought a 'high class' tone refused to sell food in their picture palaces, but by the mid-1930s, any additional source of revenue was desperately sought, and candy and popcorn concession stands entered foyers everywhere.

Although recovery was strong in the second half of the decade, the industry's experience of the Depression left studios (and their Wall Street investors) in a state of heightened financial sensitivity. This, in turn, contributed to one of the factors often associated with Hollywood's alleged 'escapist' tendencies – namely the adoption and enforcement of the Production Code. The provisions of the Code required that every script be vetted before it went into production, each detail checked against a list of articles which stated what was considered to be tasteless or morally unacceptable in American cinema. This included sexual indecency, adultery and 'perversion' (a euphemism for homosexuality), nudity, profanity, brutality and irreverence towards law and religion. Studios had originally signed up to this process of self-censorship in 1930 to ensure that various state and municipal censorship boards passed their films with as few cuts as possible and to quiet the growing clamour for federal regulation. The next three years, however, saw an abundance of 'sinful girls', horrific monsters and Mae West's innuendo, as the industry tried everything to lure Depression-hit audiences back into the theatres. The Code did tone down some of the salaciousness, but a 'staged crisis' occurred in 1934, when one of the formulators of the Code, Father Daniel Lord, campaigned to orchestrate the Catholic Legion of Decency. As Lord made priests and bishops aware of how studios were flaunting the Code, they urged millions of Catholics to join the Legion and pledge that they would boycott any film 'condemned' by the Legion's board of film reviewers. When Cardinal Dougherty in Philadelphia told his congregations to boycott *all* films, box office receipts in the city reportedly fell by 40 per cent. Complicit in this campaign was the new (and Catholic) head of the Production Code Administration (PCA), Joseph Breen, who now assured studio bosses that they could avoid further trouble *if* the Code was adhered to.[15]

A somewhat cynical 'public act of atonement' saw the industry launch a 'Better Pictures Campaign' in reaction to the furore.[16] Breen's application of the Code accepted that 'sin' and criminal behaviour were legitimate subjects for drama, and allowed immorality to still be present as story material, but insisted on 'compensating moral values' being emphasized throughout. Reinforcing 'religious teachings that deviant behaviour, whether criminal or sexual, cost violators the love and comforts of home, the intimacy of family, the solace of religion, and the protection of law', movies endorsed by the PCA increasingly took on the tenor of 'morality plays that illustrated proper behaviour to the masses'.[17]

Recent scholarship has suggested that cycles of movies such as the 'fallen women' pictures, epitomized by Jean Harlow in *Red Headed Woman* (1932) and Barbara Stanwyck in *Baby Face* (1933), and gangster films like *Scarface* (1932) and *Little Caesar* (1931) were not, in fact, 'casualties' of the Breen office. The popularity of these genres had already waned by 1934, with exhibitors and box office returns indicating that audiences had tired of films of overt sexuality and sophisticated cynicism; so the financial sacrifice of 'cleaning house' was hardly a great one.[18] Moreover, the revival of 'prestige' adaptations of classic literature and historical epics evident after 1934 (with films such as *David Copperfield* (1935), *Midsummer's Night Dream* (1935), *The Charge of the Light Brigade* (1936) and *The Private Lives of Elizabeth and Essex* (1939)) had already been sparked by the successes of *The Private Life of Henry VIII* and *Little Women* in 1933, and had more to do with the ambitions of producers like Irving Thalberg, David Selznick and Darryl Zanuck than any 'clean up'. Their high production values and costs had simply 'placed them out of reach' for most companies at the height of the Depression.[19]

These trends, however, have been interpreted as a turn to 'harmless entertainment', with the dictates of the Code 'cutting films off from the realities' of the contemporary 'American experience'.[20] By 1935, the *New York Times* was characterizing that year's adventure films and period romances (including *Captain Blood*, *Anna Karenina* and *Lives of a Bengal Lancer*) as 'avenues of escape' from the burden of 'hard times' and 'daily woes'.[21] One of the earliest works of film studies, Margaret Thorp, *America at the Movies* (1939), was firmly of the belief that 'audiences wanted to be cheered up when they went to the movies; they had no desire to see on the screen the squalor and misery of which there was all too much at home'.[22] As Hays's comment about the movies 'laughing the depression out of the public mind' suggests, this was an image that the industry itself actively promoted, making the case that Hollywood was all about 'furnishing amusement, laughter, entertainment and escape', expending its 'far-flung energy in making the world a happier place to live in'.[23]

Hostile critics also shared the belief that 'escape' was what Hollywood did best, but argued that the movies were fraudulent in their efforts, designed not so much to cheer up the people as to distract them from a reality that needed to be faced. Dwight Macdonald, for instance, took umbrage at the 'escapism' of Will Rogers' *State Fair* (1933), set in a nostalgic rural Midwest. 'At a time when the American farmer is faced with ruin, when the whole Middle West is seething with

bitterness and discontent', Macdonald found it ridiculous that
Hollywood should produce an exercise in 'studied avoidance of anything more serious in the life of the farmer than whether his hog will
win the state championship'.[24]

Film historians, however, have generally sought to turn escapism on
its head. All the ostensibly obvious vehicles of escapism (musicals,
comedies, westerns, period dramas, horror films and family fantasies)
have been revisited and revised in an effort to demonstrate that they
were not 'escapist' at all, but were sources of powerful allegories,
mirror images of modern society, or vehicles for film-makers who used
humorous or fantastic genres to deliver 'messages' that would have
provoked controversy if placed in a contemporary, realistic setting. In
such analyses, for example, the enormous popularity of Will Rogers
cannot be explained by suggesting simply that the nostalgia and folksy
humour of his movies tapped a 'forgotten public' which had 'lost interest' in 'the so-called smart films' of Mae West, the Marx Brothers or
Ernst Lubitsch.[25] As Lary May points out, Rogers had a politicized
persona, established through radio and syndicated newspaper
columns, as a 'cracker-barrel' philosopher who supported both the
New Deal and Huey Long's 'Share Our Wealth' scheme. By 1933,
commentators were referring to him as 'the Number One New
Dealer'.[26] Reading his film characters in this light, as May does, brings
a different perspective to comedies such as The County Chairman
(1935), Old Kentucky (1935) and Handy Andy (1934), observing that
it is always wealthy, elitist men who undermine small-town America,
'stealing funds for the parks and poisoning the public reservoirs' and
then blaming disorder on 'poor and marginal groups' who have no one
except Rogers 'to champion their cause'.[27] May also looks beyond the
Rogers character of State Fair to the narrative of his discontented
daughter. Unhappy about her engagement to a man who believes that
'in their home "men will decide"', her time at the fair exposes her to
ideas of greater female emancipation, and she falls instead for a young
newspaperman who (like Rogers himself) admires the radical Midwest
farmers, 'whom he calls the "Bolsheviks" of the farm belt'.[28]

While often revealing, this understandable drive to recuperate the
period's motion pictures has sometimes produced interpretations that
stretch credibility. Reading Dracula (1931) as a representation of a
'blood sucking' capitalist, for example, is only superficially satisfying,
while Martin Tropp's suggestion that the scientist and hunchback of
Frankenstein personify 'the forces of mad authority and sadistic servitude that brought disaster to the world' seems to untenably credit the

1931 film with powers of political prophecy.[29] Socio-political interpretations of *The Wizard of Oz* (1939) would also appear to run
directly against the grain of Dorothy's express desire to escape the
drabness of storm-hit Kansas to a fantasy world 'somewhere over the
rainbow' (a desire delivered so powerfully in song by Judy Garland
that it undercuts the 'no place like home' homily of the film's
ending).[30] Politicized readings of this musical do possess the impri-
matur of the movie's lyricist and co-writer Yip Harburg, an open
socialist, who subsequently insisted that 'the Emerald City was the
New Deal'.[31] It is plausible to find a contemporary 'parable' in
Dorothy and her new friends, all seeking to change their circumstances, heading off to see the Rooseveltian wizard 'because of the
wonderful things he does', while discovering that the resources they
need to overcome adversity and oppression are within them already.
However, Francis MacDonnell's reading of the Scarecrow as a representative Midwest farmer, the Tin Man as an unemployed industrial
worker and the Lion as a bankrupt businessman, is one that stretches
credibility, especially when he goes on to argue that the trophies given
by the Wizard to symbolize brains, heart and courage are symbols of
the 'three things which the New Deal promised to give America',
namely the Brain Trust, relief programmes, and FDR's assertion that
'the only thing we have to fear is fear itself'.[32] Walt Disney's short
cartoon *The Three Little Pigs* (1933) can justifiably be read as symbolic. Given its extraordinary popularity at the time, contemporaries
were alert to the parallels of 'the Big Bad Wolf representing the
Depression and the Three Little Pigs representing average citizens
desperately fighting for survival against its attempts to devour
them'.[33] Yet Richard Schickel's later assertion that because the eldest
pig 'looked a bit like Hoover', the film supports Herbert Hoover's
Republican philosophy, is rather more difficult to accept.[34]

   Still, even these less persuasive readings do not invalidate
Lawrence Levine's position that films of the 1930s have 'too frequently and too easily been characterized as "escapist"' when many
entertainments were 'deeply grounded in the realities and intricacies
of the Depression'.[35] Some were very direct about it. A Mickey
Mouse cartoon *Moving Day* (1936), for example, extended the character's general 'Chaplinesque' appeal to portray the mouse, Donald
and Goofy being evicted from their home after falling six months
behind with the rent. In *Just Around the Corner* (1938), Shirley
Temple's father loses his job as an architect as the economic collapse
hits home, while her first feature film appearance in *Stand Up and*

Cheer (1934) depicted FDR appointing a Secretary of Amusement as part of the New Deal relief strategy. And the most successful of Warner Bros.' musicals were rooted firmly in the economic context, with *Gold Diggers of 1933* and *Footlight Parade* (1933) both present- ing backstage stories of struggling girls for whom it is either the chorus-line or the breadline. In *Gold Diggers*, the opening number of 'We're in the Money' becomes cruelly ironic when the sheriff closes down the Broadway production due to unpaid debts. The finale of 'Remember My Forgotten Man' is even more hard-hitting as an evo- cation of the Bonus Marchers, as Joan Blondell sings of the veterans of the First World War, sent away with 'a rifle in his hand', now for- gotten and betrayed. Usually associated with a world of excessive visual spectacle in which dancers' bodies form kaleidoscopic pat- terns, Busby Berkeley's celebrated choreography here matches the lyrics in a powerful style, as soldiers march in circles, initially proud and virile, then wounded and bleeding, crushed by the war, then homeless and unemployed, forming lines once again but this time in a soup kitchen.[36]

Less direct but no less resonant were many of the historical dramas, most of them adaptations of novels, including *Gone With the Wind* (1939) and *Northwest Passage* (1940). Like their literary sources, these films offered models of 'heroic idealism' while assuring audiences that America had 'overcome hardships before and could do so again'.[37] With many such dramas released late in the decade, it is notable that war repeatedly provides the test of the protagonists' resilience, pro- viding a cumulative 'message' of affirmation in the face of another impending conflict:

> The nation that could conquer the wilderness (*Allegheny Uprising* (1939), *Northwest Passage*, *Brigham Young* (1939), *Union Pacific* (1939)), could win independence and establish a democratic republic (*Drums Along the Mohawk* (1939), *The Howards of Virginia* (1940)), could give birth to great leaders (*Young Mr Lincoln* (1939), *Abe Lincoln in Illinois* (1940)), who held the country together during its severest trials (*Gone With the Wind*), and could conquer the environment with science and technology (*Young Tom Edison* (1940), *Edison, The Man* (1940), *The Story of Alexander Graham Bell* (1939)), would surely continue to survive.[38]

Economic deprivation was not the only source of contemporary anxiety. Some of the most intriguing readings of films of the period emphasize other concerns, such as James Snead's racialized interpretation of *King Kong* (1931) which discusses the film, persuasively, as 'a potentially explosive allegory of racial and sexual exploitation' in which blackness is linked with monstrosity. Enslaved and brought to America in chains, only to 'run amok in New York City with a white woman he had abducted' the image of the savage, black Kong, encodes into fantasy all manner of white supremacist anxieties about the 'threat' they perceived in empowered African Americans.[39]

Yet if 'escapism' was not escapist, where does this leave the argument that enforcement of the Production Code depoliticized the industry? Generalized answers stress a change of tone from 'attacking the wrongs of society' at the start of the decade, to an emphasis on 'trying to make them right'.[40] A transition in comedy epitomizes this. The decade began with the Marx Brothers' run of films from *The Cocoanuts* (1929) to *Duck Soup* (1933) presenting madcap anarchy and chaotic disruption with endings that refuse to re-establish order. As prime minister Rufus T. Firefly in *Duck Soup*, Groucho mocks Hoover's failings, noting how 'the last man nearly ruined this place'. Yet there is no suggestion of things getting better: 'If you think this country's bad off now, just wait till I get through with it!'. Celebrating 'the collapse of the social order' for a disillusioned audience now 'capable of seeing the absurdity of the verities and relations that had been treasured before', the brothers' humour (like that of W. C. Fields and Mae West) possessed little respect for conventional morality.[41] In comparison, the later cycle of 'screwball' comedy – which included *It Happened One Night* (1934), *The Awful Truth* (1937), *Bringing Up Baby* (1938) and *My Man Godfrey* (1938) – was, as Andrew Bergman suggests, more 'warm and healing'.[42] Thus, as *It Happened One Night*'s spoiled heiress Ellie Andrews encounters working-class journalist Peter Warne and is reduced to travelling with him by bus and hitchhiking on a subsistence allowance, their emergent love for one another results in a 'levelling of class barriers', and comedy becomes 'a means of unifying what had been splintered and divided'.[43] These films were not entirely detached from the Depression. *My Man Godfrey*, for instance, ends with William Powell awakening the previously self-absorbed members of a wealthy family to their responsibilities to the poor. Chaos could still be a source of humour but the thrust was now toward the moral reconstitution of a better, 'classless and egalitarian society'.[44] Breen's requirement that amoral cynicism be toned down certainly neutered Mae West et al., and the Production Code's insistence on 'supporting the sanctity of marriage and the home' was a clear

Figure 2.3 James Cagney and Jean Harlow in *The Public Enemy* (1931: directed by William Wellman: Warner Bros./The Kobal Collection).

factor in this shift. Yet so too was the New Deal's positive spirit of asking 'the country to pull together', along with the changing taste of audiences for more affirmative entertainment at a time when possibilities for progress seemed to be renewed.[45]

The Public Enemy (1931)

As odd as it may sound, the gangster films of the early 1930s resonated with the same temper that pervaded the Marx Brothers' comedies, revelling in pervasive cynicism and displays of contempt for established authority. The vibrancy of the cinematic gangsters, their boldness and their will to act, drew audiences to urban, immigrant hoodlums like Rico in *Little Caesar* (1931), Tom Powers in *The Public Enemy* (1931) and Tony Camonte in *Scarface* (1932). Each man achieves the power and status he desires, living (for a while at least) without restraint, free 'from the fetters of normative codes'.[46] At a time when ordinary lives seemed characterized by frustration, inertia and a lack of opportunity, these films were simultaneously 'escapist', offering an exciting vicarious existence, and closely tied to contemporary reality.

The Public Enemy in particular, was heralded as a 'hard and true picture' of the contemporary scene, a 'hard-boiled' vision torn from the newspaper headlines.[47] Tom and his friend Matt were inspired by Terry Druggan and Frankie Lake, 'the first gangsters to distribute beer on a large scale in Chicago after Prohibition', while characterizations and story drew on real-life gang leaders Dion O'Bannion, Hymie Weiss and Louis 'Two-Gun' Alterie. Writers John Bright and Kubec Glasmon, who themselves had peddled prescription alcohol in Al Capone's Chicago, brought to bear a wealth of historical incidents, including the death in 1923 of Samuel 'Nails' Morton in a riding accident and Alterie's subsequent execution of Morton's horse. Even the film's celebrated moment in which James Cagney, as Tom, thrusts a grapefruit into Mae Clarke's face, was based on reports of Weiss doing the same to his girlfriend with an omelette.[48]

These specific moments certainly resonated with the city-dwelling, tabloid-reading audiences who responded to the film. But it was the narrative of Tom 'growing up tough in an Irish ghetto behind the Chicago stockyards' which really reflected back at them the ethnic urbanite experience.[49] Tom's delinquency and criminality are set against his 'good' brother, Mike, who stays 'straight', fights in the First World War, holds down a job as a trolley conductor and seeks to improve his prospects through education at night school. Governed by a solid work ethic, Mike should be the film's moral centre. Yet in *The Public Enemy*, Mike is a 'sap', with his moral voice undermined by his sanctimony and rigidity as well as the anger he directs at Tom, seemingly rooted in resentment 'at the way in which his honest life of toil has emasculated him'.[50] In contrast, Tom's life of crime empowers him, bringing him freedom, excitement and opportunities to exert his masculinity. It even affords him the status of 'breadwinner', bringing food and money back to his mother and family. With that status denied to millions of unemployed men, Tom's cynicism about the 'definitions of good behaviour and good citizenship' that rule Mike's life was much more likely to attract audience empathy than disturb it.[51]

Tom's appeal also owed much to James Cagney's performance. Tom's brutality, misogyny and irresponsibility are hardly likeable characteristics, but Cagney's jaunty insolence and genuine boyish charisma undercut them. Born in New York City's Hell's Kitchen, Cagney brought something 'fresh' to the movie, a machismo that was natural, uncontrolled and seemingly spontaneous (as when he spits beer into someone's face), and imbued with a wise-guy wit. In addition, his star persona was harnessed to a different kind of gangster to that present in *Little Caesar* and *Scarface*. Tom never displays overweening greed or ambition to control and run the gang; he is comfortable taking orders, enjoys the material gains he makes and is driven more by the freedoms and empowerment that gang-life offers him. Lacking the deviancy and calculated cold-heartedness of Rico and Tony Camonte, and possessing a greater loyalty to his friends, Tom is more of an 'everyman' character and thus much easier to relate to.

Tom's appeal, however, was precisely what others deemed 'dangerous' about this film and the genre as a whole. Taking for granted the audience's cynicism about Prohibition and the Volstead Act, *Public Enemy* directly flaunted the Production Code's stipulation that criminals should never be presented 'in such a way as to throw sympathy with the crime as against law and justice'.[52] Nor, stated the Code, should characters like Tom be allowed 'to inspire others with a desire for imitation' – yet fans 'eagerly imitated Cagney's dress and mannerisms'.[53] Warner Bros. sought to defend itself against criticism by prefacing the movie with a foreword stating that their intention was 'to honestly depict' a genuine social problem 'rather than to glorify the hoodlum or the criminal'. But the outcry of civic and religious organizations complaining about the 'corrupting' influence of Hollywood led, in September 1931, to the industry creating new guidelines which practically 'prohibited the further production of gangster films'.[54] The profitability of the genre had, in fact, dipped soon after *The Public Enemy* and, as with the 'fallen women' cycle, it is inaccurate to see the gangster picture as entirely the victim of the Production Code.[55]

However, when the genre was revived after 1934, the watchful eye of Joseph Breen was present, and it is notable that Cagney's return in *G-Men* (1935) was of a very different tone. Raised in orphanages, associating with criminals, and arrested for vagrancy and fighting, Cagney's 'Brick' Davis could easily have been another Tom Powers. Yet rather than becoming a gangster in *G-Men*, Davis becomes an FBI agent, his anger disciplined by the Bureau and directed to halt 'the march of crime'.[56] Authority was affirmed rather than seen as the problem. Criminals were an unsympathetic threat to decent people. And filmmakers had found a way to continue presenting the excesses of gangster stories, in narratives which now fitted within the Code's moral framework.

Reality Cinema

Criticism of *The Public Enemy* reflected broader concern about the ways in which Hollywood used genuine social problems as a source of entertainment. Clearly, whatever the film's foreword said about its intention to 'honestly depict an environment that exists today', the prime aim of Warner Bros. was to produce the 'roughest, toughest and best of the gang films to date'. The studio's head of production, Darryl Zanuck, argued that they needed to 'sell the idea' that 'only by the betterment of environment and education . . . can we overcome the widespread tendency toward lawbreaking'. Yet his rationale had little to do with making a contribution to social debate, and more that 'punching over a moral' message would 'do a lot toward protecting' *The Public Enemy* from the censors.[57] The orthodox image of Hollywood's political sensitivities remains Sam Goldwyn's oft-quoted aphorism, 'Pictures are for entertainment, messages should be delivered by Western Union'.

More films than might be anticipated, however, offered direct considerations of the social, economic and political ramifications of the Depression. Injustice toward the unemployed drove the plots of *I am a Fugitive from a Chain Gang* (1932), *Heroes for Sale* (1933) and *Dust Be My Destiny* (1939). *The Grapes of Wrath* (1940) dramatized the consequences of the Dust Bowl, while *Our Daily Bread* (1934) offered the collectivization of farms as a partial solution to the agricultural crisis. *American Madness* (1932) mirrored the contemporary collapse of the banking system; *Black Fury* (1935) concerned itself with the highly controversial subject of labour strikes; and *Wild Boys of the Road* (1933), *Dead End* (1937) and *Back Door to Heaven* (1939) were among a number of films which treated juvenile delinquents with understanding – indeed, when *Wild Boys* culminates in a violent clash between the police and the young tearaways, the film's sympathy is clearly with the latter. Responding to anti-lynching legislation that was working its way through Congress, *Fury* (1936), *Legion of Terror* (1936), *Black Legion* (1937) and *They Won't Forget* (1937) all made strong statements against mob law and vigilante action. Concern over the international situation also eventually reached the screen, first with *Blockade* (1938) and its reflection on the Spanish Civil War, and then with *Confessions of a Nazi Spy* in 1939. Corruption and venality in state and federal government was also a repeatedly-tapped vein, from *Washington Merry-Go-Round* (1932) and *Washington Masquerade* (1935), through to *Mr Smith Goes to Washington* (1939).

At first, this turn to films of 'social consciousness' was a matter of expediency. When the cost-cutting Warner Bros. refused to invest in buying the rights to novels and other commercial properties, their writers turned instead to news stories in the public domain as a source of inexpensive inspiration. But when a strong public response was registered at the box office, socially-minded filmmakers were encouraged to further embrace the 'setting, concerns, and dark mood' of the Depression.[58] The influx of left-wing writers from New York and Chicago, such as Clifford Odets, John Howard Lawson, Albert Maltz and Robert Rossen, also maintained a left-leaning pressure, as did the call of influential left-wing and liberal film critics for filmmakers to 'acknowledge and engage with the social turmoil of the age'.[59]

The most acclaimed of these movies is undoubtedly *I am a Fugitive from a Chain Gang*, based on Robert Burns' true personal account of the horrors of the Georgia prison system.[60] The dream of decorated war veteran James Allen is to continue serving his country, putting his skills to work in engineering projects. Unemployment, however, denies him this opportunity and he is soon destitute. Things take a further disastrous turn when Allen, unwittingly involved in the robbery of a diner, is wrongly convicted and sentenced to ten years' hard labour. Director Mervyn LeRoy's presentation of that chain gang is pitiless, with prisoners starved and brutalized by sadistic, vicious guards. Allen does manage to escape this subhuman existence, fleeing to Chicago where his diligence, skill and hard work pay off and he rises to become an executive in the construction industry. In consequence, when he is found out and the state of Georgia demands his extradition, many in the North stand by him as a prominent citizen who has proven his worth. Georgia, though, insists on a token, symbolic retribution and, on the promise of a nominal sentence and full pardon, Allen nobly agrees to return to prison. However, vindictive wardens immediately renege on the deal and condemn him to a lifetime of brutal punishment. Escaping again, Allen has no choice but a life on the run. Burns himself was still a wanted man and had to be smuggled into the studio to advise the filmmakers. Their famous ending presents the dehumanizing consequences of such unjust persecution. Encountering his former girlfriend, Allen skulks in the shadows, a 'scared, hunted animal'. Unable to reach out to him, Helen asks how he lives. Allen delivers the simple but devastating punch as he backs into the darkness: 'I steal'. For all his efforts, for all his nobility, he has been 'ground down into a bitter, twisted, criminal failure', denying any hope for the American Dream.[61]

Described variously as 'Warners' most unequivocally pessimistic picture of life in Depression America', 'the absolute nadir of hopes and possibilities as depicted in the movies' and the 'most sensational social problem film of the period', *Fugitive* has also been seen as the exception.[62] Somewhat ironically, in the light of all the 'messages' that have been read into ostensibly escapist movies, the common argument regarding Hollywood's 'social problem' films is that they were 'confused', 'fatally flawed' and 'hopelessly compromised'.[63] *Wild Boys of the Road*, for example, depicts children whose parents can no longer support them, leaving home and riding the freight trains – a grim reality for over 250,000 teenagers. Yet a 'happy ending' negates all their harsh experiences, tacking on a note of New Deal optimism when a kind judge comforts them that 'Things are going to get better now . . . all over the country'.[64] Charlie Chaplin's *Modern Times* (1936) is possessed of greater 'social realism', with factories closed down, striking crowds clashing fatally with police, men stealing or scrounging for food and firewood to keep their families alive. His Tramp is depicted as being better off in jail, where at least he receives food and protection (indeed, he tries to get himself arrested again in order to return). But even Chaplin's last scene 'softens the critique', escaping into the optimistic bromides of 'Buck up. Never say die. We'll get along', which seem unwarranted in light of what has gone before.[65]

Frank Capra's films were consistently among the most popular and acclaimed of the decade, with a clear interest in social and political topics. *American Madness* (1932), *Mr Deeds Goes to Town* (1936), *Mr Smith Goes to Washington* (1939) and *Meet John Doe* (1941) all pit their heroes – each an 'average' American male – against 'big bankers, shyster lawyers, cynical reporters, sell-out politicians and fascist tycoons', with a progressively darkening opinion about the ability of American democracy to resist these threats.[66] Their denouements, however, are frequently criticized for being unrealistic, able to resolve the situation only when characters undergo an unconvincing change of heart. *American Madness* sees a banking panic averted when the people who have been helped by kindly banker Tom Dickson (who advances loans according to need and character rather than collateral) return his trust and make deposits to save the bank. In *Mr Deeds Goes to Town*, Longfellow Deeds uses the fortune he inherits to assuage the agricultural and unemployment crisis, giving millions of ten-acre parcels of land to the needy. Up against the financial elites of New York, greedy opportunists and his corrupt attorney, Deeds is labelled insane and called before a court hearing. 'In life', Lawrence Levine observes, 'Deeds would have been

committed to an insane asylum or, at the very least, lost control of his
millions'.[67] In the film world, though, he prevails, asserting that 'the
fellas who can make the hill on high should stop once in a while and help
those who can't', thus convincing the judge that he is 'the sanest man'
who ever walked into his courtroom. *Mr Smith*, too, ultimately defends
Jefferson Smith's naively glorious vision of American ideals against the
realities of dishonesty and graft in national politics which have
corrupted his former hero, Senator Paine. Yet for most of the film, Smith
is powerless to fight back, framed and disgraced for corruption himself,
and saved only by a last-minute and unlikely confession from a con-
science-ridden Paine. Such final triumphs against the odds reveal
Capra's belief in a society that could still counter the humiliation, disillusionment and cynicism encountered in contemporary life, if only it
could 'return to the basics of the American tradition'.[68] For many commentators, however, such affirmative endings exemplify the 'fantasies'
which Hollywood perpetuated when it compromised 'realism'.

The Production Code certainly contributed to this. A prime
example of Joseph Breen 'compromising' a film's politics is *Black Fury*,
described by one commentator as 'one of the real frauds of the thirties'.[69] Dramatizing unionism, *Black Fury* presented a dark picture of
the poverty in a company mining-town and the murderous brutality
of hired detectives and strike-breakers, who kill one miner who dares
to speak out. It was based on a story by M. A. Musmano, a judge who
had investigated such situations in his own state of Pennsylvania.
However, Breen insisted upon a 'fundamental dishonesty' which
undermined its real-life basis.[70] His advice, accepted by the producers,
was that the coal industry management should not be played as
'heavies', and that the grievances of the miners should be down-
played.[71] Instead, 'outside agitators' should be blamed for stirring up
trouble among previously content workers.[72] The industrial detective
agency itself, therefore, became the villain of the piece, fomenting a
wildcat strike among miners so as to compel the otherwise benevolent
mine owners to engage its strike-breakers. Following Breen's guidance, both management and the miners become 'victims' of the 'dis-
honest intrigue of racketeers'.[73] The realities of conflict between labour
and capital are ducked, and all class antagonism evaporates as soon as
the perpetrators are revealed. Having championed the project from the
start, its star Paul Muni suggested bitterly that it might as well have
been renamed *Coal Diggers of 1935*.

Gregory Black's history of the PCA also presents evidence of Breen
persuading MGM to cancel plans to film Sinclair Lewis's anti-fascist *It*

Can't Happen Here, and his insistence that Fritz Lang's anti-lynching film *Fury* should avoid discussion of race.[74] Breen's intervention in *Black Fury* was not, however, due solely to his own political conservatism. The PCA was pressured by powerful groups, including the National Coal Association and the United States Steel Corporation, all wanting assurances that the picture would reflect 'the greatest care' in portraying their interests.[75] Even though his interference in politics seemed to go beyond the explicit remit of the Code, Breen did what Hollywood paid him to do, 'protecting' the industry from potentially influential hostile criticism.

Of course, such compromises and evasions did not quiet criticism from the Left. In fact, movies like *Black Fury* fuelled a reaction among independent documentary filmmakers, who countered 'conservative Hollywood fare' with films which showed the real struggles of labour.[76] Frontier Film's *United Action* (1939), for instance, was produced by the United Auto Workers themselves, covering their strike at General Motors. *Native Land* (begun in 1938 but not released until 1942) and Leo Huberman's *The Labour Spy Racket* dramatized the findings of Senate investigations about the harsh suppression of union movements. *Native Land*'s re-enactments included 'true-life' accounts of sharecroppers killed for meeting to ask for 10 cents more for their cotton, members of the Ku Klux Klan tarring and feathering union supporters and the murder of a union representative. It also featured images of the 1937 Memorial Day Massacre of strikers at Republic Steel's Chicago works – based on footage shot by Paramount News but suppressed by studio executives who refused to include it in their newsreels. It had only come to light when shown to a closed session of Robert LaFollette's Senate committee, but *Native Land* brought it into the open.[77]

These productions had their origins in the Communist-organized Film and Photo League (FPL), formed in 1930, which began by covering the strikes and demonstrations in which affiliated trade unions took part. Filming events such as the Bonus March and the Unemployed Council's hunger marches of 1932, the FPL staff edited together low-budget newsreels, made in opposition to Hollywood's commercial news reports, for distribution to unions. An *Unemployment Special* (1931), for example, 'treats the big United Steel Workers' strike of 1930 with explicit attention drawn to its use of footage that had been 'censored from commercial newsreels'.[78] In their revolutionary Marxist idealism, founders of the FPL even dreamed of supplanting and 'abolishing Hollywood'.[79] In reality, it released only sixteen such reels before being dissolved in 1937.

Its ambition, however, motivated more sustainable projects, most notably the production co-operative which formed around Leo Hurwitz, Ralph Steiner, Irving Lerner and Paul Strand. Rejecting the limited reportage of the FPL, they left the group to form first Nykino and then Frontier Films in the hope of creating a 'cinema of greater expressive power'.[80] They, too, wanted to challenge the commercial cinema, attempting their own left-wing alternative to *The March of Time* in *The World Today* (1936). Nonetheless, they also learned from Hollywood, expanding the documentary aesthetic by incorporating re-enactments of actual events to create, as Hurwitz described it, a 'mixture' of 'objective' 'external montage' and 'the synthetic recreation of the dramatic film'.[81] It was a development which also influenced the New Deal documentaries of Pare Lorentz (discussed in further detail in Chapter 5), and occasioned serious discussion of the artistic and political merits of documentary cinema throughout the decade, culminating in 1939 when the Museum of Modern Art launched its first retrospective on 'The Non-Fiction Film'.

Frontier Films' vision was consolidated when radical Dutch film-maker, Joris Ivens, came to America in 1936. Ivens was already producing works which combined reportage, romanticism and re-enactments (as well as subversively recutting commercial newsreels to drive home left-wing political messages), and on joining Frontier he directed one of their most successful projects, *The Spanish Earth* (1937). Sponsored by an organization that included Lillian Hellman, Archibald MacLeish and John Dos Passos, with Ernest Hemingway providing narration, *The Spanish Earth* combines battle footage of the siege of Madrid and civilians under bombardment, with the story of the civil war's effect on a single farming community. Ivens alternates shots of the Loyalists fighting back with enactments involving ordinary peasants to construct a powerful ideological picture of 'a people's war'.[82] It can be compared instructively to Hollywood's later production of *Blockade* (1938). Written by one of Los Angeles' leading Communists, John Howard Lawson, *Blockade* similarly concerned a peasant farmer, played by Henry Fonda, taking up arms to defend his farm and valley. Yet in contrast to the power of Ivens' film, all Lawson could get Warners to sanction was a speech in which Fonda finally asks 'Where's the conscience of the world?'. Even then the studio ensured that the word 'Spain' was never mentioned.[83]

The Spanish Earth, however, played in only three hundred or so theatres across the United States: 'a mere ripple in the commercial sea'.[84] The Hollywood studios' control over distribution always marginalized the distribution of documentaries, and independent productions lacked the financial resources to compete (Ivens' budget was just $18,000). In the end though, just as the 'social realist' writers experienced, the 'didactic nature' of most documentaries 'appealed mainly to the already converted'. Mass audiences may not have been adverse to politicized film, as *The Grapes of Wrath*, *I am a Fugitive* and *Mr Smith Goes To Washington* indicated, but for the most part they preferred politics 'presented in more entertaining form'.[85] Moreover, in any analysis of Hollywood's 'social' films, it is worth bearing in mind that the ostensibly happy or unrealistic endings could not totally undercut the dark and often threatening images and situations that preceded them. Levine cautions against assuming that audiences in the 1930s unthinkingly accepted Hollywood's 'happy endings', and posits the possibility 'that audiences were able to learn from the main thrust of the films they saw, even while they derived comfort and pleasure from the formulaic endings'.[86]

Sullivan's Travels (1941)

Justifying his decision to film *The Grapes of Wrath* in 1939, Darryl Zanuck claimed that 'when times are hard' audiences wanted 'dramas, heavy stuff. They don't want anyone up there on the screen being just too gay for words when the factory's closing down next week'.[87] Coming from the producer who championed Shirley Temple in the early years of the decade, this was certainly disingenuous, and *Sullivan's Travels*, written and directed by Preston Sturges, sharply punctured such pious pronouncements. A movie about making movies, *Sullivan's Travels* opens with director John L. Sullivan announcing his ambition to make his first gritty social problem film: 'a true canvas of the suffering of humanity', based on an epic novel by an author called Sinclair Beckstein (a pun on John Steinbeck and Sinclair Lewis). Studio executives are appalled, reminding him that his success has been built on escapist comedies like *Hey Hey in the Hayloft* and *So Long Sarong*, films 'about nice clean young people who fall in love, with laughter and music and legs'. His once-poor butler also disapproves of his motives, warning that 'only the morbid rich would find the topic' of poverty 'glamorous'. But Sully (Joel McCrea) is unmoved in his decision to film *O Brother, Where Art Thou?*, and when his producers point out that he knows nothing about suffering, he hits the road disguised as a tramp, determined to gain the firsthand experience he needs to make a truly meaningful film.

Sturges's own film is a 'dizzying mix' of every type of cinematic genre.[88] The first stage of Sully's journey is played out as slapstick farce, as the studio exploit his travels as a publicity stunt and his entourage chase after him in a trailer van. Madcap 'Keystone Cops' routines see motorcycle police in pursuit, jeeps crashing into haystacks and the studio personnel being thrown wildly around in their van, until Sully's black cook ends up with a 'white face' of pancake batter. It then moves into the territory of *It Happened One Night*, when the still disguised Sully meets out of work actress 'The Girl' (played by Veronica Lake). Mixed-up identities, sophisticated verbal sparring and a journey which cements their romance mimic the 'screwball' genre. The tone changes again when 'The Girl' insists on joining Sully in his search for 'trouble', but Sturges still parodies other movies as they ride the rails in cattle cars with the authentic poor. Dressed as a boy, her long hair concealed under a cap, Lake replays Dorothy Coonan's role in *Wild Boys of the Road*.[89]

Things go wrong, however, when Sully (handing out cash to the poor in a 'satiric echo' of *Mr Deeds Goes to Town*) is assaulted by a vagrant who steals his money and boots.[90] The attack leaves Sully with temporary amnesia, which eventually leads to him being arrested and sentenced to six years' hard labour in a Southern prison work camp, while everyone in Hollywood believes him to be dead. Once again this experience is mediated through the movies, revisiting *I am a Fugitive from a Chain Gang* as a ruthless warden degrades Sully and punishes him cruelly, locking him in a sweat-box to break his independent spirit. This is more 'trouble' than Sullivan ever sought to experience. But relief comes unexpectedly when the prisoners are taken to a film screening at a local black church. What they see is a Walt Disney cartoon, with Mickey Mouse's dog Pluto caught and entangled in flypaper – an image pertinent to Sullivan's situation. This elicits the most almighty and infectious laughter from the oppressed and downtrodden of society, which includes not only the convicts but also the African American rural congregation. Laughing himself, Sullivan comes to realize that the funny movies he had made but never valued actually serve a genuine therapeutic purpose in the world. 'There's a lot to be said for making people laugh', he tells his producers when he finally gets back to Hollywood and abandons his plans for *O Brother*. 'Do you know that's all some people have? It's not a lot, in this cockeyed caravan, but it's better than nothing'.[91]

Throughout *Sullivan's Travels*, characters like 'The Girl' and Sully's butler are critical of filmmakers who get 'too preachy', and Sturges has said that he possessed 'an urge to tell some of my fellow filmwrights [particularly Frank Capra] that they were getting a little too deep-dish and to leave the preaching to the preachers'.[92] Yet within this celebration of escapism, Sturges himself acknowledges the power of the 'social problem' genre, when Sully and 'The Girl' witness the hunger and desperation of America's unfortunates in Hoovervilles, soup kitchens and doss houses. Picking through garbage cans looking for scraps to eat, having to be fumigated at a homeless shelter and sleeping on the packed floor of a mission flophouse with dozens of downtrodden souls, the realities of poverty soon hit them and the audience. *Sullivan's Travels* may be a comedy that celebrates comedy but in showing the brutality of poverty and the prison system, and even in 'The Girl's' disillusioning experience of trying to 'make it' in Hollywood, it is a million miles away from *Hey Hey in the Hayloft*. Indeed, one of its most relishable ironies lies the way in which *Sullivan's Travels* draws the viewer into just the kind of 'social problem' movie that Sullivan's producers say it is impossible to get people to watch.[93]

Figure 2.4 Preston Sturges directing more trouble for Joel McCrea and Veronica Lake in *Sullivan's Travels* (1941: Paramount/The Kobal Collection).

Art or Document?

When it came to the field of photography, there were those who shared Sturges's concern over the prevalent idea that only the 'documentary' image was of value. Ansel Adams, for one, remained intensely committed to promoting photography as a fine art. He did not object to sociological uses of photography *per se*, or the use of the camera for 'gathering evidence on contemporary society'.[94] However, he did believe that the increasing emphasis on photography as a 'tool' for social and political ends was undermining its standing as an art form.

Photography in the United States had gained significant acceptance as modern art during the 1920s, in part because of the crusade begun by Alfred Stieglitz for its recognition 'as a new medium of expression, to be respected in its own right'.[95] Earlier photography had been characterized by 'pictorialism', soft-focus images that sought to gain popular credibility by emulating painting styles. Adams, though, was one of the champions of 'straight' photography, marked by precisionism, sharp focus, crisp images and glossy reproductions. The manifesto of Adams's Group f/64, founded in San Francisco in 1932, affirmed a commitment to 'pure' photography, defined as 'possessing no qualities of technique, composition or idea, derivative of any other art form'.[96] Adams's own sublime landscapes, especially those of Yosemite National Park, embodied this commitment. Critical of the 'mundane records of scenery that commonly passed for landscape' which, in his view, had 'hindered the creative development of photography as a whole', Adams developed new techniques for taking pictures that would 'reflect not only the forms, but what I had seen and felt at the moment of exposure'.[97] His black-and-white images sought an intensified and 'purified' vision of natural beauty which might infuse the viewer with the emotions that Adams had experienced as photographer.

Yet, as in most every field of culture, this modernist perspective faced a fundamental challenge during the Depression. Adams found himself criticized frequently for not dealing with the realities of contemporary society, for producing 'cold' and 'precious keepsakes for the rich' rather than contributing to the 'struggle for a meaningful art'.[98] In the debate over social documentation former 'purists', such as Willard Van Dyke, were abandoning their stance. Adams' earlier mentor Paul Strand had achieved renown for his angular, Cubist photographic compositions in the 1910s, and his abstracted close-ups of forests, plants and driftwood in the 1920s. But now he warned Adams that the artist could not 'insulate himself in some "esthetic rut", away from the world', and turned his own talents to the highly politicized documentaries of Frontier Films.[99] Sensitive to such criticism, Adams defended the legitimacy of his own interest in nature as being equally reflective of reality as were images of rural and urban suffering, and asserted that he would 'be damned' if he saw the 'rightness' of 'being *expected*' to produce pictures '*for a purpose*'.[100]

Adams was not entirely isolated in his denunciation of the documentary impulse. Hollywood's boldly stylized glamour portraits rejected the 'pseudo-realism' of conventional photography, with George Hurrell setting the standard in turning his sitters into 'dramatic sculptures'.[101] Margaret Bourke-White dominated commercial photography, making her name by turning ordinary industrial objects into extraordinary modernist images 'that not only turned viewers' heads but often made them stare and wonder just what they were looking at'.[102] Her photographs for LaSalle unexpectedly isolated components such as the front wheel cover and the egg-shaped headlight of an automobile, and succeeded in conveying the streamlined design of the whole and the vital quality of 'precision' in its engineering. She was also commissioned to produce huge abstract photomurals of radio transmission tubes and microphones for the offices of the National Broadcasting Company, while her stunning pictures of the Chrysler Building saw her take great risks in finding eye-catching perspectives as she crawled out onto the building's steel gargoyles to capture their shining, eagle-headed designs. Focused entirely on the Chrysler's architectural dominance in New York City, her photographs were largely devoid of a humanizing sensibility.

Yet the documentary aesthetic certainly dominated. In fact, it acquired a commercial value of its own. Lewis Hine had pioneered 'social photography' as early as 1909, producing harrowing pictures of urban slums and children at work in factories as evidence to help secure the passage of reformist child labour laws. In 1930 he was commissioned to photograph the Empire State Building. The use of his work to bolster capitalist enterprise was a rather sad indicator of Hine's own desperate circumstances at that time, but the commission itself attested to renewed interest in his aesthetics. Moreover, his photographs of construction workers in heroic poses (later published as *Men at Work*) still possessed his social determination to show 'that the worker is not a lower form of life'.[103] The launch of *Life* magazine in November 1936, devoted to using photography to represent news, politics and the social world, also demonstrated the growing appetite for the photodocument, boasting a weekly circulation of one million copies within just three months of its launch.

Many of the documentary photographers who worked for the government's Farm Security Administration and its Historical Section had their images reprinted in *Life*, often incorporated into five-page spreads illustrating the week's 'big special feature'. Presenting *Life* itself as a 'vital document of U.S. life', publisher Henry Luce argued that its 'real life' pictures made 'the truth about the world we live in infinitely more exciting, more easily absorbed, more alive, than it has ever been made before'.[104] As Wendy Kozol points out, it took 'the photographic language of documentary and refined it into a more commercial language of photojournalism'.[105] It also represented a turning point for Bourke-White, who produced *Life*'s first cover story. While her iconographic cover image of Fort Peck Dam seemed typical of Bourke-White's technological interests, her accompanying photoessay was something of a surprise to the editors. Rather than architectural shots, the photographs presented a human document of the dam's builders and their families, opening their lives to sympathetic public view as Bourke-White herself succumbed to the documentary impulse.[106]

Bourke-White's epiphany came in 1934, when *Fortune* sent her on assignment to the Dust Bowl and she witnessed scenes of people caught 'helpless' in 'total tragedy'. 'They had no defense', she recalled. 'They had no plan. They were numbed like their own dumb animals'.[107] Her social conscience had been awakened. Dorothea Lange's awakening came when she returned to San Francisco in 1931 after a prolonged sojourn in New Mexico, with her lack of exposure to the 'horrors of the Depression' until that time heightening her sensitivity.[108] As she watched from her studio 'an unemployed workman' stopped in bewilderment. Behind him was the waterfront, where no work was available; to his left was the financial district, symbol of the Crash; ahead of him were the courts who could offer no justice; and to his right were the flophouses. 'What was he to do?' Lange asked herself, 'Which way was he to go?'.[109] With that she abandoned her portrait studio and took to the streets herself, determined to photograph other images that could communicate America's anxieties. Ben Shahn had already been radicalized, apprenticing himself to Mexican muralist and Marxist, Diego Rivera. Yet Shahn, too, temporarily abandoned this calling for photography in 1935, persuaded that the camera's capabilities were more suited than painting to recording the struggles of the dispossessed in a way that would 'shock' middle-class Americans into action.[110]

Individual images could be highly evocative. Marion Post, who left behind a career in fashion photography when it came to seem 'tragically incongruous', took images of coal-mining families in West Virginia for the FSA, documenting their health problems. Her photograph of a packing worker's house in Florida showed 'miserable conditions' – a family with 'few amenities', its child shoeless, and the roof 'simply a tattered piece of canvas'.[111] Arthur Rothstein's 'Fleeing a Dust Storm', taken in Oklahoma in 1936, became a definitive image of the Dust Bowl, as a farmer and his sons run for shelter against the winds. Lange's well-known 'The White Angel Breadline' shows a despondent old man, waiting with the other unemployed for food, his empty cup resting in his arms. Turned away from the rest, he is isolated in the composition, solitary even in a crowd. His worn, battered hat and unshaven face suggest that he has endured poverty much longer than the others in the line. But it is open to interpretation as to whether his hands are clasped in prayer, despair or anger.[112]

Partly because of such ambiguities, the most popular mode for presenting social photography soon became the photo-book. Pictures themselves could not say all that these photographers wanted to convey. Bourke-White in *You Have Seen Their Faces* (1937) was one of the first, an album of 'human despair', with accompanying text by Erskine Caldwell. Conceived, partly, as a rejoinder to critics of Caldwell's fiction (see Chapter 1) it was a 'scathing depiction of the South and its problems', with Bourke-White's photographs depicting the 'grotesque' side of human impoverishment: elderly women suffering with goitres, malnourished mothers losing their sight.[113] Its success spurred the development of a 'new genre', and was followed by volumes such as H. C. Nixon's *Forty Acres and Steel Mules* (1938), Archibald MacLeish's *Land of the Free* (1938) with its 'prose poem' accompanying FSA photographs, Sherwood Anderson's *Home Town* (1940), which featured twenty-five of Marion Post images, and Richard Wright's *12 Million Black Voices: A Folk History of the Negro in the United States* (1941).[114] Lange worked with Paul Schuster, professor of agricultural economics at the University of California (and later her second husband), to harness her photographs to his statistics and analysis. They published *An American Exodus: A Record of Human Erosion* in 1939, with Taylor's scientific arguments for the regulation of agribusiness given a human, emotional dimension by Lange's 'masterful portraits of destitute migrant workers and tenant farmers'.[115]

Yet even within this movement, at the height of the 'objective' documentary photograph's primacy, the photograph as a 'subjective work of art' was never fully submerged. In taking her images for *You Have Seen Their Faces,* Bourke-White employed aggressive measures to capture portraits of people which matched what Caldwell already wanted to say, often waiting 'an hour before their faces or gestures have what we were trying to express', rather than producing images reflecting their 'natural' state.[116] She came in for considerable criticism for this. Lange's *American Exodus* and Walker Evans and James Agee's *Let Us Now Praise Famous Men* were both conceived in reaction to Bourke-White's 'sensationalism' and 'distortion'. Lange herself, however, had taken five pictures of Florence Thompson and the children she encountered picking peas near Santa Barbara, yet she developed only the one image which best suited her vision of the Migrant Mother's plight. Moreover, Rothstein's picture of fleeing farmers was actually staged on an ordinarily windy day. A true dust storm, with dense black clouds moving at sixty miles an hour, would have been practically impossible to photograph, the subjects would have been 'in fear of their lives', and the image would have been far less effective in conveying 'man's struggle against the elements'.[117] Ansel Adams's real complaint about the situation was that while Lange, Bourke-White, Rothstein and many others had actually created 'true works of art' in such photographs, recognition of this was lost 'within the context of social criticism' in which their images were incessantly presented and discussed.[118]

Walker Evans's experiences in the 1930s provide a particular illustration of this point. His photographs accompanied Carleton Beal's political polemic *The Crime of Cuba* in 1933, which exposed the cruelties of Gerardo Machado's dictatorship and implicated American imperialism. In 1935 he joined the Resettlement Administration, and his first assignment was documenting the New Deal's homestead projects in West Virginia and describing the material poverty they were supposed to alleviate. Then in the summer of 1936 he accompanied James Agee to Alabama to photograph the tenant farmers who became the subject of *Let Us Now Praise Famous Men*. Evans's work was thus located firmly within the social documentary context. But the photographs he actually produced were most often politically neutral, with the development of his photographic art taking precedence. Rather than going to Cuba to illustrate Beal's thesis, for instance, he went in search of 'its Latin culture' and its 'visual idiosyncrasies'.[119] When employed by the RA/FSA, he vowed 'NO POLITICS WHATEVER' before accepting the job, and then frequently ignored orders from Washington about his assignments.[120] Instead, he pursued his own photographic development, more interested in the opportunity it presented to travel the country and take pictures of factory towns, car dumps, antebellum mansions, movie theatres, public monuments and southern cemeteries. He did produce a series on soil erosion in Mississippi, but unlike most of the Historical Section's output, his images were elegantly impersonal, 'imposing aesthetic order on chaos'.[121] A number of critics have also observed that in *Famous Men* Evans often seemed more interested in people's possessions than in the people themselves. He was certainly determined not to sensationalize the sharecroppers' distress or humiliation. His portraits of the family members, for instance, are intimate but there is nothing intrinsic to encourage a particular 'social' interpretation. Rather it was the context of the book itself that encouraged contemporaries to read his image of Annie Mae Gudger as a 'single concentrated phrase of suffering', that 'gains in dignity' because she returns 'our gaze and checks our pity'.[122]

In 1938, Evans was offered a one-man retrospective of his work at the Museum of Modern Art. He arranged one hundred photographs as a complex and ambiguous 'wandering through America'.[123] They remained 'documentary' in that their aesthetic was one of seemingly unmediated photographic realism, and the title of the exhibition, *American Photographs*, suggested a sociological dimension. However, Evans brought together images in sequences of architecture, signs, buildings, people and landscapes which eschewed any evident message or topicality, 'apparently free from subjective overtones'.[124] As Ansel Adams perceived, with *American Photographs*, Evans had bridged the gap between the supposedly antithetical conceptions of art and social document, presenting photographic documents as art, not information or emotion. Yet, at the very same time, Adams was infuriated by the accompanying essay produced by Lincoln Kirstein. Defining the photographer's 'most significant purpose' as 'to fix and show the whole aspect of our society', Kirstein's comments represented, to Adams, once again the insistent context of 'social criticism' being 'foisted' upon art.[125]

Berenice Abbott and *Changing New York*

In March 1935 art magazine *Trend* invested overt political meaning in Berenice Abbott's photographic project of documenting New York's rapidly changing architecture. As Elizabeth McCausland noted:

> It is fantastic, that the Chrysler Building, the Daily News Building, the Rockefeller Centre, the Stock Exchange, and any other of a hundred similar displays of ostentatious and vulgar wealth should exist side by side with

those Central Park shanties of the unemployed which she also photographed.[126]

The problem, however, with this interpretation was that while Abbott had
taken photographs of Central Park's Hoovervilles, she had never made
them public; McCausland was only privy to them because she was Abbott's
partner, and knew that Abbott was socially aware even if her published and
exhibited photographs did not convey this. In contrast, most of Abbott's
contemporary reviews, while strongly admiring her work, wished for 'more
emphasis on the human side'.[127] Indeed, the lack of obvious 'social value'
in her photography meant that Abbott struggled throughout the 1930s to
find a sponsor for her work, rejected, for instance, by one potential patron
who noted that, 'with a large part of the population of this City almost starving . . . projects of this kind can await more auspicious times'.[128]

The 'epiphany' which came to Abbott in 1929 was not, unlike that of
Lange or Bourke-White, related to the suffering of the Depression. Rather,
when Abbott encountered New York City after an eight-year absence in
Europe, it was the massive physical transformations wrought in the 1920s
which exhilarated and shocked her. New York in late 1929 was, as her biographer Bonnie Yochelson describes, a 'tumult of construction, as hundreds
of nineteenth-century buildings fell, and cranes carried steel girders, brick
and stone aloft by the ton'.[129] Experiencing a second great boom in skyscraper building, new 1,000-foot edifices were overshadowing the old,
with both edging out 'any semblance of nature'.[130] In Paris, Abbott had
been inspired by Eugene Atget, an elderly French documentary photographer who had, from the 1880s onwards, roamed through the city, making
its changing streets and street life his 'immense subject'. Returning to
America, Abbott found her own 'immense subject' in New York, and emulated Atget, devoting one day a week to exploring the city, taking pictures
of the skyscrapers, the El trains, store fronts and bridges. At first she simply
sought to capture the 'speed and brashness' of city life, but this soon
evolved into a more complex project that would create a 'faithful chronicle
in photographs of the changing aspect of the world's greatest metropolis'.[131] The result was a study in contrasts that captured New York's 'extraordinary potentialities' in a 'state of flux'.[132]

Encouraged by McCausland and by Harding Scholle, the director of the
Museum of the City of New York, Abbott eventually found support from the
government's Federal Art Project (discussed in Chapter 5), which in 1935
provided the funds and research staff to make her creative vision of
Changing New York a reality. Over 300 images were produced, 111 of
which were exhibited in 1937 at Scholle's museum. A key thrust of these
photographs was to 'show the skyscraper in relation to the less colossal
edifices which preceded it'; 'the past jostling with the present', as Abbott
described it.[133] A series of images taken of, and from, Trinity Church in
Lower Manhattan, for instance, depict this once imposing neo-gothic
edifice now hemmed-in by the skyscrapers of Wall Street. Built in the 1840s
as a symbol of the dominance of the Christian faith, by the mid-1930s its
impact was minimized, occupying a far 'lesser place' in the city than the

new 'bastions of commerce and finance'.[134] A 1938 view of Fortieth Street juxtaposed landmarks from several generations, modern skyscrapers, 'starkly simple and functional by design', dwarfing the mid-nineteenth-century structures with 'neoclassical and neo-Romanesque flourishes' that themselves had once dominated the skyline.[135] And when Scholle secured her entry to the construction site of the Rockefeller Center, she portrayed the relationship of modernity to an even older past, juxtaposing ancient limestone formations against the man-made steel framework which now overwhelmed nature itself. Yet it was not only building demolition and sky-scraper construction which encapsulated this theme: in Abbott's vision, changing window displays in department stores were just as representa-tive of the constant transformations of the city.[136]

If Abbott was suggesting that the disorienting pace of modern develop-ment was sacrificing important values rooted in the past, a social philoso-phy could be attributed to her 'endless contrasts of old and new' and her dedication to 'subjects that were disappearing in the wake of accelerated change'.[137] However, images such as 'Brooklyn Bridge with Pier 21' (1937) did not seem particularly critical of the present, with an antiquated, wooden-wheeled horse cart in the foreground providing 'a stark contrast to the triumph of modern engineering overhead'.[138] Rather, the project as a whole seemed more an attempt to 'confront' the contemporary world objectively and realistically, to provide evidence of what Abbott called 'the now'.[139] The city that New York was becoming could be harsh, but also promising at the same time. Her photographs could be used, as they were in the 1938 exhibition *Roofs for 40 Millions*, to help focus attention on the nation's housing crisis. That they could also be published in a celebratory guidebook to coincide with the New York World's Fair suggests the extent to which there was no judgement on modernity explicit in Abbott's images. Her work, like that of Evans, was driven first by artistic ambition, to create visually compelling photographs with a 'philosophical and esthetic sym-pathy for the camera's documentary realism'.[140] Experimenting with com-position and placement, lenses and forced distortion, she found new ways of photographing skyscrapers, her images realizing the beauty and the complexity of the structures themselves. Her art was, in essence, one of 'documentary modernism'. And it proved that the photographic document could itself generate an art of 'the real world', making spectators see with 'wonderment and surprise' the city they took for granted.[141]

Further Considerations

The call for socially relevant art was practically inescapable in the 1930s. Ansel Adams himself eventually succumbed when he realized that his photography could play a vital role in the designation of Sequoia and Kings Canyon as national parks, and he took his portfolio to Washington DC to help launch the environmentalist campaign that he continued for the rest of his life. But for all that the 'social message' and the document dominates the narrative of 1930s photography and interpretations of films – both from Hollywood and independent film-makers – there is again a huge variety of movies, images and practitioners of significance which have not received treatment in this chapter. Simply asking oneself where Fred Astaire and Ginger Rogers, *The Thin Man* series, *Grand Hotel* (1932) or the Tarzan movies fit into this picture, or how to evaluate the photography of Alfred Eisenstadt and Alfred Stieglitz during this period, or the male nudes of George Platt Lynnes, would open up some very different avenues of cultural exploration.

Figure 2.5 The past jostling with the present: Berenice Abbott's 'John Watts Statue from Holy Trinity Church Courtyard' (1938: Museum of the City of New York).

Chapter 3

Music and Radio

By the close of the 1930s, twenty-eight million households (and seven million cars) boasted at least one radio set, with most tuned-in to a network or local station for an average of five hours a day. Reaching over 80 per cent of the population, and far more 'Depression proof' than the movies, radio dominated America's entertainment habits. When the listening public went crazy for *Amos 'n' Andy* at the start of the decade, cinema owners found that the only way to get audiences to come to early evening screenings was to delay the start of the feature film and pipe the radio broadcasts into theatres. Broadcasts such as President Roosevelt's 'fireside chats' revolutionized political engagement, reports like those of H. V. Kaltenborn changed the way in which news was transmitted, and the nationwide scope of the medium was felt to be transforming the country as a whole in a 'levelling' of cultural and regional differences. As the means by which most Americans heard music, radio also transformed the music industry.

The impact of the Depression tended to consolidate radio's nationwide cultural influence rather than reduce it. At the start of the decade 600 or so stations existed, but small ones lost heavily in the competition for available advertising revenues. A few survived by resorting to barter, even exchanging chickens for airtime. Most others, however, were either bought by or affiliated to the National Broadcasting Company (NBC) or the Columbia Broadcasting System (CBS), rapidly giving national dominance to these major networks (which had only come into existence in 1926 and 1927, respectively). A trio of the most powerful independent stations joined forces to launch their own Mutual Network in 1934, but by end of the decade NBC controlled 182 stations, and CBS had grown from having nineteen affiliates in 1928 to 112 in 1939. CBS's strategy was to offer affiliates free access to 'sustaining' programmes (music, advice shows and so forth) in exchange for them guaranteeing time slots in which CBS could schedule programmes paid for by commercial sponsors. In consequence, many affiliates stopped producing original material and surrendered control over content to the centre. Yet the fierce competition engendered by the Depression meant that NBC and CBS themselves lost control to commercial sponsors who took over production of individual programmes in order to protect their interests. By as early as 1931, most network programmes were developed by advertising agencies. One key example, Blackett, Sample and Hummert, even formed its own 'soap opera factory', writing and controlling the content of more than thirty daytime serials for sponsors such as Procter and Gamble.[1] With advertising spending on radio rising from $3 million in 1932 to over $100 million by 1940, this commercial influence only increased.

Network affiliations had huge implications for the music industry in the Depression economy, with radio offering both challenges and opportunities for musicians and songwriters. Any song that was played over the networks could reach many millions of listeners; but songs which did not receive airtime, which often included those by African American artists, were practically doomed to obscurity. The dominance of advertising agencies in radio programming reduced the airtime devoted to music in general, since sponsors were drawn towards serials, quizzes and big-name comedy shows which could be more readily identified with particular brand names. Still, even at the end of the decade, music programming amounted to 57 per cent of broadcast hours. This in itself could be detrimental, as musicians who worked in restaurant orchestras, for instance, found themselves replaced by 'canned' radio music. On the other hand, companies like Ford and General Motors sponsored long-running concert programmes, NBC formed its own symphony orchestra in 1937 and even agency-led shows needed in-house bands (such as the Phil Harris orchestra featured in *The Jack Benny Show*), all providing relief for some Depression-hit musicians. When recording and bandwork collapsed for clarinettist Benny Goodman, for instance, radio jobs allowed him to continue playing, and eventually gave him a major break leading the jazz segment of NBC's *Let's Dance* in 1934. Then, when Goodman's band came to lead the phenomenal swing music craze of the late 1930s, the dynamics of the broadcast industry worked in his favour. Companies wanting to attract a youth market capitalized on the trend, leading Camel Cigarettes to sign Goodman to the nationally broadcast *Camel Caravan* on CBS.

For many of the problems besetting America's musicians, however, radio was neither the cause nor the solution. Even before the Crash, over 5,000 performing musicians had lost their jobs when movies began to talk and cinema owners dispensed with accompanists and orchestras. With Prohibition also having closed many nightclubs, bars and dance-halls, music historian Kenneth Bindas estimates that 30 per cent of professional musicians were jobless before the Depression set in. When it did, the figure rose to over 65 per cent.[2] Many opera companies and orchestras were unsustainable. The sales of phonograph records plunged from $46 million in 1930 to just $5 million in 1933. In the late 1920s, it took the sale of over 350,000 records to qualify a song as a hit, whereas by 1930, a 'hit' record was lucky to sell 40,000 copies.[3] Symbolic of the reversal of fortunes, Columbia Records – which had been wealthy enough in 1927 to co-found CBS – was now bought out by CBS itself in 1938 for just $700,000.

Things did improve, particularly after Prohibition was reversed. The swing craze helped revive record sales and jukeboxes became ubiquitous (consuming thirty million records a year). Hollywood also proved 'insatiable' in its demands for music and song. But when the radio and music industries were facing the Depression with such apparently divergent fates, people naturally became exercised about their respective positions in American culture. For musicians, the most pressing concern was how to find an audience again, how to make their music 'connect' with the public. This prompted discussion not only of how appreciation for live music could be encouraged, but also of what kind of music *should* be appreciated and valued. Mirroring the perspective of proletarian writers, some composers felt that one way to reach a mass audience was 'to contribute to the work of the political Left'.[4] Others believed that a specifically 'American' musical culture needed to be created, with its roots in 'the folk'. Others still – particularly alarmed by the fact that in 1931 an average classical music recording was selling just 500 copies – were convinced that the public's musical taste needed to be raised before a recovery could occur. All were debates engendered by the sense that musicians and composers lacked any power or control over the audience. In contrast, the debates concerning radio focused around broadcasters having *too much* power and control. The medium's hold over the public seemed astonishing. Social workers reported that even the poorest families were so wedded to the radio that they would 'give up furniture or bedding or most anything', rather than their precious receiver.[5] In these circumstances, what was to be made of the power radio seemed to have to sway the public's opinions: from Roosevelt's 'chats', through the demagoguery of Father Coughlin, to the panic induced by Orson Welles' broadcast of *War of the Worlds* in 1938. What was at work in the great level of public investment in the pervasive soap operas or characters like Amos and Andy? If radio was 'levelling' cultural barriers, what sort of nation was it constructing? Such issues, hotly debated by practitioners, critics, sociologists and politicians alike, were central to the forms and directions in which America's aural culture developed.

Musical Roots

Radio's associations with advertising had already created a keen debate about whether or not the medium could contribute to the elevation of American culture, and throughout the early 1930s the networks were under pressure to demonstrate their commitment to 'public service' programming. Congress twice debated legislation (the Fess Bill in 1930 and the Wagner-Hatfield Bill in 1934) which would have reassigned a quarter of all radio channels to educational, religious and government agencies. Broadcasters fended off these challenges, in a move similar to Hollywood's self-regulation through the Production Code, with promises of 'ample time' for educational, non-profit and 'quality' programmes, which were then written in to the 1934 Communications Act.[6] The fact that advertising agencies exercised so much control over programme development made it rather difficult to meet these promises, but over the next few years the response took a number of forms. Soap opera serials, which had been denigrated as obvious examples of crass commercialism and 'debased' culture, were relegated from the primetime evening schedules to daytime slots.[7] 'Educational' programmes such as *Cavalcade of America*'s series of historical and biographical dramas were also scheduled (this particular programme serving simultaneously to improve the image of its sponsor, DuPont, which had just been investigated by the Senate for profiteering during the First World War). A third track was to develop programmes that would prove radio capable of providing 'authentically "Cultural" experiences'.[8]

In 1937, Italian conductor Arturo Toscanini became the figurehead of NBC's bid to define 'cultural' radio. Having been the artistic director of La Scala in Milan, and principal conductor of both the Philharmonic and the Metropolitan Opera of New York, Toscanini's passionate commitment to textual fidelity in performing the classics had led to his idolization as the 'First Musician' of America. His celebrity status was such that tickets for his farewell concert of 1936 had sold out on the day it was announced, with prices driven over $100 and a crowd of 5,000 descending on Carnegie Hall to fight for standing-room places. Therefore, for NBC to entice him out of retirement and bring him back to the United States by offering him his own show and orchestra, was indeed perceived as a huge cultural event, widely heralded as the 'scoop of the century'.[9] Broadcast live from a dedicated studio in New York on Saturday and Sunday evenings, Toscanini and the NBC Symphony Orchestra brought great prestige to the network and a veneer of class that its president David Sarnoff clearly relished.

Ratings for the Toscanini broadcasts were impressive, and tickets to be in the studio audience were always in great demand. So much was the conductor the 'darling of the American media' that he eventually stayed with NBC for seventeen years, and the nation's 'love' and 'reverence' for Toscanini was celebrated as evidence of a 'vast increase in the popular appetite for the greatest things that music has to offer'.[10] Nor was it an isolated example. NBC had regularly broadcast the Boston Symphony Orchestra, the Metropolitan Opera and the Rochester Philharmonic along with sponsored classical music programmes like *The Firestone Hour*. CBS likewise had the Philadelphia Symphony, the New York Philharmonic and the 'rigorously traditional' *Everybody's Music*.[11] Some critics, however, were wary of the claims made about the ability of such programmes to raise the level of the nation's 'musical literacy'. For Marxist cultural critics, 'rather than fostering critical understanding', NBC's presentations encouraged listeners to feel good about themselves simply for 'appreciating' the version of 'high culture' they were being sold. Radio music, according to Theodor Adorno's analysis, offered a 'new function not inherent in music as an art – the function of creating smugness and self-satisfaction'.[12] What worried less radical dissenters, however, was the content of Toscanini's programming, particularly his eurocentric thrust. Joseph Horowitz has calculated that Beethoven, Brahms and Wagner accounted for more than 40 per cent of Toscanini's programmes (a fact which had been a concern since his days at the New York Philharmonic, when his emphasis on European classics undermined the orchestra's earlier efforts to promote a 'greater Americanization' of its repertoire).[13] Moreover, with the exception of Howard Hanson's *Eastman School of Music Symphony* on NBC, most radio broadcasts followed Toscanini's lead and largely ignored the work of American composers.

This, of course, was of special concern to native composers themselves. Virgil Thomson railed against the attitude of 'music appreciation' exponents who seemed to present the 'same 20 pieces' of classical music as if they were 'all the music in the world worth bothering about'.[14] The implication behind Toscanini's choices – that European classical music was innately superior to anything American or modern – was particularly galling. As Aaron Copland observed, opportunities for American composers to get their works played had already been impeded by the Depression, as the public for 'modern music concerts had fallen away'. Radio, on top of this, seemed set on encouraging a taste for the 'conventional' rather than challenging popular indifference 'to anything but the established classics'.[15]

Copland, Thomson, Marc Blitzstein, George Gershwin and other leading lights of American composition had themselves earlier subscribed to the notion of Europe as the superior place to 'learn music'. Each had studied composition and harmony with Nadia Boulanger at the Conservatoire Americaine in Paris, and returned to the United States committed to developing 'modernist' music. An inclination toward 'national expression' was evident in Gershwin's *Rhapsody in Blue* and *An American in Paris*, and might also be discerned in Copland's occasional drawing on jazz in his otherwise 'dissonant, avant-garde works' of the 1920s.[16] Yet it was not until the mid-1930s that a vibrant and widespread 'national identification' became particularly apparent, as composers reacted against European models by turning to native 'folksong' in droves.

The great wave of interest in folk and rural music apparent in the 1930s had its origins in the previous decade. 1927, for instance, saw the publication of Carl Sandburg's *The American Songbag* and the signing of acts such as the Carter Family and yodelling Jimmie Rodgers to the Victor label. Commercial interest was, in part, driven by the need for record companies to diversify in order to compete with radio, but rural radio stations also picked up on both the popularity of the material and its relative cheapness (union rates did not have to be paid because the American Federation of Music had barred rural, blues and jazz musicians from membership). When the Depression came, stations which could not afford to maintain a record library gave even greater prominence to live folk and country acts instead. As exposure increased, many artists got their break on radio. Bill Monroe, known as the progenitor of 'blue grass' music, was first hired by WLS-Chicago for their 'National Barn Dance' programme; Roy Acuff, who was to become one of the best-loved stars of Nashville's 'Grand Ole Opry', rose to fame playing the fiddle on WROL-Knoxville; and Woody Guthrie landed a programme on Los Angeles station KFVD in 1937, co-starring with singer 'Lefty Lou' (Maxine Crissman) and delivering a distinctive mix of old folk songs and his own contemporary adaptations.[17]

More significantly for composers, there was also a drive to preserve folk music material for posterity. Both Sandburg and A. P. Carter had wandered isolated parts of the country collecting and transcribing old songs, hymns and lyrics (which Sandburg published and Carter arranged for his family to perform). Such efforts were formally endorsed by the government when the Library of Congress established the Archive of American Folk Song in 1928, and the project was expanded greatly in the following decade. Most notable was the work of John Lomax and his son Alan, who travelled through forty-seven states in search of folk material, making accurate recordings in the field. Their *American Ballads and Folk Songs*, published in 1934, represented the 'rich musical heritage of rural America' like never before, and broadened the canon to include 'African-American blues, spirituals and work songs'.[18] The Lomaxes also collected prison songs, bringing particular attention to bluesman Huddie Ledbetter, who achieved fame as 'Leadbelly'. Alan also played a key role in bringing Guthrie to national attention, recording his songs and stories for the Archive in 1940. 'Grand Ole Opry' and the 'National Barn Dance' were generally thought to be 'debased' by commercial interests (NBC's broadcasts, for instance, included singing cowboys and the heavily-accented balladeer, Olaf the Swede); but Guthrie, Leadbelly and the like, retained qualities that were seen as 'authentic' elements in a tradition of 'home-made hand-me-downs in words and music'.[19]

This legitimation of vernacular folk music fed into new 'artistic' compositions on a remarkable scale, especially as publications and research made their musical notations more accessible than ever before. Virgil Thomson's score of Pare Lorentz's documentary film, *The Plow That Broke the Plains*, quoted tunes transcribed in John Lomax's *Cowboy Songs and Other Frontier Ballads*. Lincoln Kirstein slipped Copland 'two slim collections of Western tunes' when he commissioned the ballet *Billy the Kid* in 1938, from which the composer incorporated the melodic material of 'The Old Chisholm Train', 'The Dying Cowboy' and 'Trouble for the Range Cook' among others.[20] Morton Gould, *Cowboy Rhapsody* (1941) similarly transferred melodies such as 'Home on the Range' into the symphonic realm. And Elie Siegmeister was so inspired by Sandburg's *Songbag* that, as well as drawing blues and folk melodies into compositions such as *American Holiday* (1933), he even formed his own professional folk group, the American Ballad Singers, to travel the country in 1939.

Roy Harris became a particular symbol of the movement, not only because he was always 'aiming to produce an American masterpiece', but because his roots in Oklahoma and California were held to imbue him with 'natural' credentials 'untouched by the artificial refinements of Europe or the stultifying commericalism of cosmopolitan New York'.[21] Critic Paul Rosenfeld, for instance, characterized Harris as one who had 'heard the peasant tunes preserved by his stock all through his childhood'.[22] Much of this was a fiction, and his *Symphony: 1933* – supposedly commissioned as a 'great symphony from the American West' – actually lacked 'any specifically western references' or folk melodies.[23] Yet it still spoke to a widespread desire to champion a music that was characteristically 'American' and connected to 'the people'. Harris himself readily embraced the label of 'the Log Cabin composer', turning his attention to 'western' compositions such as *A Farewell to Pioneers* (1935) and *Cimarron* (1941), while his most famous folk-based work, *Folksong Symphony* (1942), was produced with the support of the Lomaxes.

There was something of a political undertone to this call to 'discover America'. A common component of Popular Front ideology was evident in musicologist Charles Seeger's urging that the composer should 'celebrate his oneness' with the American people and 'not his difference from them'.[24] Seeger's own enthusiasm for folk music sprang, in part, from his failure to 'reach' the working classes with the 'mass chants' he composed for Communist organizations in the early years of the Depression.[25] But his call also tapped broader anxieties about the 'danger of working in a vacuum', and composers such as Copland did see the turn to folk music as a way of making their compositions 'simpler' and more accessible. Copland in particular recognized that the radio and cinema had created an 'entirely new public for music' beyond the traditional concert halls, which could be captured if the composer made 'the effort' to reach out to them.[26] Adapting identifiably 'American' material became one part of a successful strategy for Copland, which also included composing for radio (as in *Music for the Radio* commissioned by CBS in 1937) and writing film scores for *Of Mice and Men* (1939) and *Our Town* (1941).

Of course, often it was not so much an authentic folk culture that was being preserved in this music, rather the compositions were commonly celebrating mythical pioneers and cowboys. Yet in this attempt to 'break the barrier between the highly trained composer and the audience', folk-based compositions represented a notable rejection of European and 'modernist' musical idioms.[27] Siegmeister, for instance, renounced his early compositions as 'obtruse, over-dissonant, and intellectualized', to favour instead 'contact with the simple, human, quality of our folk tradition' which he celebrated as a 'healthy stimulating factor'.[28] If the 'Toscanini cult' threatened to perpetuate the American sense of cultural inferiority, this new 'musical national identity' was thus cultivated in a spirit of 'release' from Europe. Indeed, according to Roy Harris, the vitality of national music did not just depend on the 'folk', for the United States itself possessed particular 'patterns' of culture which gave 'a unique valuation of beauty and a different feeling for rhythm, melody and form' to 'indigenous' composers (as well as an equally natural distaste for 'the warmed-over moods of eighteenth- and nineteenth-century European society').[29] Certainly by the end of the decade, and on into the patriotic years of the Second World War, champions of the national culture could point to the breadth and depth of a cultivated music that was also distinctly American.

George Gershwin and *Porgy and Bess* (1935)

Even before George Gershwin had completed the score, *Porgy and Bess* was being touted as an original 'American Folk Opera' – a label that spoke directly to the currents at work in the musical culture. Opera's tragic qualities were inherent in the source material provided by South Carolinan poet and author DuBose Heyward.[30] Heyward's 1925 novel and 1927 play, both entitled *Porgy*, told of the ill-fated love affair between the eponymous crippled black beggar and Bess, a 'loose' woman under the domination of brutish stevedore Crown. When Crown flees town wanted for murder, Porgy offers Bess shelter. Together they take in a child who is orphaned in a hurricane, but their idyll is then shattered by Crown's return. Protecting his 'family', Porgy strangles the stevedore, and although he is detained by the police they never suspect that a cripple could be capable of the crime. On his release, however, he learns that Bess has been enticed to New York by the flashy gambler and drug-pusher, Sportin' Life. At the story's end, Porgy heads to the city in his goat-drawn cart, searching desperately for his woman. With crimes of passion, murder, rape, infidelity and heartbreak, it had all the ingredients for grand opera. On the other hand, *Porgy and Bess* was also a product of 'folk culture', drawing on Heyward's own observations of the 'Catfish Row' community when he was a poor white youth in South Carolina, working among African Americans as a cotton-checker for a steamship company. Heyward and Gershwin further emulated the 'fieldwork' of folklorists by travelling in the summer of 1934 to Folly Island near Charleston. There they attended 'Gullah church services, revival meetings and funerals', to listen to local people.[31] The intent, at least, was to present African Americans as 'bona fide American folk, rather than minstrel caricatures', and thereby construct an 'authentic' version of Southern black folklife.[32]

By this time, Gershwin had become a key exponent of employing folk styles in 'the creation of American art-music'. In 1933 he was arguing that 'the great music of the past in other countries has always been built on folk music', and that American composers needed to see 'jazz, ragtime, Negro spirituals and blues, southern mountain songs, country fiddling, and cowboy songs' as legitimate sources for serious work.[33] Such legitimacy was a matter of personal concern, since many commentators did not regard Gershwin as a 'serious' composer. His jazz-infused orchestral works – *Rhapsody in Blue* (1924), *An American in Paris* (1928), *Variations on 'I Got Rhythm'* (1934) – were popular but not always acknowledged by his peers. This was largely because of his close and concomitant association with Broadway, where hits like *Strike Up The Band* (1927), *Girl Crazy* (1930) and *Of Thee I Sing* (1931) proved Gershwin and his brother Ira to be masters of musical comedy theatre.[34] *Porgy and Bess*, however, presented Gershwin with the opportunity to realign his work alongside Bizet's *Carmen*, Puccini's *Madame Butterfly*, or composers like Stravinsky and Dvorak who, as he argued, had always 'used elements of native folk materials in many of their most successful works'.[35]

Elements of African American folk music are certainly identifiable in Gershwin's compositions, retaining 'the quality of the Negro chant, the spiritual, the wail, the jazz and the blues', as one contemporary critic put it.[36] The sultry lullaby of *Summertime* is rendered in 'the jazz-blues idiom'; Sportin' Life's sacrilegious sermon *It Ain't Necessarily So* parodies the fervent call-and-response singing and the 'speaking in tongues' witnessed by Gershwin at the Gullah services; and a large part of the score consists of spirituals and funeral songs. Yet, as Raymond Knapp has discerned, this material is blended with both opera and popular song. *Summertime* draws on the harmonics of Wagner's *Tristan and Isolde*, for instance, while *It Ain't Necessarily So*, in contrast, is often seen as almost a vaudevillian 'number', closer in spirit to 'standard Broadway fare'.[37] Some critics accepted Gershwin's assertion that *Porgy* was an effort to 'create a new form'.[38] For others, however, the eclecticism was off-putting and deemed responsible for the mixed reception the work received. Rather more problematic in the long term, however, was the composer's own statement that he had 'decided against the use of original folk music because I wanted the music to be all of one piece'. 'Therefore', said Gershwin with the utmost presumption, 'I wrote my own spirituals and folk songs'.[39]

As Ray Allen argues, this statement made Gershwin a 'white interloper', claiming the ability not only to 'write black songs' but also to 'incorporate them into the more "serious" operatic form'.[40] It raised serious questions about white appropriation of African American culture, and about the 'authenticity' of all American classical compositions which drew on popular idioms. Virgil Thomson (implicitly defending his own appropriation of 'cowboy' songs) denounced *Porgy and Bess* as 'fake folk-lore' and effectively declared African American folk material as 'off limits' to white composers stating: 'Folklore subjects recounted as an outsider are only valid so long as the folk in question is unable to speak for itself, which is certainly not true of the American Negro in 1935'.[41] As those who worked with Gershwin attested, including the production's African American cast, he expressed genuine respect for the subject, but he did tend to imbue 'black' music with specific racial characteristics. African American musical styles, he suggested, were appropriate to opera in allowing the 'mood' to 'change from ecstasy to lyricism plausibly, because the Negro had so much of both in his nature'. He drifted further into stereotyping when arguing that 'folk song' introduced to opera 'the humor, the superstition, the religious fervor, the dancing, and the irrepressible high spirits of the race'.[42] The opera's images of black men shooting craps, drinking and snorting 'happy dust' only compounded the problem.

Alternative assessments can be advanced. One straightforward defence is that, despite its limitations, *Porgy and Bess* moved beyond the prevalent minstrel characterizations of the 1930s to expose white audiences to 'something closer to genuine southern culture' and that it sympathetically presented a southern black community as 'illustrative of American life'.[43] Accepting Gershwin and Heyward's genuine admiration for black culture, the production can also be situated valuably within the Popular Front's re-envisioning of the nation in a more inclusive manner. That 'a New York Jewish composer', argues Allen, 'in tandem with a WASP librettist and a cast of conservatory-trained African American singers . . . could forge a great American folk opera' was the quintessence of 'populist dreams of a diverse and inclusive melting pot'.[44] Heyward and Gershwin also insisted that it should always be performed by an all-black cast to 'permit the interpretation of the story by the race with which it was concerned', somewhat compensating for the fact it was a white man's version of black experience.[45] However, the suggestion that he had composed his 'own folk songs' always left Gershwin vulnerable to Duke Ellington's damning criticism that *Porgy and Bess* simply was 'not the music of Catfish Row or any other kind of Negro'.[46]

Blackface Culture

Porgy and Bess was not the only cultural phenomenon which raised concerns over appropriation, authenticity and race. The emphasis placed on Roy Harris's 'western' roots, for instance, constituted a claim that his use of folk music was more legitimate than the compositions of those 'city boys' who became 'folksong authorities after reading in a public library for a few weeks' or who 'take a short motor trip through our land and return to write the Song of the Prairies'.[47] A jibe at Aaron Copland's *Saga of the Prairie* (1937), this issue could take on a rather anti-Semitic tone, as in the suggestion of John Tasker Howard's 1941 evaluation of *Our Contemporary Composers*, that 'while Harris reflects the prairies and vastness of the West' Copland 'embodies the Russian-Jewish element transplanted to American soil'.[48] There was also, as Beth Levy observes, a racial charge to the description of Harris as 'the white hope' of American music; with the popular, if mystical, notion that Harris somehow derived his inspiration from 'the land', implicitly denigrating the compositions that others, like Gershwin, had derived from 'black' sources.[49]

In fact, cultural appropriation was a central feature of two the decade's biggest crazes. On radio, the portrayal of African American characters *Amos 'n' Andy* by two white actors raised questions about the perpetuation of demeaning blackface minstrelsy. In popular music, the rise of swing bands, led by white bandleader Benny Goodman, prompted concern as to whether African-American jazz music was being 'whitened' for a commercial mass market. From a race-conscious perspective after the Second World War, the conclusion was obvious: *Amos 'n' Andy* had been 'a nightly racial slur', and swing was 'the historical enemy of authentic black music'.[50] In the 1930s, however, the appeal of these cultural phenomena could not be dismissed so readily and occasioned a much more diverse reaction.

On the face of it, the case against *Amos 'n' Andy* is simple. Its creators and performers, Freeman Gosden and Charles Correll were white men who had travelled with minstrel companies in the years after the First World War . Comedy performed in blackface make-up had been an essential feature of these shows since the 1830s and relied on belittling stock caricatures such as 'Jim Crow' (a childlike, stupid plantation slave) and 'Zip Coon' (an ostentatious northern character who thought he was as smart as whites, but was really all bluster). First with *Sam 'n' Henry* for WGN-Chicago from 1925 to 1929, and then with *Amos 'n' Andy* for WMAQ-Chicago and NBC, the characters created for radio by Gosden and Correll drew on this tradition. Andy/Henry was characterized as pretentious and cocky, with his malapropisms (using words like 'regusting' instead of 'disgusting') and his false logic revealing his essential ignorance. Amos/Sam was meek, wide-eyed and credulous, frequently duped into hard work by the lazy Andy. Since the show was on radio no physical blackface was involved, but 'blackness' was instead conveyed vocally through dialect and the mangled language associated with minstrel performance. In 1931 it prompted the African American-owned *Pittsburgh Courier* to lobby for *Amos 'n' Andy* to be

Figure 3.1 Freeman Gosden and Charles Correll in blackface as *Amos 'n' Andy* (c. 1949: Hulton Archive/Getty Images).

banned from the airwaves for its negative effect on the 'self-respect and general advancement of the Negro in the United States'.[51]

What angered the *Courier*'s editor Robert Vann most, however, was the great enthusiasm that African Americans themselves displayed for *Amos 'n' Andy*. By 1930, the show was reaching an audience of

40 million; and, as J. Lawrence Freeman wrote that year, most black families in Harlem 'did just what whites did every evening at seven: they laid aside what they were doing, gathered around the radio, and observed fifteen minutes of absolute silence'. Each episode 'provided fodder for conversation the next day' among African Americans 'ranging from ministers and doctors to servants and laborers'.[52] Indeed, the popularity was such that, in contrast to the *Courier*, the nation's leading black newspaper the *Chicago Defender* even organized a parade and picnic to honour Gosden and Correll. Vann's campaign failed to drum up any significant opposition to the show (though given that he was arguing that the 'insult' of the programme lay in 'Amos and Andy telling us how ignorant we are', Vann did himself few favours by chastising other African Americans for being 'too dumb' to see that insult).[53]

Part of *Amos 'n' Andy*'s success was that it was one of the first original serials to be devised for the radio. Gosden and Correll were pioneers in developing an approach which fashioned an 'entirely self-contained fictional world' 'out of their own voices'.[54] Proving to the industry that 'serialized narrative drama' could be a 'basic building block of the new medium', the show inspired the development of subsequent 'soap opera' serials such as *The Rise of the Goldbergs, Just Plain Bill* and *The Romance of Helen Trent* and situation comedies like *Lum and Abner* or *Fibber McGee and Molly*.[55] The format encouraged 'the development of an intimate emotional bond between the characters and the listeners', who could 'easily imagine' that 'they were *there* in the taxicab office or the rooming house or the lunchroom *with* Amos and Andy, listening in on the conversation of friends'.[56] However, to achieve this kind of identification, Amos and Andy had to be more than minstrel caricatures. Indeed, Elizabeth McLeod's recent commentary demonstrates how Gosden and Correll 'set themselves apart from old-fashioned blackface' by constructing their broadcasts 'on a foundation of solid characterization', instead of minstrelsy's derogatory jokes and punch lines.[57]

Early programmes did make comedy out of the boys' migration from the South to Chicago (and later New York), presenting them as easy prey for urban hucksters such as the 'Kingfish'. Michele Hilmes argues that their ineptitude in assimilating to the city allowed other ethnic groups in the audience, who had experienced similar problems, to still laugh and 'feel themselves superior' to the 'unassimilable' black characters.[58] However, this was not a source of humour for long. With six fifteen-minute programmes every week, the stories moved on quickly and the characters developed. Stories such as Andy's problems with an amorous widow and Amos being falsely accused of murder gripped the nation. Amos in particular, became the emotional heart of the show, with audiences hooked by the ups and downs of his romance with Ruby Taylor. This 'simple love story', observes McLeod, 'brought out the best' in the characters: 'Amos fought back his natural shyness to stammer out his feelings, while Andy muttered sarcastic asides, which by their very tone revealed his own loneliness'.[59] It was not until 1936 that Amos and Ruby got married, but the obstacles put in their way transformed Amos from 'fumbling, naive and self-conscious' to a 'mature, responsible man . . . supporting himself and his family by the operation of a viable small business'. This in itself repudiated 'minstrel stereotypes of laziness, shiftlessness and dishonesty'.[60] Moreover, the social situations experienced by the central characters, through Andy's financial misadventures or Amos's struggles to work hard and better himself, were matters in which *Amos 'n' Andy* evoked universal rather than 'racial' qualities. Even Roy Wilkins, a future director of the NAACP, praised the show for possessing 'all the pathos, humor, vanity, glory, problems and solutions that beset ordinary mortals', black or white.[61]

Gosden and Correll also portrayed a self-sufficient and layered black community. Though voicing all the characters themselves, they presented a number of intelligent figures from the black middle classes, including lawyers, doctors, policemen and entrepreneurs. Ruby's father was depicted as a college-educated man who owned a construction company, a clothing store, a garage and a chain of lunch rooms. The show could certainly be accused of creating a false image, ignoring the real ghetto's problems of racial intolerance, segregation and discrimination. However, to an audience 'accustomed to servile, irresponsible blackface caricatures', *Amos 'n' Andy* showed that African-Americans could be dynamic, accomplished and successful.[62] This helps explain why many African Americans accepted that Gosden and Correll's intentions were good, even if they were not 'authentic'. There were difficulties, however, with the characterization of Kingfish and his black fraternity of the Mystic Knights of the Sea, which presented a selection of rogues and 'amiable thieves' who could be seen as a racial insult. The character of Lightnin' also came closer than any other to representing a pure blackface stereotype: slow-witted, lazy and drawling, he was very much in the vein of cinema's Stepin Fetchit. Unfortunately, these negatives were exacerbated in the late 1930s when, under pressure from sponsors, a weekly 'minstrel' and variety show was introduced (under the conceit that it was a 'fundraiser' being put on by the Mystic Knights), and *Amos 'n' Andy* gradually lost the goodwill it had inspired among many African Americans in its early years.[63]

Perhaps because the tradition of minstrelsy was long-established, the fascinating fact of white audiences identifying with African American characters played (or at least voiced) by white men did not occasion much debate at the time. With the swing phenomenon, however, the fact that white audiences were listening and dancing to African American music played by white men prompted an outpouring of academic, religious, political and media speculation about its significance. From the outset, swing music was invested with a whole series of ideological meanings pertaining to race.

Since the 1920s, white big-band leaders like Paul Whiteman had tried to synthesize dance music with jazz, but with little success. Instead, the pioneers were African American bandleaders such as Duke Ellington, whose orchestra recorded *Don't Mean a Thing If It Ain't Got That Swing* in 1932, and Count Basie, whose style of 'swinging the blues' came to the fore in front of black Kansas City audiences years before it became a national obsession.[64] Rather than the collectively-improvised music that purists knew as jazz, swing was more tightly structured with written arrangements that drew on Tin Pan Alley style songs, and possessed an infectious rhythm. Fletcher Henderson's versions of *King Porter Stomp* (1932) and *Wrappin' It Up* (1934) were masterpieces that shaped the early swing era, with hard-driving arrangements that ensured the music's jazz roots were not submerged. The subsequent craze soon saw these African Americans achieve fame in their own right, with Ellington and Henderson, along with Fats Waller, Cab Calloway and Jimmie Lunceford all proving profitable by 1937. Indeed, Lunceford became the first African American to be awarded a commercially-sponsored radio programme.

Against this, however, lies the fact that the national recognition of African American musicians came only after the success of white bands who 'colonized' their sound. Much of Goodman's triumph was built on the genius of Henderson's arrangements, but the bandleaders designated as the successive 'Kings of Swing' by the media – Benny Goodman, Artie Shaw, Tommy Dorsey and Glenn Miller – were all white men leading predominantly white orchestras. Moreover, by the end of the decade, when white bands were playing a music that 'struck many listeners as indistinguishable from that of their black counterparts', black performers 'were the first to be pushed out' of a glutted market.[65] There was also a sense that swing was deliberately 'whitening' the jazz idiom for mass appeal. The rage for interpreting classical music with a swing tempo (including Alec Templeton's *Bach Goes to Town* and Jimmy Dorsey's jazzed version of Strauss's *Blue Danube*) has been seen as an attempt to 'elevate' jazz and deny its black roots by 'associating it with the established canon of European art music'.[66] Goodman's famous concert at Carnegie Hall in 1938, which placed swing within a setting of 'high culture' could also be interpreted in this light.

It is difficult, however, to separate the question of appropriation from the nexus of commercial interests that promoted and capitalized on swing music, and the prejudice which faced black artists throughout the country. Segregation often prevented black bands from performing in front of white audiences (Cab Calloway, for example, was beaten when he tried to enter the segregated Pla-Mor Ballroom in Kansas City). Since radio broadcasts often came from 'whites-only' hotels, they were also denied access to such public airtime. Few other opportunities were available on commercial radio because few sponsors were happy to have their products linked with African American performers. Further, when artists were signed to record labels, they were either under-promoted (as with Victor's recordings of Henderson in 1932) or exploited. Count Basie's recording contract with Decca was one of the worst, offering his entire band just $750 for twelve records a year, with no royalties.

Still, both detractors of swing and its most fervent proponents ensured that the music's genesis in African American culture were not forgotten or ignored. For its denouncers, the 'jitterbugging' dance antics of America's swing-obsessed youth was the same immoral 'contagion spread by insidious rhythms' that jazz had represented in the 1920s. References to 'cannibalistic rhythmic orgies' painted the music with the racial slur of primitivism.[67] On the other side, particularly on the revitalized Left of the Popular Front, music critics such as John Hammond repeatedly praised swing as 'a national art form created by blacks and adopted by a pluralistic society'.[68] Hammond did much to make this pluralist vision a reality. His work at Columbia introduced vocalist Billie Holiday to the music world and secured her a contract with Artie Shaw's orchestra. He also urged Goodman to integrate his orchestra, who responded first by forming a quartet with pianist Teddy Wilson and vibraharpist Lionel Hampton, and then in 1941 hired Fletcher Henderson and guitarist

Charlie Christian to perform in his main band, directly challenging barriers against racial integration. Gene Krupa followed suit by hiring Roy Eldridge as his trumpeter. Goodman's Carnegie Hall concert also challenged expectations. In 'direct contrast' to Whiteman's similar Aeolian Hall concert of 1924, Goodman 'did not attempt to refine jazz by incorporating classical elements'. Instead, his orchestra 'blasted out uncompromising swing' and stressed its racial origins by featuring sets with Wilson, Hampton and Ellington's soloists, and a jam session with Count Basie.[69] Eleven months later, Hammond acquired Carnegie Hall again as the venue for *From Spirituals to Swing*, integrating swing, jazz, blues and Gospel in a celebration of African-American music as the potential basis for 'a new American culture' of racial harmony.[70]

Indeed, it was in this context that swing acquired a whole range of Popular Front associations. As a phenomenon of youth culture, it was seen as a challenge to patrician 'standards', representing the 'voice of youth striving to be heard in this fast-moving world'.[71] It was celebrated, too, as a source of racial pride in the cultural accomplishments of 'black heroes and heroines' at time when African-Americans were otherwise 'mostly excluded from politics and suppressed in economics'.[72] Given that among swing's celebrities Goodman and Shaw were children of immigrant Jewish garment workers and Dorsey was the son of a Pennsylvania coal-miner, the phenomenon was also defined as the epitome of the 'melting pot', transcending racial, ethnic and class barriers.[73] Of course, the racism of the industry and of some audiences represented a serious challenge to the Left's interpretation of swing as a bridge between the races, but as David Stowe argues it is important to 'distinguish the "colonizing" impulses of swing as an industry' from individual artists like Goodman 'who went out of his way' to credit Basie and other black musicians on his Camel Caravan radio broadcasts.[74] Moreover, the actions taken by Goodman, Shaw, Krupa and others in integrating their bands and showcasing black performers offered concrete examples of mutual respect, admiration and tolerance. The public crazes for *Amos 'n' Andy* and swing music, at opposite ends of the 1930s, were both testament to white America's 'long-standing fascination for African-American culture'; but swing, at least, demonstrated that such fascination could be met 'without the protective coloration of blackface'.[75] Moreover, as the recording of *Strange Fruit* in 1939 suggests, swing also created a context for advancing even more racially-charged statements.

Strange Fruit

Southern trees bear a strange fruit,
Blood on the leaves and blood at the root,
Black body swinging in the Southern breeze,
Strange fruit hanging from the poplar trees.

Pastoral scene of the gallant South,
The bulging eyes and the twisted mouth,
Scent of magnolia sweet and fresh,
Then the sudden smell of burning flesh!
Here is a fruit for the crows to pluck,
For the rain to gather, for the wind to suck,
For the sun to rot, for a tree to drop,
Here is a strange and bitter crop.

This bleak and harrowing metaphor of lynched Southern blacks as 'strange fruit' was penned and set to music by New York schoolteacher and Communist sympathizer Abel Meeropol (pen-name Lewis Allan) in 1937. As the work of a white Jewish intellectual, what *Time* magazine was to name in 1999 as 'the best song of the century' could easily have been dismissed as another example of an 'outsider' mediating black experience. Certainly some African Americans, including Paul Robeson, disliked *Strange Fruit* because it perpetuated the image of blacks as victims. Yet it rose above this when Billie Holiday made it her own. Indeed, it became 'her' song to such an extent that, reversing the usual direction of racial appropriation, Holiday's autobiography *Lady Sings the Blues* falsely claimed she had written it herself.[76] Though understandably aggrieved by this, Meeropol himself acknowledged that it was Holiday's 'startling' and 'dramatic' interpretation that gave *Strange Fruit* the power to 'jolt an audience out of its complacency' and 'fulfilled the bitterness and shocking quality I had hoped the song would have'.[77]

Holiday first performed it at the unique left-wing, racially-integrated Café Society in New York's Greenwich Village. There, as David Margolick records in his excellent 'biography' of the song, 'the doormen wore rags', the 'bartenders were all veterans of the Abraham Lincoln Brigade', and 'blacks and whites fraternized on stage and off'.[78] Proprietor Barney Josephson had engaged John Hammond to organize the music and, as Hammond's protégé, Holiday became a featured artist. *Strange Fruit* became the song with which she closed her show three nights a week; staged with the audience silenced, drinks service halted and all lights out except for one spotlight on Holiday. 'There were no encores after it', insisted Josephson. 'My instruction was to walk off, period. People had to remember *Strange Fruit*, get their insides burned with it'.[79] Sometimes people walked out because 'they said, we don't call this entertainment',[80] but most audiences were indeed 'burned' by it. As one who experienced

Holiday's performance later wrote, 'all of us sat as if stunned, immobilized by the intensity of our emotion'.[81]

The impact, as Samuel Grafton described it in the *New York Post*, was 'as if a game of let's pretend had ended and a blues singer who had been hiding her true sorrow in a set of love ditties had lifted the curtain and told us what it was that made her cry'.[82] Columbia Records rejected the song because of its subject matter, but in April 1939, Milt Gabler's independent Commodore label captured Billie's performance. Devoid of the histrionics that could easily have accompanied the lyrics, Holiday brought things 'down to a starker "I'm-gonna-tell-it-like-it-is" level', as if driven by the thought, 'So you want to hear about lynching, do you? Well then I'm really going to give it to you!'.[83] The ugliness of racist violence and the blood of lynch victims 'gliding from the leaves down the trunks and on to the roots', were portrayed with a 'chilling tautness' in her voice. In describing the 'pastoral' South she spits out the word 'gallant'. Intensity increases as the song progresses, until Holiday reaches the final words, 'bitter crop'.[84] Then, as Studs Terkel notes, 'The voice goes up – crah-ah-OP – like a scream . . . She leaves the last note hanging. And then – bang – it ends. That's it. The body drops'.[85]

Between 1930 and 1939, 130 lynch killings had been officially recorded, with 119 African Americans murdered, although many more were committed and hushed up. Those that came to attention were often accompanied by a gruesome 'carnival-like atmosphere', and involved much more than murder.[86] Victims were burned, tortured, dragged behind wagons; often their genitals were cut off, and they were hung while still alive. *Strange Fruit* was inspired by a picture of lynch victims Thomas Shipp and Abram Smith. Beaten to death and then strung up, the mob had posed with them for 'souvenir' photographs. In 1934, when Claude Neal was kidnapped from jail, one local newspaper even advertised the event ahead of time, with the headline 'Florida to Burn Negro at Stake . . . Will Be Mutilated, Set Afire'. Florida's governor ignored the NAACP's calls to intervene. Neal was tortured for two hours before being hanged, but the governor only acted when the mob began storming the jail to take another victim.[87] Every year from 1909 until the late 1940s, the NAACP led the fight for lynching to be made a federal crime, with the Communist Party joining the campaign in the late 1920s. It was in this context that *Strange Fruit* became a 'prime piece of musical propaganda', as proponents of the federal legislation sent copies of the song direct to congressmen. It did not, however, have the desired result of making them feel 'the deepest shame of racist America'.[88] In both 1937 and 1940, the House of Representatives passed a bill but on each occasion, as had happened in the past, it was defeated by Southern senators.[89]

Indeed, the wider impact of *Strange Fruit* was limited. By 1945, the recording had sold 50,000 copies, but most radio stations found it 'too sensitive to put on the air', and WNEW would not let Holiday perform it during a live hook-up from Café Society.[90] As Gunther Schuller notes, without radio exposure 'most Middle-America white swing fans never heard it and went on discovering Glenn Miller instead'.[91] Yet for those who did play the recording or witnessed the live performance, 'not only did you see the "fruit" evoked in all its graphic horror, but you saw in Billie Holiday the wife or sister or mother of one of the victims beneath the tree, almost prostrate with sorrow and fury'. And when Billie 'wrenched the final word from her lips, there was not a soul in her audience, black or white, who did not feel half strangled'.[92]

Figure 3.2 'You saw in Billie Holiday the wife or sister or mother of one of the victims': Billie Holiday sings Lewis Allan's *Strange Fruit* (William P. Gottlieb Collection, Library of Congress; www.jazzphotos.com).

Politics, Power and Panic

The exclusion of *Strange Fruit* from the airwaves is generally considered as symptomatic of the radio industry's conservatism, rather than as a weakness of the cultural Left. Significant aspects of American music were infused with left-wing politics, but they rarely received the national exposure that radio could have given them. Organizations affiliated with the Communist Party, such as the Workers' Music League and its Composers' Collective, sought to develop music 'to inspire revolutionary fervor' in the working classes, with the likes of Copland even setting May Day poems to music.[93] Swing music was also embraced by the Popular Front. *New Masses* sponsored Hammond's *From Spirituals to Swing* and Goodman participated in anti-fascist benefits like 'Stars for Spain' (prompting the FBI to label him 'an ardent Communist sympathizer').[94] Marc Blitzstein's opera *The Cradle Will Rock* challenged the escapism of Broadway by taking the CIO's struggles to unionize steelworkers as its subject and 'exploring the possibilities of theatre music for expressing social commentary'. Each middle-class character in *Cradle* – the doctor, the college president, even the church minister – is given a song expressing how they had 'prostituted' themselves to the power of 'Mister Mister', the boss of Steeltown.[95] Alan Lomax made the collections of the Archive of American Folk Song available to Music League publications such as Lawrence Gellert's *Negro Songs of Protest* (1936), and also championed figures like Woody Guthrie whose modern folk songs captured the hardships of the dispossessed with potent resonance. Singing at migrant camps and picket lines in California, Guthrie used songs such as 'Pretty Boy Floyd', 'If You Ain't Got the Do Re Mi' and 'So Long, It's Been Good To Know Ya', to inspire working people and farmers in the struggle for social justice.

Yet the compositions which dominated radio airplay were love songs like *Night and Day*, *Blue Moon* and *Cheek to Cheek*, and novelties like *Santa Claus is Coming To Town*. The decade was a 'golden age' for songwriting for the likes of Cole Porter, Irving Berlin, Hoagy Carmichael, Johnny Mercer, Dorothy Fields and Lorenz Hart, whose work achieved a 'stunning level of variety and sophistication', and proved to be particularly commercial, publicized both on the radio and in the movies.[96] One of the few commercial hits of the Popular Front was the revue show of *Pins and Needles*, produced and performed by the International Ladies Garment Union. Intended both as entertainment for the workers and to promote a positive image of unionism, it included songs such as *One Big Union for Two*, which turned labour relations into romantic liaisons, and *We'd Rather Be Right*, which 'poked pins and needles' into conservative '100-percent Americans' intent on making 'America bigoted and better'. Far beyond the expectations of its creators, it transferred to Broadway and became the longest running musical of the decade. However, in contrast to *The Cradle Will Rock*, *Pins* was perceived as 'non-threatening' in its politics, sacrificing its bite in its effort to entertain.[97] Indeed, its producer all along insisted that what the public wanted, even from a union production, was 'amusement and not class consciousness'.[98]

It was a sentiment undoubtedly shared by the nation's radio producers. The networks were not entirely devoid of progressive politics. After two years at Los Angeles-KFVD, Guthrie was introduced to the nation by Lomax on *Columbia School of the Air* and Norman Corwin's *Pursuit of Happiness* series. Corwin's show also brought to public attention the Popular Front's unofficial anthem, *Ballad for Americans*, as sung by Paul Robeson. Mild political satire featured in some comedy programmes, especially in Fred Allen's *Town Hall Tonight* series; and it has been demonstrated that soap operas were not as conservative as critics supposed, but raised repeatedly the socially significant subjects of female sexuality, dysfunctional marriages and even crime.[99] Overtly political statements, however, were usually confined to one-off dramas, such as Corwin's reaction to Spanish Civil War atrocities in *Words Without Music*'s 'They Fly Through the Air' (CBS, 1938) and the anti-fascist verse play by Archibald MacLeish, *Fall of the City* (CBS, 1937).

Many observers blamed the commercialization of mass culture for the lack of opportunities available to socially conscious artists. Critics put the lack of exposure down to the business-related need to appeal to the lowest common denominator in order to reach the broadest audience. As music critic B. H. Haggin saw it at the time, the consequence was that most producers 'made sure safe, simple musical forms dominated the air'.[100] Left-wing commentators like James Rorty believed the problem to be more insidious, with the networks giving little time to anyone who questioned the capitalist ideals of corporate America. Big business was appeased, according to this analysis, not only because of radio's dependence on advertising revenues, but also because the networks had become 'big businesses in their own right . . . owned by the same huge financial powers that controlled many of America's banks, power trusts and corporations'.[101] Radio, it was alleged, 'gave capitalism an additional, influential means of promoting its own ideals', and created a 'conspiracy of silence regarding all those aspects of the individual and social life that do not contribute to the objectives of the advertising'.[102] Certainly, it was true that those whose opinions courted controversy could find themselves silenced. When Alexander Wollcott devoted an edition of his *The Town Crier* to 'acid comments on Hitler', the sponsor Cream of Wheat simply cancelled the series.[103]

   Sometimes, however, politics could be profitable, and it was not only corporate advertisers who could afford to pay for airtime. To pay for the broadcasts of his sermons from the Shrine of the Little Flower in Michigan, Father Charles Coughlin organized a Radio League of the Little Flower, with members making donations of $1 a year for him to buy time first on WJR-Detroit, and then on CBS in 1930. CBS became concerned when Coughlin moved from the subject of the Bible to attacking Wall Street bankers and the Hoover administration. His broadcasts, though, had stimulated such a flow of donations to his church that by the point CBS tried to ease him off the air, Coughlin had raised sufficient funds to buy time from twenty-six stations across the United States and effectively created his own 'ad hoc independent network'.[104] Reaching a radio congregation estimated at over ten million by the mid-1930s, Coughlin's invective widened to include Jewish financiers, Communists and 'Franklin Double-Crossing Roosevelt', prompting great anxiety about the power that radio could bestow upon such a demagogue. Indeed, in 1935 he used his influence with listeners to challenge Roosevelt directly, denouncing the President's request for Senate to approve American affiliation with the World Court. His broadcasts launched a startling avalanche of telegrams and letters on Congress – 200,000 by Coughlin's own estimate – and were credited with pressuring senators into rejecting the proposal.[105] Public support also kept Coughlin from being censored: CBS was overwhelmed with letters of protest when it tried to 'muzzle' the priest, and when WMCA of New York and WDAS of Philadelphia attempted to enforce an order compelling Coughlin to submit his scripts to the network prior to broadcast, 'listeners erupted in violent protest, forming picket lines before the two stations'.[106] It was not until 1939, when Coughlin's ever-increasing admiration for Hitler reached its zenith, that the National Association of Broadcasters declared his bigoted statements to be 'an evil unworthy of American radio' and effectively cut him off from the airways.[107]

   Coughlin's radio power, however, was exaggerated. Despite his efforts to turn his personal popularity into a political movement, the

Union Party of 1936 polled less than 900,000 votes and letters from his audience suggested that, while he was much admired for his forthrightness, he 'could never turn [Americans] against our president'.[108] Roosevelt himself, after all, had used radio to build up an even greater national following than Coughlin, exploiting the medium's political potential. Like Coughlin's broadcasts, his 'fireside chats' exploited the ability of radio to create intimacy between broadcaster and audience. These short broadcasts – of which he delivered only fourteen before the war – could reach upwards of sixty million listeners, or almost 80 per cent of the American population, including millions who 'were unable to read or lived in areas not served by newspapers'.[109] For the administration, radio was also the ideal way to bypass the conservative newspaper owners and editors who were often hostile to the New Deal. Delivered not as formal 'addresses' but as if they were informal, person-to-person conversations, these broadcasts allowed the President to examine the banking crisis, outline the New Deal relief programmes and discuss unemployment figures in such a way that he seemed to be taking the nation into his confidence. To the public, it felt as if Roosevelt 'was talking to them directly as individuals, knew their problems and was interested in them'.[110] As well as the chats, FDR made over 300 radio addresses during his presidency and, with the kind of 'drawing power' he possessed, the networks were 'eager to carry his voice' whether or not they agreed with his politics. Indeed, the industry adopted a 'right of way' policy in which 'all national and regional networks would drop prior commitments and link together in one huge chain', giving the President access to as many as 600 stations at once.[111] FDR's political manager, James Farley, was of the opinion that the 'influence of radio' in determining his election victories could 'hardly be overestimated'.[112] Moreover, 'fireside chats' that boosted New Deal programmes such as the Tennessee Valley Authority or the National Recovery Administration, prompted hundreds of thousands of Americans to press the President's cause, implicitly sending Congressional representatives the message that he was 'stronger in the country than they were'.[113]

Critics, of course, also regarded this as demagoguery. They felt the same way about Huey Long, when the senator from Louisiana used the networks to promote his radical 'Share Our Wealth' programme to public attention. Indeed, Long delivered his first address just days after Roosevelt's first 'fireside chat' in March 1933, seeking to manoeuvre the President into making a stronger commitment to the redistribution of wealth. When the administration moved slowly on the issue, Long again used the radio to take his cause to the people in February 1934, making his 'Every Man a King' address. Rhetoric overwhelmed the flaws in his economic plans and by the spring of 1935 over seven million Americans had formed their own 'Share Our Wealth' societies in response, providing an impressive base for an anticipated presidential bid which was only derailed by his assassination later that year. One interesting aspect of Long's use of radio is that NBC 'rushed to give him free time'.[114] The usual explanation is that Long attracted big audiences, and that broadcasting his 'radical' speeches also served as a demonstration that radio was not censored. However, given that some NBC executives resented New Deal policies and Roosevelt's use of their network, historians have also speculated that the prospect of Long splitting the Democrat vote in 1936 may have had a role to play in their 'generosity'.[115]

At the end of the 1930s, the two key strands influencing radio's political outlook – the conservatism of sponsors and executives and the growing concern about the power of radio to shape public opinion – converged in the policies governing news programming. The power of advertising agencies had militated against extensive news coverage; few commercial sponsors at the start of the decade were interested in associating their products with news programmes, and those that did retained the power of veto. Sponsored bulletins tended to be in the form of broadcasts such as Lowell Thomas's genial commentaries for *Literary Digest* on NBC, or, most famously, the popular dramatizations of *The March of Time*, produced by Henry Luce's media conglomerate for CBS. However, massive nationwide audiences and acclaim attended coverage of events such as the 1932 election, the kidnapping of Charles Lindbergh's baby son in 1933 and the subsequent trial of Bruno Hauptmann in 1935. Consequently, when the Associated Press and the American News Publishers Association temporarily banned the sale of news material to radio stations, viewing them as a competitive threat to the print media, the networks stepped up their own news-gathering activities. Paul White at CBS pioneered the practice of setting up correspondents in all major cities, paying them for material as it was used. As world affairs deteriorated after 1936, these operations were extended internationally.

H. V. Kaltenborn played a crucial role in this transformation. Originally paid just $100 per week for two broadcasts from Europe, in 1936 he headed into Spain to observe the civil war firsthand. Via shortwave radio set up in an evacuated farmhouse in the midst of the battle of Irun, Kaltenborn broadcast for 'the first time in history' the sounds of a war actually happening, to 'people sitting in the safety of their homes an ocean away'.[116] His frontline reports demonstrated clearly – in sharp contrast to the accounts circulated by the Hearst press – that the Germans and Italians were giving Franco direct support. Following these unique broadcasts, CBS committed fourteen staff to Europe, with William Shirer covering Chamberlain's appeasement of Hitler, Edward Murrow broadcasting from Vienna as Austria was annexed by the Nazis and CBS engineers setting-up short-wave stations for the Czechoslovakian government itself as the threat against it escalated. While it took over twenty-four hours for photographs of the German invasion of Poland to reach the newspapers, and a further two days before the newsreels were ready, radio broadcasters provided immediate coverage. During the Munich crisis, Kaltenborn himself 'threaded the drama together', commentating, explaining and even translating Hitler's speeches 'instantaneously as they came through his headset'.[117] Every time Kaltenborn had a report to make, CBS uniquely gave him priority over scheduled commercial programming.

Few broadcasts brought network radio as much prestige and critical distinction. But as the coverage of Munich transfixed audiences, news now attracted the attention of corporate sponsors, which brought new pressures as well. Kaltenborn was first aware of them when an executive from sponsors General Mills asked him to avoid further discussion of Spain. CBS supported Kaltenborn by ending GM's association as soon as their thirteen-week contract expired, but the situation arose in the midst of considerable debate about the role of news commentators. Kaltenborn's reports from Irun had gained their power from being 'frankly personalized', chronicling not only the war but also his own 'rising personal indignation' about fascist duplicity.[118] Radio's ability to report the news more 'directly, personally, concisely and full of human energy' had given it the edge over the print media.[119] But as war broke out, network executives became anxious. In 1939, CBS determined that a policy of 'straight, objective' reporting was necessary to avoid accusations that the power of radio was being used to push the United States into the conflict. As Barnouw suggests, announcing that they would have only 'news analysts', not 'news commentators' effectively instituted a 'kind of neutrality law for radio'.[120]

That the policy was unsuccessful was testament to the talents of the radio journalists and the nature of the medium. Ed Murrow's reports from London during the Blitz in the summer of 1940 carefully avoided any direct attempt to influence opinion. But his seemingly objective

Figure 3.3 Orson Welles broadcasting *The War of the Worlds* (1938: Kobal Collection).

efforts to present the reality of circumstances facing ordinary Londoners, taking his microphone onto the streets to allow his American listeners to hear the shrieks of air raid sirens, or broadcasting from a rooftop during a Luftwaffe raid, served to undermine his listeners' sense of 'remoteness from the European struggle'. His 'vivid, eyewitness accounts' put Americans in the shoes of those who were suffering under Hitler's onslaught and conveyed, without the need for any direct comment, 'the pressing need to aid England'.[121] According to David Culbert, Roosevelt himself believed that 'Murrow's broadcasts had helped greatly in making Americans accept the possibility of a declaration of war'.[122] Of course, it was this perceived power, not only to inform but to persuade, that had made network bosses nervous in the first instance.

The War of the Worlds (CBS, 1938)

The infamous hysteria generated by Orson Welles's production of *War of the Worlds* loomed large in the anxieties of radio executives in 1939. Broadcast by CBS on Halloween 1938 as part of *Mercury Theater of the Air*, this adaptation of H. G. Wells' fantasy about a Martian invasion of Earth had sparked pockets of panic across the country. New York police reported 'frightened citizens' shouting that they 'had seen enemy planes . . . heard the president order evacuations, or . . . seen poisonous gas coming over the Hudson'.[123] Twenty families in Newark fled their homes with wet towels over their faces as makeshift gas masks. In Indianapolis, a woman rushed into a church service screaming that the world was coming to an end, and a man in Pittsburgh came home to find his wife holding a bottle of poison and shrieking, 'I'd rather die this way than that!'.[124] Priests had calls from people seeking confession, thousands telephoned newspapers seeking instruction and at least twenty adults were treated in hospitals for shock or hysteria. News of the panic reached CBS before the broadcast had even ended, compelling Welles to announce that the programme was nothing more than a 'holiday offering' – 'the Mercury Theate's own radio version of dressing up in a sheet, jumping out of a bush and saying Boo!'.

'Describing the programme as a practical joke', writes Welles's biographer Simon Callow, 'was an idea improvised on the spot as a sop to the panic'.[125] Welles's real intention had been to develop a new style of drama that made full use of radio techniques 'to liven up a dull book'.[126] Thus, as well as transferring the setting of *War of the Worlds* to modern-day New Jersey, scenarist Howard Koch was instructed to imitate 'the form of radio itself' and present the story in the form of a series of emergency news bulletins. His script, therefore, repeatedly interrupted a fake broadcast of music from a New York hotel, with 'breaking news' from mystified reporters in the field who urgently narrated the horrific invasion as it unfolded. It drew upon Kaltenborn's recent commentaries on the Munich Crisis, as well as the reporting of the 1937 *Hindenburg* explosion when Herb Morrison had testified in horror as the hydrogen-filled dirigible crashed to the ground in flames, killing thirty passengers and crew. In *War of the Worlds*, as the Martians emerged to annihilate all humans, actor Frank Readick emulated Morrison's 'graduation from comfortable report, through growing disbelief, to naked horror'.[127] The testimony of an array of fictional military, scientific and political experts, unexpected breakdowns in transmission and innovative sound-effects, all added to the verisimilitude.

Yet from the outset, statements were made to inform listeners that the play was a dramatization, and the second half of the production changed style significantly as Welles documented the aftermath of the invasion in a far less sensational first-person narration. The hysteria derived less from a deliberate effort to fool the audience than from an accident of timing. The majority of those who panicked had actually been listening instead to NBC's improbably popular ventriloquist show *Edgar Bergen and Charlie McCarthy*. At fifteen minutes into *Charlie McCarthy*, however, millions reached for the dial to avoid the commercials, and suddenly heard Readick describing the horrific alien creature as it emerged. For a moment, at least, an estimated 1.7 million listeners believed that it was a real news broadcast.[128]

Many of the explanations that appeared in the press immediately after the panic attributed it to 'incredible stupidity'.[129] One prominent psychologist theorized that 'no intelligent person would be taken in'.[130] Yet at least one university professor telephoned the press to 'verify reports of the alien invasion', and two geology lecturers set out in search of the 'falling meteors' featured in the broadcast.[131] The seemingly illogical reaction became the subject of study for Hadley Cantril of Princeton University, who had already co-authored *The Psychology of Radio* in 1935. His account of *The Invasion from Mars*, published through the American Institute of Public Opinion in 1940, confirmed that highly-educated people had joined in the panic and suggested that the radio techniques used by Welles had aroused in them 'false standards of judgment'.[132] Audiences had only recently become accustomed to the authority of special 'on-the-spot' news flashes and, with the extensive coverage of the Munich Crisis and the Anschluss, the interruption of programming for emergency announcements was expected. Indeed, since radio had also made Americans aware that Germany was readying for war, Cantril found that a number of panicked listeners had assumed that what was being reported was really 'an invasion by the Nazis with a terrifying new weapon'.[133]

Finding that 'it was the people who were closest to the borderline of economic disaster who were most apt to take the program as news', Cantril concluded his study with the socially-minded argument that such hysteria could be avoided in the future if Americans were 'less harassed by the economic insecurities which stem from underprivileged environments'.[134] However, with the print media promoting the idea that the real 'menace' lay in radio's potential for demagogic manipulation of an unthinking public, the immediate response came in the industry's public display of self-regulation. That CBS ruled against the future use of the 'technique of a simulated news broadcast' was not surprising, but the networks also required all announcers to 'handle news without the slightest color or melodrama', keeping 'horror, suspense and undue excitement' out of their coverage – thus, introducing the 'neutrality' policy that sought to govern news broadcasting in the lead up to the Second World War.[135] Rather than the root causes of the panic, it was again the 'power and the force of radio' that dominated the debate over *War of the Worlds*.[136]

Further Considerations

There are still major areas to explore in the aural cultures of the 1930s. While contemporary opinion remained divided as to whether radio was a dangerously 'powerful propaganda machine', or a 'supremely democratic arena' with 'audiences controlling the medium by voting with their tuning dials', recent scholarship tends to focus instead on the complexity of listeners' investment in shows like *Amos 'n' Andy*.[137] The comedies of Jack Benny and Fred Allen, thriller serials like *The Shadow* and *Fu Manchu*, children's programmes such as *Little Orphan Annie*, and the daytime chat shows of Margaret McBride, have all prompted intriguing research and comment. The consistent portrayal of corrupt government institutions in the adventures of *The Green Hornet*, for example, has been read as a conservative challenge to the New Deal's claims to moral authority'; while the soap operas that contemporary critics dismissed as the 'touchstone of discredited, feminized, commercialized mass culture', have since been treated seriously as a 'place where women could hear their unique concerns addressed'.[138]

In terms of the development of American music, a lengthier consideration of the decade should evaluate the popularity of 'sweet' music as well as swing, for the bands of Guy Lombardo, Rudy Vallee and Eddie Duchin were capable of drawing crowds as large as Goodman's. Bing Crosby's rise to prominence as the nation's premier radio 'crooner' is also easier to appreciate in that context. The legacy of musical theatre is also of huge significance. Greater justice needs to be done to the acclaimed work of Irving Berlin (in both stage revues like *As Thousands Cheer* and movies like *Top Hat*) and, in particular, the perspective on 'high society' that Cole Porter perpetuated, to explore the appeal of his particular evocation of a sophisticated 'world of pleasure, travel, wealth, promiscuity' and erotic love in the midst of the Depression.[139] Attention to Hollywood film scores is also warranted, including Erich Korngold's work at Warner Bros. on films such as *Robin Hood* and *Elizabeth and Essex*, and Max Steiner's masterful score for *Gone With the Wind*. Moreover, what is one to make of the adoption in March 1931 of *The Star Spangled Banner* as the official national anthem; was its selection simply a reflection of 'a desire for national unity in troubled times'?[140]

Perhaps of even greater significance in the long term is the fact that in 1935, the Radio Corporation of American announced substantial investment in the new medium of television. By the end of the decade, both CBS and NBC had developed their own television studios and mobile units. Although the Second World War meant that such developments were temporarily put into storage, the relationship between radio and television was such that when special telecasts were made from the 1939 New York World's Fair, the subjects chosen for the inaugural pickups were radio's most popular figures: Correll and Gosden in their *Amos 'n' Andy* blackface and President Franklin Roosevelt himself.

Chapter 4

Art and Design

In 1936, Walter Benjamin in 'The Work of Art in the Age of Mechanical Reproduction' suggested that film and photography had become more than artistic media in their own right: they had altered fundamentally the concept of art itself. Benjamin observed that in permitting the reproduction of all other works of art, the technologies of photography, cinema and the phonograph had 'profoundly modified the effect' of art on upon the public.[1] Original works had once possessed an 'aura'; their very unique existence and presumed cultural value inspired a sense of awe in those who experienced them. Mass reproduction, however, substituted this with a 'mass existence' in copies of the original artwork which could now be encountered in a wide variety of situations.[2] Choral performances could be played in your own home. The *Mona Lisa* could be seen in books, on magazine covers, or even bought as a postcard. Film, Benjamin noted, was a form of art in which no original actually existed; its 'artistic character determined entirely by its reproducibility', cinema audiences only ever saw a mass-reproduced print.[3] The 'aura' around art was, therefore, 'withering'. Some critics were anxious about this, but Benjamin saw it as an ambiguous development. Mass consumption of the reproduced image could well make the artwork so familiar as to undermine critical reflection. Yet reproducibility could also 'emancipate the work of art', freeing it from the grip of elitist critics and the 'cultist' sanctums of galleries and museums and, in allowing the beholder to form their own opinions, make art more accessible and more democratic.[4]

Although the German philosopher's essay was not disseminated widely in the United States until after the war, Benjamin's conclusions were in accord with the ways in which many American artists and designers were contemplating their own work in the 1930s. His assertion that the loss of aura presented Communists with an opportunity to bring politicized art to the masses, was already apparent in the didacticism of left-wing 'proletarian art' and 'Socialist Realism'. This was especially true of the cartoons on labour strife and the social inequities of capitalism that were being disseminated directly by 'mechanical reproduction' in publications like New Masses.[5] Throughout the decade, however, the concept of 'accessible' and 'democratic' art affected the development of most every school of artistic expression, as the Depression gave urgency to the artist's desire to connect with 'the people'.

Quite simply, the economic collapse had all but destroyed the existing art market. Collectors and museums had limited cash for new purchases, private patronage largely vanished and many galleries closed or cut their exhibition schedules. Marxist theorists presented this as an opportunity for the artist to 'redeem' himself from dependency on the 'bourgeois' and 'decadent' collector's market, and end his 'isolation' from 'the people'.[6] Yet even without this political spin, most every artist realized that to simply to survive, a new market for art needed to be found or created among the general public. The Associated American Artists (AAA) group, formed in 1934, represented one such response to the Depression, selling lithographs and etchings by its members through department stores and by direct mail for just $5. Although it still sought to maintain an artistic aura through 'limited editions', publicity for the AAA specifically offered 'original works of art which once only museums and the rich could afford', as 'yours to live with at home'.[7] The rhetoric of 'the people' replacing the wealthy as patrons reached its greatest expression in the New Deal arts projects, which sought to suggest that the artistic patronage of a representative government constituted the creation of a 'cultural democracy'.[8] Mural painting, in particular, came to be regarded as the 'people's art'. Conceived for the public, and displayed to them in post offices, schools, hospitals and department stores, murals epitomized the endeavour to make art 'connect'.

Benjamin had further asserted that the modernist notion of 'art for art's sake' had been a reactionary, undemocratic doctrine adopted by elites to protect the 'aura' of fine art. This had particular relevance to the Left, but it also resonated among some Regionalist and American Scene painters, who denounced the influence of New York's art critics and patrons as the self-appointed arbiters of 'taste'. Thomas Hart Benton was particularly vocal in condemning the 'intellectuals and aesthetes' who staged 'exhibitions of esoteric art incomprehensible to the general public'.[9] The Regionalist movement of the 1930s was framed as a call for art that conformed not to the standards of New York or Europe but which came from the 'rural and small-town' heartland of America and 'represented American life'.[10] What Benton desired, he stated, 'more than anything else, [is] to make pictures, the imagery of which would carry unmistakeably American meanings for Americans and for as many of them as possible'.[11] While the politics of Regionalism may have been very different from that of Socialist Realism, both schools shared the perception that 'a work which does not make contact with the public is lost'.[12]

In the design world, commercial imperatives made the need to 'make contact' even more pressing. Graphic design, of course, was always dependent on its ability to communicate ideas and advertise products effectively, but the decade also saw new developments in manufacturing design, precipitated by the slump in consumer demand. Economic desperation led manufacturers to think again about 'enhancing product appearance', and their search for ways 'to make a product so new it would be irresistible' brought prominence to 'industrial designers' such as Raymond Loewy, Henry Dreyfuss and Norman Bel Geddes.[13] Under their guidance, 'modernism' and 'streamlining' became design tools used to make functional items from cars and trains to pencil sharpeners and dinner plates, appear more desirable. Perhaps the ultimate in 'mechanical reproduction', industrial designers were creating '*for* the machine, providing patterns to be mechanically reproduced endlessly'.[14] Their philosophy, however, was also animated by the populist sentiment that 'good design was for everyone'.[15] As suggested by the Rockefeller Center's skyscraper city, or Frank Lloyd Wright's 'Broadacre' plans for new suburban development, it was an outlook also shared by the decade's leading architects. Interestingly, though, in the light of Benjamin's essay, it was Hollywood that really reproduced modernist design and architecture and introduced it to the American public: in the on-screen trains and ocean liners that brought the streamlined aesthetic to millions; in the modernistic Art Deco nightclubs and hotel ballrooms in which Fred Astaire and Ginger Rogers danced; and in the tubular chrome furniture and the white Bakelite phones used by cinema's sophisticates. Hollywood's exposure of audiences to the 'modern' look contributed to its association with affluence and taste, at the same time as the designers themselves made it more affordable and accessible.

This chapter focuses on three areas of contemporary debate in which concerns about connecting the artist and designer to 'the people' were particularly influential, namely: art affected by the politics of

Marxism; the Regionalist art movement; and the vogue for 'streamlin-ing' in industrial design and architecture. It is important, however, not to reduce the artistic achievements of the 1930s to just these three lines. The case studies included here, of Joe Jones, Edward Hopper and the Rockefeller Center in Manhattan, each illustrate areas of overlap, dissent and eclecticism.

Social Art

Hugo Gellert's *Secret of Primary Accumulation* was a prime example of unabashedly pro-Communist art, a response to the slogan that 'Art is a Weapon in the Class Struggle!'.[16] His image of a gigantic Henry Ford amassing his factories, while towering over a solitary worker, was one of sixty prints illustrating *Karl Marx's 'Capital' in Lithographs* (1934), in which the drawings sought to 'capture the current political relevance' of the text and make it possible for the working classes to understand the fundamentals of Marxism.[17] Significantly, although Ford is pre-sented as god-like, the worker does not convey passive acceptance of the capitalist's hold over the means of production. Rather, his compact frame and solid bulging muscles present him as an 'Americanized vision of the new Soviet man . . . the virile worker as a proletarian hero'.[18] Gellert's industrial worker is a potential David to Ford's Goliath – and, at least as the radical artist imagined it, a collective army of such heroic men could readily overcome the crisis of capitalism.

Like its literary counterpart, proletarian art sought to raise classic consciousness by conveying a Marxist social vision through simple and direct devices. The use of cartoons was particularly appropriate; com-municating through a visual language understood by even the illiter-ate, and reproducible at minimal expense in newsprint and pamphlets to reach potentially a far greater audience than even mural painting could hope to affect. To that end Gellert had helped found the *New Masses* in 1926 and became its art editor in 1928, with artists William Gropper, Anton Refregier and Nicolai Cikovsky among his regular contributors of prints and cartoons. Though better remembered for his mural work, Refregier insisted that 'doing cartoons was not a sep-arate activity from our painting or from our lives'.[19]

The narrative of politicized art in the 1930s is commonly aligned with the shifting trajectory of Communist Party policy. Art historians seek to distinguish between 'Socialist Realism' and 'social realism', with the former officially sanctioned by Moscow as the 'artistic depic-tion of reality' devoted to 'the task of ideologically transforming and

Figure 4.1 Hugo Gellert, *The Secret of Primary Accumulation* (1934: Mary Ryan Gallery, New York).

educating the workers in the spirit of Socialism'.[20] Significant numbers of artists, like Gellert and Refregier, certainly considered themselves 'movement artists', and the Party made considerable efforts to support them. The John Reed Clubs (JRCs) (founded in 1929) provided art schools and exhibition opportunities, while members produced publications like *Art Front* and formed the Artists' Union to lobby the government for new and expanded work programmes. When the philosophy of the Popular Front rendered the JRCs too sectarian and they were disbanded in 1935, they were replaced by the broadly progressive organization of the American Artists' Congress (AAC). Although not a term used at the time, 'social realism' commonly serves as the 'catch-all' label for the work of the left-leaning artists brought together by the Popular Front, 'regardless of their relationship to the Communist Party'.[21] Exhibitions such as *Dedicated to the New Deal* in 1938 marked this spirit of the uniting of Communists and progressive liberals in support of Roosevelt's administration. Disillusionment for many, however, came in 1940 when the AAC's governing board issued a statement exonerating the Soviet Union for its invasion of Finland and thereby revealed the Communist Party's continuing dominance over the group.

Of course, the distinction between 'Socialist' and 'social' realism is a slippery one. Communist organizations did not hold a monopoly on social commentary, and the circumstances of the Depression compelled many artists to address themselves to matters of dehumanizing poverty, violence against striking workers and racial injustice. Communist initiatives did channel artistic output toward particular subject matter, with JRC shows encouraging artists to engage with themes such as the *Struggle for Negro Rights*, and AAC exhibitions emphasizing the Communist Party's new priorities, such as *War and Fascism* and *To Aid Democracy in Spain*. Some of the exhibited works were explicitly Communist, as in Jacob Burck's five-panel celebration of the Soviet Union as utopia, in *Socialist Construction in the USSR*. Yet even exhibitions such as the 1933 *Social Viewpoint in Art* incorporated artists whose sympathies were not Marxist, but only 'swinging leftward'.[22]

In various shades of political commitment, the majority focused on conditions in America and visible evidence of the failure of the capitalist system, as if that were sufficient argument for socialism in itself. William Gropper's *Miners* (1935), for instance, dramatized the tyranny of industrialists and the suppression of unionism, depicting a miner forced back to work at the point of a bayonet. Burck's ironically titled *The Lord Provides* (1933) showed a female demonstrator arrested by armed police for demanding 'Work or Bread' for the unemployed. Both artists used their skills as cartoonists to convey urgency and immediacy in their generalized images. Other painters like Edward Laning created powerful works by representing more specific instances of repression: *Unlawful Assembly, Union Square* (1931) shows the Communists' International Unemployment Day protest of

1930 being broken up violently by mounted police. The 'Memorial Day Massacre' at Republic Steel in 1937 prompted an angry resurgence of such imagery, after Chicago police shot into a crowd of 2,000 strikers and their supporters. Philip Evergood responded with one of the 'most radically revolutionary' works of its type: the bloody melee of *American Tragedy* (1937), in which 'cruel-eyed police' attack protestors indiscriminately.[23] In the centre, however, one white worker takes his stand, seeking to defend a small, pregnant Latina woman against a thuggish armed officer – an inspiring image of inter-racial solidarity and strength in the face of brutality.

Political causes championed by the Left also led to the creation of works such as Ben Shahn's *The Passion of Sacco and Vanzetti* (a series of twenty-three gouaches begun in 1931), and Philip Guston's powerful evocation of the Spanish Civil War in *Bombardment*. Moreover, almost every significant artist of the decade felt compelled to present their condemnation of lynching, with congressional hearings on anti-lynching legislation prompting two exhibitions in New York in 1935: the JRC's *Struggle For Negro Rights* and the NAACP's *An Art Commentary on Lynching*. The competing exhibitions reflected the tensions between the Communist Party and the NAACP at this time, with the militancy of the CPUSA prompting most artists to contribute to the NAACP's exhibition instead – but the statements were no less powerful for that.[24] Harry Sternberg's expressionistic lithograph of *Southern Holiday* was particularly disturbing, depicting a black man lashed to a broken pillar, blood dripping from where his genitals have been cut off. The details of Sternberg's setting implicate the whole Southern system in this gruesome image: the pillars, as Andrew Hemingway suggests, symbolize the 'decaying Southern aristocracy', with the factories of the industrial 'New South' towering behind, and the Church 'complicit in this order of things'.[25] Isamu Noguchi created a towering chrome sculpture in *Death*, his figure's taut and twisted limbs copied from a photograph of the burned body of a Texas lynch mob's victim. In *This Is Her First Lynching* (1934), Reginald Marsh turned from the victim to focus instead on the ghoulishly enthusiastic crowd who eagerly hold a young girl high to 'get a better view of the gala proceedings'.[26]

Less transparently polemic were paintings of conditions in American industry and agriculture, but artists still critiqued urgent social problems. The struggle of the American farmer, especially in the Dust Bowl, saw representation in the likes of Gropper's *The Last Cow*, Joe Jones' *Our American Farms* and Evergood's *Sorrowing Farmers*

(1938). Others exposed oppressive working conditions, the misery of sweatshops and the life-threatening situations faced in some industries. Eugene Morley in *Hard Coal Landscape* (1935), for example, reveals a broken human skeleton as the 'grim aftermath' of a collapsed mine tunnel.[27] Evergood's painting on the same subject, *Mine Disaster* (1935) divided the canvas into three, with the left-hand side showing 'Labor in Darkness' as miners drill for ore, and the right-hand side showing the 'Tragedy of Entombment' as a cave-in buries them alive. The centre section depicts a rescue squad ready to descend, but their doomed efforts are foretold by a black coffin placed near a wounded miner.[28] By exposing such dangerous conditions, Evergood hoped to effect change; others such as Irwin Hoffman simply sought to stir empathy in the viewer, with his *Miner's Child* (1933) rendering a mother's heartbreaking grief over the ghostly body of her dead son.

Such images, however, tended to promote an image of victimhood, rather than resistance. Dejection and apathy were common motifs in artistic treatments of unemployment. *No Work* by Blanche Gramb (1935) was an empathic depiction of despair, but her image of an anonymous man sitting in the gutter, possessed little to inspire the masses to action. A distinction could be made between the portrayal of homeless bums of Raphael Soyer's *In the City Park* (1934) and the slightly more politicized mix presented in Marsh's *Park Bench* (1935), of white and black men of different classes all reduced to the same circumstances. Yet in both paintings the figures seem simply to be 'waiting for the Depression to come to an end'. As Erika Doss suggests, this was an accurate reflection of the 'resignation and sense of stasis' pervasive in the early 1930s; but as social criticism it was subdued and muted.[29] As Jerome Klein wrote of the Soyer brothers in the pages of *Art Front*, these were artists who had 'looked out from the studio into the street', but had 'not yet stepped down into it' to capture 'the will to struggle'.[30] To Klein, this was the distinction between 'Socialist Realism' and other social art.

Some critics argue that this was a result of artists feeling compelled to document what they saw around them, but not subscribing to any specific ideological dogma. Philip Evergood, for example, characterized fellow artist Reginald Marsh as one whose work projected 'tragic hopelessness' because he did not believe in socialist utopianism; for Marsh, the condition of the unemployed and underprivileged 'was inevitable'.[31] Others suggest, however, that whatever the artist's ideological commitment, the 'little pictures' of easel art were inherently limited as social critiques, making it difficult to portray both the problem and the solution simultaneously. This was one of the reasons why mural work was so lauded in the 1930s, especially when the Mexican mural renaissance of the previous decade provided rich inspiration. Not only were murals situated to confront a public that might never visit a gallery, but their scale also provided the opportunity to convey a narrative. The left-hand side of Joe Jones' 1934 *Social Protest in Old St Louis*, for example, presented unemployed, dejected workers lounging outside a pawnshop, just as the Soyers might have depicted them. Yet the 'will to struggle' appears in the right-hand side of the mural, as an 'African-American baptism . . . merges into a Communist-led demonstration'. It depicts a real strike among nutpickers in St Louis in 1932, when the CPUSA had successfully mobilized African-American women 'from a passive religious outlook to militant unionism' – an event that Jones represents as an 'exemplary' instance of the party's labour organizing.[32] Similarly, Bernard Zakheim's controversial design for the Public Works of Art project in Coit Tower, San Francisco, turned the 'unpropitious theme of the public library' into a narrative of burgeoning political consciousness. The image of the absorbed patrons of a reading room, to the left of the *Library* mural, seems innocuous. But on the right-hand side, these readers have moved on to newspapers with provocative headlines about the banking crisis, farm foreclosures and industries breaking the NRA Codes. In a 'dawning consciousness', one man reaches for a volume of Marx's *Capital* from the shelves, while another displays the 'resolution to act', crumpling up his newspaper and preparing to head outside, armed with his new knowledge. Such 'readable' narratives made murals seem 'almost the necessary form for a revolutionary art', and help explain why so many left-wing artists embraced the Federal Arts Projects in which the decoration of public buildings played a major role.[33]

Unsurprisingly, this emphasis on accessibility and readability in 'revolutionary' art, promoted the same hostility among Marxist critics toward modernism as seen in literary circles. There was the same tendency to regard modernistic art as symptomatic of bourgeois, self-absorbed decadence and to hold it responsible for the gulf between the artist and the masses. Abstract art in particular was criticized for falling 'beyond the comprehension of most people'.[34] However, a number of artists did remain insistent that the modernist idiom was a vital resource for any socially conscious art. Stuart Davis was the most vocal proponent of abstract expressionism as a 'direct progressive social force', arguing that it 'liberated' people from their 'familiar reality' to consider the 'new lights, speeds, and spaces which are uniquely real to our time'.[35] It took, however, the greater spirit of tolerance encouraged by the Popular Front to occasion a broader shift in assessment: *Art Front*'s dismissal of Salvador Dali's work as an escapist 'flight from external reality into phantasy' in 1936, saw a notable about face in 1937 when the journal began to praise surrealism for its techniques in representing the 'destructive and creative processes of the subconscious mind'.[36] Rehabilitated as a 'new humanistic social art', the AAC's exhibitions now included surrealist panels such as Refregier's *Fascism Over Spain*. Davis also found a much more responsive audience to his argument that abstract art was inherently political because, in a time of opposition to Fascism, it 'celebrated the most progressive aspect of American democracy' – its 'Freedom of Expression'.[37]

Of course, 'Socialist Realism' was no more realistic than any of Davis's paintings. The kind of resistance depicted in Evergood's *An American Tragedy* has no basis in the eyewitness accounts of the actual Memorial Day massacre. Nor did the heavily muscled, masculine labourers, idealized in images like Gellert's *Secret of Primary Accumulation*, bear much relation to the realities of mass unemployment, and they deliberately ignored the roles women had taken in the workforce. Rather than realism, these were utopian visions, perpetuating myths of 'heroic proletarianism' and projecting the social ideals for which the Left claimed to stand.[38] The dejected pessimism of the Soyer brothers' paintings, driven more by the 'documentary impulse' than by Marxism, was arguably more 'realistic'. In the end though, it was the express intent of American artists to interpret the contemporary circumstances that most energized social art in the 1930s. As one of the most recent accounts of the subject has argued, the key to understanding 'social realism' is that – whatever their approach or style – 'artists of the Depression era believed that their art *became* realistic by engaging the great economic and political issues of society'.[39]

Joe Jones

Housepainting is a good way to learn the feel of a brush, the mixture of colors. It also gives one plenty of time to think. Housepainter Adolf Hitler thought up Naziism.[40]

Among American artists, probably only Joe Jones could have prompted *Time* magazine to reach for a connection between art and Depression-era politics that was simultaneously so disturbing and trite. By mid-decade, Jones' former identity as a housepainter, apprenticed by his father in St Louis, Missouri, had become inseparable from his then-current status as the nation's foremost proletarian artist. In contrast to Philip Evergood, who had studied at Eton, or Reginald Marsh, a Yale graduate raised by affluent parents in a New Jersey artists' colony, Jones was the 'genuine article': a self-taught, working-class artist, whose paintings expressed his 'unique solidarity' with 'the kind of people who earned their living by the sweat of their brow'.[41] With an open and vocal commitment to Communism as well, he immediately became 'the darling of the social realist set'.[42]

The image of an impoverished yet outspoken youth, with a raw, natural talent, first attracted his hometown's socialite art lovers, such as Elizabeth Green, who effectively 'adopted' Jones. They encouraged him to exhibit at the St Louis Art Guild, where he won his first awards, and in the summer of 1933 they sent him to Provincetown, Massachusetts, where he was expected to 'acquire the polish and patina of the fine arts'.[43] Instead, as Jones said himself, he returned with 'class consciousness' and a Communist Party membership card. In truth, it was no overnight conversion. Already in his 1932 mural for the local KMOX radio station he had defined the theme of 'Progress' in terms of 'job opportunities for the unemployed'.[44] After 1933, though, he played the role of proletarian artist with greater deliberation. Green continued to support him, helping him establish the Unemployed Art Group which produced his *Social Protest in Old St Louis* mural. However, he provoked deliberate outrage by decorating the rotunda of the city's Old Court House with Soviet posters, pushing St Louis's Director of Public Safety into closing the project.

Leaving for New York, Jones turned this into a *cause célèbre*, claiming that he had been driven to Manhattan by the oppressive conservatism of the Midwest. The American Artists' Congress welcomed him with open arms, as he delivered a hard-hitting address on 'The Repression of Art in America'. An exhibition at the American Contemporary Artists (ACA) Gallery further cemented his reputation, with symbols of his working-class solidarity in pictures such as *We Demand!* and *Demonstration*, and criticism of the New Deal and its agricultural policy in *Capitalism*, which depicted a farmer 'plowing under' his crops. Associated with vigorous and powerful images, he rapidly became not only the 'best-known social protestor painter of the decade', but also the most credible.[45] In his own analysis, his work differed from that of other social realists, because for him the 'revolutionary element' was 'natural'.[46]

Yet having been feted as the 'outstanding artistic discovery' of 1935, Jones seemed to change direction entirely.[47] By February 1936, he appeared more interested in wheatfields than workers. Of fourteen paintings exhibited at the uptown Maynard Walker Gallery, eleven were rural landscapes painted in the fields near St Louis. Also, rather than remaining critical of the New Deal, he appeared to have been co-opted by it when employed by the government's Resettlement Administration to illustrate 'social conditions in the Midwest'.[48] Moreover, he continued to paint studies of harvest scenes even after this commission and, unlike the angry political statements of his earlier work, his 'golden icons' of waving grain and 'the bounty of the plains' now presented 'reassuring signs that out there in the heartland, everything might turn out for the best'.[49]

This caused considerable problems in interpretation for the champions of Jones' social realism. Scenes of Midwest agriculture were the particular focus of the Regionalist movement, as in Grant Wood's idylls of Iowa, John Steuart Curry's renditions of Kansas farming and Thomas Hart Benton's depiction of harvests in Missouri. Yet such Regionalism was regarded by the Left as profoundly conservative, denying the social realities of the impoverishment of the farmer and ignoring the desperate need for collective political organization and action. Seeking to draw a distinction, most defenders of Jones' agricultural studies noted that he continued to emphasize men engaged in physical labour, arguing that his paintings were more than empty landscapes. When the ACA exhibited *Wheat Threshing in St Charles County* in 1937, for instance, it was captioned as 'one of a series on the relationship of the worker to his job'.[50] The murals he painted for government post offices in Missouri, Kansas and Arkansas also depicted solid, working men, 'tending their mules and machinery, and gathering in the harvest with almost ritualistic solemnity', thus bearing some comparison with his earlier paintings of the industrial proletariat.[51]

Other paintings, however, required more convoluted explanations to suggest social content. *Wheat*, for example, depicted a vast, abundant field of grain harvested by a tractor. The harvester might well be the 'kind of mechanized agriculture' which 'never intrudes' in Wood's romanticized images of Iowa; but to claim that the tractor, in itself is 'redolent . . . of a whole process of technological change and social dislocation' is hardly persuasive.[52] Arguing that the inclusion of a farmer's fist is 'a probably deliberate paraphrase of the communist salute', testifies less to the artist's political consciousness than to the straining of contemporaries to find evidence that Jones's 'placid agricultural studies were really just as inflammatory as the strike scenes of old'.[53]

In 1938 Jones himself admitted, with some regret, that his 'youthful ardour had cooled' and 'my active political life is almost negligible'.[54] There did remain, however, the determination that was shared by social realists, proletarian cartoonists, and Regionalists alike, to 'give art back to the ordinary folks and to make art a meaningful element in their daily lives'.[55] In post office murals, prints distributed by the Associated American Artists, and even paintings for a chain of St Louis bar rooms, Jones demonstrated a commitment to art 'for the people', depicting the region and the existence they knew, in forms they could encounter as part of their every-day surroundings. Perhaps more than his Communist militancy, it was this goal that made Jones an emblematic artist of the 1930s.

Painting America

That supporters of Joe Jones felt the need to dissociate his portrayal of agricultural activity from notions of Regionalism suggests the ideological baggage imposed on this idiom. On one level, the regionalist current in painting, concentrating on 'rural motifs' and celebrating 'plain, down-home virtues', could be seen as simply a rural counterpoint to the urban images produced by artists like Marsh and the Soyers, an alternative artistic version of the 'American Scene'.[56] John Steuart Curry, for instance, saw little difference between his images of Kansas farmers and the works of those who depicted 'elevated stations, subways [and] butcher shops', arguing that 'we are one and all painting out of the fullness of our life and experience'.[57] Yet the Left accorded a hostile reception to the work of the Regionalists, especially that of Curry, Grant Wood and Thomas Hart Benton.

A protracted exchange in *Art Front* in 1935, between Curry, Benton, Stuart Davis and Jacob Burck, was only the most vitriolic of various attempts to dismiss Regionalism as a conservative movement. First, it was held to be devoid of social significance. Benton's mural of *America Today* (1930), for instance, presenting a variety of episodes from prize-fighting to men at work in the foundries, was attacked as a 'meaningless' presentation of 'picturesque Americana', satisfied with 'mere surface appearances' and lacking a message.[58] Secondly, Regionalism was deemed guilty of escapism, offering false, utopian views of rural life which exploited the nostalgic feelings of Americans who had migrated from the countryside to cities in recent years. In this analysis, Wood's stylized landscapes, presenting Iowa as a lush and sensuous 'great green quilt', were a perverse denial of the contemporary realities of drought and the Dust Bowl.[59] His 1930 *Stone City*, for example, presented a thriving town amidst 'pristine geometric trees, sensuous, gently rolling hills and lush vegetation', even though the real Stone City had been deserted since its limestone quarry closed at the turn of the century.[60] Finally, and perhaps most damagingly, Regionalism was linked to the 'tide of national chauvinism'.[61] This claim was given substance not so much by specific artworks, but by the way *Time* had introduced Regionalism to the public in December 1934 as a 'native-born' movement conceived in opposition to Europe's 'crazy parade of Cubism, Futurism, Dadaism [and] Surrealism'.[62] Benton's subsequent association with one of the Left's *bêtes noires*, anti-Semitic art critic Thomas Craven, furthered the extreme parallels detractors drew between the regionalist's 'anti-modern art views' and 'celebration of the common folk', and similar prejudices 'in the official state of Nazi Germany'.[63]

Part of the problem was that the term was linked with the Southern Agrarians, whose literary manifesto of *I'll Take My Stand* (1930) had held the 'essential' agrarian values of the South to be superior to those of the rest of the country. Regionalism in painting did possess something of this attitude. Wood, for instance, spoke of 'reemphasizing the fact that America is agrarian as well as industrial'.[64] Regionalism also depicted itself as a reaction against the dominant influence of New York City in defining America's artistic values. This was given voice in Wood's 1935 essay, 'Revolt Against the City', and in Benton's autobiography, *An Artist in America*, which presented Regionalism as his 'escape' from 'narrow metropolitan intellectualism'.[65] It was also frequently populist: *Time*'s dismissal of 'foreign abstraction' and Benton's attack on New York dealers and critics enamoured of 'esoteric art incomprehensible to the general public', served to present Regionalism as an idiom of 'representational common sense', understandable by the 'ordinary' American.[66] Also like their southern literary counterparts, Wood, Benton and Curry each became involved in 'boosterism' for their region and its culture: Wood sought to establish an art colony at Stone City in 1932; Benton was commissioned to paint murals for the Missouri State Capitol in 1936; and Curry became the first artist-in-residence at the University of Wisconsin.

However, Wood's philosophy differed from that of the Southern Agrarians in that he rarely claimed that the Midwest's values were superior to others. In fact, contrary to the accusations of their detractors, the work of the Midwest triumvirate was not uncritical or naively celebratory. There was an evident distaste and satiric intent in Wood's *Daughters of the American Revolution* (1932), and his now iconic *American Gothic* was also regarded by Iowans with suspicion. Produced in 1930, *American Gothic* presented an old-fashioned couple in austere clothing, posed in front of a Carpenter Gothic farmhouse from the 1880s. Many from outside the state interpreted the work as a 'devastating satire' on the insularity of small-town midwestern Puritans who regarded modern society with suspicion.[67] When it was reproduced in the Des Moines *Register*, a number of locals felt the same way too, taking offence at being portrayed as 'morose and backward' (modern farmers, after all, used mechanical haying equipment, not the pitchfork carried by the man in the painting). Wood sought to assure local citizens that he regarded the depicted characters as 'good and solid people' who had, in an attribute deemed positive by the Regionalists, resisted the pressure 'to move to the cities'.[68] Yet whatever spin was put on them, the figures were archaic. Moreover, although the couple are often perceived as man and wife, Wood asserted that they were 'father and spinster daughter', suggesting that the sense of repression in *American Gothic* stems, in part, from the woman's unfulfilled sexuality, with the man's pitchfork warning against potential trespass.[69]

Curry, too, could certainly paint idealized images of agricultural abundance, yet he tended more often to be drawn not to the 'tranquillity' of the region, but to more violent subject matter. He proved expert at capturing the 'brute struggle for survival' faced by Kansas farmers and 'the elemental terror of storms' that swept the prairie – his 1935 *The Line Storm* being a stunning example.[70] His work also extended to direct social criticism, as in *Manhunt*'s depiction of a lynch mob, exhibited at the NAACP's show. Erika Doss has argued strongly that Benton's work similarly contains a 'reformist political' vision. Many of his lithographs were as concerned with the rural poor, Southern blacks and industrial workers as any of those by artists of the Popular Front; and in grander murals such as his 1933 *Social History of the State of Indiana*, Benton challenged the state's boosters by including a cross-burning by the Ku Klux Klan in his visual narrative, warning viewers 'of the dangers of a decline in thinking citizenship and liberalism'.[71] One panel of *The Social History of Missouri* in 1936 also showed a lynching and the beating of a slave, and caused such uproar in Missouri that Benton received no further mural commissions until the next decade. In fact, it was not until *Time* cast these painters as local heroes that Regionalist art was truly embraced by 'the people' it claimed to represent.

In further contrast to the Southern Agrarians, Wood's Regionalism was a notably pluralist vision. Although he spoke of his childhood growing up on a farm in Iowa as an 'archetypal rural American experience', he saw it as only one 'strain of the national culture' that, if probed, could be 'as rich and colorful as that of any other region or period in history'.[72] Rather than claim pre-eminence for the artistry of the Midwest, he envisaged instead a network of regional art centres or colonies, like the one he tried to establish at Stone City, operating throughout the country, each developing 'characteristics of their own'. There would be competition between these regional schools, but from their combined efforts a 'rich American culture' could grow.[73] This was no narrow 'fascist' conception of a national culture, but a democratic, pluralist one, in tune with concerns that stretched far beyond this particular trio of painters. Regionalism thus conceived meant an art which not only responded to a given region, but which could 'transcend regional boundaries to communicate to all Americans'.[74]

Importantly, as Wood saw it, it would also be a 'genuine' and 'authentic' culture. He viewed his own artistic renderings of Iowa not simply as 'regional', but as a reaction against 'touristic' artists who had previously painted areas such as the western frontier, or Taos, or Cape Cod without any insight into 'the life of a given locality'.[75] What Wood sought to promote was art that derived from rooted experience and local knowledge. This was a popular conception, inherent also in *Time*'s effort to classify Charles Burchfield and Reginald Marsh as 'regional' artists, by virtue of their affinity with specific American locales, from the villages of Ohio to the city of Manhattan, respectively.[76] Not all artists embraced this idea, of course, but Roosevelt's administration did, and sought to make this type of regional expression a vital component of national culture through the New Deal's Federal Art Project (FAP) and its Community Art Centres (discussed in greater detail in Chapter 5). With efforts focused in particular on the southern and western stretches of the country, over eighty CACs had been created by 1940, animated by the belief that a 'cultural erosion . . . quite as serious as the impoverishment of the soil' had occurred.[77] As the organizers saw it, America's 'best talent' had been lured away 'to the strange pavements of the big city' – but the government now had an opportunity to reverse that process, bringing artists back to 'the native soil of the small town'. Just as Wood convinced Benton and Curry to return to the Midwest, so the FAP claimed success in encouraging painters and sculptors to return as 'artists-in-residence' to home towns like Laramie, Greensboro, Memphis and Charleston, and championed the project of 'reinstating' an 'authentic' and indigenous 'cultural diversity across the body of the Nation'.[78]

Some independent local movements also associated themselves with this philosophy. A school of water-colour painting, for example, rose to prominence in California, centred around students from the Chouinard School of Art, the Los Angeles-based California Water Color Society, and the centre built up by Millard Sheets at the art department of Scripps College, Claremont. Involving artists such as Tom Craig, Emil Kosa and James Fitzgerald, the characteristic style was one of strong, rich colours and bold brushwork undertaken on large canvases, purportedly to convey the 'vigorous immediacy' of the Golden State. As one exponent described it, the medium of water-colour was itself 'organic' to the region (and more broadly applicable to the nation) in that its 'swift fluidity fits our experience and outlook. We go fast, we decide quickly. We may not go deep, but we are not as rooted in an acre or a belief as a European is likely to be'.[79] Similarly,

Texas was credited with a 'Lone Star Regionalism', which found an identity in the Free Public Art Gallery's 1932 *Exhibition of Young Dallas Painters* which included Jerry Bywater, Thomas Steel, Alexandre Hogue and William Lester among its contributors. This movement was further promoted by the informal forum of the Dallas Artists League (1932–6), with Bywater emerging as its leading spokesman.[80]

Yet while plenty of 'localized subject matter' was in evidence, it is difficult to identify styles which were truly 'typical of particular sections of the country'.[81] Regionalism was often a media creation, making unwarranted linkages between artists of disparate styles and aims. It was New York critics who responded to the 1932 exhibition in Texas by misleadingly labelling the local artistic community as 'The Dallas Nine', even though the group of active painters, print-makers and sculptors in the state was considerably larger and more diverse. Some works certainly celebrated the Lone Star state, as Florence McClung's *Squaw Creek Valley* (1938), but there was also a tendency toward social criticism, as with Hogue's *Drought Stricken Era* (1934) in which a derelict farm is threatened by a dust storm. Likewise the subject matter of California's water-colourists ranged from Fitzgerald's rural homily of *Spring Plowing*, to Craig and Kosa's depictions of urban Los Angeles. Even the application of the Regionalist label to Benton, Curry and Wood was problematic. As Benton suggested with murals such as *Arts of Life in America*, in which he devoted panels to 'the South', 'the West' 'the City' and 'Indian arts', his subject matter 'ranged north and south and from New York to Hollywood', seeking a composite 'picture of America in its entirety'.[82]

A later generation of artists, including Benton's student Jackson Pollock, were to find the very idea of 'an American art' as 'absurd as an American mathematics or American physics'.[83] Yet it is worth observing that for a time in the 1930s, a good many artists found the label of 'regionalist artist' more useful than restrictive. Years before the Midwest tried to proclaim itself America's artistic heartland, New Mexico and Arizona had offered artists the opportunity to challenge the 'centrality of Manhattan', and commune with the 'indigenous traditions' of the Southwest.[84] Artist colonies such as the one established by Mabel Dodge at Taos in 1919 suffered somewhat from the perception that the artists who painted there were often 'tourists', but even this qualified association served Georgia O'Keeffe well in the 1930s. In a marked departure from the images of magnified flowers for which she was best known, she unveiled in 1931 a series of still lives of the bleached animal bones she found in the Southwest's deserts. One iconic painting of the dead, empty gaze of a cow's skull on a blue background, framed by red stripes – entitled *Cow's Skull: Red, White and Blue* (1931) – may have been O'Keeffe's 'joke on the American scene', but in total the series presented a provocative juxtaposition of bones and antlers against the 'vast radiant space' of New Mexico's landscape.[85] She also painted repeatedly the area around Ghost Ranch, after she discovered it in 1935. Its 'magisterial valleys, strange towering landforms' and pink-red siltstone hills became a world she 'adopted as her own', as much as Wood adopted Iowa.[86] As Wanda Corn suggests, O'Keeffe had resented the way in which critics saw her floral art only as the embodiment of 'female feelings and sexuality'. Now she exchanged 'fleshiness for dryness and hardness', and 'fluid forms for strong iconic statements'. Consistently claiming that the 'skull works' were all about 'place and region', O'Keeffe's 'second signature body of work' became a conscious effort to 'change the paradigm' from 'woman painter' to 'regional painter'.[87] In this respect, Regionalism allowed O'Keeffe to challenge her critics to reconsider the limiting gendered interpretations they had ascribed to her work. In such circumstances, the designation of 'regionalist artist' could even serve as a liberating identity.

Figure 4.2 Edward Hopper, *Cape Cod Evening* (1939: National Gallery of Art, Washington DC).

Edward Hopper, *Cape Cod Evening* (1939)

Edward Hopper was one artist who strongly resisted the reductivism of contemporary labels. Because many of his paintings depicted the lives of ordinary people in a manner evocative of the 'dispirited mood' of the Depression, some critics linked him with social realism, but Hopper angrily disavowed any political intent.[88] Still more critics aligned him with Regionalism, as his many paintings of Cape Cod and New England conveyed an 'Americanness' which made him one of decade's 'most fashionable of painters', yet Hopper asserted that such an association made him 'mad'.[89] Indeed, although he benefited from the acclaim that stemmed from his perceived contemporaneity, Hopper was often irritated by the parochial attitudes that adhered to such categories. *Cape Cod Evening*, his last oil painting of the decade, serves to illustrate why.

In the heated critical debate that sought to distinguish between specifically American traits and so-called 'French' tendencies, Hopper had been feted as early as 1927 as a 'vigorous and eminently native painter', held to have 'fulfilled all the requirements of what was meant by racial quality in American art: Puritan austerity, nothing in excess, [and] an emotional response to his native environment'.[90] It was partly for this reason that he was featured in the Whitney Museum's first Biennal of American Art in 1932, and why the 1933 retrospective at the Museum of Modern Art presented him as a 'typically American painter'.[91] His fascination with Cape Cod certainly seemed to compound this with a regionalist emphasis. Every summer between 1930 and 1933, he and his wife Jo rented a cottage in South Truro, at the east end of the Cape, and in 1934 he built his home and artist's studio there. The vistas and buildings of the region featured in his work throughout the decade, from *South Truro Church* (1930) to *Cape Cod Afternoon* (1936) and *Cape Cod Evening* (1939); and even when he became restless with that subject matter, he still affected a New England Regionalism by making excursions to Vermont instead, painting landscapes such as *Sugar Maple* (1938).

Cape Cod Evening, however, possesses none of the 'boosterism' that Hopper associated with the Regionalist movement. This is no idyllic, tranquil scene of a couple enjoying the evening sunshine outside their home. Nature itself seems somewhat forbidding. Rather than golden in the autumn sunlight, the grass is pale yellow as if dying, yet it has also grown far too high, unattended by the owners of the house. The dark density of the trees on the left also disturbs, with the tree in the mid-foreground having encroached to tap on the window pane. The 'dark, solid impenetrable wall' of trees recalls Hopper's earlier *House at Dusk* (1935), which presented a pale apartment block with a gloomy park behind.[92] Rural landscapes in the Regionalist idiom usually offered a positive contrast to America's impersonal, alienating city environments. But in *Cape Cod Evening*, rural life is not an escape, only a continuation of the existence available to the urban inhabitants of *House at Dusk*.

Such an existence is not inspiring. The man sits on the doorstep, trying to attract the attention of his dog. The woman stands a few feet away, her arms folded, looking toward the man, but not really looking *at* him. There is no sense of togetherness between them, and neither is smiling. Engaged in their own thoughts, they are oblivious to whatever the dog has sensed. The lack of interaction between the people (and indeed the dog) was quintessentially Hopper. *Room in New York* (1932) conveyed a similar lack of emotional connection in an urban setting, with a man reading his newspaper, 'while the woman he is ignoring turns half-heartedly toward a piano and picks out a tune'.[93] Such qualities of characterization, in understated scenes suggestive of alienation or loneliness, prompted many social readings of Hopper's art. One Marxist critic has suggested, for instance, that the sorrowful lone woman, nursing her coffee in the 'sparse, cheerless café' of Hopper's *Automat*, was probably 'out of work', while the man sitting on the empty sidewalk in *Sunday* conveys the impression 'that his life too is empty and meaningless as he stares vacantly across the street'.[94] Yet *Automat* was painted in 1927, and *Sunday* in 1926. Hopper's paintings may have been embraced in the 1930s as evocations of the 'sense of human hopelessness that characterized the Great Depression', but they resist such simplistic readings because he had invoked this sentiment long before the Wall Street Crash and would continue to do so until his death in 1967.[95]

Indeed, as *Cape Cod Evening* suggests, the sense of a psychological undercurrent between the people is what transcends the contemporary scene in Hopper's work. He keeps us wondering what the story behind the picture is. In *Hotel Room* (1931), he hooks the spectator into speculating about a piece of paper held by a partially-dressed woman seated on the edge of a bed. In *Cape Cod Evening* we speculate about the couple. What is the woman thinking? What does that look in her eyes mean? Have they been arguing, or is the distance between them symptomatic of a failing marriage? Are they even married? And what is it that the dog has seen? The house offers little clue to their existence, with its door shut and windows covered. But the painting puts the observer in the position of a voyeur – aware that we are intruding on a private moment of introspection, yet intrigued to know more. As many commentators on Hopper have noted, his paintings often function like the frozen frames of a movie.[96] They make us think of the narrative from which these frames are excerpted, 'demanding of us to imagine the stories of the people who appear in them'.[97] Hopper had no need to make his work either politically relevant or expressive of regional or national pride for an audience to engage with it. An avid moviegoer himself, Hopper knew the thrall of the voyeuristic narratives which drew tens of millions of Americans to the cinema every week – and he mastered that technique in painting.

The Design Decade

It was difficult to discern a particular 'American spirit' in design at the start of the 1930s. 1931 saw the publication of the first *Annual of American Design*, but the majority of the works it illustrated were executed in the imported style of Art Deco, derived from the 1925 *Exposition International des Arts Decoratifs et Industriel Modernes* in Paris. That exhibition's implicit assumptions about the luxurious superiority of French taste still held sway in the design community's catalogue of hand-crafted ceramics, unique pieces of furniture and the home decor of 'upper-class Manhattanites' like the Rockefellers. The 'ultimate Art Deco interiors' of the film-sets designed by Cedric Gibbons at MGM and Van Nest Polgase at RKO extended the connotation of Deco with decadence.[98] Hollywood's repeated use of Deco aesthetics for nightclubs, hotels, ocean liners and sky-scrapers indelibly linked polished black surfaces, tubular chrome furniture and geometric motifs with luxury, youth, sexuality, con-sumerism and affluence. Some effort had been made to 'Americanize' the *style moderne*, by utilizing the skyscraper as the nation's own symbol of modernity. The ziggurat silhouette of Manhattan's skyline became emblematic on everything from Miami Beach hotels to custom-made fabrics, with designer Paul Frankl asserting that the skyscraper was 'a more vital contribution to the field of modern art than all the things done in Europe'.[99] The Chrysler Building itself represented a stunning display of Deco aes-thetics, integrating stylized versions of the automobile company's hubcaps and hood ornaments into its architecture. However, it took the Depression for a distinct and purportedly democratic 'American tendency' to really come to the fore.

The *Annual of American Design* did reveal the desire of many designers and architects to change the situation. In contrast to the book's images of current commissions, the majority of contributors looked to the future and wrote of the need for a 'new national style' that was no longer 'subservient' to the demands of the 'irresponsible and the sophisticated'.[100] This was a dual-edged challenge, directed not only against the 'foreignness' of Deco but also against the blow that had been dealt to designers by their own government when it had refused to participate in the Paris *exposition*, on the basis that 'American manufacturers and craftsmen had almost nothing to exhibit conceived in the modern spirit'.[101] The response of American design-ers, as it evolved over the decade, was the displacement of the *style moderne* of Art Deco with the specifically American *streamlined moderne*.[102] Characterized by unbroken surfaces, 'uncluttered' tapering lines, and 'simpler, more useful objects', and popularized in the futuristic designs for ships, trains, cars and houses presented by Norman Bel Geddes in *Horizons* in 1932, streamlining came to epitomize American modernity for both the public and the designers themselves.[103]

As unlikely as it might seem, the Depression supplied the necessary context for this development. Former advertising artists William Teague and Raymond Loewy, and theatrical designers Bel Geddes and Henry Dreyfuss, had each opened industrial design offices in New York in the late 1920s. They operated as independent 'art directors' for corporations, employed to give products a style or appearance that would distinguish them from their competitors in an oversaturated market. When, however, that market collapsed, manufacturers turned to these men with new urgency, desperate to get frightened consumers to buy at all. Advertising agencies pushed their clients toward designers as well, realizing that if products were made more attractive, they stood a better chance of mounting an effective ad campaign. Dramatic stories such as one company's sales of hearing aids doubling after a restyling by Joseph Sinel, prompted corporate executives to proclaim the 'redesign movement' as the solution to 'all the nation's economic problems'.[104] The panic induced by economic woes gave industrial designers the influence they needed to enact their ambitions.

Over the decade, industrial designers remodelled stoves, tractors, alarm clocks, food mixers, radios, shop fronts, cruise liner cabins and locomotives. They also redesigned packaging and advertising formats, seeking a unity of design that might foster brand loyalty by making the manufacturers themselves appear stylish and modern. Yet the designers intended the process to be more than just a commercial face-lift for any given product. Many insisted on working closely with company engineers, ensuring that their proposals were suited to the production process and that their designs would actually 'improve the things people live with'.[105] Dreyfuss, in particular, was concerned with functionality, asserting that the elimination of 'aggravations' and 'irritations' in product design could itself improve people's lives.[106] Bel Geddes's transformation of Standard Gas's kitchen stoves served to demonstrate that good design could not only 'eliminate drudgery' in 'objects of daily use' but make them more economical to produce.[107] The existing range of over a hundred separate models was reconfigured entirely into a modular system of just twelve standardized components which could be attached to different skeletal frames in different ways to produce sixteen models. Much more economical, it was also redesigned for ease of cleaning too; a combination which Standard Gas marketed, in the spirit of the times, as 'a complete New Deal for the forgotten kitchen!'[108]

Streamlining, as a style, certainly served the commercial interests of industrial design through its psychological connotations. The smooth curve of the teardrop or bullet shape was borrowed from the technology of aviation, inspired by airplanes and zeppelins, and thus possessed the sense of modernity, speed and glamour that had accrued to their aerodynamic design. The first products to capture the nation's imagination were streamlined trains: the *Zephyr* of the Burlington Line, and the M-100,000 of the Union Pacific, both unveiled at the Chicago World's Fair of 1933. Both companies adopted the new design for commercial reasons, in an attempt to counter the competition that airlines now represented in the travel market. But they also used aluminium and stainless steel to reduce the weight of the trains and so improve their speeds, with the sleek, bullet-shaped casings conveying that improvement even more dramatically.[109] When other rail companies quickly engaged designers to rethink their rolling stock, Dreyfuss's torpedo-shaped *20th Century Limited* became famed not only for its luxury but for the speed of its overnight run between Chicago and New York. The style, thus, quickly came to represent the 'visual implications of frictionless technological progress', and proved to be a powerfully seductive image for a nation 'mired in the stasis' of the economic downturn.[110]

In many ways it did become just a marketing vogue. Sweeping teardrop lines were applied to pedal cars and vacuum cleaners, soda siphons and electric fans, telephones and pencil sharpeners alike. One advertiser even sought to claim that one-piece underwear was streamlined; while, as David Hanks points out, the occupant of a 1937-designed streamlined coffin was surely 'no longer in a hurry' to get anywhere.[111] Likewise the application of streamlined motifs to architecture was often superficial. The streamlined piers used to support flagpoles above the entrance to Hollywood's Pan-Pacific Auditorium, for instance, were certainly exuberant in their style, but the visual implication of aerodynamic structure was meaningless. Writing to Bel Geddes in 1934, the director of the Museum of Modern Art justifiably criticized this trend as an 'absurdity', and noted that the 'blind concern with fashion' made it 'difficult to take the ordinary industrial designers seriously'.[112] Critics were also disturbed by the way in which manufacturers now thought of design as a way of creating 'artificial obsolescence'. The head of advertising agency Calkins & Holden defined the purpose of 'restyling' as early as 1930 as:

> to make the consumer discontent with his old type of fountain pen, kitchen utensil, bathroom or motor car, because it is old-fashioned, out-of-date . . . We no longer wait for things to wear out. We displace them with others that are not more effective but more attractive.[113]

William Teague experienced this attitude when he was requested, every year from 1933 to 1938, to submit a new design for an oil-burning heater to American Gas Machine, who wanted annual model changes simply to stimulate sales. It cut directly against his philosophy of finding the 'perfect form' for a given object, but Teague complied anyway.[114]

Streamlined design, however, could possess functionality. In architecture, curved lines could be conceived to aid 'traffic control' in public buildings, while for store-front designs 'inward flowing lines' at the entrance directed pedestrians to look toward the interior and 'increased the chance that he or she would enter'.[115] The design of the Church and Dwight factory in New Jersey, built in 1938, successfully meshed streamlining with both expressionism and functionalism: its white brick bands suggested 'the purity' of the baking soda produced there, while the curves of the building followed the seven-storey industrial tank that was housed within.[116] In every-day products, moreover, streamlining seemed eminently suited to modern industrial processes. Curved contours allowed forms to be pressed out of single sheets of steel and aluminium, avoiding the need to weld joints and, thus, reducing both costs and points of weakness. Rounded corners were also ideal for plastics manufacturing, allowing for moulds to be finished by machine rather than by hand. This prompted Bakelite to invest heavily in industrial design, and saw plastics move into the mainstream of American design. Often, as in Loewy's mimeograph for Sigmund Gestetner, designers did not change the existing machine much, yet by encasing previously-exposed gears and levers in a smooth plastic shell they made it easier to clean and less dangerous to operate. Such encasements also served to restore to the operator a 'feeling of confidence' over the complex machine.[117] Industrial design such as this combined both a visual and a functional simplification.

Indeed, designers advanced a broad philosophy that defended streamlining even in its least practical forms. On one level it was a rejection of European Deco, now declaimed as a style of 'effete luxuriousness' on which the Depression-hit nation ought to turn its back.[118] Streamlining, in contrast, was perceived as a stripped-down, 'pure' form, designed for purpose and with graceful aesthetics that could make society 'cleaner and [more] efficient'.[119] Moreover, given how entwined streamlined design had become with commercial production, the style became intrinsic to the industrial designer's ambition to modernize the nation's taste. Unlike Deco, which was applied to unique luxury items, streamlining (and indeed industrial design as a whole) was bringing 'style' to mass-produced goods, and was capable, therefore, of transforming the aesthetic values of millions of ordinary Americans. In fact, some even advanced the idea that if everyone agreed on adopting the streamline aesthetic as a common style, America would be transformed into a designer's utopia; a 'unified and modish environment' in which 'good taste' was affordable and possessed by all.[120]

Though this utopia never came to pass, the 'democratization of design' was a widely-embraced vision among designers, whether working in the streamlined idiom or not. Donald Deskey, for example, moved from designing exclusive interiors for wealthy New Yorkers such as Abby Aldrich Rockefeller and Gilbert Seldes, to concentrate more and more on mass-produced objects such as table lamps and waste baskets decorated with machine-part motifs. Gilbert Rhode applied himself to creating multifunctional and economical designs which could be mass-produced by big furniture companies like Herman Miller. Russel Wright, in particular, championed the notion that 'good design was for everyone', and ambitiously sought to establish an 'American Way' consortium of over a hundred designers to develop stylized products sold at prices 'within the means of the average American family'.[121] Although this fell through, Wright continued his determination to bring unified design into people's homes, creating affordable modular furniture and a range of co-ordinated flatware and ceramics entitled 'Modern Living', in an approach that continues to inform homeware design today.

It was a vision also embraced by America's foremost architect, Frank Lloyd Wright. Most accounts of his work in the 1930s emphasize Fallingwater: a truly extraordinary private house, built directly over a waterfall in Bear Run, Pennsylvania, which made innovative use of concrete cantilever beams to create the building as a series of terraces projected into space above the stream.[122] Yet while Fallingwater returned Wright to the limelight and brought him a series of new commissions, it was his Usonian homes and his creation of the Johnson Wax office building in Wisconsin that best epitomized the dominant design vision of the decade. Usonian houses represented the populist dimension of bringing 'good design' to ordinary people. Low-cost suburban dwellings, each was built to order but with a 'standard vocabulary' of common architectural features such as an L-shaped plan enclosing a garden, flat roofs and a large family living room. One customer had challenged Wright to meet the nation's need for a 'decent $5,000 house', and each Usonian house used modern materials to fulfil this demand, providing under-floor heating built into a concrete slab foundation, using thin 'sandwich' walls of wood and batten, and replacing the garage with a cantilevered carport.[123] Several were built in locations across the country between 1936 and 1941, and each was adapted to the owner's unique needs; yet Wright's scheme for modern living echoed the goals of the industrial designers, as built-in seating, cabinets, bookshelves and lighting contributed to a unified decorative scheme and ensured that all elements in a Usonian home were integrated into one design.

The S. C. Johnson Administration Building, on the other hand, represented perhaps the most profound application of streamlining to architecture. Commissioned in 1936, in response to Herbert Johnson Jr's desire to 'eliminate the drabness and dullness we so often find in office buildings', Wright created a streamlined masterpiece: built to a low-profile, emphasizing sinuous, horizontal lines picked out in alternating bands of brick and glass tubing, and almost devoid of any rectilinear form.[124] At the heart of it was the 'Great Workroom': a dazzling, soaring space, suggestive of a cathedral and vaulted by a forest of giant pillars. Made of hollow reinforced concrete, these pillars themselves were curved, growing like mushrooms from a base of just nine inches (22.8 cm) in diameter, to large circular caps which formed the ceiling. Skylights of Pyrex filled the spaces in between, providing natural illumination. The circles formed by light and concrete were extended to custom furnishing, with Wright again ensuring complete integration by designing even the desks and chairs in elegant curves (with the legs of the desks tapered to reflect the aesthetics of the columns). However, the Johnson Wax building took streamlining far beyond applied ornamentation. The narrow-based pillars provided the maximum of floor space and visibility in the workroom. Pyrex tubing

Figure 4.3 Raymond Hood's RCA Building at the Rockefeller Center (c. 1945: George Enell, Getty Images).

replaced windows, letting in light but preventing users of the building from looking outside at the building's ugly industrial location, thus turning everything inward into a clean, self-contained environment. And thinking about the administrative work, the lines of the building itself were created to suggest expedient routes that would 'promote the most efficient flow of information through the building'. One study shortly concluded that efficiency did indeed improve by 15 per cent in the new building.[125]

As Wright later wrote of his Johnson Wax design, it was 'time to give our hungry American public something truly streamlined . . . so sure of itself, and clean for its purpose . . . that anybody could see the virtue of this thing called Modern'.[126] The industrial designers who contributed to the vision of the 'World of Tomorrow' displayed at the end of the decade at the New York World's Fair, felt similarly driven. Streamlined dynamism featured everywhere, from the oval-shaped hall commissioned from Loewy by Chrysler with its 'rocketport to the future', to the monolithic, curving facade of Bel Geddes's General Motors building. And both Bel Geddes and Dreyfuss presented their imagined communities of *Futurama* and *Democracity*, respectively, each a meticulous model of 'a perfectly integrated, futuristic metropolis'.[127] In the end, however, little that seemed to be the 'wave of the future' in 1939 – including streamlined design itself – was to survive the Second World War.[128]

The Rockefeller Center

For all that streamlining, Regionalism and radicalism dominated artistic discussion in the 1930s, the Rockefeller Center serves as an important reminder that the realities of art and design were much more varied. Mural painting, abstract art, sculpture, Art Deco design, industrial design, modernist architecture, photography, Marxism, high-brow culture and the mass media of radio and cinema all intersected and overlapped at the Rockefeller. Outside the Federal Arts Projects, no other undertaking united 'so many arts in a common enterprise'.[129] Certainly, no other was more eclectic and yet representative of the decade.

It reflected broader cultural trends, for instance, when what was originally intended to be an elitist cultural institution became instead a national centre for mass entertainment. While conceived in the late 1920s as a more 'fashionable' home for New York's Metropolitan Opera than its original Broadway location, the Wall Street Crash forced a change of plans. The Met withdrew and John D. Rockefeller Jr's eleven-acre real estate investment was only saved when the Radio Corporation of America (RCA) moved in instead, converting the main building into the nation's best recording studios and the new headquarters of NBC. Rather than an opera house, the centre's principal entertainment venue became the Radio City Music Hall; and even that abandoned cultural forms like ballet for popular culture in 1933, becoming the city's pre-eminent first-run movie theatre and home to the Rockette showgirls.

Also apparent was the design world's rejection of Deco, with the RCA Building itself stripped of ornamentation, after the Chrysler's Art Deco aesthetics had been dismissed as *passé*. The 71-floor, 872-feet high skyscraper, designed by architect Raymond Hood, was given only a simple face of Indiana limestone, with decoration reduced to dark aluminium spandrels connecting one floor's windows to the next. Though distinctly lacking in curves, some contemporaries did regard it as 'streamlined' in that form so closely followed function. Informed by the Center's project manager that any office space which did not receive natural sunlight was proving impossible to rent, Hood designed the RCA from the 'inside-out', creating an ingenious series of setbacks that ensured 'not a single point in the rentable area of the building' was ever 'more than 22 feet away from a window'.[130] With five elevator shafts located in the very centre of the building, each serving different sets of floors (1–15, 16–30 and so on), Hood was able to cut the building back to the core each time an elevator shaft ended, so that the profile of the skyscraper narrowed as it climbed. In the restricted real estate market of the time, moreover, Hood's slender silhouette actually gave the RCA 2.3 million square feet of rentable space, exceeding the 1.8 million square feet enclosed in the much taller Empire State (then being pilloried as the 'Empty State Building').

In contrast, however, the rest of the complex embraced, rather than rejected, European styles. Its overall plan recalled the monumental arrangement of public squares in European cities, with symmetrical buildings flanking a grand thoroughfare, gardens and a sunken plaza, as suggested to Rockefeller by architect John Russell Pope, a fervent worshipper of the European 'Beaux Arts' tradition. The integration of art and sculpture was also characteristic of the Beaux Arts school and, despite Hood's own inclinations, many of the commissions were executed in a Deco style. Friezes and mosaics throughout the Center produced an Art Deco 'parade of Hellenistic, Roman, Assyrian, Egyptian, Mayan and Indian figures', in bold angular designs and colours.[131] Even the entrance to Hood's skyscraper was adorned by a 37-ft high gilded limestone tableau of the god-like figure of 'Wisdom' grasping a draftsman's compass and pointing to light- and sound-waves. Its sculptor, Lee Lawrie, further contributed the giant statue of Atlas that stands at the entrance on Fifth Avenue. Though denigrated by many contemporary designers, Deco evidently remained popular with wealthy patrons and, indeed, much of the American public.

Of course, the most legendary commission of the Rockefeller Center was not a Deco piece, but a very contemporary work of 'socialist realism': Diego Rivera's fresco mural for the lobby of the RCA, destroyed in 1934 because it contained a portrait of Vladimir Lenin. As a *cause célèbre* of the Left, it was presented as the struggle of a skilled Communist painter against the artistic philistinism of 'the royal family of the free market'.[132] In truth, the Rockefellers were quite familiar with Rivera's Marxism. Rockefeller's wife, Abby, already owned several of his works, and the mural commission had been awarded on the basis of a detailed pencil rendering and textual description which made Rivera's politics very plain: 'It will', he had said, 'show the Workers of the Cities and the Country inheriting the world', with their 'heroic ranks . . . rallied in front of the walls of the Kremlin'.[133] Abby and her son Nelson Rockefeller had accepted this. Rather, as Daniel Okrent argues, the controversy was deliberately provoked by Rivera. Having earlier been expelled from the Communist Party for 'trading with the enemy' in his acceptance of rich patronage, Rivera added the confrontational image of Lenin at the very last minute and unveiled it to the press before the Rockefellers knew about it. Creating embarrassing headlines, such as 'Rivera perpetuates scenes of Communist activity and Rockefeller Jr. foots the bill', Rivera provoked the family into firing him, and thus stage-managed a heated scandal that 're-established his revolutionary credibility'.[134]

Yet while this scandal resulted in the Rockefeller family becoming the focus of the art world's scorn for a while, the inflammatory equation of radical protestors that 'Hitler and Rockefeller stifle culture' was absurd.[135] Twenty-one of 'America's leading artistic lights' were commissioned simply to decorate the Radio City Music Hall itself.[136] Works completed for the Center ranged from the neo-classical muscle-bound sculptural reliefs of Gaston Lachaise, to the modernist abstractions of Stuart Davis's mural *Men Without Women*. Paul Manship sculpted the eighteen-foot recumbent Prometheus placed above the sunken plaza's fountain, while Isamu Noguchi created the first large piece of sculpture ever cast in stainless steel for the Associated Press Building, with figures carrying cameras, telephones and typewriters. Huge photographic murals were commissioned from Edward Steichen for the Center Theatre and from Margaret Bourke-White for the NBC offices. The Center also championed industrial design, hosting a 'glittering showcase' for Teague, Wright, Loewy and over one hundred others, in reaction against MoMA's snobbish refusal to present the work of commercial designers in its 1934 'Machine Art' exhibition.[137]

The Rivera controversy, did, however, reinforce the fact that, first and foremost, the Rockefeller Center was an international symbol of capitalism. Critics were torn, applauding the opportunities that the Center provided but remaining regretful that its great artistic undertakings were ultimately not the 'organic product of American culture', but 'the result of a fortune seeking to find monumental expression'.[138] However, it must also be understood that in the midst of the Depression, this in itself was part of the Rockefeller Center's appeal. The very public display of wealth and the 'tingle of metropolitan success' in the heart of New York gave the Center a particular sheen, keeping alive 'an American dream of providing elegance and drama for everybody'.[139]

Further Considerations

To the list of those who contributed to the Rockefeller Center, one could add artists Erza Winter and Frank Brangwyn, ceramicist Henry Varnum Poor, sculptors William Zorach, Robert Laurent and Gwen Lux, textile artist Ruth Reeves, architects Walter Harrison and Julian

Everett and designer Donald Deskey (who created the spectacular interior of the Music Hall), and still not do full justice to the creative spirit of the 1930s. In addition to the artists discussed in this chapter, students of the decade could also consider the social politics in the art of Louis Guglielmi, Rockwell Kent or Ben Shahn, or the sexual politics of the paintings of Elizabeth Bishop and Paul Cadmus. Nor was Stuart Davis the only exponent of abstract expressionism: Charles Biderman, Gertrude Greene, Rosalind Bengelsdorf and William De Koonig merit further attention, as does the pioneer of 'kinetic sculpture', Alexander Calder. Of particular significance too, is the work of African-American artist Aaron Douglas, and the Native American art that developed around the Oklahoma group of the 'Kiowa Five' and the Studio School founded in Santa Fe in 1932 which included artists James Auchiah, Stephen Mopope and Gerald Nailor. One should also note the importance of graphic illustration in the decade, from the sixty-seven *Saturday Evening Post* covers executed by Norman Rockwell, through the corporate commissions accepted by Georgia O'Keeffe and Isamu Noguchi to promote Dole pineapple juice, to the first of Haddon Sundblom's iconic paintings of Santa Claus for Coca-Cola in 1931.

What also needs to be appreciated is the ever-growing influence of artists and designers who emigrated to the United States to escape the worsening situation in Europe. This massive exodus included over 700 artists, almost 400 designers and 100 graphic designers in the 1930s alone.[140] This had an impact on design at every level, from the whole new approach to magazine design taken by Alexey Brodovitch at *Harpers* and Mehemed Fehmy Agha at *Vanity Fair*, to the championing of the austere, rectilinear International Style in architecture by the former directors of Germany's Bauhaus, Ludwig Mies van der Rohe and Walter Gropius. Indeed, as far as American architecture was concerned, while the streamlined visions of Bel Geddes and Dreyfuss dominated the New York World's Fair, it was the International Style of Alvar Aalto's Finnish Pavilion that more accurately predicted the look of 'the World of Tomorrow'.

Chapter 5

New Deal Culture

Numbers mattered in the New Deal. There were 168 symphony orchestras, thirty-five choral groups and thirty chamber ensembles formed by the Federal Music Project. Thirty million people attended shows put on by Federal Theatre companies in forty cities in twenty-two states. The Federal Writers Project produced 1,200 publications, 31,000 pages of which were in the *American Guide* series alone. Five thousand artists were employed by the Federal Art Project to produce 108,000 easel paintings, 2,500 murals, 17,700 sculptures and 11,200 print designs. A further 400 murals and 6,800 easel works were created in five months under the Public Works of Art Project, with another 1,200 murals commissioned by the US Treasury's Section of Painting and Sculpture. There were also 77,000 photographs taken for the Historical Section of the Farm Security Administration. As evidence of 'value for money' from the unprecedented use of federal tax dollars to promote American art and culture, these were the numbers which justified the government's projects. They also demonstrate just how much of the artistic and literary outpouring of the Depression years was fostered by the patronage of Roosevelt's New Deal. Devoting a separate chapter to the federally-sponsored arts is not to present them as an aside to the culture of the 1930s (indeed, from Zora Neale Hurston to Joe Jones, Orson Welles to Berenice Abbott, many of the talents already discussed in this book made important contributions to the projects); rather it is a measure of their significance and of the fact that they were unique to this decade.

It was, of course, the Depression which transformed the scope of the government's largesse, with the quartet of the Federal Art, Theatre, Music and Writers projects (collectively known as Federal One) created in 1935 to find ways of employing some of the many thousands of creative artists who were among the 'one third of the nation' that was 'ill-fed, ill-clad and ill-housed'.[1] Federal patronage did exist before these projects, but it tended to be confined to architecture and monumental art – an investment which itself expanded in the 1930s when buildings for the Department of the Interior, the Federal Reserve, the National Archives and numerous other offices of government were constructed in Washington DC. At the determination of the Treasury, all of these were completed in a 'neo-classical style' to provide a unity of design, even when its application to John Russell Pope's Jefferson Memorial raised controversy about the appropriateness of creating monuments of 'imperial splendour' in the seat of democratic government.[2] However, with 1 per cent of the construction costs of public buildings automatically set aside for decoration, the physical expansion of government itself created unprecedented opportunities for artists to challenge such conventionality. When the Public Works Administration put the unemployed to work on 1,300 different construction projects, Treasury Department official Edward Bruce and artist George Biddle responded with the temporary Public Works of Art Project (PWAP), employing artists and sculptors between December 1933 and March 1934 to create works to ornament new schools, court houses and hospitals. When 1,100 new post offices were also built, Bruce was able to create a Section of Painting and Sculpture within the Treasury itself, eventually holding competitions throughout the country to commission artists to execute friezes, murals, reliefs and free-standing sculpture. Indeed, in June 1939, the Section launched a '48 States Competition', to find artists to decorate one post office lobby in every state of the Union, thus 'blanket[ing] America in murals'.[3] Bringing art into communities across the United States, and with contracted artists as diverse as regionalist John Steuart Curry, social realist William Gropper and surrealist Peter Blume, the Section (for a time at least) also effectively ended the isolation of 'official' painting from the 'stream of contemporary art'.[4]

Significant as this was, paying 850 artists an average of $725 for their work was clearly inadequate as a response to the Depression. The Treasury acknowledged this by also establishing its own relief art project (TRAP), similarly embellishing small federal buildings but only using artists from the unemployment rolls. TRAP's assistance, however, extended to just 440 persons. The Works Progress Administration (WPA) Federal Arts Projects, in contrast, created work for thousands. The New Deal's earlier Civil Works Administration (CWA) had recognized the need among desperate artists, and undertook ventures such as sponsoring community choruses and employing actors to put on marionette and vaudeville shows in hospitals and schools. Yet the CWA had been a short-term effort, based on the expectation that the private economy would revive to generate new jobs. The nine million employable people still without work in 1935 crushed this hope, but also prompted the more socially ambitious Second New Deal and the WPA. Through the WPA, the 3.5 million people on the relief rolls were to be offered employment through the government, rather than the dole, providing not only immediate sustenance but also the long-term preservation of their skills and self-confidence. Out of the WPA's initial appropriation of $5 billion, administrator Harry Hopkins set aside $27.3 million for Federal One, acknowledging that 'if the Depression continued for very long, a generation of artists would be lost and a fatal blow would be dealt to American culture'.[5]

The first of the projects to be established was the Federal Music Project (FMP), directed until 1939 by the former conductor of the Cleveland Symphony, Nikolai Solokoff. As well as forming orchestras to employ over 6,000 musicians, the FMP established an Education Branch to address the high level of unemployment among music teachers, encouraging them to organize community groups, offer free classes and set up music therapy projects. Arthur Cohn supervised 100 music copyists in Philadelphia, preparing manuscripts and providing scores for performing units. Efforts were also made to compile an authoritative 'Index of American Composers', providing biographical information on every composer from colonial times to the present day (although never completed, more than 2,200 records were deposited at the Library of Congress). Contemporary composers were encouraged too, not only in orchestral premieres of works like *At the Tomb of the Unknown Soldier* by Dent Mowry or Morris Hutchins Ruger's operatic *Gettysburg*, but also in the Composer-Forum Laboratories. Launched in New York in October 1935, and taken up in other cities, these Laboratories allowed composers such as Roy Harris, Aaron Copland and Marion Bauer to have new works presented by an FMP orchestra and then discuss them with the audience, 'introducing the American people to the composition process'.[6]

The challenge of directing the Federal Art Project (FAP) was taken on by Holger Cahill, then the director of exhibitions at the Museum of Modern Art and known for his interest in folk art. The FAP reflected this in its nationwide effort to create an 'Index of American Design', employing 400 artists to draw and reproduce artefacts of vernacular design from across the country, from glassware and toys, to furniture, weathervanes and quilts. Community Art Centres were also established in eighty-four towns, creating a network of sites offering free lectures, classes and exhibitions, intent on 'drawing out' the artistic talents that were 'hidden there'.[7] Divisions were created for murals, easel painting, graphic arts, sculpture and children's work, and commonly paralleled the PWAP and Section in providing artworks for courthouses, libraries, schools, prisons and WPA housing projects. Moreover, one hundred FAP artists, including Philip Guston, Ruth Reeves and Seymour Fogel, produced works for the walls and arcades at the New York World's Fair. The project also developed influential graphic design units, producing posters for other federal agencies and innovating with printing techniques and high-impact geometric designs. FAP accomplishments even prompted *The Nation* to remark that the crash of 1929 might prove to have been the best thing that ever happened to American art.[8]

Appointed to the Federal Theatre Project (FTP) from the Vassar Experimental Theatre, director Hallie Flanagan realized the necessity not only of creating work in the short-term, but of stimulating an interest and nurturing an audience throughout America in order to ensure theatre remained viable once the economic crisis had passed. Thus, to determine what kind of productions would 'excite the tastes of the public' the FTP presented countless dramas, both modern and classical, developed children's theatre, broadcast plays on radio, staged pageants and musicals, supported vaudeville and puppet shows and even operated a circus in New York.[9] Eugene O'Neill and George Bernard Shaw were both sufficiently impressed to release their plays to FTP for nationwide production at a rate of only $50, and Sinclair Lewis adapted his own novel, *It Can't Happen Here*, for a spectacular premiere of twenty-one simultaneous openings across the United States in October 1936. Dance units in New York, Chicago, Philadelphia and Tampa staged original ballets, while seventeen different 'Negro units' were established in active support of minority theatre (Chicago's swing version of *The Mikado* and Orson Welles's imaginative staging of a 'voodoo' *Macbeth* for an African American cast in Harlem were particularly celebrated). The FTP's most original creations, however, were the 'Living Newspapers', which forged drama out of headlines, congressional speeches and sociological studies to engage with issues of national controversy, such as slum housing in *One-Third of a Nation* or the New Deal's agricultural policy in *Triple-A Plowed Under*.

Henry Alsberg became national director of the Federal Writer's Project (FWP), and while 'journalist', 'sometime play-producer', 'would-be novelist' and 'philosophical anarchist' might not seem the most promising of resumés, he was widely credited with possessing a 'missionary zeal' that made the FWP 'much more ambitious and exciting than it otherwise would have been'.[10] Its most influential venture, the *American Guide* series, involved not only travel writing but the comprehensive description of the history and culture of every state, including encyclopaedic essays on localized literature, education and industry, as well as socio-ethnic studies of African American and Native American cultures. Project staffers also collected urban and rural folklore and oral histories. Their interviews with former slaves were published in the influential *Lay My Burden Down: A Folk History of Slavery*, while the groundbreaking *These Are Our Lives* documented overlooked aspects of 'Southern' identity in its stories of tenant farmers, sharecroppers, miners, vagrants and sales girls. Ranging from *The Italians of New York* to *Baseball in Chicago*, from children's books to bibliographical indexes, FWP stimulated the production of almost 14,000 manuscripts, an estimated 1,200 of which saw publication. Opportunities for creative writing were rather limited, but a one-volume collection of poems and stories was published in 1937 as *American Stuff*, including contributions from Richard Wright and Claude McKay, and several state projects produced their own literary magazines. Moreover, the FWP's factual projects served some writers in their subsequent fiction; with Ralph Ellison, for one, acknowledging the debt that *Invisible Man* owed to his work on the FWP oral history projects.[11]

It should be remembered, too, that not all New Deal culture was 'WPA art'. As discussed in Chapter 2, for instance, the government also entered the film industry, sponsoring the documentaries of Pare Lorentz and Joris Ivens and, in 1938, creating the United States Film Service. The documentary photography project of Roy Stryker's Historical Section was also located outside the WPA, operating within the Resettlement Administration and its successor, the Farm Security Administration (FSA). Bringing together figures now regarded as among the most significant in the history of American photography, it included Dorothea Lange, Walker Evans, Marion Post Wolcott, Russell Lee and Carl Mydans, with Stryker's placement of FSA images in national magazines such as *Life*, *Look*, *Fortune* and *US Camera*, making this venture central to the very definition of documentary photography as it emerged in the 1930s. The rest of this chapter, however, is not so much focused on the specific cultural contributions made by the various New Deal projects. Rather, reflecting the uniqueness of these projects and the circumstances and motivations behind their existence, it examines three major aspects of the qualities (both positive and negative) that government sponsorship itself brought to the production of culture.

Patronage as Relief

The Federal Arts Projects were a particularly unusual form of government patronage. While the Treasury Section stressed the quality of art in awarding its contracts, the employment of out-of-work artists was the WPA's primary goal, not the fulfillment of any specific commission. Certainly, each of the national directors possessed objectives of their own: Sokoloff, for instance, shared Toscanini's faith in programming classical music to encourage more 'cultivated' tastes in American audiences. Also each project operated within its own 'specific cultural history': Flanagan's ambitions for the Federal Theatre stemmed from anxiety that theatre in the United States was on the verge of becoming a 'museum product', stifled by the commercialism of Broadway and unable to compete with film and radio.[12] Yet while such factors were influential, the WPA's mission of relief was always paramount.

Congress impressed this upon the national directors by attaching several conditions to government money: 90 per cent of those employed had to be drawn from local welfare rolls; and 90 per cent of the funding had to be spent on wages. It was also stipulated that the Arts Projects could not compete with private industry. Orchestras, opera companies, theatres, galleries and publishing houses were suffering enough without government-subsidized ventures undercutting them. The projects should not get in the way of recovery, especially when it was always expected that those whose talents were being maintained would be absorbed back into private enterprise as soon as the economy improved. To encourage this, WPA salaries were therefore set below the minimum wage. Later, concerned that the relief projects should not become a permanent feature, Congress also legislated that no one could be employed on a WPA project for longer than eighteen months.

It was a measure of both the creativity and the vision of the project directors that these restrictions could sometimes be turned into opportunities. The Federal Theatre Project's Living Newspaper productions were a case in point. As experimental, alternative theatre, they avoided competition with commercial Broadway-style productions, and served too as a practical way of putting large numbers of theatre people to work. *One Third of a Nation*, for one, not only incorporated 195 different characters on stage, but also employed former journalists and secretarial workers to undertake the research into court records, newspaper stories and public speeches which provided the script's raw material. The 'ring-fencing' of money for wages caused difficulties in that expenditure on the other costs of producing theatre, such as scenery, costumes and advertising, had to be limited; but the originality of the Living Newspaper scripts meant that there were no royalties or performance rights to negotiate, and the plays themselves were designed not to rely on scenery or special effects. Actors were simply supported with innovative music, lighting and slide projections. The format also circumvented problems associated with the talent available among those claiming relief. In consequence of the shame attached to having been reduced to 'pauperism', many unemployed professionals had not registered themselves on the rolls and were therefore not eligible. Many of those who were on relief, such as former vaudeville comedians, possessed talents that were not particularly suited to dramatic roles. And because theatre had long been concentrated in major cities, directors outside areas like New York and Chicago found it difficult to find theatrical workers on the local rolls; meaning that in much of the country, projects were often staffed by interested amateurs. The Living Newspapers, however, could accommodate this 'plethora of amateur talent': 'Rather than having one actor carry the play with a few well-delivered monologues', the Living Newspapers presented 'short scenes in rapid-fire succession to make the news come alive. Thus individual talent was not as important as the holistic presentation of the play'.[13] Indeed, it has been argued that the very surplus of actors suited the project's politicized style, allowing for a diversity in casting that enabled 'many kinds of people' in the audience to identify with the characters' struggles to 'understand the natural and social and economic forces around them'.[14]

Similar ways to adapt to the bureaucratic stipulations were found by all the projects. The FAP's Index of American Design, for instance, was explicitly conceived as a labour-intensive project that could 'employ hundreds of art workers as copyists', thus putting to work 'personnel not considered accomplished enough for the easel or mural programs'.[15] In the FMP, Sokoloff's reaction to the availability of talent on relief was conservative, in that he generally restricted orchestra places to registered members of the American Federation of Musicians. However, the Composer-Forum Laboratories represented a more creative response. They compensated for the fact that the FMP could not pay American composers (since few if any were on relief) by giving them instead a much-needed chance to 'get a hearing for their new works', while allowing them virtually unlimited rehearsal time with as many FMP performers as they required.[16]

The Writers' Project probably faced the most difficult situation, with fewer than 10 per cent of employees having previously earned money putting words to paper. The North Carolina FWP director, for example, examined the unemployment rolls to find 518 teachers, three librarians, but 'not a single name of a writer, journalist, or otherwise professionally qualified person'.[17] Yet the format of the State Guides allowed the FWP to employ individuals with varied talents – clerks, typists, lawyers, map-makers, scholars, even people whose only experience was to write for their school magazine – to research the data which could then be written up by 'the few real writers' and edited at the national office.[18] In consequence, the FWP was able to take 6,500 people from the relief rolls nationwide. Moreover, the pyramid structure worked to the benefit of the Guides themselves, first compiled by local people already familiar with their subject matter, then refashioned by editors with a more consistent style and an overall perspective on the significance of the material. The Guides also satisfied the criteria of not competing with private industry since, in the Depression, no American publishing house was capable of such an expansive undertaking.

The nature of government-sponsored art was also affected by the ways in which artists themselves aligned with the New Deal itself. This was often a genuine reflection of enthusiasm for the government's liberal agenda, as well as of gratitude. As artists and actors on the projects acknowledged, 'without projects suited to their talents' they would only have been able to find work as 'unskilled construction workers and manual laborers'.[19] Moreover, most creative artists had never before experienced regular, predictable employment, making Federal One the first time that so many of them were 'employed continuously to produce art'.[20] Subsequently, cultural essays in the States Guides often included zealous descriptions of the Arts Projects themselves, sanctifying them as the culmination of artistic development in each state. The FAP's murals at the New York World's Fair, including Seymour Fogel's *Relation of WPA to Rehabilitation* and Anton Refregier's eight-panel *Cultural Activities of the WPA*, were similarly celebratory: Refregier portrayed the arts and education projects, and Fogel depicted more generally 'how people can be raised from starvation and hopelessness to self-support and self-reliance'.[21] The Treasury

Section also witnessed similar enthusiasm for the New Deal's under-takings in positive depictions of the Tennessee Valley Authority (TVA) in David Stone Martin's *Electrification* mural for Lenoir City, Tennessee, and of the CCC in Hollis Holbrook's *Reforestation* for Haleyville, Alabama. Ben Shahn also painted two direct representa-tions. One, *The Meaning of Social Security*, was painted for the Department of Health and Social Services, contrasting the 'social causes of insecurity with the benefits to be expected from this land-mark New Deal program'.[22] The other was a mural for the Jersey Homesteads, an agricultural co-operative community built by the gov-ernment for Jewish garment workers who had lost their jobs. Shahn's mural not only celebrated the creation of the Homesteads by con-trasting the freedoms enjoyed by Jews in America with the anti-Semitism then seen in Nazi Germany, but it also memorialized the congressmen and union organizers who had made the project possible, seating them beneath a campaign poster for Roosevelt's re-election.[23]

In the Theatre Project's Living Newspapers such enthusiasms extended into what could well be considered 'New Deal propaganda'. *Triple-A Plowed Under* (1936), for instance, set itself directly against the recent Supreme Court decision invalidating the New Deal's Agricultural Adjustment Act. *One-Third of a Nation* took its title from FDR's second inaugural, to endorse specific housing legislation to end urban slums. Harry Hopkins himself personally supported *Power*'s engagement with the controversy surrounding the TVA in the spring of 1937. With a major struggle underway between the TVA and a host of private electric utility companies, *Power* presented a series of 'highly theatrical scenes' depicting how 'electricity had been co-opted by private interests and business trusts', in a powerful argument in favour of public ownership.[24] With the TVA dams generating hydro-electric power as a by-product, New Dealers believed it was in the con-sumer's interests to have access to that inexpensive source of energy, especially in rural areas where private enterprise had ignored the needs of farmers. The Living Newspaper, as Barry Witham notes, 'supported TVA without reservation'. Indeed, *Power* was 'startling' in 'the degree to which the private sector [was] hounded and vilified', shown stoop-ing to 'bribery, blackmail and lying to get their way'.[25] All the content was drawn from factual sources, speeches and actual incidents, but with the amplified off-stage 'Voice of the Living Newspaper' cajoling, mocking and questioning official characters, the construction put upon those facts left little doubt as to where *Power* sought to direct audience sympathies.

While rare in the arts projects, the proselytizing of the Living Newspapers was not out of place when considered against the government's sponsorship of Pare Lorentz's films and Roy Stryker's photographic unit. Technically, Stryker's Historical Section was supposed to be 'documenting' the problems of the Depression, developing a central file of images that could be supplied to congressional committees, government publications and newspaper reports. But for the Resettlement Administration (RA), it was the persuasiveness of the image that mattered most. With radical plans to 'remove poor farmers from unproductive land' and resettle them in new government housing co-operatives, build utopian suburbs for 'refugees from the shattered industrial cities' and provide shelters for thousands of migrant families in government labour camps, the RA was probably the most controversial of the New Deal agencies.[26] It certainly faced serious challenges in Congress and the concerted opposition of Southern landowners and western agribusiness interests. Dorothea Lange's images of government migrant camps were therefore used to convince the public and Congress of their importance and undercut the opposition of California landowners. Her photographs of 'farmers being gradually displaced by machines' proved 'particularly compelling'.[27] Arthur Rothstein responded to RA instructions to 'include evidence of land misuse and mismanagement', with stark photographs of a sun-bleached steer skull on the scorched soil of drought-ridden South Dakota; even moving the skull when composing the image to further suggest that the cracked earth was the 'direct result of overgrazing'.[28] Other photographs sought to show the positive benefits of the RA/FSA programmes, with Russell Lee, for example, photographing the Jersey Homesteads. Countering criticism that the 'American taxpayer [was] putting up $1,800,000 to create a model of a Russian commune', Lee's photographs deliberately downplayed the co-operative dimension to focus instead on individual workers in the Homesteads' garment factory, demonstrating how their skills were being maintained.[29]

Indeed, both the Historical Section and Lorentz's film unit existed primarily to provide 'visual arguments for the implementation of rural relief' and images of suffering, despair and injustice that could help justify federal assistance.[30] Lorentz received his first commission for *The Plow That Broke the Plains* directly from the RA's director Rexford Tugwell in 1935, to demonstrate the need for soil conservation in the Midwest. His second film, *The River* (1938), was just as explicit as the Federal Theatre's *Power* in its support of the TVA,

Figure 5.1 *The Plow That Broke the Plains* (1936, directed by Pare Lorentz: Resettlement Administration/The Kobal Collection).

explaining the need for flood control in the Mississippi Valley. Given the TVA's controversial authority to appropriate privately-owned property for its massive dam-building enterprise and order thousands of people living in the area to be resettled, Lorentz both immortalized the TVA as a monumental and heroic undertaking, and provided dramatic images to 'prove' its necessity. It was, as Roosevelt saw, a powerful means to reach beyond a hostile press and enable the public to 'see' why radical action was needed. In this context, it is perhaps only surprising that there were not more productions like *Power*.

Pare Lorentz, *The Plow That Broke the Plains* (1936)

Though *The Plow That Broke the Plains* was the first film he ever made, Pare Lorentz came to it with a strong belief in the persuasive power of cinema and its ability to make people face up to reality. As a film critic and co-author of *Censored: The Private Life of the Movies* (1930), he had frequently indicted Hollywood for 'censoring' the public's access to information about 'tough contemporary facts'.[31] Thus, when the Resettlement Administration asked him to make Americans aware of the necessity of its programmes, he leapt at the chance and convinced Rex Tugwell of the need, not for short public information films but for a new kind of 'dramatic/informational/persuasive movie' that would be 'worthy of commercial distribution'.[32]

By 1934, the Dust Bowl extended from Texas to North Dakota, with reports that over 180 million acres had already been ruined for agricultural cultivation and that a further 775 million were at risk. Lorentz had already proposed a film about the appalling cost of this situation to Hollywood. Having been rebuffed, he only became more determined to use the RA's support to command the public's attention. As many film historians have noted, he succeeded in producing a seminal film, both 'politically committed and aesthetically ambitious', that shaped the American documentary tradition.[33] Presenting The Plow as 'a record of the land' and 'a picturization of what we did with it', the prologue immediately conveys a sense of collective national guilt. Each section is carefully orchestrated, with poetic narration delivered by operatic singer Thomas Chalmers and visuals edited to Virgil Thomson's musical score to unite the film as a lyrical whole. Idyllic shots of tall waving grass show 'the richness of the western plain lands before their abuse', and serve as the measure of the ensuing disaster.[34] Homesteaders, farmers and the frenzy of mechanized harvesting prompted by the agricultural profits available during the First World War, contribute in turn to an ever-expanding exploitation of the land. A dramatic montage juxtaposing tractors on the home front with tanks on the Western Front foreshadows the destruction which Lorentz soon marks with images of dead animals and bleached bones on parched, depleted soil. His most powerful footage, however, is of the violent dust storms themselves, blocking out the sun, bringing the terror of the 'black blizzards' to 'millions who had only read about what was happening far away on the Great Plains'.[35]

The last few minutes humanize the story with a family of 'Okies', 'baked out, blown out and broke', their home turned into a 'nightmare of swirling dust, day and night'. They have no choice but to head for migrant camps in California in 'a desperate gamble for a day's labor in the fields'. In its original form, The Plow ended by stating clearly that the Resettlement Administration (RA) was these people's only hope, with a depiction of the government's work in relocating 4,500 families to sustainable farms in new 'beltville' communities. However, soon after The Plow's release, the RA became part of the Farm Security Administration and, with the 'beltville' concept never fully realized, this epilogue was dropped. This absence has led some to question The Plow's effectiveness as New Deal propaganda. Certainly, as it stands the ending lacks in comparison to the exultant celebration of the Tennessee Valley Authority at the end of Lorentz's subsequent film, The River (1938). However, even without its epilogue, The Plow still served the RA's argument that farming in such areas, characterized by 'little rain' and 'high winds and sun', was simply unsustainable. 'One feels the waste, the irresponsibility, the failure in planning' in its account of the land's past use.[36] Indeed, in its sanctioning of government intervention, FDR apparently considered sending the film to Congress 'as a presidential message'.[37]

In fact, Lorentz's fervent support of the RA and the New Deal was itself the source of several problems. The filmmakers he hired to undertake location camerawork – Paul Strand, Leo Hurwitz and Ralph Steiner – were founding members of Nykino, and were all politically to the left of Lorentz. Feeling it 'their duty to hew the artistic product as closely as possible to the anticapitalist line', they clashed with Lorentz's New Deal perspective.[38] While prepared to indict greed in general, he refused to accept their analysis of 'how lousy our social system was', and their emphasis on 'capitalism's anarchist rape of the land'.[39] Things got so difficult that in the end he could only work with Steiner. On the other hand, although it may have lacked the 'force and specificity' wished by Strand and Hurwitz in particular, *The Plow* was certainly propagandist enough for Hollywood studios to refuse to distribute it on the basis that the film was 'New Deal electioneering'.[40] In the end Lorentz could only circumvent this by taking *The Plow* direct to independent theatre operators, touring the Midwest to drum up bookings. Through such efforts it eventually played in more than 3,000 cinemas. Political opponents, however, gained further leverage in charging that some of the film's statements were false. Even the RA's own regional administrator in Texas suggested that *The Plow* 'unduly magnifies the true situation', in that 'extreme wind erosion' was only localized.[41] The repeated statement in the film that the region was 'without rivers, without streams' also conveniently overlooked the Missouri, Yellowstone, Platte and Arkansas rivers. Attacked in some quarters as 'a libel' on the region, *The Plow* was eventually taken out of official circulation in 1939.[42]

Of course, as Richard Dyer McCann has argued, if *The Plow* had been a straightforward account of 'the facts', its intensity would have been greatly diluted.[43] Indeed, for Lorentz it was not a 'documentary' as such. He always preferred the term 'Films of Merit', and the 'merit' of *The Plow* lay in making the problem clear, and compelling audiences to endorse the government's progressive actions. Moreover, in the spirit of much of the New Deal, it casts such actions in a thoroughly patriotic light. Despite the fact that human actions are at the root of the problem, the narration still conveys an 'awe of the American land'. Even in the sequence of tractors and tanks, there is still 'a celebratory pride in America'.[44] Thomson's music, too, drawing on folk tunes and hymnals, adds to this dual-edged sensibility. His evocation of *All People That on Earth Do Dwell* over the images of the terrible dust storms may suggest an ironic comment on the hymn's lyric that God's 'mercy is forever sure'; but the lyric also speaks of a spirit which 'shall from age to age endure'. Indeed, despite *The Plow*'s indictment of what Americans had done to the land, it maintains the faith that 'these still-proud refugees' will get back on their feet, and that 'Americans can and will marshal their talents to beat the drought'.[45]

Cultural Nationalism and Cultural Democracy

Throughout the short history of these projects, the nature of federal sponsorship set up continuous tensions between provincial, regional and national cultural identities. The scope of New Deal patronage, directed from Washington DC, represented a unique opportunity to document, nurture and define a 'national' culture. This was indeed embraced, with undertakings such as the theatre project's Festival of American Dance or the FMP's contributions to the American Music Festival and National Music Week in 1938.[46] At the FAP, Holger Cahill argued that the ultimate goal of the Index of American Design was to bury forever the perception that American culture was inadequate, by documenting folk and craft objects deemed to be of 'a distinctive American character' and thus retrieving a 'rich native design heritage which we had all but forgotten in our frantic and fashionable search for aesthetic fragments of European and Asiatic civilization'.[47] In the PWAP, too, Edward Rowan made it clear that he expected murals to reflect 'the American Scene', commissioning artists who possessed 'the imagination and vision to see the beauty and the possibility for aesthetic expression in the subject matter of his own country'.[48]

Yet, the projects also needed to operate through regional, federated structures. The FMP, for instance, began with ten regional and city projects and then assigned directors to each state in 1936; while the Federal Theatre split the country into East, West, Midwest and South, New York, Los Angeles and Chicago. Moreover, always dependent on WPA funding being allocated by Congress on an annual basis, the projects needed to win the support of the public's elected representatives in every state. The fact that the FTP proved unable to establish theatres in twenty-nine states meant that it was hit particularly hard when cuts began to be made in appropriations; unless their constituency had benefited, congressmen had little reason to support the project. In contrast, the State Guides project served the FWP particularly well, since it involved every part of the union and gave local politicians, representatives and senators pride in their own state's guide and, therefore, created a desire to see the series through to completion. Similarly, given that post office murals would be a 'permanent presence' in communities, symbolic of their relationship with the federal government, the Treasury Section insisted that 'wherever possible' artists should consult 'leading citizens about the choice of subject matter'.[49] This often resulted in images of 'idiosyncratic local lore', including 'dubious "firsts", peculiar doings, and the humble origins of heroes who attained national fame elsewhere'.[50] Yet most artists, like sculptor Carl Schmitz, were happy with the process, agreeing that citizens would get 'local pride out of a design having to do with their own activities'.[51]

Though such claims to local distinctiveness might seem to work against the grain of national identity, many of the New Dealers saw it differently, rationalizing local and regional heterogeneity as a positive manifestation of the nation's pluralism.[52] In this vision, each community, state and region was deemed to have unique cultural characteristics of its own. The cultural nationalism for which New Deal officials strove was, in essence, one that constructed America as a 'nation of communities'. In consequence the most important and progressive work that the arts projects could do was to make the cultures of those communities manifest, and then provide opportunities for them to transcend local boundaries and make their contribution to the national culture: showing 'New York to Texas and Texas to New York' as FSA photographer Russell Lee phrased it.[53] The New Deal's cultural vision of 'America' allowed it to be diverse and united simultaneously.

This process was certainly encouraged, even if only partially realized. Opportunities for local artists were created by the Section's regional competitions and by the FAP's establishment of Community Arts Centers in places as diverse as Spokane, Washington and Melrose, New Mexico. The Index of American Design itself validated the crafts of localized 'folk' traditions – including embroidery, ceramics and woodwork – as authentic American arts, possessed of a 'forthright quality and honesty' that is 'simply the genuine voice of the people'.[54] From a similar perspective, FMP fieldworkers drove across the country to record and transcribe folk ballads and spirituals, while the expansion of Composer-Forum Laboratories to Detroit, San Francisco, Tulsa and other cities provided unique outlets for local composers. In the FTP, Flanagan exhorted each region to develop its own 'indigenous drama and native expression', reflecting 'its own landscape and regional materials, producing plays of its past and present, in its own rhythm of speech and its native design'.[55] The Oklahoma FTP in particular, under John Dunne's direction, worked enthusiastically with the state university to collect indigenous histories and folklore and supply them to playwrights for dramatization. Various Native American groups provided information and stories, while the unit proactively used the Southwest's radio stations to put out a call for regional source material. Dunne himself used the results to write *Beyond Tomorrow*, about the West after the civil war; John

Woodworth told the story of female outlaw Belle Star in *Cheat and Swing*; and the Tulsa unit used accounts of pioneer life in the state to produce *Riding for the Cherokee Strip*. Through the FTP's National Play Bureau, these plays were then made available to other units (with, for instance, Robert Whitehead's *Precious Land*, portraying 'an Oklahoma farmer's unwillingness to sell his land to oil speculators', finding favour in Florida).[56] Others saw publication in FTP volumes, furthering the ambition to make this material known to the rest of America.

On the Writers' Project, the national office advised States Guides to essay the contributions 'racial and foreign groups' had made 'to the culture of the State' and 'what survivals of [their] earlier folkways still persist'. The Massachusetts guide, for instance, recorded how 'Slavic, Semitic, and Celtic influences have permeated Massachusetts' thought, enriching folkways, enlivening speech, and giving a new perspective to graphic art, music and literature'.[57] Alsberg also engaged Benjamin Botkin and John Lomax as folklore experts to guide this. While Lomax emphasized traditional and rural material, Botkin's interest was in contemporary 'living lore', often urban, which existed in forms of 'folksay', or 'what people have to say about themselves'. As the *Manual for Folklore Studies* he produced for the FWP suggested, Botkin believed that this kind of folklore 'could help Americans achieve a deeper understanding of the nation's multicultural context'.[58] FWP guidelines also insisted that 'anything of interest that is peculiar to the community or its region should be treated more fully'.[59] Fieldworkers frequently delivered, allowing Alsberg to celebrate their work as material that had 'actually been collected locally, on the spot by Guide workers who are native to the location and catch its real spirit'.[60] Indeed, when the completion of the series was marked with 'American Guide Week' in 1941, Roosevelt himself praised the publications for marrying the 'ideals and traditions shared by all Americans' to 'the diverse local patterns of thought and behaviour'. To the President, mindful of what fascism had wrought in Europe, this was what 'distinguished our free and democratic way of life'.[61]

Indeed, the overarching ambition of the arts projects was often seen to be the establishment of a 'cultural democracy' – even if the phrase meant different things to different people.[62] On one level, it simply meant involving communities in the art works, as Section artists did in soliciting local opinions about prospective mural content, in a 'process of democratic negotiation and compromise'.[63] Others interpreted cultural democratization as a process of taking art out of elitist domains where, in FDR's words, it was only seen 'in a guarded room on holidays or Sundays', to make it 'accessible' to the whole of the American public.[64] Post office murals, Community Art Centers and free theatrical productions in public parks were just some of the means by which federal sponsorship was perceived as having achieved this. Indeed, it was estimated that of the thirty million theatregoers who attended FTP performances, 65 per cent were 'seeing theatre for the first time'.[65]

'Cultural democracy' was also constructed in terms of inclusiveness, of encouraging more Americans to give voice to their own artistry, particularly those who had before been under-represented. The Section, for instance, included Native American artists Stephen Mopope, Richard West, Gerald Nailor and Acee Blue Eagle in its commissions, some for post offices in Oklahoma, others for the Department of the Interior. It also awarded one-sixth of its commissions to female artists. Barbara Melosh points out that it is difficult to determine whether these 162 artists signified 'a few or many'; but it certainly represented an effort to 'redress the sexual imbalance of public art'.[66] In 'opening up a space' for the representation of women in mural art itself, the Section also challenged the objectification of the female body that was otherwise 'common in easel painting, film and advertising'.[67] Instead, artists of both sexes were prompted to portray women engaged in historical pioneering ventures, rural activity, or even in 'heroic labour' alongside men in a 'comradely ideal', taking their place in 'the narrative of social life that was the heart of American scene painting'.[68] Some murals, indeed, were dominated by female characters, such as *The Wealth of Sutter County* by Lulu Hawkin Braghetta in which the 'settlement that followed the boom and bust of the gold rush' is depicted as the result of women's efforts.[69]

The African American experience of the WPA arts programmes has been the subject of most study. So-called 'Negro Art Centers' were established by the FAP, providing considerable new exposure for African American artists; one in Jacksonville, Florida, for example, boasted 40,000 attendees over its three years of operation. The music project formed black concert units in New York, California, Ohio, Illinois, Pennsylvania and Missouri, and one in Richmond, Virginia. Choruses such as the 100-strong Miami WPA black choir were also formed, and Solokoff sanctioned swing and dance bands for African American performers, even as he opposed them for white musicians. 'Negro Theatres' were established in sixteen cities (three of them in the South) and included drama, choral, youth, vaudeville, musical and operetta units. The FTP also encouraged several new plays by

Figure 5.2 Zora Neale Hurston with publications of the Federal Writers Project (Library of Congress, Prints and Photographs Division, LC-USZ62-126945).

African American authors, including Theodore Ward's *Big White Fog* (Chicago, 1938), Theodore Brown's *Natural Man* (Seattle, 1937) and Hughes Allison's *The Trial of Dr Beck* (New Jersey, 1937). Alsberg, too, signalled his intentions by appointing African-American poet and Howard University professor Sterling Brown to the FWP national office, to 'oversee and ensure adequate coverage' of black history and culture in the guides (he similarly appointed D'Arcy McNickle to oversee work on Native Americans).[70] He also made Richard Wright New York's Editor for Negro Affairs in 1937, and encouraged Zora Neale Hurston to join the Florida unit, suggesting that she be put in charge of editing *The Florida Negro*, bringing to bear her knowledge of the region's racial folklore.

Yet for all that could be celebrated, there were some severe limitations. The FWP, for instance, possessed the worst record on African-American employment. White staff in the regions often 'simply refused to work in the company of blacks'.[71] Even in northern states, local administrators 'feared that placing black writers on the FWP staff would antagonize white colleagues, sponsors and the public'.[72] In order to increase black employment in several states, the government instead resorted to separate 'Negro Units' rather than challenge segregation. Sterling Brown also had to contend with blatantly racist passages that appeared in some guide copy, such as the Alabama FWP's positive references to the Ku Klux Klan and its suggestion that the 'dismal living conditions' of African Americans were only to be expected 'among an illiterate people suddenly thrown on their own resources'.[73] North Carolina writers also resisted requests to 'expand the volume and detailed texture of copy on black lives and institutions', claiming that Brown was asking them to 'overemphasize the Negro'.[74] Hurston experienced discrimination in Florida from the outset, as the state's WPA supervisors sidestepped Alsberg's directive, paying her more but refusing to put a black woman in an editorial position. Moreover, while she worked with Botkin toward 'adding imaginative and colourful African American lore' to the guide's tour sections, her detailed essays on black folk religion and a masterful work on 'the theme of primitive man's need to create folklore to explain the world around him', were never included in *The Florida Negro*.[75]

The pluralist vision of cultural democracy thus only extended so far, despite the noble ambitions of project directors. But it was not only in the matter of Southern racism that the centre's perspective was challenged. When it came to the stress on cultural diversity, for instance, the director of Minnesota FWP professed himself 'baffled by the tendency of all the federal editors to regard us as inhabiting a region romantically different from any other in the country'.[76] Indeed, Christine Bold demonstrates that the 'diverse local patterns' supposedly 'revealed' in the American Guides were constructed more by the national directors than by fieldworkers in the regions. Insisting that anything 'that is common to all or many communities in America should be given little space', they edited copy to conform to their preconceived ideas, imprinting it with their own worldview.[77] This was rationalized, as Flanagan argued at the FTP, in the belief that 'only a national plan can emphasize and correlate different parts of the country as parts of a nationwide pattern', but it was nevertheless a paternalistic point of view that was not always welcomed.[78]

In the end, though, whatever their limitations, the New Deal arts projects did attempt to give each region and locality a chance to develop its own cultural expression. FAP work and Section commissions also gave opportunities to female, African American, Native American and working-class artists that galleries and private patrons had rarely offered.[79] Publications such as *The Negro in Virginia, The Armenians in Massachusetts* or *The Albanian Struggle in the Old World and New* were driven by the desire to change the status 'of disparaged and ignored groups of Americans', and sought to foster among readers a wider understanding of both cultural differences and common ground.[80] Productions addressed audiences that had not been previously been catered to, with the Federal Theatre staging plays in Yiddish, Chinese, Spanish and other languages, and the few plays that were written by African American authors at least undercut the usual 'white interpretations of black life' that were seen on the stage.[81] Also, even while segregation persisted in the creation of 'Negro units', there were some projects like the Federal Art Center in St Louis that were open to everyone without restriction, fusing 'various racial, religious and cultural backgrounds into a common creative endeavour'.[82] Quite how 'American unity would emerge from a knowledge of diversity' was always more of a 'hopeful faith' than a 'clearly communicated ideal', but for all the difficulties faced by the projects, it was, nevertheless, a sustaining and progressive commitment.[83]

Hallie Flanagan

Hallie Flanagan had been the director of theater at Vassar College for ten years when Harry Hopkins asked her to head the Federal Theatre Project in 1935. Some critics questioned the wisdom of appointing a college and art theatre director to the task; and it was certainly true that her main interest in accepting the position had less to do with putting the unemployed to work, than with the opportunities government sponsorship provided for extending experimental theatre across the nation. Indeed, she always wanted to develop a national theatre that would be able to continue even after the federal subsidy ended. Yet it was this wider vision and zeal that, for Hopkins at least, made her the ideal candidate.

Flanagan's vision was the product of several complementary influences. 'Under no obligation to the commercial stage', she was one of several leaders of community and university theatres who had already propounded the idea of a 'national federation of regional theatres' at the 1931 National Theatre Conference.[84] Many of those she involved in the FTP, like Elmer Rice and E. C. Mabie, shared the concern that millions of Americans outside major cities had never even seen a play, and that theatre was being rendered obsolete by radio and the movies. From the start, therefore, Federal Theatre was committed to bringing theatre 'to every segment of the population'.[85] Indeed, initial plans called for the creation of new theatre centres in 100 communities across the country, with repertory companies 'recruited from the ranks of the unemployed'.[86] It was also conceived explicitly as 'federal', not 'national', since to Flanagan 'national' implied an 'attempt to have one theatre expressive of one national view'. 'Federal', on the other hand, meant 'bringing together for purposes of mutual benefit', and Flanagan believed that such benefit was to be had in developing local talent and producing plays articulating local issues and distinctive experiences.[87]

Such plans, however, proved beyond the capacities of the WPA. In reality, the FTP was eventually limited to just four regional and three major city projects, with several states having no units at all. The pre-existing concentration of theatrical workers in New York City also thwarted the ambition, when Flanagan's regional directors found few theatre people on local relief rolls, simply because professional actors and directors had already deserted their regions for the lure of Broadway. Despite such frustrations, however, Flanagan's dynamism ensured that in 1936 twenty-two theatres from Boston to Birmingham opened their productions of *It Can't Happen Here* by Sinclair Lewis simultaneously. Indeed, she specifically fought against the New York unit in order to make it happen, 'furiously challenging' their attitude that the productions in other cities were only 'tryouts in hick towns'. Devised to test 'the health of Federal Theatre units outside of New York', the great success of *It Can't Happen Here* offered a clear demonstration of what the FTP could achieve 'in both its national and regional aspects'.[88]

Creating a 'National, Regional and American' theatre was not, however, the only way in which Flanagan hoped to rejuvenate theatre in the United States. Her mentor, George Pierce Baker, a key figure in America's prewar 'new theatre' movement, had always encouraged American dramatists to emulate the vitality of European playwrights like Shaw, Ibsen and Maeterlinck, and create theatre that would provoke 'lively discussions of human problems'.[89] Touring Europe at Baker's suggestion in 1926, Flanagan encountered this vitality for herself, especially at Vsevolod Meyerhold's productions in Russia where, as she wrote in *Shifting Scenes*, she witnessed 'the most alive audience I have seen in any country'. 'Full-blooded, vigorous, coarse . . . shouting approval or disapproval', it was so far removed from the restrained, upper-middle-class patrons of theatre in the United States, that she returned determined to find ways of engaging the potentially vast working-class, ethnic and rural audiences that American theatre did not reach.[90] This perspective was at the heart of Flanagan's first address as project director, criticizing the way in which commercial theatre clung 'to sentimentality', telling in 'polite whispers its tales of small triangular love stories in small rectangular settings'.[91] Broadway, in this diagnosis, was stifled by the profit motive, staging only light entertainment and 'tried and true' classics; but the Federal Theatre was freed from concern with profits.[92] The Living Newspapers, in particular, became Flanagan's 'antidote' to commercialism, incorporating modernist staging and cinematic ideas of montage and pastiche to present theatrical equivalents of newsreels, while seeking to win new audiences with 'lively discussions' of contemporary social and political issues.[93] In this regard, FTP was successful. Not only was it estimated that twelve million New Yorkers saw at least one Living Newspaper, but critics observed that these audiences were very much like Meyerhold's: 'far from passive, they yelled back at the stage and often left the theatre arguing loudly about what had taken place'.[94] Responses like this seemed to support Flanagan's assertion that the theatre could indeed win a broader audience if it created drama that spoke to their concerns and gave them something 'which they cannot get in any other form of entertainment'.[95]

Flanagan's position, however, was under fire from the start. The Hearst press had already attacked her during her time at Vassar, using her authorship of *Shifting Scenes* to suggest that when students put on plays from the nascent worker's theatre movement, Flanagan had become 'an authorized disseminator of Communist propaganda'.[96] Flanagan was no Communist or fellow-traveller, but she was caught up in Popular Front ideology. She openly sympathized, for instance, with project workers who went on strike when Congress cut the WPA's appropriations. Moreover, when cuts did have to be implemented, she preferred to close projects doing 'old plays in old ways' and save experimental units like the Living Newspapers even as they were giving ammunition to the WPA's conservative critics.[97] In part, this explains why, when opponents in the House of Representatives determined to end the FTP's funding in 1938, WPA administrators told her that they would not be mounting an effort to save it. Her determination though was such that she and her team organized their own counter-attack to line up congressional support. Moreover, this characteristically became a fight not just to save the FTP but to 'get the public to recognize that artists counted, that their talents were essential to the nation's well-being'.[98] In the end it was to no avail. Yet before she retired back to Vassar to write the story of the FTP, published as *Arena* in 1940, Flanagan still drew up a plan that went 'beyond anything she had thought of for the Federal Theatre', envisioning a government Department of the Arts that would underwrite national touring programmes, produce annual theatre festivals and use WPA labour to build new theatres.[99] Naive perhaps, but as John Houseman later eulogized, it was precisely such optimism and vision in the first place that had turned 'a pathetic relief project' into 'what remains the most creative and dynamic approach that has yet been made to an American National Theatre'.[100]

Free, Adult and Uncensored?

Government patronage always carried with it the inherent spectre of censorship. That was apparent from the outset, even in the fact that it had to be denied repeatedly, as in Harry Hopkins's assurance that the Federal Theatre was going to be 'free, adult and uncensored', or the way in which administrators 'unhesitatingly, unanimously and without qualification' promised that 'Yes!' artists would exercise freedom and autonomy on the Public Works of Art Project.[101] Predictably, such promises soon rang hollow.

For the PWAP, controversy erupted in the summer of 1934, over murals for the Coit Tower in San Francisco where twenty-five artists had been commissioned to paint local scenes of city life, agriculture and industrial production. A month before the Tower was due to open, it was discovered that several changes had been made to the approved designs: Victor Arnautoff had added copies of the *New Masses* and *Daily Worker* to a newsstand in his *City Life* mural; Bernard Zakheim featured *Das Kapital* prominently in his *Library*; and Clifford Wight had included a hammer and sickle and the slogan 'Workers of the World Unite' in one of his panels. Each of these artists had previously worked with Diego Rivera, and given that they were painting at the time when Rivera's Rockefeller Center mural was demolished, these new details may have been intended as a show of solidarity. They also reflected the artists' sympathy with San Francisco's waterfront workers at a time of great tension between them and the city's shippers – in fact, just forty-eight hours before the murals were meant to be unveiled, two strikers were killed by police. This politically explosive atmosphere, however, made the PWAP even less prepared to accept the unauthorized additions, with Bruce indeed insisting that the 'objectionable features must be removed'. When the Artists and Writers' Unions responded by picketing Coit Tower, the city's Parks Commission actually ordered its closure – raising fears that the murals, like Rivera's, would be destroyed. Although only Wights' Soviet emblem was erased in the end, the charge of censorship had become very vocal, with Wight raising the legitimate point that since 'no one censored the press for admitting the existence of communism', 'why should the artist be denied the freedom allowed the journalist?'.[102]

Similarly, the directors of the Federal Theatre intervened on several occasions. The very first Living Newspaper, *Ethiopia*, was cancelled at the request of the White House itself, since the administration feared that a dramatization of Mussolini's invasion of Ethiopia would antagonize the Italian government. Thereafter sensitive to Roosevelt's priorities, the national office also pressed the New York ballet unit to remove overt political symbols from its production of *Guns and Castanets*, a version of Bizet's *Carmen* set against the Spanish Civil War. With the ballet clearly favouring the Loyalists, administrators warned that 'inasmuch as the government for this country had decidedly not come out for one side or the other, we as a government sponsored agency certainly have no right to do so'.[103] The most famous case, though, was *The Cradle Will Rock*, as the production by Orson Welles and John Houseman of Marc Blitzstein's new opera fell victim to major cuts in WPA appropriations. Intended as the FTP's major premiere of 1937, its positive support of union-organizing in the fictional city of 'Steeltown USA' became 'political dynamite' when pitched battles broke out in June between strikers and Republic Steel's company police. In this context, the WPA's sudden decree that due to 'budgetary problems' all new productions would be postponed, seemed to be targeting *Cradle* specifically. Certainly WPA officials also ensured that Actors Equity would not permit their members in the production to appear on stage, and sealed off the theatre with security guards. Welles, however, smuggled out the score, relocated to an empty theatre, and encouraged members of the cast to perform their roles from the auditorium while Blitzstein played the score alone on stage. It was a masterstroke which turned *Cradle* into the greatest theatrical *cause célèbre* of the decade, and a major embarrassment for the arts projects.[104]

Not all the constraints facing government artists, however, came from above. For all the hopes and good intentions, the very notion of 'cultural democracy' could present a problem in itself when 'the people' actually spoke. Stuart Davis produced a stunning abstract mural, entitled *Swing Landscape*, for a WPA low-income housing development in Brooklyn, but residents rejected it as 'too modern'.[105] Joseph Vorst was compelled to repaint his Section post office mural in Paris, Arkansas, when local civic pride demanded that instead of the 'tumbledown cabin' which Vorst had painted from reality, he give them a 'modern and progressive' (and imaginary) picture of the town 'packed with houses, barns, stables and gins, all of them spanking new'.[106] Likewise rejected was Fletcher Martin's *Mine Rescue* design for Kellogg, Idaho, which depicted two lead miners carrying an injured worker out on a stretcher. Edward Rowan himself thought it the strongest design in the whole of the 48 States Competition, aesthetically 'comparable to some of the great religious paintings of the past' and a great tribute to 'the sacrifice which a good citizen makes in faithfully carrying out his humble duties'.[107] Officials of the Mine Workers and Smelt Workers union praised the work in similar terms. However, when the town's industrialists objected that it was 'not in harmony with existing conditions', Section policy required the establishment of a local advisory committee, which reported back that 'to hang a picture depicting such an accident' on permanent display would 'prove a torture to the families of victims', and give 'work in Kellogg a permanent pall of tragedy'.[108] Censored by public opinion, Martin eventually substituted a far less powerful painting of prospector Noah Kellogg discovering the mine upon which the town was founded: 'noncontroversial' and of 'purely local' interest.[109]

The bureaucratic organization of the WPA also caused particular problems; indeed, Barry Witham describes it as the 'principal cause of censorship' within the projects.[110] Although funding and salary allocations were devolved to State WPA offices, Hopkins had placed artistic control and decisions about who to hire in the hands of the national directors. Many local WPA personnel resented this as a challenge to their authority, generating ill feeling from the outset. In Birmingham, Alabama, for instance, the WPA Director of Professional and Service Projects 'sabotaged' the entire Federal Theatre operation in her city in order to pursue her own plans for 'a drama program through the local Parks and Recreation Board'.[111] California's WPA state administrator, Colonel Connelly, directly challenged Flanagan's authority in cancelling a production of Elmer Rice's anti-Fascist drama, *Judgment Day*, while Seattle's Don Abel closed an African-American adaptation of *Lysistrata* after just one performance because his wife had been 'offended by the sight of black people performing a sexually suggestive comedy'.[112] Even within the arts projects themselves, local directors sometimes undermined the national goals. Cahill discovered late in the day that the selection of Mary Curran to head the Philadelphia FAP had been a mistake. Rather than sharing his ambition to bring 'art to the millions', Curran blocked efforts to allocate project art works to schools and hospitals and, out of a 'misplaced' devotion to 'the sacredness of the artist', sought to place them in exclusive museums instead.[113]

In the end though, the greatest obstacles, and indeed the final act of censorship, came from Congress. Many Republicans and conservative Democrats were already critical of the WPA's work-creation 'boondoggling'; and the art projects were a soft target for the New Deal's opponents. Having already decided for himself that the Theatre and Writers projects were both part of a 'vast and unparalleled New Deal propaganda machine' and a 'branch of the Communistic organization', New Jersey Republican J. Parnell Thomas led the call for their investigation in July 1938, and hearings began in the autumn, chaired by Texas Democrat Martin Dies.[114] Under Dies, the House Committee of Un-American Activities (HUAC) treated unsubstantiated allegations from disgruntled former project workers as objective evidence, including

Wallace Stark's claim that he had been fired from the Living Newspaper for objecting to plays advocating 'the overthrow of the government'.[115] Committee members also asked leading questions, such as 'would you say that the Federal Writer's Project is being converted into an agency to spread communism throughout the United States', or 'is it the uniform policy [of the States Guides] to array class against class?'.[116] Their knowledge of the actual productions of the projects was cursory. Congressman Starnes' ignorance that Christopher Marlowe was a sixteenth-century playwright and not, as he presumed, 'a Communist', reflected a philistinism that Flanagan found more disturbing than amusing.[117]

The allegations, however, possessed just enough basis in reality to be damaging. The New York FWP, for instance, had done little in its first year of operation except publish mimeographed 'Trotskyite leaflets' under the direction of Orrick Johns, a former editor of the *New Masses*.[118] A minor scandal had also been provoked by the Massachusetts' State Guide when paragraphs concerning the Sacco–Vanzetti case were leapt upon by local Republicans as evidence of 'federal funds' being 'used for official Communist propaganda'.[119] A children's show called *The Revolt of the Beavers* also embarrassed the FTP through the evident Marxist overtones of its tale of animals over-throwing their chief to establish a communal society. And it was diffi-cult to deny that Living Newspapers like *Power* were not, indeed, 'New Deal propaganda'. Moreover, while most FAP artists gratefully tolerated the programme's 'inconsistencies' while waiting for the economy's return to health, a vocal minority of radicals theorized that it was the *right* of workers to 'work at an occupation for which [they] had talent and interest', and that the government had an obligation to ensure such jobs.[120] Thus, when cuts in WPA appropriations meant cuts in project employment, these radicals became militant in fighting for their 'rights'. Particularly in New York, project artists joined orga-nizations such as the American Artists Union and the Workers Alliance, and responded to freezes in the relief programme with sit-down strikes, hunger strikes and the occupation of WPA offices. In June 1937, workers dismissed from the FWP even held Federal One's Harold Stein hostage in his office. Futile in their attempts to reverse WPA rulings, such actions only fed sensational news coverage that gave 'the impression that the writers, musicians, actors and artists of America had become anarchists'.[121]

In examining the evidence emphasized by HUAC, however, Jerrold Hirsch has advanced a persuasive argument that it was not just

'Communist' or 'New Deal' propaganda that concerned the Committee's members. Excerpts from the galleys of the New Jersey and Montana Guides came under particular scrutiny when they made sympathetic comments about the labour movement in their histories of state industry. To Dies' mind, a reference to 'men of greater means' establishing Montana's mining industry, while 'the worker took wages instead of metal for his labours', was a statement intent on 'fostering class hatred'.[122] Similarly, Dies interpreted Richard Wright's essay on 'The Ethics of Jim Crow' in *American Stuff* as evidence of the FWP 'promoting racial hatred'.[123] As Hirsch suggests, while FWP officials believed that theirs was a progressive vision, incorporating the realities of working-class and black experience into a more inclusive national picture, 'for Dies and a majority of the HUAC members, mentioning the history of labor and African Americans was an unpatriotic act promoting disunity'.[124] Not everyone in the 1930s shared the New Deal vision of what constituted 'American' identity.

An effort was mounted to save the projects by divorcing the government's patronage from relief efforts. Congressman William Sororvich and Senators John Coffee and Claude Pepper each advocated a permanent Bureau of Fine Arts, asserting that the projects had already proved conclusively that 'there exists in the United States, the potentialities for a great and flourishing culture which will, if properly developed, make our country a greater nation'. Their bill also claimed that such a Bureau would give 'our people as a whole the occasion to exercise with democratic equity their cultural aspirations'.[125] Although the plans achieved a good deal of support in the arts world, they were subjected to 'ruthless ridicule' in the House, and defeated by 195 votes to thirty-five.[126]

The Federal Theatre was the first to be axed. The House Subcommittee on Appropriations had followed HUAC's report by investigating how the WPA spent its funding; and in June 1939 Flanagan's project was held hostage, with the House refusing to pass the 1939–40 Relief Bill unless the FTP was abolished. Association with New Deal propaganda had made it a particular target. For the same reason the same measure was used to kill the United States Film Service (USFS) the following year. Dramatizing the government's public health initiatives, USFS's *The Fight for Life* (1940) attracted the same charges of electioneering that had been levelled at *The Plow* and *The River*, prompting Congress to use the 1940–1 Relief Bill to deny Lorentz any further funds.[127] The other projects were allowed to continue, but only in modified form. The Writers Project was only saved because of the overwhelmingly positive reception awarded to the States Guides, and the fact that there were still volumes to complete. Alsberg himself was fired. Further provisions attached to the 1939–40 Bill meant that anyone employed on WPA projects for more than eighteen months had to be dismissed, and loyalty oaths were required of any new workers. With control also transferred to the states, these constraints effectively drained the projects of any grand ambition to transform American culture.

In the end though, it was the Second World War as much as censorship which ended the unique experiments of the 1930s. Cahill sought to preserve the FAP by demonstrating its value to national defence, with art workers decorating service clubs, building training aids and making posters for local military bases.[128] But creative arts thereby gave way to practical arts and, with over 80 per cent of FAP work relating to defence studies and public information by March 1942, it became the Graphics Section of the War Services Program. Likewise, once the American Guides were completed in 1941, the FWP was soon split into the tortuously named Writers' Unit of the War Service Division of WPA and the Writers' Phase of the Morale Service Project of the War Services Program. Only a few individual Music Projects continued by performing at Army camps. Stryker's Historical Section briefly survived a transfer to the Office of War Information in 1942, shifting its focus toward 'optimistic' photographs of American workers in an effort to capture a sense of the nation's determination; but even this ended in 1943. Indeed, as early as 1939, the Treasury's Section's Edward Bruce was conscious of a feeling in communities that, in the light of the growing emergency, 'we don't want to be bothered with art and now is the time to close out this fancy piece of French pastry'.[129] This sentiment only intensified after Pearl Harbor. With post offices the centre of recruitment drives and the sale of war bonds, local postmasters were justifiably anxious about any sign of 'unnecessary' government expenditure. Murals such as Stefan Hirsh's painting on the 'importance of communication to wartime morale' for Bonneville, Mississippi, sought to mark the Section's patriotic value. But the fact that the government was also cutting back its building programme left the Section with little to paint, and it was not long before appropriations for 'decoration' were denied. Edward Bruce's death in 1943, following a heart attack, ended the battle to save the Section. In any accord, all the projects had been reduced significantly as the artists themselves left to take jobs in defence plants or join the military.

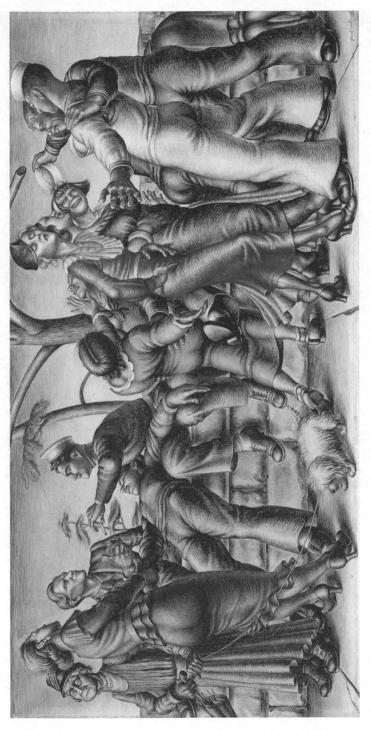

Figure 5.3 'What shall we do with the drunken sailor?' Paul Cadmus's controversial *The Fleet's In!* (1933: Naval Historical Center, Washington Navy Yard, Washington DC).

Paul Cadmus, *The Fleet's In!* (1933)

Amidst all the furore over government-sponsored art, it is easy to get the impression that politics was everything when it came to censorship in the 1930s. Paul Cadmus's *The Fleet's In!*, however, serves as a reminder that 'traditional' controversies surrounding sex and sexuality were never fully eclipsed.

In one of the most blatant acts of artistic censorship in the decade, Cadmus's oil painting of sailors on shore leave was confiscated by the United States Navy, just days before its intended display at the Corcoran Gallery in Washington DC in April 1934. The exhibit had been organized by Edward Bruce, showcasing nearly 500 works with a view to generating enthusiasm for the PWAP. Cadmus, then an unknown, unemployed artist living in New York, had completed two canvases while working for the PWAP on a salary of $34 a week, and was invited to display them both. *Greenwich Village Cafeteria* provided 'a rowdy account of Stewart's Cafeteria on Christopher Street', while *The Fleet's In!* was an equally raucous depiction of sailors cavorting in Riverside Park, near the US Navy's anchorage on the Hudson River.[130]

Riverside Park was 'notorious' in the 1930s as a 'destination for sailors in search of sexual companionship'.[131] Having grown up on Riverside Drive, Cadmus had seen this himself, watching and envying 'the freedom of their lives and their lack of inhibitions'.[132] With acidic colours accentuating 'fleshy urgency', Cadmus's painting captured a mob of muscular sailors, clearly the worse for drink, carousing with prostitutes. In the centre, one gets a slap for groping a woman. Two others stand in the path of three women, who sport 'expressions of idiotic glee, flirtation and feigned disinterest respectively'.[133] A fourth sailor has collapsed in an intoxicated stupor across an officer's lap, while a curvaceous blonde attempts to hoist him up. Few faces are on view, and the sightline is set not at eye-level but at the level of the figures' waists, emphasizing their buttocks and groins. Cadmus admitted putting the sailors into skin-tight bell-bottoms, 'tighter clothes than they sometimes wore', because he 'loved the nude'.[134] The anticipation is that they will not be wearing those clothes for long.

The carousing, moreover, is not entirely heterosexual. The emphasis on male 'gluteal preponderance' was itself testimony to Cadmus's erotic idealization of the masculine body; and on the left is a well-dressed male civilian who seems to share that viewpoint. George Chauncey in *Gay New York* quotes a 1933 study of 'sexual abnormalities', that listed the characteristic features of the male homosexual as including 'plucked eyebrows, rouged cheeks' and 'marcelled, blondlined hair'.[135] Wearing a bright-red tie as a further period sign of the so-called 'pansy', Cadmus's civilian personified this entirely; and he proffers a Lucky Strike cigarette to an interested marine. As one recent commentator has put it, *The Fleet's In!* suggests more than one answer to the question, 'what shall we do with the drunken sailor?'.[136]

For incensed retired admiral Hugh Rodman, Cadmus's 'disgraceful orgy' was a 'libel' that he wanted 'immediately destroyed'.[137] At his urging, the assistant secretary of the navy, Henry Latrobe Roosevelt, removed the canvas from the Corcoran and took it to his home. It became, of course, a media *succès de scandale*. Having had the painting professionally photographed, Cadmus was able to provide newspapers with good reproductions, which then appeared on front pages across the country. Suppression made it famous. It also generated a national discussion about what sailors really did get up to on shore leave. Rodman and official publications such as *Our Navy* challenged the 'truth' of the painting, claiming it was 'utterly without foundation in fact', and making counterclaims about the 'virtues of the American sailor' as morally fit, sober and self-restrained.[138] Most of the press coverage, however, ridiculed this. The *New York Daily News* was typical in declaring that 'the shore-leave activities so vividly pictured by Mr Cadmus go with the fighting man's trade'. Libidinousness and drunkenness were, in fact, celebrated as 'salty proof' of the sailor's virility.[139] The bulging muscles that Cadmus painted were read not as homoeroticism, but a 'sign of masculine vitality'. Asking quite directly 'Should Sailors Be Sissies?' editorials mocked Rodman, suggesting that the sailors he seemed to valorize, those who 'hurry alone to the Public Library or the museums on shore leave', were not 'he-men' enough to defend the country.[140] As Richard Meyer notes, in the 'greatest irony', Cadmus's painting was thus 'defended as a scene of normative masculinity', while the admiral's sanitised image of the sailor was 'ridiculed as effeminate'.[141]

The homosexual encounter in the left-hand side was always absent from contemporary discussion of the painting. Even as Rodman attacked Cadmus for his 'sordid, depraved imagination', Cadmus's own homosexuality remained unspoken.[142] But he certainly recognized the scandal for the impetus it gave his career. Cadmus followed *The Fleet's In!* with a string of ambitious paintings including others which played with homoeroticism as in *Horseplay* (1935) and *Gilding the Acrobats* (1935). His first one-man exhibition, at New York's Midtown Galleries, broke attendance records and sold all works on display. He also caused a stir with his 1938 post office mural for Richmond, Virginia, when the immodesty of one of the Native American men in *Pocahontas Rescues John Smith* was covered only by the particularly long nose of a fox-skin loincloth.[143] However provocative, Cadmus was vital enough to be counted by *Life* as one of the 'five most prominent American painters', and by *Newsweek* as one who would 'someday inherit the togas of Benton, Wood and Curry'.[144] After the Second World War, however, his fortunes declined sharply. His literary, illustrationist style fell out of critical favour, and it was not until the 1970s that Cadmus was reclaimed by America's gay community. In 1980, the government finally retrieved *The Fleet's In!* from the private club to which Henry Roosevelt had illegally 'bequeathed' it in 1936. In a final irony, it was officially awarded to the Department of the Navy and installed in the public galleries of the Naval Historical Center in Washington DC; continuing, as Meyer suggests, to 'satirize "the hard-earned experience" of navy life that the center seeks to enshrine'.[145]

Further Considerations

One major issue that I have specifically not addressed in this chapter is the matter of quality. 'Accounts of the various projects', as Bruce Bustard notes, 'are filled with stories of inept or long-in-the-tooth individuals passing themselves off as actors, writers, artists, or musicians, so they could receive relief payments'.[146] It was true that many 'mediocre' artistic objects filled government storerooms as a result of project directors being swayed more by a person's desperate need than their skills. Yet artists like Cadmus, Shahn, Refregier and writers like Wright and Ellison undercut the claim of New Deal opponents that relief workers were only unemployed because they lacked talent.

With a weekly pay cheque coming from a democratically-elected government, many relief-artists worked with the sense that 'the people' themselves were their patrons, and much of the energy and vibrancy displayed in project works can be attributed to this sensibility. As Robert Cronbach said of his time as a WPA sculptor, the New Deal artist often believed that he was 'part of an important art movement'. Knowing that his project work 'would be seen by his peers, and also by a fair section of the public and the art world', Cronbach was convinced that 'Project sculpture should at this time be his major sculpture'.[147] Generalizations about the lack of 'masterpieces' produced with government money seem to forget about Davis's *Swing Landscape*, Lange's *Migrant Mother* or Welles's 'Voodoo' *Macbeth*. It should also be considered that the 'search for masterpieces' itself ran against the grain of the projects' ambitions. Cahill, for instance, considered such an attitude to be a critic's idea that bore little relation to what 'the people' wanted from art. As he saw it, the greatest contribution of the arts projects was to emphasize 'the principle that it is not the solitary genius but a sound and general movement which maintains art as a vital functioning part of any cultural scheme'.[148]

The quality of artworks produced under government patronage is something which can only truly be determined by considering the merits of any individual piece, or the value of what was documented. Hundreds of thousands of plays, books, murals, sculptures, recordings and designs exist to be examined. Books like *Such as Us: Southern Voices of the Thirties* (1978) have also compiled project work that was collected but never published at the time, and much more has now been made accessible through the Internet. This chapter has mentioned just a few examples, but hopefully serves as a framework for placing other works into context and for considering the complex factors that shaped them.

The Cultural Legacy of the 1930s

Determining the cultural legacy of any given decade can become something of a parlour game, observing those aspects which have survived into the present day. David Hanks, for example, identifies the Nike Airmax and its 'Swoosh' trademark as a continuation of the connotation of streamlined aesthetics with speed, while Michele Hilmes rightly measures the debt that soap operas and sitcoms owe to the innovations of *Amos 'n' Andy*.[1] Among the most enduring creations of the 1930s, one would definitely have to count Mickey Mouse (even if Mickey was somewhat displaced in the Second World War by Donald Duck, whose indignantly aggressive temperament suited the national mood) and Monopoly (which, intriguingly, was used as an educational game at Columbia University by Rex Tugwell and Roy Stryker before being redesigned by unemployed plumbing engineer Charles Darrow and sold to Parker Brothers in 1935).[2] Moreover, from his appearance on the cover of *Action Comics* No. 1 in June 1938, Jerry Siegel and Joe Shuster's creation of Superman has remained an inspiring phenomenon, translated through comic books, radio serials, television series, graphic novels, toys, cartoons and films, with *Superman Returns* (2006) being the latest instalment in the cinematic franchise, referencing its 1930s origins in elements such as the Frank Lloyd Wright-inspired design of the Daily Planet offices.

Ranked alongside such ostensibly 'trivial' survivals, the political legacy of the 1930s appears much more substantial. The concrete achievements of the New Deal are still imprinted on the political economy of the United States, from the regulation of the banking sector, through the price-support loans provided to farmers, to the framework of labour–industrial relations established by the Wagner Act. Despite concern as to its long-term sustainability, Social Security remains the 'heart' of the Rooseveltian reform legacy, even proving

impervious to George W. Bush's efforts to make its 'partial privatization' the centrepiece of his domestic agenda.[3] Indeed, perhaps even
more than its liberal defenders, the critics of the New Deal have credited it with a far-reaching legacy: whether having 'sustained the hege-
mony of corporate capitalism' (which, from the New Left perspective
of the 1960s was an undesirable consequence), or having set the
American economy 'inexorably on the wrong course' by creating a
broker state wherein 'interest groups simply bid up the level of government spending to benefit themselves' (as right-wing critics have
argued since the 1970s).[4] In addition, William Leuchtenberg's *In the
Shadow of FDR* (1983, revised 2001), serves to remind readers of
Franklin Roosevelt's transformation of the presidency itself, and how
his posthumous reputation has affected all his successors.

Isolating the 1930s

There remains, however, a sense of the 1930s as 'boxed off' from the
rest of the twentieth century, with the Second World War demarcating
a cut-off point. This is true of political history, as in Alan Brinkley's
analysis of *The End of Reform* which observes that in the postwar
years, 'few liberals any longer expressed much interest or faith in many
of the reform ideas that had once been central to the New Deal'.[5] The
flurry of social legislation that marked Lyndon Johnson's 'Great
Society' in the 1960s certainly extended the welfare state, but postwar
liberalism rejected earlier 'radical' concerns with 'restructuring the
economy' or experimenting in 'statist planning', and committed the
government instead to 'providing a healthy environment in which
the corporate world could flourish and in which the economy could
sustain "full employment" '.[6] Likewise, by 1945 the potentially radical
labour movement of earlier years was 'on its way to assuming its
modern form as a highly bureaucratized interest group'.[7]

In most cultural assessments of the 1930s, this feeling of movements
coming to an end or accommodating themselves to the demands of
wartime and the postwar world, is even more pronounced. The Second
World War definitely had an effect. The remaining Federal Arts
Projects, for instance, directed their energies toward defence work,
with artists producing posters, writers developing civil defence
brochures and bands performing at Army camps, until the WPA itself
ended in 1943 as enlistment and defence contracts alleviated unemployment. The war also affected the swing phenomena, as swing bands
and musicians enlisted, joined USO tours and made 'V'-discs (records

produced, by arrangement with the government, for the use of US military personnel overseas). As Lewis Erenberg notes, though, the swing units led by Artie Shaw in the Pacific and Glenn Miller in Europe altered the music's relation to American society: 'no longer was swing an outsider to the establishment'.[8] Moreover, the music became 'more organized as well as more sentimental', with increasingly 'regimented' arrangements and limited freedom for individual expression. This watered-down version, seemingly 'symptomatic of the lost energy' of the 1930s craze, in itself created disaffection. Young black musicians like Dizzie Gillespie, in particular, reacted against it with 'bebop' jazz: a frenetic, anxious and almost abstract style which 'reinvigorated the improvisatory power of the individual'.[9]

Postwar affluence also made Depression-era culture seem remote and out-of-date. The industrial design profession may have come of age, as designers and industry 'rushed into schemes for addressing the pent-up material desires of a population that had endured more than fifteen years of economic hardship'.[10] Yet, writes Jeffrey Miekle, as the 'consumption of flashy new products increased exponentially', the emphasis on 'structure and simplicity' in industrial design fell by the wayside. Characteristic of the 'explosion of products available in a lurid rainbow of colours and a steadily changing array of styles', the pastel colours, chrome ornamentation and ostentatious tailfins of 1950s automobiles encapsulated the desire of newly-empowered consumers to put the austerity of the prewar years behind them.[11] Architecture, on the other hand, saw a move in the opposite direction, embracing the austere lines of the International Style and its glass-box, steel-frame construction which emphasized 90-degree angles, in contrast to the flowing curves and nature-inspired architecture of Wright's prewar work. The first International Style skyscraper had actually been built in the 1930s, with the Philadelphia Saving Fund Society building in 1932 designed by George Howe and William Lescaze. But it was the building boom beginning in 1948 that elevated the 'anonymous glass box' to *the* architectural expression of corporate America's bullish desire to get on with 'the business of progress'.

Prosperity also delivered a setback to the film and radio industries. As average family incomes rose by 30 per cent, and three out of five Americans came to enjoy 'middle-class' status in the 1950s, television took a hold in more than thirty-five million homes. It competed directly with radio for advertising revenues, and many housewives treated the television set as a direct replacement, listening to it as they did their housework. Many primetime programmes subsequently abandoned radio for television. Hollywood was hit even harder. Between 1946 and 1960, the average weekly attendance at American cinemas fell from ninety to forty million patrons. It was not only television that caused this: the growth of suburbia took audiences away from downtown cinemas, and the public had the income to indulge in alternative leisure pursuits. In any event, the postwar years saw the end of America's 'intense love affair' with the movies and the radio that had so characterized the 1930s.[12]

Most significant though in seeking to consign the decade's culture to the past, was the deliberate denigration of the Popular Front's achievements during the climate of Cold War anti-communism. By the late 1940s, many of the cultural developments of the previous decade had been repainted in stark shades of 'Red' and subsequently repudiated, 'even by those who created them'.[13] The Hollywood blacklist was just the most prominent example of this in operation, instigated after the House Un-American Activities Committee came, first in 1947 and then in 1951, to allege that members of the Communist Party had turned the movies into 'subversive' propaganda. As several hundred witnesses from the industry were called to testify to their past political sympathies, former involvement with Popular Front organizations proved harmful to their careers, unless they renounced that past and demonstrated a 'change of heart' by naming colleagues who had also associated with the cultural Left in the 1930s. The process was not only encouraged by right-wing anti-communists like Eugene Lyons or Joseph McCarthy, but also by former socialists themselves, especially those who had been repelled by the authoritarianism of Stalinism. The 'standard narrative' of postwar liberal anti-communists became a 'morality tale', depicting the 1930s as a time when many writers were 'intense, horatory, naïve, simplistic and passionate but, after the Moscow trials and the Soviet Nazi pact, disenchanted and reflective'.[14] It supported the impression of a 'Red Decade' in which 'ideological commitment' was presumed to have been central to the arts (rather than just the limited experience of a few New York intellectuals), and in which the Communist Party had been a 'powerful direct cultural patron'.[15] As early as 1942, Alfred Kazin in On Native Grounds claimed that in the 1930s the left-wing writer had 'surrendered his craft' to political considerations 'beyond literature'; while Philip Rahv dismissed all social realist writing as 'the literature of a party [the CPUSA] disguised as the literature of a class'.[16] Such a characterization only exacerbated hostility toward the dominant currents of prewar culture, isolating 'the thirties' as an aberrant moment 'when politics captured the arts, when writers went left, Hollywood turned Red, and painters, musicians and photographers' had abandoned 'art' for 'social-minded' work.[17]

When the postwar years saw a broader denial of the value of the 'political' in art, the culture of the 1930s was further marginalized. For example, the school of New Criticism, named by John Crowe Ransom in 1941 but originating in Cleanth Brooks and Robert Penn Warren's 1938 textbook, *Understanding Poetry*, reacted against the Marxist trope of criticism which judged 'past and current literature according to its awareness of and involvement in the class struggle'.[18] The dominant trend by mid-century, the New Criticism was one of pure aestheticism, rejecting the study of literature in political terms, or indeed in any terms other than as a 'work of art'. Art criticism also aligned itself with this objective, with the modernist abstractions of painters such as Jackson Pollock, Willem de Kooning, Mark Rothko and Arshile Gorky championed as work which 'referred only to itself', presenting the 'arrangement of and invention spaces, surfaces, shapes, colors, etc., to the exclusion of anything outside of itself', especially the exclusion of anything explicitly political.[19] With this about-turn in critical commentary, proponents of abstract art were particularly disparaging of Regionalism and social realism. Regionalism was seen as diametrically opposed to abstract art, given the determination of practitioners like Benton to produce 'inspiring' work which 'reflected the American people's life and history in a way which the people could comprehend'.[20] Likewise criticized for being driven by 'a message', the prewar mural movement was dismissed as 'a debacle of class-conscious art, regional scene painting, Americana, WPA history and other "communicating modes"'.[21] Lumping together all those who 'had been trying to paint society' as 'Marxists', Harold Rosenberg presented the artistic endeavours of the 1930s as having been stunted by Communist art theory. When, according to Rosenberg, artists like Jackson Pollock 'decided to paint . . . just to paint', the 'gesture on the canvas' thereby became 'a gesture of liberation'.[22]

This celebration of avant-garde modernism also led to an assault on Popular Front culture as 'hopelessly middlebrow'.[23] It was a critique that again originated in the 1930s itself, with the German-Marxist émigrés of the Frankfurt School, most notably Theodor Adorno and Max Horkeimer, critical of the 'low level of aesthetic complexity and intellectual content' in the cultural products of film, radio and publishing.[24] It was then, however, expanded by America's anti-Stalinist intellectuals, particularly Clement Greenberg, Dwight Macdonald and

Robert Warshow. Greenberg championed the avant-garde by defining it in opposition to what he called 'kitsch': that which 'predigests art for the spectator and spares him the effort', providing 'a short cut to the pleasures of art' by specifically 'telling' the spectator how he should respond to it.[25] This chimed with Adorno's criticism of 'music appreciation' radio programmes which encouraged listeners to feel good about themselves simply for 'appreciating' the version of 'high culture' they were being sold. In Macdonald's analysis, such cultural forms, characterized by standardization, formula and the built-in reaction, became the 'Midcult'; neither 'mass culture' nor 'high culture', but an 'inauthentic' bastardization of both. *Our Town* by Thornton Wilder (see Chapter 1) was cited by Macdonald as a prime example in its theatricalized manipulation of an audience's sentiments.[26] Finally, in his 1947 essay defining 'The Legacy of the 30s', Warshow linked the 'Midcult' explicitly to the culture of the Popular Front. For Warshow, works like *The Grapes of Wrath*, both novel and film, were guilty of being designed first and foremost to provoke a 'conventionalized' social–political reaction. In his analysis the 'Communist–liberal–New Deal movement of the 1930s' was to blame for creating a fundamentally disingenuous culture.[27] Clearly, such a perspective suggested, the culture of the 1930s was not worthy of a 'legacy'.

Recovering the 1930s

The 'return of the repressed' began, with considerable nostalgia, in the folk music revival of the late 1950s and early 1960s. The catalyst for the 'great boom' was the Kingston Trio's recording of *Tom Dooley* in 1958, which placed folk back in the cultural limelight and prompted an intense burst of revivalism that lasted until 1965 at least. The emergence of Bob Dylan, as the self-created 'heir' to Woody Guthrie, generated new interest in the earlier Dust Bowl balladeer, especially when Dylan's *Song to Woody* 'placed him among the folk heroes who had "come with the dust and are gone with the wind"'.[28]

Interest in folk music had not ended in the 1930s; indeed, Pete Seeger's folksong quartet, The Weavers, had made hits in 1950 of Guthrie's *So Long, It's Been Good to Know Ya* and Leadbelly's *Goodnight, Irene*. However, the career of The Weavers had soon been terminated by McCarthyism when Seeger merited thirteen citations in *Red Channels: Communist Influence on Radio and Television*. Alan Lomax, too, found it expedient to spend much of the 1950s in England, away from the anti-communist witch-hunt. This short suppression, though, served to make the subsequent 'revival' seem even more 'fresh' and 'vital' – exploding onto the scene as a 'bracing contrast to McCarthyism and the consumption-obsessed culture of the 1950s'.[29] Some commentators have also argued that the discontinuity inflicted by the 'Red Scare' meant that much of the ideological freight that had been attached to folk music in the 1930s had, by 1958, been largely 'suppressed, abandoned, forgotten or lost', allowing the music to be rearticulated for a new generation without its Depression-era baggage.[30] Certainly many who were 'newly attracted' to the music did shun its political connections, but equally there were those like Dylan who aimed at being topical (if not expressly 'political'), writing songs about current events including the Civil Rights movement.[31] Notably, too, providing a further link to the Popular Front, it was John Hammond who produced Dylan's first album and convinced Columbia to sign him.[32]

This all helped to fuel renewed awareness of the culture of the 1930s. The novels of Nathanael West, Henry Roth, Horace McCoy and Daniel Fuchs were 'rediscovered', while Agee and Evans' *Let Us Now Praise Famous Men* finally found its audience after the 1941 edition had sold little over 1,000 copies and 'fizzled out of print'.[33] In fact, the 1960 reissue of *Famous Men* became something of a 'bible' for the thousands of white students who participated in the 1964 Freedom Summer campaign to register Mississippi's black voters. One such civil rights worker, Mary King, recalled how she 'could identify' with Agee's anxiety about his ability 'to convey the reality of the people about whom he was writing', and how this 'limned my own struggle to be effective as I worried that I might be an inter-loper'.[34] Such a sense of identification with the dispossessed of the 1930s was also vibrantly extended by Arthur Penn's 1967 film of *Bonnie and Clyde*. This account of Bonnie Parker and Clyde Barrow, who, in 1932, had gone on a 'two-year binge of robbery and murder in the Southwest and Midwest', presented an undeniably 'romantic' view of the truly vicious desperadoes, but Robert Newman and David Benton had deliberately crafted their screenplay to capture the imagination of a youthful audience that in the 1960s was growing increasing alienated from society.[35] Early scenes of Clyde and an evicted farmer (straight out of *The Grapes of Wrath*) taking turns to shoot at a bank's notice of foreclosure, established the sense of the outlaws' acts expressing 'the legitimate frustrations of many under-privileged Americans', and celebrated their 'defying the Establish-ment'.[36] In Newman and Benton's minds, Parker and Barrow had

Figure C.1 Counter-culture heroes of the 1930s? Warren Beatty and Faye Dunaway in Arthur Penn's *Bonnie and Clyde* (1967: Warner Bros./The Kobal Collection).

been 'cultural rebels': 'people whose style sets them apart from their time and place so that they seemed odd and aberrant to the general run of society'.[37] They rewrote history to that effect with a scene in which C. W. Moss (a fictionalized member of the Barrow gang) incurs his father's outrage, not because of his involvement in crime, but because he has acquired a tattoo. It is *this* transgression which leads his father to sell out Bonnie and Clyde to the police, setting up their fatal ambush. That the 'luckless couple' are betrayed because their 'freakish style' offended a father's 'sense of propriety', was a moment carefully calculated to resonate with a generation whose 'parents were "offended" by long hair, Woodstock, rock and roll, smoking pot and dropping out'.[38] It was an approach that clearly worked, with one critic even going as far as to suggest that there 'is an unmistakable affinity between the euphoria of LSD and the kicks that Bonnie and Clyde get from robbing banks'.[39] The film was so enthusiastically received by young audiences that it even prompted a 1930s-inspired revival in fashion, with maxi-dresses, wide-lapelled pin-stripe suits and fedora hats becoming all the rage.

The opening frames of *Bonnie and Clyde* defined the period setting by interspersing the credits with sepia-tinted photographs, portraits of poor and desperate families taken from the Farm Security Administration files. Now elevated to iconography of 'the thirties', these too had been 'recovered' in the 1960s, when curator Edward Steichen mounted an exhibit of FSA photographs at the New York Museum of Modern Art, entitled *The Bitter Years, 1935–1941*. Appropriately the exhibition coincided with renewed interest in government support for the arts. In the 1950s, when Nelson Rockefeller, then an undersecretary in Eisenhower's Department of Health, Education and Welfare, had proposed the formation of a National Council of the Arts, it had been widely derided in Congress. But Jacqueline Kennedy's love for the arts had helped change some attitudes in Washington, evident in the creation in 1963 of the 'Art in Architecture' programme. Like the Public Works of Art programme before it, this mandated the allocation of 0.5 per cent of the construction costs of federal buildings toward artistic decoration. Then, forging ahead with the Democrat dominance in Congress that followed John F. Kennedy's assassination, Lyndon Johnson was able to sign the National Foundation on the Arts and Humanities Act of September 1965, creating both the National Endowment for the Arts (NEA) and the National Endowment for the Humanities (NEH) as part of his 'Great Society'.

With emergency relief no longer a consideration, advocates of the NEA and NEH could openly draw on the philosophies and ambitions which the New Deal project directors had sought to express in more difficult circumstances. Roosevelt's wish to increase accessibility to the arts was repeated in the NEA's vision of making 'artistic excellence available to all Americans'.[40] Hallie Flanagan's insistence that only a 'free people' could have created the arts projects and that they were 'a democratic answer to both fascism and communism', found resonance in Johnson's affirmation that during the Cold War the government had a duty to encourage 'freedom of thought, imagination and inquiry' by sustaining the nation's 'creative talent'.[41] The 1965 legislation also gave even more attention to the issue of cultural pluralism, affirming art's ability to foster 'mutual respect for the diverse beliefs and values of all persons and groups', while strengthening the nation's 'rich cultural heritage'.[42] Since its foundation, the NEA has made more than 120,000 grants, including critical support for the American Film Institute, the Sundance Film Festival, PBS's *Great Performance Series*, and a long-running Folk Arts programme that has funded many local festivals (and which, for many years, was headed by Bess Lomax Hawes, sister of Alan Lomax). It has also helped fulfil at least part of Flanagan's ambitions, supporting the expansion of non-profit professional theatres in the United States from just fifty in 1965 to 'a network of 600 today'.[43] Recent plans by the NEH, moreover, revisited the concept of community art centres when, in 1998, William Ferris announced an initiative to 'establish ten regional humanities centers around the United States'. An updated version of the American Guides series was also proposed, in the form of 'online encyclopedias for each state'. 'Embodying many of the goals the FWP had articulated earlier', the NEH embraced the idea that through exploring 'how a "sense of place" infuses and enriches American history, culture and traditions', we 'discover our cultural roots and affirm our common bonds as Americans'.[44]

Revisiting the 1930s

Since the 1960s, subsequent revisitations have continued to address issues raised both by the cultural debates of the 1930s and by the 'suppression' of the decade's culture in the postwar discourse. Woody Allen in *The Purple Rose of Cairo* (1985), for instance, evaluates the meaning of escapism in popular entertainment. For Cecilia, an unemployed woman with an unfaithful husband living in Depression-hit New Jersey, the cinema becomes a refuge. 'The Purple Rose of Cairo' is itself the title of a 'champagne comedy' of elegance and adventure which the infatuated Cecilia watches again and again as a 'desperate evasion' of reality.[45] It is, as David Grimsted observes, the very definition of 'kitsch'.[46] Cecilia, however, realizes the inauthenticity of the cinematic illusion when one of the characters in the movie, Tom Baxter, magically steps out of the screen into her world. Tom is 'honest, dependable, courageous, romantic and a greater kisser', but he is a fictional creation, recognized by Cecilia as 'some kind of phantom'. This is reinforced when Gil Shepherd (the actor who plays Tom) comes to try and compel Tom to return to his place in 'The Purple Rose'. Cecilia now sees both sides of the Hollywood illusion. Tom takes her into the screen, into a montage of a 'night on the town' which is 'as beautiful and romantic' as Cecilia expects, but in which 'the champagne is really ginger ale'. She understands 'the overplotted, falsely reassuring, pretty unreality which the screen projects'.[47] On the other hand, Gil puts on the charm to woo Cecilia in a deceitful effort to get her to choose him over Tom, and thus persuade Tom to go back to the screen. When

Cecilia's dreams of escaping to Hollywood are then shattered by Gil, she is made cruelly aware of the film star's 'egotism, complete untrustworthiness, and real indifference to the audience of which she is a part'.[48] Yet Allen ends his film with a 'stunningly ambiguous effect'.[49] Reluctant to give into her misery and return to her husband, Cecilia wanders numbly back into the cinema, where the 'new attraction' of *Top Hat* sees Fred Astaire singing Irving Berlin's *Cheek-to-Cheek* to Ginger Rogers. 'Despite all she's learned of the duplicity and fraudulence existing on both sides of the screen', Cecilia's joy and adulation is rekindled, and she is once more able to 'forget her troubles a little'.[50] But she is not an unthinking dupe of the mass culture of kitsch. Indulging the illusion and the glamour once again is a choice she makes consciously because of the consolation it provides, a dream of 'heaven' and 'happy endings' that 'protects her from cynicism and despair'.[51]

For Arthur Miller, it was the illusions that the Great Depression had shattered, rather than the ones it created, that mattered most. *The American Clock*, first performed in 1980, assesses how the Depression shook 'the structure of the world' in general, and America's confidence 'in its own discourse of progress' in particular.[52] Like Allen, Miller recognizes that the 'stagnating and defeated spirit' of the Depression had been 'intolerable', and that Americans had 'found hope where we could, in illusions too, provided they showed promise'.[53] A 1986 staging of the play appropriately combined the text with upbeat songs of the 1930s, such as *Life's Just a Bowl of Cherries*, underlining Miller's thesis that 'America improvised her way through' without giving into despair.[54] However, the central image of the play is of time running out on a society where the myth of 'the individual, with no obligation beyond self-definition' was no longer sustainable.[55] *The American Clock* explores how Americans survived the Depression by arriving at a 'new sense of interdependence' in which 'connections and responsibilities had to be acknowledged in order for everyone to survive'.[56] Adapted from the oral histories collected in Studs Terkel's *Hard Times* (itself part of the 'recovery' of the decade, published to great acclaim in 1970), Miller conveyed this sense of shared experience by creating an ambitious 'montage' in which the personal stories of forty-six named characters overlap. These range from an African American woman who believes in Communism 'as a sane response to the times', to a cartoonist drawing Superman whose world is 'largely built upon well-meaning fantasy'. Lee Baum is Miller's own autobiographical counterpart, who needs to sign on for relief before he can join the Federal Writers Project.[57] Baum's story becomes central, for the 'significance' of the Depression had never left Miller. His own father, the successful owner of a garment factory in New York, had lost his business in the Crash and then lost the family home. Miller could never forget how his father succumbed to a sense of hopelessness, and the strain this put on his parents' relationship. The shadow of this experience not only informed his plays, but also his belief that the Depression had fundamentally changed American culture – expressed in *The American Clock* as the pervasive fear 'that suddenly, without warning, it may all fall apart again'.[58] Miller created *The American Clock* concerned that, in the self-absorption of the 1970s and the 'return to selfish and heedless attitudes' in the wealth-driven 1980s of Reagan's America, those 'brutal lessons' learned in the Depression were in danger of being forgotten.[59]

Tim Robbins has also shared Miller's determination not to let the past be repeated. When in 1995 the NEA was threatened with 'outright elimination' by the Republican-dominated Congress and its *Contract With America*, Robbins responded with *Cradle Will Rock* (1999). To comment on the new moral censorship aroused by the NEA's funding of artists such as Robert Clark Young, Andres Serrano and Robert Mapplethorpe, he revisited the politicized censorship of the 1930s, weaving together not only the cancellation of Marc Blitzstein's musical play, but also the desecration of Diego Rivera's Rockefeller Center mural and the determination of the Dies Committee to shut down the Federal Theatre Project. Concluding with a scene of a small coffin, representing the 'death' of the Federal Theatre, being carried from the past into modern-day Times Square with all its garish advertising signs, *Cradle Will Rock* expresses concern that 'art' again faced a death sentence from the combined forces of 'right-wing congressmen, rich industrialists and tawdry commerce'.[60]

The following year, Joel and Ethan Coen released a rather more light-hearted 'romp' through Depression-era folk culture in *O Brother, Where Art Thou?* (2000), borrowing their title from the movie John L. Sullivan intended to make in *Sullivan's Travels* (see Chapter 2). The Coen Brothers' story of three escaped convicts who inadvertently become country music stars playfully throws in references to various 1930's films as well as real life aspects of the decade such as 'Baby Face' Nelson and the TVA. Yet there is also a serious side in its engagement with questions of cultural authenticity. Homer Stokes, a duplicitous 'reform' politician who is also the head of the Ku Klux Klan, reveals his hatred of 'miscegenated music' when he exposes the presence of a black performer, Tommy Johnson, among the hugely popular 'Soggy Bottom

Boys'. Yet in an earlier scene when Stokes and his Klansmen are about to lynch Tommy, the KKK themselves join in a chorus of 'O Death': a song that had been popularized by bluegrass singer Ralph Stanley, but which derived originally from an African American slave spiritual.[61] Thus, as Sean Chadwell suggests, questions about racial appropriation and the white South's hypocritical denial of its racially mixed cultural heritage (issues which had provoked debate in the 1930s from *Porgy and Bess* to the States Guides) come to bear again in *O Brother*.

Most commonly, however, Hollywood's recent reconstructions of the 1930s have used sporting events to convey symbolic narratives of the Depression years. *The Legend of Bagger Vance* (2000) depicts it through golf, *Cinderella Man* (2005) with boxing and *Seabiscuit* (2003) uses horse-racing. Given that the idea of a 'New Deal' itself drew on the metaphor of a card game, sporting analogies are not entirely inappropriate, and it is true that Americans in the Depression did invest such sports events with socio-political significance. The legendary 1938 rematch between boxers Max Schmeling and Joe Louis was widely portrayed as a fight between 'a Nazi whose defeat was essential' and a black American whom the nation rallied behind as 'a symbol of democracy' (somewhat ironically, given the segregated status of African-Americans at the time).[62] *Cinderella Man* makes a similar case for Jim Braddock's 1935 victory over Max Baer. Director Ron Howard, however, extended the symbolism further, 'fascinated by the way Braddock's story seemed to illuminate how the nation coped – by hanging tight to the thinnest threads of strength, optimism and commitment'.[63] Thus, Braddock's life is inflated to *the* story of the Depression. Injured in 1929, his life falls apart to the point where he is unable to support his family without swallowing his pride and applying for relief; until, 'just as Roosevelt's New Deal began to kick into high gear', he is once again given a fighting chance.[64] Likewise, *Seabiscuit* (2003) makes a 'populist celebration of the "underdog" who overcomes enormous odds', out of the true story of the eponymous racehorse who became a national sensation in 1937 when he took on the champion 'War Admiral' in a much-anticipated match-race.[65] Gary Ross's film turns that race into a pointed contest of the 'East Coast establishment' of bankers and their thorough-breds, against the 'ragtag team' of a 'horse that's too small, a jockey too tall, a trainer too old, and an owner too dumb to realize it'.[66] Even more than *Cinderella Man*, *Seabiscuit* insists on the parallels between this story and that of the New Deal, using historian David McCullough to explain how 'men who were broken' by the Depression, in the same way that

'Seabiscuit' was written off by her original owners, were given a
second chance to demonstrate their skills and their fighting spirit. A
sequence in which jockey Red Pollard is 'adopted' by millionaire
Charles Howard and receives a much-needed decent meal, is followed
immediately by a series of historical photographs of soup kitchens
and people receiving government relief, with McCullough's voiceover
stressing that 'for the first time in a long time, someone cared'. A final
photograph of Roosevelt meeting a grateful farmer makes it clear who
that someone was. As Graham Barnfield observes, the subtext seems
to be, 'If only it was more like that now'.[67]

Indeed, this now appears to be the 'official' cultural memory of the
1930s, as embodied and sanctified in the Franklin Delano Roosevelt
Memorial in Washington DC. Not that the memorial was without controversy. First authorized in 1946, it took until 1959 to agree on a site
on the edge of the Tidal Basin, and until 1975 to agree on a design.
Planned by San Francisco landscape architect, Lawrence Halprin, the
expansive memorial park was finally dedicated in May 1997. As the
National Park Service acknowledges, it is 'a memorial not only to FDR,
but also to the era he represents'.[68] Halprin's design involves a series of
open air 'rooms' which progress from the president's inauguration and
'messages of hope to a bewildered nation', through the array of New
Deal social programmes, their names and images inscribed on pillars
and bas reliefs; to a ten-foot statue of Roosevelt, commanding over a
world at war; and finally to a relief depicting his funeral cortege, encapsulating the 'sense of loss and grief' which came with the death of 'a
much-loved president on whom so many had counted'.[69] In historian
Robert Dallek's mind, at least, the effect is to capture 'the man's buoyant
optimism, his confidence in himself and his country; his refusal to
believe that America had seen its best days; [and] his conviction that the
nation's future greatness would exceed its past achievements'.[70]

Yet by the early 1990s, when construction began, complaints arose
that the memorial made no mention of FDR's disability. The National
Organization on Disability, in particular, began lobbying hard, insisting that the nation should not ignore 'his extraordinary courage in
achieving so much for the country and the world despite his paralysis'.[71] Some amends were made when small wheels were added to the
back of the chair on which Neil Estern's imposing, larger-than-life
statue is seated. By 1997, however, it was clear that this was not enough
to appease critics and President Clinton mandated the creation of an
additional statue of Roosevelt in a wheelchair, with Halprin adding a
new room to his design as a 'Prologue'. Those who opposed this move

Figure C.2 Contrasting statues of the 32nd President by Robert Graham and Neil Estern at the Franklin D. Roosevelt Memorial in Washington DC.

criticized it as 'political correctness', but those who favoured it emphasized an interpretation of the 1930s that narratives like *Seabiscuit*,
Cinderella Man, *The American Clock* and countless other representations have understood: that it had been a time when the nation 'desperately wanted to believe in miracles'.[72] Once Roosevelt had become
a presidential candidate, he had falsely but persuasively projected an
image of 'successful rehabilitation' from his polio-inflicted disability,
and he maintained this image for virtually all his presidency.[73] Most
people in the 1930s believed 'he had fully recovered from his paralysis'. It was that belief, that miraculous recoveries were indeed possible,
that gave Roosevelt his 'special hold on a country trying to overcome
the Depression'.[74]

The narrative implied by the two statues now at the Roosevelt
Memorial – from the frail, diminutive and crippled Roosevelt of the
'Prologue', to the imposing figure of powerful bearing, seemingly possessed of a 'kind of sublime confidence', steering the country through
the Depression and the Second World War – is itself suggestive of the
popular cultural myths of the 1930s. It is not far removed from the
'miracle' of the human, frail, everyman Clark Kent transforming into
Superman, the saviour of 'truth, justice and the American way'. Was it
by chance that Estern chose to model his statue on a photograph of
Roosevelt wearing a cape? Certainly, it is no coincidence that
Roosevelt on one hand and Superman on the other, have always
remained the most resonant icons of the 1930s.

Notes

Introduction

1. Terry A. Cooney, *Balancing Acts: American Thought and Culture in the 1930s*, p. 211; Lawrence Levine, The Folklore of Industrial Society: Popular Culture and Its Audience', *The American Historical Review*, 97.5 (December 1992), 1399.
2. David Kennedy, *Freedom from Fear: The American People in Depression and War, 1929–1945* (New York: Oxford University Press, 1999), p. 52.
3. Ibid., pp. 351–2.
4. James Patterson, *America's Struggle Against Poverty 1900–1980* (Cambridge, MA: Harvard University Press, 1981), pp. 41–2.
5. Kennedy, *Freedom from Fear*, p. 168.
6. Ibid., p. 311.
7. Cooney, *Balancing Acts*, p. 211.
8. Kennedy, *Freedom from Fear*, p. 222.
9. Richard Pells, *Radical Visions and American Dreams: Culture and Social Thought in the Depression Years* (New York: Harper and Row, 1973), p. 169.
10. George Novack, 'American Intellectuals and the Crisis', *New International* 3.1 (February, 1936), available at: http://www.marxists.org/archive/novack/1936/02/x01.htm.
11. Robert Schulman, *The Power of Political Art: The 1930s Literary Left Reconsidered* (Chapel Hill: University of North Carolina Press, 2000), p. 16.
12. Ibid., p. 20.
13. Quoted in ibid., p. 221.
14. Graham Barnfield, 'A Reversal of Fortune: *Culture and the Crisis*, Yesterday and Today' (December 2003) available at *Working Papers on the Web*: http://extra.shu.ac.uk/wpw/thirties/thirties%20barnfinal.html.
15. J. S. Hoffmann quoted in Albert E. Stone, 'Seward Collins and the *American Review*: Experiment in Pro–Fascism, 1933–37', *American Quarterly* 12.1 (Spring 1960), 6.
16. Steve Leikin, 'The Strange Career of Lawrence Dennis: Race and Far-Right Politics in the Great Depression', unpublished paper, 2007, p. 15.
17. Ibid., p. 5; Stone, 'Seward Collins', p. 7.
18. Leikin, 'The Strange Career', p. 18.
19. Quoted in Stone, 'Seward Collins', p. 8.

20. Kennedy, *Freedom from Fear*, pp. 236–9.
21. Collins, quoted Stone, 'Seward Collins', p. 7.
22. James P. Shenton, 'The Coughlin Movement and the New Deal', *Political Science Quarterly*, 73.3 (September 1958), 367.
23. See Alan Brinkley, *Voices of Protest: Huey Long, Father Coughlin and the Great Depression* (New York: Knopf, 1982).
24. Ibid., p. 260.
25. Michael Parrish, '1921–1941', in Stephen Whitfield (ed.), *A Companion to 20th Century America* (London: Blackwell, 2007), p. 48.
26. Paul Buhle, 'Louis C. Fraina/Lewis Corey and The Crisis of the Middle Class', *New Politics*, 5.17 (Summer 1994), available online at: http://www.wpunj.edu/newpol/issue17/buhle17.htm.
27. Pells, *Radical Visions*, p. 77.
28. Ibid., p. 77.
29. League of Professional Groups for Foster and Ford, *Culture and the Crisis* (1932), reprinted in Albert Fried (ed.), *Communism in America: A History in Documents* (New York: Columbia University Press, 1997), p. 11.
30. Ibid., p. 29.
31. Ibid., p. 11.
32. Ibid., p. 18.
33. Ibid., p. 29.
34. Ibid., p. 5.
35. Novack, 'American Intellectuals', n.p.
36. Buhle, 'The Crisis of the Middle Class', n.p.
37. Michael Denning, *The Cultural Front: The Laboring of American Culture in the Twentieth Century* (London: Verso, 1998), p. 102.
38. Buhle, 'The Crisis of the Middle Class', n.p. See Lewis Corey, 'Marxism Reconsidered', *The Nation*, Vol. 150, (February–March 1940), 245–8, 272–5, 305–7.
39. Barnfield, 'A Reversal of Fortune'.
40. Ibid.
41. Quoted in Kennedy, *Freedom from Fear*, p. 282.
42. Ibid., pp. 279–80.
43. Ibid., pp. 283–4.
44. Ibid., p. 276.
45. See Kennedy, *Freedom from Fear*, chapters 5 and 9.
46. Alan Brinkley, *The End of Reform: New Deal Liberalism in Recession and War* (New York: Vintage, 1996), p. 6.
47. See Paul S. Hudson, 'A Call for "Bold Persistent Experimentation": FDR's Oglethorpe Commencement Address, 1932', *Georgia Historical Quarterly*, 77.2 (Summer 1994), 361–75.
48. See Arthur M. Schlesinger Jr, *The Crisis of the Old Order, 1919–1933* (Houghton Mifflin, edition 2003), pp. 130–2.
49. Wilfred McClay, 'Ideas', in Stephen Whitfield (ed.), *A Companion to 20th-Century America* (London: Blackwell, 2007), p. 439.
50. Paul Conkin, *The New Deal* (Arlington: Harlan Davidson, 1992 [1967]), pp. 10–12; Richard Hofstadter, 'Franklin D. Roosevelt: The Patrician as Opportunist', in *The American Political Tradition and the Men Who Made It* (New York, 1948), p. 311. See also Kennedy, *Freedom from Fear*, p. 122.

51. Brinkley, *End of Reform*, p. 5.
52. Tugwell quoted in Brinkley, *End of Reform*, p. 34; Johnson quoted in Kennedy, *Freedom from Fear*, p. 179.
53. See Brinkley, *End of Reform*, p. 70.
54. Eccles quoted in Brinkley, *End of Reform*, p. 80.
55. 'A Survey of the Purposes, Accomplishments and Failings of the NRA: March 5, 1934', in *The Public Papers and Addresses of Franklin D. Roosevelt: Volume 3, The Advance of Recovery and Reform* (New York: Random House, 1938), p. 125.
56. Brinkley, *End of Reform*, p. 9.
57. Ibid., p. 10.
58. Kennedy, *Freedom from Fear*, pp. 353–4.
59. Howard Kershner, *The Menace of Roosevelt and His Policies* (New York: Greenberg, 1936), quoted in Robert Higgs, 'The Mythology of Roosevelt and the New Deal', *The Freeman* (September 1998), 557.
60. David Weingast, 'Walter Lippmann: A Content Analysis', *Public Opinion Quarterly* 14.2 (Summer 1950), 299; John Patrick Diggins, 'From Pragmatism to Natural Law: Walter Lippmann's Quest for the Foundations of Legitimacy', *Political Theory* 19.4 (November 1991), 531.
61. Martin Rubin, 'The Crowd, the Collective, and the Chorus', in John Belton (ed.), *Movies and Mass Culture* (London: Athlone, 1996), p. 66.
62. Rubin, 'The Crowd', p. 65.
63. Charles Beard, *The Myth of Rugged Individualism* (New York: John Day, 1932).
64. Warren Susman, *Culture as History: The Transformation of American Society in the Twentieth Century* (New York: Pantheon, 1973), p. 168.
65. Quoted in Kennedy, *Freedom from Fear*, p. 247.
66. Roosevelt quoted in Kennedy, *Freedom from Fear*, p. 249.
67. Brinkley, *End of Reform*, p. 7.
68. Denning, p. xvii.
69. Quoted in Kennedy, *Freedom from Fear*, p. 299.
70. Sidney Hillman quoted in Kennedy, *Freedom from Fear*, p. 306.
71. Denning, *The Cultural Front*, p. 152.
72. Badger, *The New Deal*, p. 6.
73. Kennedy, *Freedom from Fear*, p. 113.
74. Kenneth S. Davis, *FDR: The Beckoning of Destiny, 1882–1928* (New York: Putnams, 1972).
75. Mark H. Leff, 'Franklin D. Roosevelt', in Alan Brinkley and Davis Dyer (eds), *The American Presidency* (Boston: Houghton Mifflin, 2004), p. 349.
76. Kennedy, *Freedom from Fear*, p. 378.
77. Leff, 'Franklin D. Roosevelt', p. 345.
78. Susan Ware, 'Franklin D. Roosevelt', in James McPherson (ed.), *The American Presidents* (New York: Agincourt Press, 2004), p. 226.
79. Kennedy, *Freedom from Fear*, p. 96; Leff, 'Franklin D. Roosevelt', p. 347.
80. Kennedy, *Freedom from Fear*, p. 96.
81. Eleanor Roosevelt, *This I Remember* (London: Hutchinson, 1950), p. 31; Ted Morgan, *FDR: A Biography* (London: Grafton, 1986), p. 259.
82. Leff, 'Franklin D. Roosevelt', p. 349.
83. 'New York State Takes the Lead in the Relief of the Unemployed: August 28, 1931', in *The Public Papers and Addresses of Franklin D. Roosevelt: Volume 1,*

The Genesis of the New Deal 1928–32 (New York: Random House, 1938), pp. 457–8.

84. 'Annual Message to Congress: January 3, 1938', in *The Public Papers and Addresses of Franklin D. Roosevelt: 1938 Volume, The Continuing Struggle for Liberalism* (New York: Macmillan, 1941), p. 14.
85. Quoted in Kennedy, *Freedom from Fear*, p. 116.
86. Paul Conkin, for example, argues that the New Deal was 'an exceedingly personal enterprise . . . unified only by the personality of Franklin D. Roosevelt'. (Conkin, *The New Deal*, p. 1). A similar verdict is delivered in James MacGregor Burns, *Roosevelt: The Lion and the Fox* (New York: Harcourt Brace, 1956).
87. Leff, 'Franklin D. Roosevelt', p. 354.
88. Schlesinger's three-volume study of *The Age of Roosevelt* includes *The Crisis of the Old Order*, *The Coming of the New Deal* and *The Politics of Upheaval*.
89. Susman, *Culture as History*, p. 157.
90. Parrish, '1921–1941', p. 49.
91. Susan Hegeman, *Patterns for America: Modernism and the Concept of Culture* (Princeton: Princeton University Press, 1999), p. 103.
92. Susman, *Culture as History*, pp. 159–60.
93. Parrish, '1921–1941', p. 48.
94. Cooney, *Balancing Acts*, p. 101.
95. Perry Miller, *The New England Mind: The Seventeenth Century* (Cambridge: Harvard University Press, 1939).
96. Michael Kammen, *Mystic Chords of Memory: The Transformation of Tradition in America* (New York: Knopf, 1991), pp. 303–4.
97. Ibid., p. 308.
98. Hegeman, *Patterns for America*, p. 93.
99. Wanda Corn, *The Great American Thing: Modern Art and National Identity, 1915–1935* (Berkeley: University of California Press, 1999), p. 315.
100. Alfred Haworth Jones, 'The Search for a Usable Past in the New Deal Era', *American Quarterly* 23.5 (December 1971), p. 723.
101. Christine Bold, *The WPA Guides: Mapping America* (Jackson: University of Mississippi Press, 1999), p. 31.
102. Hegeman, *Patterns for America*, p. 130.
103. Ibid., p. 129.
104. Jerrold Hirsch, *Portrait of America: A Cultural History of the Federal Writers Project* (Chapel Hill: University of North Carolina Press, 2003), p. 23.
105. Laura Browder, *Rousing the Nation: Radical Culture in Depression America* (Amherst: University of Massachusetts Press, 1998), p. 176.
106. Quoted in McClay, 'Ideas', p. 438.
107. Quoted in Kammen, *Mystic Chords*, p. 409.
108. Denning, *The Cultural Front*, p. 9.
109. Hegeman, *Patterns for America*, p. 128.
110. See chapter 4 of Cooney, *Balancing Acts*.
111. Bold, *The WPA Guides*, p. 31.
112. Quoted in Cooney, p. 199. For a fuller statement of these views, see John Dewey, *Freedom and Culture* (London: Unwin, 1940).
113. Constance Rourke, *American Humor: A Study of the National Character* (New York: Harcourt Brace, [1931] 1959). A hypertext version of *American Humor* is

available at: http://xroads.virginia.edu/~HYPER/rourke/cover.html. All subsequent references refer to this online book.

114. Rourke, *American Humor*.
115. Quoted in Joan Shelley Rubin, *Constance Rourke and American Culture* (Chapel Hill: University of North Carolina Press), p. 114.
116. Rourke, *American Humor*.
117. Van Wyck Brooks, *America's Coming of Age* (New York: Doubleday, [1915] 1958), p. 3.
118. Van Wyck Brooks, *The Ordeal of Mark Twain* (New York: Dutton, 1920), p. 96. See Sean Zwagerman, 'Book Review: *American Humor*', *Journal of Popular Culture* 38.3 (2005), 600–1.
119. Rourke, *American Humor*.
120. Quoted in Rubin, *Constance Rourke*, p. 59.
121. Quoted in Joan Shelley Rubin, 'Constance Rourke in Context: The Uses of Myth', *American Quarterly*, 28.5 (Winter 1976), 584.
122. Rubin, *Constance Rourke*, p. 40.

1. Literaure and Drama

1. Warren French, 'Introduction' to *The Thirties: Fiction, Poetry, Drama* (Deland: Everett Edwards, 1967), p. 2.
2. David Mintner, *A Cultural History of the Novel: Henry James to William Faulkner* (Cambridge: Cambridge University Press, 1994), p. 204.
3. Richard Ruland and Malcolm Bradbury, *From Puritanism to Postmodernism: A History of American Literature* (London: Penguin, 1991), p. 332.
4. Paul Buhle and Dave Wagner, *Radical Hollywood: The Untold Story Behind America's Favorite Movies* (New York: New Press, 2002), p. 74.
5. Quoted in Michael Denning, *The Cultural Front: The Laboring of American Culture in the Twentieth Century* (London: Verso, 1998), pp. 207–8.
6. Quoted in Denning, *The Cultural Front*, p. 120.
7. Ralph Bogardus and Fred Hobson, 'Introduction', in *Literature at the Barricades: The American Writer in the 1930s* (Tuscaloosa: University of Alabama Press, 1982), p. 3.
8. Mike Gold, 'Proletarian Realism', in Michael Folsom (ed.), *Mike Gold: A Literary Anthology* (New York: International Publishers, 1972), p. 206.
9. Gold quoted in Mintner, *A Cultural History of the Novel*, p. 185.
10. James Gilbert, quoted in Susan Hegeman, *Patterns for America: Modernism and the Concept of Culture* (Princeton: Princeton University Press, 1999), p. 131.
11. Peter Conn, *Literature in America: An Illustrated History* (Cambridge: Cambridge University Press, 1989), p. 399.
12. Colette Hyman, *Staging Strikes: Workers' Theatre and the America Labor Movement* (Philadelphia: Temple University Press, 1997), p. 71.
13. Alan Wald, 'Revolutionary Intellectuals: *Partisan Review* in the 1930s', in Bogardus and Hobson (eds), *Literature at the Barricades*, p. 190.
14. Barbara Foley, *Radical Representations: Politics and Form in U.S. Proletarian Fiction, 1929–1941* (Durham: Duke University Press 1993), p. 354.
15. Irving Howe, 'The Thirties in Retrospect', in Bogardus and Hobson (eds), *Literature at the Barricades*, p. 25.

16. James T. Farrell, 'The End of a Literary Decade' [1939], reprinted in Bogardus and Hobson (eds), *Literature at the Barricades*, p. 205.
17. See Robert Schulman, *The Power of Political Art: The 1930s Literary Left Reconsidered* (Chapel Hill: University of North Carolina Press, 2000), pp. 266–9.
18. Ibid., p. 204.
19. Ibid., p. 184.
20. Ibid., p. 204.
21. Jordan Y. Miller, 'Maxwell Anderson: Gifted Technician', in Warren French (ed.), *The Thirties: Fiction, Poetry, Drama* (Deland: Everett Edwards, 1967), p. 187.
22. Schulman, *The Power of Political Art*, p. 96.
23. Ibid., pp. 86, 90.
24. Ibid., p. 131.
25. Donald Pizer, *John Dos Passo's U.S.A: A Critical Study* (Chartlottesville: University Press of Virginia, 1988).
26. Gail McDonald, *American Literature and Culture 1900–1960* (London: Blackwell, 2007), p. 72.
27. Conn, *Literature in America*, p. 408.
28. McDonald, *American Literature and Culture*, p. 77.
29. Ibid., p. 72.
30. Quoted in David Peeler, *Hope Among Us Yet: Social Criticism and Social Solace in Depression America* (Athens: University of Georgia Press, 1987), p. 184.
31. Schulman, *The Power of Political Art*, p. 9.
32. William Blazek and Laura Rattray (eds), *Twentyfirst Century Readings of 'Tender is the Night'* (Liverpool: Liverpool University Press, 2007), p. 3.
33. Quoted in Peeler, *Hope Among Us Yet*, p. 162.
34. Quoted in Sylvia Jenkins Cook, 'Steinbeck, the People and the Party', in Bogardus and Fred Hobson (eds), *Literature at the Barricades*, p. 92.
35. Quoted in Peeler, *Hope Among Us Yet*, p. 162.
36. Quoted in Mintner, *A Cultural History of the Novel*, p. 189.
37. Quoted in Peeler, *Hope Among Us Yet*, p. 178.
38. Ibid., pp. 156–7.
39. Quoted in Denning, *The Cultural Front*, p. 259.
40. William Stott, *Documentary Expression and Thirties America* (Chicago: University of Chicago Press, 1973).
41. Quoted in Cook, 'Steinbeck', p. 92.
42. Quoted in Stott, *Documentary Expression*, p. 119.
43. Peeler, *Hope Among Us Yet*, p. 14.
44. Ibid., p. 21.
45. James Rorty, quoted in Peeler, *Hope Among Us Yet*, p. 34.
46. Ibid., p. 17.
47. Mintner, *A Cultural History of the Novel*, p. 187.
48. Quoted in Eric Mottram, 'Poetry', in Stephen Baskerville and Ralph Willett (eds.), *Nothing Else to Fear: New Perspectives on America in the Thirties* (Manchester: Manchester University Press, 1985), p. 151.
49. Peeler, *Hope Among Us Yet*, p. 69.
50. Laura Browder, *Rousing the Nation: Radical Culture in Depression America* (Amherst: University of Massachusetts Press, 1998), p. 8.
51. Cook, 'Steinbeck', p. 83.

52. Ibid., p. 94.
53. Browder, *Rousing the Nation*, p. 8.
54. Minter, *A Cultural History of the Novel*, p. 200.
55. Farrell, 'End of a Literary Decade', p. 209.
56. Denning, *The Cultural Front*, p. 231.
57. Andrew Wiget, *Native American Literature* (Boston: Twayne, 1985). See also Carol Hunter, 'The Historical Context in John Joseph Mathews' *Sundown*', *Melus* 9.1 (Spring 1982), 61–72, and Louis Owens, 'The Red Road to Nowhere: D'Arcy McNickle's *The Surrounded* and *The Hungry Generations*', *American Indian Quarterly*, 13.3 (Summer 1989), 239–48.
58. Langston Hughes, *Not Without Laughter* (London: Macmillan, [1930] 1969), p. 240.
59. Richard Wright, *Native Son* (London: Jonathan Cape, [1940] 1970), p. 102.
60. Ibid., p. 340.
61. Michael Awkward, *New Essays on Their Eyes Were Watching God* (1990), p. 10.
62. Brooks Atkinson, 'Riggs Worships Great Spirit', *New York Times*, 21 June 1932, 19.
63. Connelly, quoted in Nick Aaron Ford, 'How Genuine is *The Green Pastures?*', *Phylon Quarterly* 20.1 (1959), 68.
64. Walter Daniel, '*De Lawd*': Richard B. Harrison and 'The Green Pastures' (Westport: Greenwood, 1986).
65. Zora Neale Hurston, *Their Eyes Were Watching God* (London: Virago, [1937] 2003), p. 69.
66. Ibid., p. 112.
67. Ibid., p. 286.
68. See Sherley Anne Williams, 'I Love the Way Janie Crawford Left Her Husbands: Zora Neale Hurston's Emergent Female Hero', in Cheryl Wall, *Zora Neale Hurston's Their Eyes Were Watching God: A Case Book* (Oxford: Oxford University Press, 2000), pp. 27–40.
69. Nellie McKay, 'Crayon Enlargements of Life: Zora Neale Hurston's *Their Eyes Were Watching God* as Autobiography', in Awkward, *New Essays*, p. 55.
70. Quoted in Wall, *Case Book*, p. 8.
71. Ibid., p. 8.
72. Hurston, *Their Eyes*, p. 81. For discussion of 'signifying' see Henry Louis Gates's essay 'Zora Neale Hurston and the Speakerly Text', in Wall, *Case Book*, pp. 59–116.
73. Hurston, *Their Eyes*, p. 111.
74. Ibid., p. 123.
75. Ibid., p. 200.
76. Quoted in Hazel Carby, 'The Politics of Fiction, Anthropology and the Folk: Zora Neale Hurston', in Wall, *Case Book*, p. 124.
77. Awkward, *New Essays*, p. 12.
78. Quoted in Wall, *Case Book*, pp. 10, 18.
79. Alice Walker, 'Foreword' to Robert Hemenway, *Zora Neale Hurston: A Literary Biography* (London: Camden Press, 1986), p. xii.
80. See Robert Amer, 'The Black, Memorable Year 1929: James Thurber and the Great Depression', *Studies in American Humor* 3.2–3 (1984), 239.
81. Michael Gold, 'Thornton Wilder: Prophet of the Genteel Christ', in Samuel Sillen (ed.), *The Mike Gold Reader* (New York: International, 1954), pp. 45–50.

82. James Thurber, 'The Secret Life of Walter Mitty', in *The Thurber Carnival* (Hammondsworth: Penguin, 1983), pp. 69–74.
83. Amer, 'The Black, Memorable Year', p. 248.
84. Lawrence Levine, 'The Folklore of Industrial Society: Popular Culture and Its Audiences', *The American Historical Review*, 97.5 (December 1992), 1375.
85. Quoted Levine, 'Folklore of Industrial Society', p. 1375.
86. French, p. 10.
87. Walter Edmonds, *Drums Along the Mohawk* (New York: Syracuse University Press, [1937] 1997), p. xi.
88. Allen, quoted in 'The Disinherited', online at: http://www.geocities.com/brine_ig/anthony.html.
89. Lawrence Levine, 'American Culture and the Great Depression', *Yale Review* 74 (January 1985), 209.
90. Mintner, p. 212.
91. Ibid., p. 204.
92. Margaret Mitchell, quoted in Richard Harwell, *Gone With the Wind as Book and Film* (Columbia: University of South Carolina Press, 1983).
93. Malcolm Cowley, 'The 1930s Were an Age of Faith', *New York Times Book Review*, 13 December 1964, 14.
94. See James P. Jones, 'Nancy Drew: WASP Super Girl of the 1930s', *Journal of Popular Culture* 6.4 (Spring 1973), 707–17.
95. Quoted in David Manning, *Popular Culture* (New York: Ayer, 1975), p. 34 [reprint of 12 March 1970, *New York Times* article].
96. Mintner, *A Cultural History of the Novel*, p. 171.
97. Carl Malmgren, 'The Crime of the Sign: Dashiell Hammett's Detective Fiction', *Twentieth Century Literature* 45.3 (Fall 1999), 371, 375.
98. Lee Horsley, *The Noir Thriller* (London: Palgrave, 2001), p. 25.
99. Ralph Willett, *Hard-Boiled Detective Fiction* (Halifax: British Association for American Studies, 1992), p. 29
100. See Daniel Singal, *William Faulkner: The Making of a Modernist* (Chapel Hill: University of North Carolina Press, 1997), chapter 8.
101. Ben Railton, ' "What Else Could a Southern Gentleman Do?": Quentin Compson, Rhett Butler, and Miscegenation', *Southern Literary Journal* 35.2 (Spring 2003), 44.
102. Kingsley Widmer, 'The Sweet Savage Prophecies of Nathanael West', in French, *The Thirties*, pp. 97–106; Hegeman, *Patterns for America*, pp. 147–57.
103. See Jopi Nyman, *Men Alone: Masculinity, Individualism, and Hard-Boiled Fiction* (Atlanta: Rodopi, 1997), pp. 245–57.
104. Browder, *Rousing the Nation*, p. 69.
105. Thornton Wilder, *Our Town* (London: HarperCollins, 2003), p. 21.
106. Gold, 'Wilder', pp. 47, 48, 50.
107. See Bert Cardullo, 'Whose Town Is It, Anyway? A Reconsideration of Thornton Wilder's *Our Town*', *CLA Journal* 42.1 (September 1998), 71–86.
108. Wilder, *Our Town*, p. 22.
109. Rex Burbank, *Thornton Wilder* (Boston: Twayne, 1978).
110. Wilder, *Our Town*, pp. 117, 115.
111. Cardullo, p. 80.
112. See Winfield Townley Scott, '*Our Town* and the Golden Veil', *Virginia Quarterly Review* 29.1 (Winter, 1953) 103–17.

2. Film and Photography

1. David Peeler, *Hope Among Us Yet: Social Criticism and Social Solace in Depression America* (Athens: University of Georgia Press, 1987), p. 69.
2. Jonathan Spaulding, *Ansel Adams and the American Landscape: A Biography* (Berkeley: University of California Press, 1998), p. 120.
3. Peeler, *Hope Among Us Yet*, p. 79.
4. Belinda Rathbone, *Walker Evans: A Biography* (New York: Houghton Mifflin, 1995), p. 109.
5. Robert Dance and Bruce Roberston, *Ruth Harriet Louise and Hollywood Glamour Photography* (Berkeley: University of California Press, 2002), p. 119.
6. Quoted in George Custen, *Twentieth Century's Fox: Darryl F. Zanuck and the Culture of Hollywood* (New York: Basic Books, 1997), p. 199.
7. Charles Eckert, 'Shirley Temple and the House of Rockefeller', *Jump Cut 2* (July–August 1974), 1.
8. Jennifer Pricola, 'Age of Lost Innocence: Photographs of Childhood Realities and Adult Fears During the Depression', (2003), available at:http://xroads.virginia.edu/~MA03/pricola/FSA/index.html.
9. Astrid Boger, *People's Lives, Public Images: The New Deal Documentary Aesthetic* (Tubingen: Gunter Narr Verlag, 2001), p. 168
10. Peeler, *Hope Among Us Yet*, p. 80.
11. James Snead, 'Shirley Temple', in *White Screens/Black Images: Hollywood from the Dark Side* (New York: Routledge, 1994), p. 14.
12. Quoted in Spaulding, *Ansel Adams*, p. 121.
13. Quoted in Andrew Bergman, *We're in the Money: Depression America and its Films* (Chicago: Ivan Dee, 1971), p. 30.
14. See Tino Balio, *Grand Design: Hollywood as a Modern Business Enterprise, 1930–1939* (Berkeley: University of California Press, 1995).
15. Breen's complicity is detailed in Gregory Black, *Hollywood Censored: Morality Codes, Catholics, and the Movies* (Cambridge: Cambridge University Press, 1996), pp. 170–4.
16. Richard Maltby, 'More Sinned Against than Sinning: The Fabrications of "Pre-Code Cinema"', *Senses of Cinema* (November 2004), available at: http://www.sensesofcinema.com/contents/03/29/pre_code_cinema.html; Balio, p. 189.
17. Gregory Black, *The Catholic Crusade Against the Movies, 1940–1975* (Cambridge: Cambridge University Press, 1998), p. 13.
18. Balio, *Grand Design*, p. 237.
19. Ibid., p. 189.
20. Arthur Schlesinger Jr, quoted in Bergman, *We're in the Money*, p. 61.
21. Quoted in David Mintner, *A Cultural History of the Novel: Henry James to William Faulkner* (Cambridge: Cambridge University Press, 1994), p. 149.
22. Quoted in Balio, *Grand Design*, p. 2.
23. Stanton Griffis, quoted in Kathleen Moran and Michael Rogin, 'What's the Matter with Capra?: *Sullivan's Travels* and the Popular Front', *Representations* 71 (Summer 2000), 127.
24. Quoted in Bergman, pp. 71–2.
25. Quoted in Peter C. Rollins, 'Will Rogers and the Relevance of Nostalgia:

Steamboat Round the Bend (1935)', in John E. O'Connor and Martin Jackson (eds), *American History/American Film: Interpreting the Hollywood Image* (New York: Ungar, 1976), p. 82.

26. Lary May, *The Big Tomorrow: Hollywood and the Politics of the American Way* (Chicago: University of Chicago Press, 2000), p. 45.
27. Ibid., p. 33.
28. Ibid., p. 35.
29. Martin Tropp, *Mary Shelley's Monster: The Story of Frankenstein* (London: Houghton Mifflin, 1976). There may be more contemporary resonance in the figure of Dracula's lawyer, Renfield, as a 'self-possessed and prosperous individual' who is reduced to servitude, penury and terror in his encounter with the Count; or in seeing Frankenstein's monster as a literal 'collection of misused human beings', a symbol of the Depression's dispossessed masses whose 'rage and rejection' threatens society. Thomas Doherty, *Pre-Code Hollywood: Sex, Immorality and Insurrection in American Cinema, 1930–1934* (New York: Columbia University Press, 1999), p. 300.
30. See Salman Rushdie, *The Wizard of Oz* (London: BFI, 1992).
31. Quoted Frances MacDonnell, 'The Emerald City was the New Deal: E. Y. arburg and *The Wonderful Wizard of Oz*', *Journal of American Culture* 13.4 (1990), 72.
32. Ibid., p. 74.
33. Steven Watts, *The Magic Kingdom: Walt Disney and the American Way of Life* (New York: Houghton Mifflin, 1997), p. 80.
34. Richard Schickel, *The Disney Version: The Life, Times, Art and Commerce of Walt Disney* (London: Pavilion, 1986), p. 154.
35. Lawrence Levine, 'Hollywood's Washington: Film Images of National Politics During the Great Depression', in *The Unpredictable Past: Explorations in American Cultural History* (New York: Oxford University Press, 1993), p. 231.
36. Martin Rubin, *Showstoppers: Busby Berkeley and the Tradition of Spectacle* (New York: Columbia University Press, 1993), p. 105.
37. John E. O'Connor, 'A Reaffirmation of American Ideas: *Drums Along the Mohawk* (1939)', in John O'Connor and Martin Jackson (eds), *American History/American Film: Interpreting the Hollywood Image* (New York: Ungar, 1976), p. 101.
38. Ibid., p. 115.
39. James Snead, *White Screens/Black Images: Hollywood from the Dark Side* (New York: Routledge, 1994), pp. 8, 21.
40. Joanna Rapf, '"What Do They Know in Pittsburgh?": American Comic Film in the Great Depression', *Studies in American Humor* 3.2–3 (1984), 193.
41. Bergman, *We're in the Money*, p. 33.
42. Ibid., p. 132.
43. Joseph McBride, *Frank Capra: The Catastrophe of Success* (New York: Faber and Faber, 1992), p. 305; Bergman, *We're in the Money*, p. 134.
44. Rapf, 'What Do They Know in Pittsburgh?', p. 194.
45. Ibid., p. 193.
46. Jonathan Munby, *Public Enemies, Public Heroes: Screening the Gangster from Little Caesar to Touch of Evil* (Chicago: University of Chicago Press, 1999), p. 54.
47. Quoted in Lee Grieveson (ed.), *Mob Culture: Hidden History of the American Gangster Film* (New Brunswick, NJ: Rutgers University Press, 2005), p. 42.

48. Henry Cohen (ed.), *The Public Enemy* (Madison: University of Wisconsin Press, 1981), p. 17.
49. Munby, *Public Enemies*, p. 51.
50. Fran Mason, *American Gangster Cinema: From 'Little Caesar' to 'Pulp Fiction'* (London: Palgrave Macmillan, 2002), p. 20.
51. Munby, *Public Enemies*, p. 52.
52. Quoted in Balio, *Grand Design*, p. 284.
53. Richard Maltby, *'The Public Enemy'*, *Senses of Cinema* (November, 2003), available at:http:/www.sensesofcinema.com/contents/cteq.03/29/public_enemy. html.
54. Richard Maltby, 'The Production Code and the Hays Office', in Balio, *Grand Design*, p. 52.
55. Balio, *Grand Design*, p. 285.
56. Indeed, Warner Bros. 'treated Cagney's conversion to the right side of the law as an event of national significance'; Balio, *Grand Design*, p. 290.
57. Quoted in Maltby, *'The Public Enemy'*.
58. Richard Slotkin, *Gunfighter Nation: The Myth of the Frontier in Twentieth-Century America* (Norman: University of Oklahoma Press, 2000), p. 259.
59. Charles Maland, *'Modern Times* (1936), Charlie Chaplin', in Jeffrey Geiger and R. L. Rutsky (eds), *Film Analysis* (New York: Norton, 2005), p. 244.
60. See John E. O'Connor (ed.), *I am a Fugitive from a Chain Gang* (Madison: University of Wisconsin Press, 1981).
61. Nick Roddick, *A New Deal in Entertainment: Warner Brothers in the 1930s* (London, BFI, 1983), p. 125.
62. Roddick, *A New Deal*, p. 123; Bergman, *We're in the Money*, p. 96; Balio, *Grand Design*, p. 281.
63. Colin Shindler, *Hollywood in Crisis: Cinema and American Society, 1929–1939* (London: Routledge, 1996), pp. 70, 72.
64. Ibid., pp. 168–9.
65. Maland, 'Modern Times', p. 255.
66. Frank Stricker, 'Repressing the Working Class: Individual and the Masses in Frank Capra's Films', *Labor History* 31 (1990), 455.
67. Levine, 'Hollywood's Washington', p. 252.
68. Ibid., p. 251.
69. Bergman, *We're in the Money*, p. 105.
70. Ibid., p. 107.
71. Quoted in Black, *The Catholic Crusade*, p. 100.
72. Steven Ross, 'American Workers, American Movies: Historiography and Methodology', *International Labor and Working Class History* 59 (Spring, 2001), 89.
73. Quoted in Shindler, *Hollywood in Crisis*, p. 184.
74. See Black, *The Catholic Crusade*, pp. 260–8.
75. Quoted in Shindler, *Hollywood in Crisis*, p. 189.
76. Ross, 'American Workers, American Movies', p. 91.
77. William Alexander, *Film on the Left: American Documentary Film from 1931 to 1942* (Princeton: Princeton University Press, 1981).
78. Boger, *People's Lives, Public Images*, p. 185.
79. Paul Buhle and David Wagner, *Radical Hollywood: The Untold Story Behind America's Favorite Movies* (New York: New Press, 2002), p. 75.

80. Charles Wolfe, 'The Poetics and Politics of Nonfiction: Documentary Film', in Balio, *Grand Design*, p. 360.
81. Quoted Nicole Huffman, 'New Frontiers in American Documentary Film', available at: http://xroads.virginia.edu/~ma01/huffman/frontier/history.html.
82. Thomas Waugh, 'Men Cannot Act before the Camera in the Presence of Death: Joris Iven's *The Spanish Earth*', in Barry K. Grant and Jeanette Sloniowski (eds), *Documenting the Documentary: Close Readings of Documentary Film and Video* (Detroit: Wayne University Press, 1998), p. 147.
83. Buhle and Wagner, *Radical Hollywood*, p. 40.
84. Waugh, 'Men Cannot Act', p. 149.
85. Ross, 'American Workers, American Movies', p. 92.
86. Levine, 'Hollywood's Washington', p. 253.
87. Quoted in J. P. McEvoy, 'He's Got Something', *Saturday Evening Post*, 1 July 1939, 67.
88. See Moran and Rogin, 'What's the Matter with Capra?', pp. 119–21.
89. E. Rubinstein, 'Hollywood's Travels: Sturges and Sullivan', *Sight and Sound* (Winter, 1977), 51.
90. Rapf, 'What Do They Know in Pittsburgh?', p. 198.
91. See Brian Henderson (ed.), *Five Screenplays By Preston Sturges* (Berkeley: University of California Press, 1985).
92. Quoted in Moran and Rogin, 'What's the Matter with Capra?', p. 127.
93. Indeed, Kathleen Moran and Michael Rogin call it 'the last 1930's social protest film'; p. 111.
94. Spaulding, pp. 118–19.
95. Quoted in Jonathan Green (ed.), *Camera Work: A Critical Anthology* (New York: Aperture, 1973).
96. See Therese Thau Heyman (ed.), *Seeing Straight: the f/64 Revolution in Photography* (Oakland, CA: Oakland Museum, 1992).
97. Spaulding, *Ansel Adams*, p. 122.
98. Ibid., p. 162.
99. Quoted in Spaulding, *Ansel Adams*, p. 120.
100. Quoted in Peeler, *Hope Among Us Yet*, p. 88 (original emphasis).
101. Dance and Robertson, *Ruth Harriet Louise*, p. 220.
102. Melissa McEuen, *Seeing America: Women Photographers Between the Wars* (Lexington: University Press of Kentucky, 2000), p. 248.
103. Freddy Langer, 'Lewis Hine, Man and Work', in Lewis Hine, *The Empire State Building* (Munich: Prestel, 1998), p. 20.
104. Quoted in William Stott, *Documentary Expression and Thirties America* (New York: Oxford University Press, 1973), p. 130
105. Wendy Kozol, *LIFE's America: Family and Nation in Postwar Photojournalism* (Philadelphia: Temple University Press, 1994), p. 34.
106. Paula Rabinowitz, 'Margaret Bourke-White's Red Coat; or Slumming in the Thirties', in Ardis Cameron (ed.), *Looking for America: The Visual Production of Nation and People* (Oxford: Blackwell, 2005), p. 161.
107. Quoted in McEuen, *Seeing America*, p. 197.
108. Peeler, *Hope Among Us Yet*, p. 61.
109. Quoted in Milton Meltzer, *Dorothea Lange: A Photographer's Life* (New York: Farrar, Strauss, Giroux, 1978), pp. 69–70.

110. Peeler, *Hope Among Us Yet*, p. 79.
111. Ibid., pp. 74, 80.
112. McEuen, *Seeing America*, p. 110.
113. Ibid., pp. 148, 238.
114. Peeler, *Hope Among Us Yet*, p. 59.
115. Boger, *People's Lives, Public Images*, p. 53.
116. Quoted in Ibid., p. 52.
117. James Curtis, *Mind's Eye, Mind's Truth: FSA Photography Reconsidered* (Philadelphia: Temple University Press, 1989), p. 84.
118. Spaulding, *Ansel Adams*, pp. 118, 165.
119. Rathbone, *Walker Evans*, p. 111.
120. Gilles Mora and John Hill, *Walker Evans: The Hungry Eye* (London: Thames and Hudson, 2004), p. 132.
121. Ibid., p. 134.
122. Lionel Trilling, quoted in Boger, p. 71.
123. Gilbert Seldes, quoted in Alan Trachtenberg, *Reading American Photographs: Images as History* (New York: Hill and Wang, 1990), p. 246.
124. Mora and Hill, *Walker Evans*, pp. 160–1.
125. Spaulding, *Ansel Adams*, p. 165.
126. Quoted in Bonnie Yochelson, *Berenice Abbott: Changing New York* (New York: New Press, 1997), p. 12.
127. Lewis Mumford, quoted in Yochelson, *Berenice Abbott*, p. 11.
128. Samuel Untermyer, quoted in Yochelson, *Berenice Abbott*, p. 9.
129. Mora and Hill, Walker Evans, p. 4.
130. McEuen, *Seeing America*, p. 266.
131. Yochelson, *Berenice Abbott*, pp. 4, 6.
132. Julia Van Haaften, 'About Changing New York', available at: www.nypl.org/research/chss/spe/art/photo/abbottex/about.html; Yochelson, p. 5.
133. Quoted in Yochelson, *Berenice Abbott*, p. 15.
134. McEuen, *Seeing America*, p. 269.
135. Ibid., p. 281.
136. Ibid., p. 295.
137. Yochelson, *Berenice Abbott*, p. 17, 6.
138. See the online exhibition of *Changing New York* at http://www.mcny.org/collections/abbott/a225.htm.
139. Quoted McEuen, *Seeing America*, p. 295.
140. Van Haaften, 'About Changing New York'.
141. Yochelson, *Berenice Abbott*, p. 4.

3. Music and Radio

1. See Michele Hilmes, *Radio Voices: American Broadcasting 1922–1952* (Minneapolis: University of Minnesota Press, 1997), pp. 164–75.
2. Kenneth Bindas, *All of this Music Belongs to the Nation: The WPA's Federal Music Project and American Society* (Knoxville: University of Tennessee Press, 1995), pp. 1–2.
3. William H. Young and Nancy K. Young, *Music of the Great Depression* (Westport: Greenwood, 2005), p. 19.

4. Barbara Tischler, *An American Music: The Search for an American Musical Identity* (New York: Oxford University Press, 1986), p. 92.
5. Terry A. Cooney, *Balancing Acts: American Thought and Culture in the 1930s* (New York: Twayne, 1995), p. 90.
6. Erik Barnouw, *The Golden Web: A History of Broadcasting in the United States: Volume 2 – 1933 to 1953* (New York: Oxford University Press, 1968), p. 26.
7. Michele Hilmes, *Only Connect: A Cultural History of Broadcasting in the United States* (Boston: Wadsworth, 2002), pp. 107–8.
8. Hilmes, *Radio Voices*, p. 212.
9. Joseph Horowitz, *Understanding Toscanini: How He Became an American Culture-God and Helped Create a New Audience for Old Music* (Minneapolis: University of Minnesota Press, 1988), pp. 142, 158.
10. Quoted in Horowitz, *Understanding Toscanini*, p. 167.
11. Young, *Music of the Great Depression*, p. 176.
12. Quoted in Horowitz, *Understanding Toscanini*, p. 232.
13. Ibid., p. 137.
14. Ibid., p. 245.
15. Aaron Copland, 'Composer from Brooklyn: An Autobiographical Sketch (1939)', in Richard Kostelanetz (ed.), *Aaron Copland: A Reader, Selected Writings 1923–1972* (London: Routledge, 2004), p. xxvii.
16. Tischler, *An American Music*, p. 92.
17. See Young, *Music of the Great Depression*, pp. 146–58.
18. Ray Allen, 'An American Folk Opera? Triangulating Folkness, Blackness, and Americaness in Gershwin and Heyward's *Porgy and Bess*', *Journal of American Folklore* 117 (2005), 249.
19. Alan Lomax, preface to *Folk Song USA* (New York: Duell, Sloan and Pearce, 1947), p. vii.
20. Kostelanetz, *Aaron Copland*, p. 239.
21. Beth Levy, ' "The White Hope of American Music"; or, How Roy Harris Became Western', *American Music* 19.2 (2001), 131.
22. Quoted in Levy, 'The White Hope', p. 141.
23. Ibid., p. 146.
24. Quoted in Levy, 'The White Hope', p. 155.
25. Michael Denning, *The Cultural Front: The Laboring of American Culture in the Twentieth Century* (London: Verso, 1998), p. 284.
26. Bindas, *All of This Music*, p. 63.
27. Ibid.
28. Elie Siegmeister, *The Music Lover's Handbook* (New York: Morrow, 1943), p. 773.
29. Roy Harris, quoted in Levy, 'The White Hope', p. 154.
30. See James Hutchisson, *DuBose Heyward: A Charleston Gentleman and the World of Porgy and Bess* (Jackson: University of Mississippi Press, 2000).
31. Allen, 'An American Folk Opera?', p. 250.
32. Ibid., p. 256.
33. Quoted in Allen, 'An American Folk Opera?', p. 248.
34. Virgil Thomson, for example, underscored the prejudice against Gershwin when stating: 'I don't mind his being a light composer and I don't mind his trying to be a serious one. But I do mind his falling between two stools'. Quoted in David Horn, 'Who Loves You Porgy? The Debates Surrounding Gershwin's Musical',

in Robert Lawson-Peebles (ed.), *Approaches to the American Musical* (Exeter: University of Exeter Press, 1996), p. 111.

35. Quoted in Allen, 'An American Folk Opera?', p. 254.
36. Marcia Davenport's review in *The Stage*, quoted in Allen, 'An American Folk Opera?', p. 251.
37. Raymond Knapp, *The American Musical and the Formation of National Identity* (Princeton: Princeton University Press, 2005), pp. 200–3.
38. Howard Pollack, *George Gershwin: His Life and Work* (Berkeley: University of California Press, 2007), p. 102.
39. Quoted in Allen, 'An American Folk Opera?', p. 250.
40. Ibid.
41. Quoted in Richard Crawford, 'Where Did *Porgy and Bess* Come From?', *Journal of Interdisciplinary History* 36.4 (2006), p. 710.
42. Gershwin, quoted in Ibid., pp. 705, 732.
43. Allen, 'An American Folk Opera?', pp. 253–5.
44. Ibid., p. 255.
45. Heyward, quoted in Allen, 'An American Folk Opera?', p. 426. David Horn notes that 'black performers themselves have sometimes confessed to mixed emotions at performing in *Porgy and Bess*', but found their 'reservations about the work . . . overcome by the sheer quality of the cast'. See Horn, 'Who Loves You Porgy?', p. 119.
46. Quoted in Ray Allen and George Cunningham, 'Cultural Uplift and Double-Consciousness: African-American Responses to the 1935 Opera *Porgy and Bess*', *Music Quarterly* 88.3 (2005) 361.
47. Quoted in Levy, 'The White Hope', p. 158.
48. Ibid., p. 152.
49. Ibid., pp. 132, 143.
50. William Manchester, *The Glory and the Dream: A Narrative History of America 1932–1972* (New York: Little, Brown, 1974); David Stowe, *Swing Changes: Big Band Jazz in New Deal America* (Boston: Harvard University Press, 1994), p. 244.
51. Quoted in Melvin Ely, *The Adventures of Amos 'n' Andy: A Social History of an American Phenomenon* (New York: Free Press, 1991), p. 174.
52. Ibid., p. 164.
53. Ibid., p. 177.
54. Elizabeth McLeod, *The Original Amos 'n' Andy: Freeman Gosden, Charles Correll and the 1928–1943 Radio Serial* (London: McFarland, 2005), p. 58.
55. Hilmes, *Radio Voices*, p. 82.
56. McLeod, *The Original Amos 'n' Andy*, p. 58 (original emphasis).
57. Ibid., p. 115.
58. Hilmes, *Radio Voices*, pp. 90–1.
59. McLeod, *The Original Amos 'n' Andy*, p. 60.
60. Ibid., p. 157.
61. Quoted in Ely, *The Adventures of Amos 'n' Andy*, p. 171.
62. McLeod, *The Original Amos 'n' Andy*, p. 118.
63. Ibid., p. 197.
64. Lewis Erenberg, *Swingin' the Dream: Big Band Jazz and the Rebirth of American Culture* (Chicago: University of Chicago Press, 1998), p. 100.

65. Stowe, *Swing Changes*, p. 122.
66. Ibid., p. 97.
67. Archbishop Francis Beckman, quoted in Erenberg, *Swingin' the Dream*, p. 37.
68. Erenberg, *Swingin' the Dream*, p. 38.
69. Ibid., p. 65.
70. Ibid., p. xv.
71. Ibid., p. 35.
72. Pittsburgh *Courier* editorial, quoted in Erenberg, *Swingin' the Dream*, pp. 114–15.
73. Denning, *The Cultural Front*, p. 330; Stowe, *Swing Changes*, pp. 13–14.
74. Stowe, *Swing Changes*, p. 130.
75. Ibid., p. 245.
76. Nancy Kovaleff Baker, 'Abel Meeropol (a.k.a. Lewis Allan): Political Commentator and Social Conscience', *American Music* 20.1 (2002), 52–3.
77. Quoted in David Margolick, *Strange Fruit: Billy Holiday, Café Society, and an Early Cry for Civil Rights* (London: Canongate, 2001), p. 48.
78. Ibid., p. 42.
79. Quoted in Denning, *The Cultural Front*, p. 327.
80. Margolick, *Strange Fruit*, p. 91.
81. Ibid., p. 120.
82. Quoted in Margolick, *Strange Fruit*, p. 77.
83. Gunther Schuller, *The Swing Era: The Development of Jazz, 1930 through 1945* (New York: Oxford University Press, 1989), p. 543.
84. Margolick, *Strange Fruit*, p. 68.
85. Quoted in Margolick, *Strange Fruit*, p. 90.
86. Ibid., pp. 37, 61.
87. See James Allen (ed.), *Without Sanctuary: Lynching Photography in America* (Santa Fe: Twin Palms, 2000).
88. Margolick, *Strange Fruit*, pp. 76, 109.
89. Baker, 'Abel Meeropol', p. 54.
90. Margolick, *Strange Fruit*, p. 23.
91. Schuller, *The Swing Era*, p. 543.
92. Jack Schiffman, quoted in Margolick, *Strange Fruit*, p. 101.
93. Tischler, *An American Music*, p. 112.
94. Erenberg, *Swingin' the Dream*, p. 129.
95. See Knapp, *The American Musical*, pp. 110–18.
96. Young, *Music of the Great Depression*, p. 36.
97. See Colette Hyman, *Staging Strikes: Workers' Theatre and the America Labor Movement* (Philadelphia: Temple University Press, 1997).
98. Quoted in Hyman, *Staging Strikes*, p. 93.
99. Hilmes, *Only Connect*, pp. 108–11.
100. Quoted in Bruce Lenthall, 'Critical Reception: Public Intellectuals Decry Depression-era Radio, Mass Culture, and Modern America', in Michele Hilmes and Jason Loviglio (eds), *Radio Reader: Essays in the Cultural History of Radio* (London: Routledge, 2002), p. 46.
101. Ibid., p. 53.
102. Ibid., p. 54; Barnouw, *The Golden Web*, p. 35.
103. Barnouw, *The Golden Web*, p. 35.

104. Hilmes, *Only Connect*, p. 127.
105. James Shenton, 'The Coughlin Movement and the New Deal', *Political Science Quarterly* 73.3 (1958), 360.
106. Robert Brown, *Manipulating the Ether: The Power of Broadcast Radio in Thirties America* (London: McFarland, 1998), p. 86.
107. Ibid., p. 88.
108. Shenton, 'The Coughlin Movement', p. 362.
109. Brown, *Manipulating the Ether*, p. 11.
110. Barnouw, *The Golden Web*, p. 7.
111. Brown, *Manipulating the Ether*, pp. 21, 14.
112. Kathleen Jameson Hall, *Packaging the Presidency: A History and Criticism of Presidential Campaign Advertising* (New York: Oxford University Press, 1996), p. 26.
113. Brown, *Manipulating the Ether*, p. 11.
114. Barnouw, *The Golden Web*, p. 49.
115. See Alan Brinkley, *Voices of Protest: Huey Long, Father Coughlin and the Great Depression* (New York: Knopf, 1982).
116. Ibid., p. 74; Brown, *Manipulating the Ether*, p. 158.
117. Barnouw, *The Golden Web*, p. 81; Brown, *Manipulating the Ether*, p. 167.
118. Barnouw, *The Golden Web*, p. 74.
119. Brown, *Manipulating the Ether*, p. 131.
120. Barnouw, *The Golden Web*, p. 137.
121. Brown, *Manipulating the Ether*, p. 188.
122. David Culbert, *News for Everyman: Radio and Foreign Affairs in the Thirties* (Westport: Greenwood, 1976), p. 194.
123. Edward Miller, *Emergency Broadcasting and 1930s American Radio* (Philadelphia: Temple University Press, 2003), p. 107.
124. Brown, *Manipulating the Ether*, p. 221.
125. Simon Callow, *Orson Welles: The Road to Xanadu* (London: Jonathan Cape, 1995), p. 406.
126. Ibid., p. 400.
127. Ibid.
128. Brown, *Manipulating the Ether*, p. 219.
129. Dorothy Thompson, quoted in Hadley Cantril, *The Invasion from Mars: A Study in the Psychology of Panic* (Princeton: Princeton University Press, 1940), p. 127.
130. Ibid.
131. Brown, *Manipulating the Ether*, p. 225.
132. Cantril, *The Invasion from Mars*, p. 67.
133. Denning, *The Cultural Front*, p. 382.
134. Ibid.; Cantril, *The Invasion from Mars*, p. 205.
135. Brown, *Manipulating the Ether*, pp. 224–5.
136. Frank McNinch, chair of Federal Communications Commission, quoted in Brown, *Manipulating the Ether*, p. 242.
137. Lenthall, 'Critical Reception', pp. 55, 58.
138. Alexander Russo, 'A Dark(ened) Figure on the Airwaves: Race, Nation, and *The Green Hornet*' in Hilmes and Loviglio (eds), *Radio Reader*, pp. 257–76; Hilmes, *Only Connect*, p. 108.

139. John Lahr, 'King Cole: The not so merry soul of Cole Porter', *The New Yorker*, 12 July 2004.
140. Young, *Music of the Great Depression*, p. 48.

4. Art and Design

1. Walter Benjamin, 'The Work of Art in the Age of Its Technological Reproducibility', in Michael Jennings (ed.), *Walter Benjamin: Selected Writings. Volume 3 – 1935–1938* (Cambridge: Harvard University Press, 2002), pp. 101–33. A slightly different translation, 'The Work of Art in the Age of Mechanical Reproduction', is available online at: http://bid.berkeley.edu/bidclass/readings/benjamin.html.
2. Jennings, *Walter Benjamin*, p. 104.
3. Ibid., p. 109.
4. Ibid., p. 106.
5. See Helen Langa, *Radical Art: Printmaking and the Left in 1930s New York* (Berkeley: University of California Press, 2004).
6. David Peeler, *Hope Among Us Yet: Social Criticism and Social Solace in Depression America* (Athens: University of Georgia Press, 1987), p. 195.
7. Erika Doss, *Twentieth-Century American Art* (Oxford: Oxford University Press, 2002), p. 111.
8. Jane De Hart Mathews, 'Arts and the People: The New Deal Quest for a Cultural Democracy', *Journal of American History* (September 1975), pp. 316–39.
9. Matthew Baigell, *Thomas Hart Benton* (New York: Abrams, 1974), p. 138.
10. Wanda Corn, *The Great American Thing: Modern Art and National Identity, 1915–1935* (Berkeley: University of California Press, 1999), p. 340.
11. Quoted in Baigell, *Thomas Hart Benton*, p. 87.
12. Grant Wood, quoted in Barbara Haskell, *The American Century: Art and Culture, 1900–1950* (New York: Whitney Museum of Art, 1999), p. 224.
13. Neil Harris, 'Artists of Capitalism', *Reviews in American History*, 9.1 (March 1981), p. 106.
14. Jeffrey Meikle, *Twentieth-Century Limited: Industrial Design in America, 1925–1939* (Philadelphia: Temple University Press, 1979), p. 38.
15. Patricia Bayer, *Art Deco Interiors: Decoration and Design Classics of the 1920s and 1930s* (London: Thames and Hudson, 1990), p. 117.
16. Andrew Hemingway, *Artists on the Left: American Artists and the Communist Movement, 1926–1952* (New Haven: Yale University Press, 2002), p. 29.
17. A hypertext edition of Gellert's *Karl Marx's 'Capital' in Lithographs* is available online at: http://www.graphicwitness.org/contemp/marxtitle.htm.
18. Paula Rabinowitz, *They Must Be Represented: The Politics of Documentary* (New York: Verso, 1994), p. 248, n. 29.
19. Quoted in Hemingway, *Artists on the Left*, p. 48.
20. Quoted in Anthony Lee, 'Workers and Painters: Social Realism and Race in Diego Rivera's Detroit Murals', in Alejandro Anreus et al. (eds), *The Social and the Real: Political Art of the 1930s in the Western Hemisphere* (Philadelphia: Pennsylvania State University Press, 2006), p. 204.
21. Alejandro Anreus, Diana Linden and Jonathan Weinberg (eds), *The Social and*

the Real: Political Art of the 1930s in the Western Hemisphere (Philadelphia: Pennsylvania State University Press, 2006), pp. xv, xvii.

22. Jacob Burck, quoted in Anreus et al., *The Social and the Real*, p. xviii.
23. Patricia Hills, 'Art and Politics in the Popular Front: The Union Work and Social Realism of Philip Evergood', in Anreus et al., *The Social and the Real*, p. 183; Peeler, p. 201.
24. See Marlene Park, 'Lynching and Anti-Lynching: Art and Politics in the 1930s', in Alejandro Anreus, et al. (eds), *The Social and the Real: Political Art of the 1930s in the Western Hemisphere* (Philadelphia: Pennsylvania State University Press, 2006), pp. 155–77.
25. Hemingway, *Artists on the Left*, p. 65.
26. Park, 'Lynching and Anti-Lynching', p. 166.
27. Langa, *Radical Art*, p. 79.
28. Hemingway, *Artists on the Left*, p. 61.
29. Doss, *Twentieth-Century American Art*, p. 105.
30. Quoted in Hemingway, *Artists on the Left*, p. 71.
31. Ibid., p. 142.
32. Ibid., p. 35.
33. Ibid., pp. 95, 27.
34. Virginia Marquardt, 'Art on the Political Front in America: From *The Liberator* to *Art Front*', *Art Journal* 52.1 (Spring, 1993), 79.
35. Quoted in Peeler, *Hope Among Us Yet*, p. 219.
36. Marquardt, 'Art on the Political Front', p. 80.
37. Quoted in Haskell, *The American Century*, p. 280.
38. Langa, *Radical Art*, p. 91.
39. Cover text of Anreus, et al., *The Social and the Real*.
40. 'Housepainter', *Time*, 3, June 1935, available online at: http://www.time.com/time/magazine/article/0,9171,883403,00.html.
41. Karal Ann Marling, 'Joe Jones: Regionalist, Communist, Capitalist', *Journal of Decorative and Propaganda Arts* 4 (Spring 1987), 47.
42. Peeler, *Hope Among Us Yet*, p. 234.
43. Marling, 'Joe Jones', p. 48.
44. Ibid.
45. Ibid., p. 50.
46. Quoted in Hemingway, *Artists on the Left*, p. 36.
47. 'Workers and Wheatfields', *Time*, 3 February 1936, available online at: http://205.188.238.109/time/magazine/article/0,9171,755755,00.html.
48. Hemingway, *Artists on the Left*, p. 37.
49. Marling, 'Joe Jones', pp. 51–2.
50. Hemingway, *Artists on the Left*, p. 138.
51. Marling, 'Joe Jones', p. 54.
52. Hemingway, *Artists on the Left*, p. 37.
53. Archibald MacLeish, quoted in Marling, 'Joe Jones', p. 52.
54. Quoted in Marling, 'Joe Jones', pp. 53–4.
55. Ibid., p. 56.
56. Weiland Schmied, *Edward Hopper: Portraits of America* (Munich: Prestel, 1995), p. 8.
57. Quoted in James M. Dennis, *Grant Wood: A Study in American Art and Culture* (New York: Viking Press, 1975), p. 194.

58. Quoted in Hemingway, *Artists on the Left*, p. 52.
59. Doss, *Twentieth-Century American Art*, p. 108.
60. Jane De Hart Mathews, 'Grant Wood's Vision of the American Scene', *Reviews in American History* 4.4 (December 1976), 593.
61. Hemingway, *Artists on the Left*, p. 30.
62. Quoted in Wanda Corn, *Grant Wood: The Regionalist Vision* (New Haven: Yale University Press, 1983), p. 35.
63. Ibid., p. 58.
64. Quoted in Dennis, *Grant Wood*, p. 161.
65. Baigell, *Thomas Hart Benton*, p. 139.
66. In truth, Benton's employment of 'brash Cubist dynamism' and Wood's abstraction of trees and hills into pristine geometric shapes, suggests that their criticism of modern art was less about defining the regionalist style than in disputing elitist snobbery toward the Midwest. See Karal Ann Marling, *Wall-to-Wall America: Post Office Murals in the Great Depression* (Minneapolis: University of Minnesota Press, 2000), p. 10.
67. Steven Biel, *American Gothic: A Life of America's Most Famous Painting* (New York: Norton, 2005), p. 59.
68. Ibid., p. 61.
69. Doss, *Twentieth-Century American Art*, p. 109.
70. Dennis, *Grant Wood*, p. 168.
71. Erika Doss, 'New Deal Politics and Regionalist Art: Thomas Hart Benton's *A Social History of the State of Indiana*', *Prospects* 17 (1992), 373.
72. Corn, *Grant Wood*, p. 2
73. Quoted in Dennis, *Grant Wood*, p. 196.
74. Susan M. Anderson, *Regionalism: The California View, Watercolors 1923–1945* (Santa Barbara Museum of Art, 1988), available online at: http://www.tfaoi.com/aa/3aa/3aa23.htm.
75. Dennis, *Grant Wood*, p. 195.
76. See Susan Hegeman, *Patterns for America: Modernism and the Concept of Culture* (Princeton: Princeton University Press, 1999), p. 139.
77. Jonathan Harris, 'Nationalizing Art: The Community Art Centre Programme of the Federal Art Project 1935–1943', *Art History* 14.2 (June, 1991), 258.
78. Ibid., p. 254.
79. Arthur Millier, quoted in Anderson, *Regionalism: The California View*.
80. See Rick Stewart, *Lone Star Regionalism: The Dallas Nine and Their Circle* (Austin: Texas Monthly Press, 1985).
81. See Matthew Baigell, *The American Scene: American Painting of the 1930s* (New York: Praeger, 1974).
82. Quoted in Doss, 'New Deal Politics and Regionalist Art', p. 356.
83. Richard McKinzie, *The New Deal for Artists* (Princeton: Princeton University Press, 1973), p. 107.
84. Corn, *The Great American Thing*, p. 253.
85. Quoted in Doss, *Twentieth Century American Art*, p. 90.
86. Emily Ballew Neff, *The Modern West: American Landscapes, 1890–1950* (New Haven: Yale University Press, 2006), p. 192.
87. Corn, *The Great American Thing*, pp. 248, 271.
88. Schmied, *Edward Hopper*, p. 14.

89. Gail Levin, *Edward Hopper: The Art and the Artist* (New York: Norton, 1980), p. 7.
90. Andrew Hemingway, 'To "Personalize the Rainpipe": The Critical Mythology of Edward Hopper', *Prospects* 17 (1992), 383; Helen Appleton Read, 'Edward Hopper', *Brooklyn Daily Eagle*, 5 November 1933, available online at: http://www.americanart.si.edu/hopper/p17-news-museum.html.
91. Schmied, *Edward Hopper*, p. 7.
92. Ivo Kranzfelder, *Edward Hopper 1882–1967: Vision of Reality* (Koln: Taschen, 1995), p. 94.
93. Levin, *Edward Hopper*, p. 60.
94. Harry Whittaker, 'The Hopper Exhibition' (August 2004), available online at: http://www.marxist.com/hopper-exhibition-tate-2.htm.
95. Kranzfelder, *Edward Hopper*, p. 67.
96. See Brian O'Doherty, 'Hopper's Look', in Sheena Wagstaff (ed.), *Edward Hopper* (London: Tate Publishing, 2004), p. 92.
97. Schmied, *Edward Hopper*, p. 40.
98. Bayer, *Art Deco Interiors*, p. 148.
99. Quoted in Jeffrey Meikle, *Design in the USA* (Oxford: Oxford University Press, 2005), p. 96.
100. Ibid., p. 101.
101. Ibid., p. 95.
102. Leland Roth, *American Architecture: A History* (Oxford: Westview Press, 2001), p. 374.
103. Martin Greif, *Depression Modern: The Thirties Style in America* (New York: Universe, 1975), p. 25.
104. Meikle, *Twentieth-Century Limited*, p. 68.
105. Loewy quoted in Meikle, *Twentieth-Century Limited*, p. 62.
106. Ibid.
107. Donald Bush, *Streamlined Decade* (New York: George Braziller, 1975).
108. Meikle, *Twentieth-Century Limited*, p. 102.
109. Ibid., pp. 158–62.
110. Ibid., p. 4.
111. David Hanks and Anne Hoy, *American Streamlined Design: The World of Tomorrow* (Paris: Flammarion, 2005), p. 21.
112. Alfred Barr, quoted in Meikle, *Twentieth-Century Limited*, p. 181.
113. Earnest Elmo Calkins, quoted in Arthur Pulos, *The American Design Adventure: 1940–1975* (Cambridge, MA: MIT Press, 1938), pp. 357–8.
114. Meikle, *Twentieth-Century Limited*, p. 80.
115. Ibid., p. 176.
116. Greif, *Depression Modern*, p. 34.
117. Meikle, *Twentieth-Century Limited*, p. 186.
118. Greif, *Depression Modern*, p. 16.
119. Dreyfuss argued that the style should be called 'cleanlining' instead of stream-lining. See Pulos, *The American Design Adventure*, p. 393.
120. Hanks, *American Streamlined Design*, p. 20.
121. Bayer, *Art Deco Interiors*, p. 117; Pulos, *The American Design Adventure*, p. 408.
122. See Donald Hoffmann, *Frank Lloyd Wright's Falling Water: The House and Its History* (New York: Dover, 1978).

123. Kathryn Smith, *Frank Lloyd Wright: America's Master Architect* (New York: Abbeville, 1998), p. 89.
124. Jonathan Lipman, *Frank Lloyd Wright and the Johnson Wax Buildings* (New York: Dover, 2003), p. 1.
125. Ibid., pp. 93–4.
126. Quoted in Brendan Gill, *Many Masks: A Life of Frank Lloyd Wright* (London: Heinemann, 1988), pp. 371–2.
127. Meikle, *Twentieth-Century Limited*, p. 190.
128. Ibid., p. 209.
129. Hemingway, *Artists on the Left*, p. 82.
130. George Douglas, *Skyscrapers: A Social History of the Very Tall Building in America* (New York: McFarland, 2004), p. 133.
131. Norbert Messler, *The Art Deco Skyscraper in New York* (New York: Lang, 1986), p. 147.
132. Daniel Okrent, *Great Fortune: The Epic of Rockefeller Center* (New York: Penguin, 2003), p. 288.
133. Ibid., p. 304.
134. Ibid., pp. 310, 307.
135. Quoted in Okrent, *Great Fortune*, p. 316.
136. Bayer, *Art Deco Interiors*, p. 154.
137. Pulos, *The American Design Adventure*, p. 357.
138. Quoted in Hemingway, *Artists on the Left*, p. 82.
139. Frederick Lewis Allen, quoted in Okrent, *Great Fortune*, p. 399; Douglas, *Skyscrapers*, pp. 137–8.
140. R. Roger Remington, *American Modernism: Graphic Design 1920 to 1960* (London: Laurence King, 2003), pp. 52–60.

5. New Deal Culture

1. President Franklin D. Roosevelt's Second Inaugural Address, 20 January 1937, quoted in David Kennedy, *Freedom From Fear: The American People in Depression and War, 1929–1945* (New York: Oxford University Press), p. 287.
2. Lois Craig, *The Federal Presence: Architecture, Politics and Symbols in United States Government Buildings* (Cambridge, MA: MIT Press, 1978), pp. 310, 323.
3. Karal Ann Marling, *Wall-to-Wall America: A Cultural History of Post Office Murals in the Great Depression* (Minneapolis: University of Minnesota Press, 1982), p. 81.
4. Robert Cronbach, 'The New Deal Sculpture Projects', in Francis O'Connor (ed.), *The New Deal Art Projects: An Anthology of Memoirs* (Washington, DC: Smithsonian Institution Press, 1972), p. 147.
5. Marlene Park and Gerald Markowitz, *Democratic Vistas: Post Office and Public Art in the New Deal* (Philadelphia: Temple University Press, 1985), p. 5.
6. Kenneth Bindas, *All of this Music Belongs to the Nation: The WPA's Federal Music Project and American Society* (Knoxville: University of Tennessee Press, 1995), p. 66.
7. Alan Lawson, 'Brief Renaissance: A Depression Memory', *The New Arcadia Review* 3 (2005), 11.
8. Jonathan Harris, *Federal Art and National Culture: The Politics of Identity in New Deal America* (Cambridge: Cambridge University Press, 1995), p. 42.

9. Rena Fraden, *Blueprints for a Black Federal Theatre, 1933–1939* (Cambridge: Cambridge University Press, 1994), p. 34.
10. Lawson, 'Brief Renaissance', p. 12; Christine Bold, *The WPA Guides: Mapping America* (Jackson: University Press of Mississippi, 1999), p. 23.
11. Daniel Aaron, *Writers on the Left: Episodes in American Literary* Communism (New York: Harcourt Brace, 1961), p. 28.
12. Jane De Hart Mathews, *The Federal Theater: Plays, Relief and Politics* (Princeton: Princeton University Press, 1967), p. 43.
13. Andrew McCain, 'Audiohistory: An Experiential Model for Teaching 30s Era American Culture', available online at: http://www.xroads.virginia.edu/~MA04/mccain/audiohist/intro.htm. McCain's website includes an audio re-enactment of the Living Newspaper *Triple-A Plowed Under*.
14. William Stott, *Documentary Expression and Thirties America* (New York: Oxford University Press, 1973), p. 108.
15. Harris, *Federal Art and National Culture*, p. 85.
16. Barbara Tischler, *An American Music: The Search for an American Musical Identity* (New York: Oxford University Press, 1986), p. 144.
17. Bold, *The WPA Guides*, p. 20.
18. Petra Schindler-Carter, *Vintage Snapshots: The Fabrication of a Nation in the WPA American Guide Series* (New York: Lang, 1999), p. 28.
19. Cedric Larson, 'The Cultural Projects of the WPA', *Public Opinion Quarterly* 3.3 (July 1939), 493.
20. Cronbach, 'The New Deal Sculpture Projects', p. 139.
21. Olive Lyford Gavert, 'The WPA Federal Art Project and the New York World's Fair, 1939–1940', in Francis O'Connor (ed.), *The New Deal Art Projects: An Anthology of Memoirs* (Washington, DC: Smithsonian Institution Press, 1972), p. 256.
22. Park and Markowitz, *Democratic Vistas*, p. 62.
23. See Diana Linden, 'Ben Shahn's New Deal Murals: Jewish Identity in the American Scene', in Alejandro Anreus et al. (eds), *The Social and the Real: Political Art of the 1930s in the Western Hemisphere* (Philadelphia: Pennsylvania State University Press, 2006), pp. 241–60.
24. Barry Witham, *The Federal Theatre Project: A Case Study* (Cambridge: Cambridge University Press, 2003), p. 79.
25. Ibid., p. 80.
26. Melissa McEuen, *Seeing America: Women Photographers Between the Wars* (Lexington: University Press of Kentucky, 2000), p. 103; Kennedy, *Freedom from Fear*, p. 379.
27. Astrid Boger, *People's Lives, Public Images: The New Deal Documentary Aesthetic* (Tubingen: Gunter Narr Verlag, 2001), p. 156.
28. James Curtis, *Mind's Eye, Mind's Truth: FSA Photography Reconsidered* (Philadelphia: Temple University Press, 1989), p. 71.
29. Ibid., p. 97.
30. Boger, *People's Lives, Public Images*, p. 145.
31. William Alexander, *Film on the Left: American Documentary Film from 1931 to 1942* (Princeton: Princeton University Press, 1981), p. 95.
32. Jack Ellis and Betsy McLane, *A New History of Documentary Film* (London: Continuum, 2005), p. 81; Alexander, p. 96.

33. Charlie Keil, 'American Documentary Finds Its Voice: Persuasion and Expression in *The Plow That Broke the Plains* and *The City*', in Barry K. Grant and Jeanette Sloniowski (eds), *Documenting the Documentary: Close Readings of Documentary Film and Video* (Detroit: Wayne University Press, 1998), p. 120.

34. Robert Snyder, *Pare Lorentz and the Documentary Film* (Norman: University of Oklahoma Press, 1968), p. 27.

35. Ibid., p. 37.

36. Alexander, *Film on the Left*, p. 105.

37. Richard Dyer MacCann, *The People's Films: A Political History of U.S. Government Motion Pictures* (New York: Hastings House, 1973), p. 79.

38. Alexander, *Film on the Left*, p. 99.

39. Quoted in Boger, *People's Lives, Public Images*, pp. 194–5.

40. Alexander, *Film on the Left*, p. 105; Snyder, *Pare Lorentz*, p. 44.

41. Quoted in MacCann, *The People's Films*, p. 81.

42. Ibid., p. 80.

43. Ibid., p. 82.

44. Alexander, *Film on the Left*, p. 108.

45. Ibid.

46. Solokoff was probably the least nationalistic of the project directors, responding to critics that 'simply because a piece of music had an American author did not mean it was to be performed' (Bindas, *All of this Music*, p. 5). Even so, by 1940, FMP orchestras had featured over 7,000 works by more than 2,000 American composers.

47. Quoted in Harris, *Federal Art and National Culture*, pp. 91, 96.

48. Quoted in Bruce Bustard, *A New Deal for the Arts* (Washington, DC: University of Washington Press, 1997), p. 24.

49. Park and Markowitz, *Democratic Vistas*, pp. 11, 14.

50. Marling, *Wall-to-Wall America*, p. 20.

51. Quoted in Park and Markowitz, *Democratic Vistas*, p. 8.

52. Marling, *Wall-to-Wall America*, p. 192.

53. Quoted in Bustard, *A New Deal for the Arts*, p. 34.

54. Harris, *Federal Art and National Culture*, p. 96.

55. Hallie Flanagan, *Arena: The History of the Federal Theater* (New York: Blom, 1965), p. 371.

56. George Kazacoff, *Dangerous Theater: The Federal Theater Project as a Forum for New Plays* (New York: Lang, 1989), pp. 214–17.

57. Jerrold Hirsch, *Portrait of America: A Cultural History of the Federal Writers' Project* (Chapel Hill: University of North Carolina Press, 2003), pp. 133–4.

58. Pamela Bordelon, *Go Gator and Muddy the Water: Writings by Zora Neale Hurston from the Federal Writers Project* (New York: Norton, 1999), pp. 24–5.

59. Quoted in Bold, *The WPA Guides*, p. 30.

60. Quoted in William McDonald, *Federal Relief Administration and the Arts: The Origins and Administrative History of the Arts Projects of the Works Progress Administration* (Columbus: Ohio State University Press, 1969), p. 695.

61. Quoted in Bold, p. 14.

62. See Jane De Hart Mathews, 'Arts and the People: The New Deal Quest for a Cultural Democracy', *Journal of American History* 62.2 (September 1975), 316–39.

63. Marling, *Wall-to-Wall America*, p. 3; Barbara Melosh, 'Images of the 1930s', *Reviews in American History* 13.4 (December 1985), 497.
64. Quoted in Bustard, *A New Deal for the Arts*, p. 21.
65. Kazacoff, *Dangerous Theater*, p. 300.
66. Barbara Melosh, *Engendering Culture: Manhood and Womanhood in New Deal Public Art and Culture* (Washington, DC: Smithsonian Institution Press, 1991), pp. 205, 220.
67. Ibid., p. 204.
68. Ibid., pp. 47, 208.
69. Ibid., p. 214.
70. Bordelon, *Go Gator and Muddy the Water*, p. 29.
71. Ibid.
72. Schindler-Carter, *Vintage Snapshots*, p. 33.
73. Quoted in Schindler-Carter, *Vintage Snapshots*, p. 143.
74. Bold, *The WPA Guides*, p. 134.
75. Bordelon, *Go Gator and Muddy the Water*, pp. 26, 30.
76. Bold, *The WPA Guides*, p. 30.
77. Quoted in Bold, *The WPA Guides*, p. 30.
78. Quoted in Witham, *The Federal Theatre Project*, p. 50.
79. Melosh, *Engendering Culture*, p. 227.
80. Hirsch, *Portrait of America*, p. 150.
81. Evelyn Quita Craig, *Black Drama of the Federal Theater Era: Beyond the Formal Horizons* (Amherst: University of Massachusetts Press, 1980), p. 11.
82. Harris, *Federal Art and National Culture*, p. 62.
83. Hirsch, *Portrait of America*, p. 59.
84. Craig, *Black Drama*, p. 2; Joanna Bentley, *Hallie Flanagan: A Life in the American Theater* (New York: Knopf, 1988), p. 190.
85. Bonnie Nelson Schwartz, *Voices from the Federal Theater* (Madison: University of Wisconsin Press, 2003), p. xii.
86. Elmer Rice, *The Living Theater* (Westport: Greenwood, 1972), p. 150.
87. Quoted in Fraden, *Blueprints for a Black Federal Theatre*, p. 35.
88. Flanagan, *Arena*, p. 119.
89. Bentley, *Hallie Flanagan*, p. 31.
90. Hallie Flanagan, *Shifting Scenes of the Modern European Theatre* (London: Harrap, 1929), p. 98.
91. Quoted in Schwartz, *Voices from the Federal Theatre*, p. xiv.
92. Kazacoff, *Dangerous Theatre*, p. 297.
93. Quoted in Schwartz, *Voices from the Federal Theatre*, p. xiv.
94. Laura Browder, *Rousing the Nation: Radical Culture in Depression America* (Amherst: University of Massachusetts Press, 1998), p. 13.
95. Quoted in Fraden, *Blueprints for a Black Federal Theatre*, p. 38.
96. Bentley, *Hallie Flanagan*, p. 177.
97. Ibid., p. 247.
98. Ibid., p. 340.
99. Ibid., p. 294. The plan is discussed in further detail in Witham, *The Federal Theater Project*, pp. 150–2.
100. John Houseman, *Run-Through: A Memoir* (New York: Simon and Schuster, 1980).

101. John O'Connor and Lorraine Brown, *Free, Adult, Uncensored: The Living History of the Federal Theater Project* (Washington DC: New Republic Books, 1978), p. 26; Richard McKinzie, *The New Deal for Artists* (Princeton: Princeton University Press, 1983), pp. 21–2.
102. Raymond Wilson, 'The Northern Scene', in Ruth Westphal and Janet Blake Dominik (eds), *American Scene Painting: California, 1930s and 1940s* (Irvine: Westphal, 1991), p. 163.
103. Elizabeth Cooper, 'Dances About Spain: Censorship at the Federal Theatre Project', *Theatre Research International*, 29.3 (2004), 241.
104. Mathews, *The Federal Theater*, pp. 122–5.
105. Karen Wilkin, 'Stuart Davis in Philadelphia', *The New Criterion*, 23.8 (April 2005), 44.
106. Marling, *Wall-to-Wall America*, p. 113.
107. Quoted in Marling, *Wall-to-Wall America*, p. 180.
108. Richard McKinzie, *The New Deal for Artists*, (Princeton: Princeton University Press, 1973) p. 71; Marling, *Wall-to-Wall America*, pp. 176–7.
109. Park and Markowitz, *Democratic Vistas*, p. 179.
110. Barry Witham, 'Censorship in the Federal Theatre', *Theatre History Studies* 17 (June 1997), 3.
111. Ibid., p. 5.
112. Ibid., p. 8.
113. Harris, *Federal Art and National Culture*, p. 35.
114. Mathews, *The Federal Theater*, p. 196.
115. Bindas, *All of this Music*, p. 28.
116. Quoted in Schindler-Carter, *Vintage Snapshots*, p. 116.
117. Flanagan, *Arena*, p. 342.
118. Bold, *The WPA Guides*, p. 93.
119. Schindler-Carter, *Vintage Snapshots*, p. 108.
120. McKinzie, *The New Deal for Artists*, p. 86.
121. Ibid., p. 102.
122. Quoted in Schindler-Carter, *Vintage Snapshots*, p. 206.
123. Hirsch, *Portrait of America*, p. 206.
124. Ibid., p. 208.
125. Harris, *Federal Art and National Culture*, p. 125.
126. James Dennis, 'Government Art: Relief, Propaganda, or Public Beautification', *Reviews in American History* 2.2 (June 1974), p. 280.
127. Charles Wolfe, 'The Poetics and Politics of Nonfiction: Documentary Film', in Tino Balio (ed.), *Grand Design: Hollywood as a Modern Business Enterprise, 1930–1939* (Berkeley: University of California Press, 1995), p. 372.
128. Milton Meltzer, *Violins and Shovels: The WPA Projects* (New York: Delacorte, 1976), p. 141.
129. Quoted in Park and Markowitz, *Democratic Vistas*, p. 22.
130. Richard Meyer, *Outlaw Representation: Censorship and Homosexuality in Twentieth-Century American Art* (New York: Oxford University Press, 2002), p. 37.
131. Ibid., p. 44.
132. Quoted in Meyer, *Outlaw Representations*, p. 57.
133. Franklin Einspruch, 'Cadmus's *The Fleet's In!* Still Relevant', *Coral Gable's Gazette*, 12 January 2000, available online at: http://www.einspruch.com.

134. Paul Cadmus, Oral History (March 1988), available online at: http://www.aaa.si.edu/collections/oralhistories/transcripts/cadmus88.htm.

135. George Chauncey, *Gay New York: The Making of the Gay Male World 1880–1940* (London: Flamingo, 1995), p. 64.

136. Einspruch, 'Cadmus's *The Fleet's In!*', n.p.

137. McKinzie, *A New Deal for Artists*, p. 30.

138. Meyer, *Outlaw Representation*, p. 47.

139. Ibid., p. 52,

140. Jonathan Weinberg, *Male Desire: The Homoerotic in American Art* (New York: Abrams, 2004), p. 128.

141. Meyer, *Outlaw Representation*, p. 52.

142. Ibid., p. 47.

143. Weinberg, *Male Desire*, p. 73.

144. Richard Meyer, 'Profile: Paul Cadmus', *Art Journal* 57.3 (Fall 1998), 82.

145. Meyer, *Outlaw Representation*, p. 56.

146. Bustard, *A New Deal for the Arts*, p. 17.

147. Cronbach, 'The New Deal Sculpture Projects', pp. 139–40.

148. Quoted in Michael Szalay, *New Deal Modernism: Literature and the Invention of the Welfare State* (Durham: Duke University Press, 2000), p. 65.

Conclusion

1. David Hanks and Anne Hoy, *American Streamlined Design: The World of Tomorrow* (Paris: Flammarion, 2005), p. 200; Michele Hilmes, *Radio Voices: American Broadcasting 1922–1952* (Minneapolis: University of Minnesota Press, 1997), p. 82.

2. See Philip Orbanes, *Monopoly: the World's Most Famous Game, and How it Got That Way* (New York: DaCapo Press, 2006).

3. See Jeffrey Miron and Kevin Murphy, 'The False Promise of Social Security Privatization' (May 2001). Available at Social Science Research Network: http://www.ssrn.com/abstract=270245.

4. Anthony Badger, *The New Deal: The Depression Years, 1933–1940* (London: Macmillan, 1989), pp. 1–4.

5. Alan Brinkley, *The End of Reform: New Deal Liberalism in Recession and War* (New York: Vintage, 1996), p. 265.

6. Ibid., p. 7.

7. Ibid., p. 224.

8. Lewis Erenberg, 'Things to Come: Swing Bands, Bebop and the Rise of a Postwar Jazz Scene', in Lary May (ed.), *Recasting America: Culture and Politics in the Age of Cold War* (Chicago: University of Chicago Press, 1989), p. 235.

9. Ibid., pp. 236, 238.

10. Jeffrey Meikle, *Design in the USA* (Oxford: Oxford University Press, 2005), p. 133.

11. Ibid., pp. 156, 159.

12. Garth Jowett, *Film: The Democratic Art* (Boston: Little, Brown, 1976), p. 338.

13. Michael Denning, *The Cultural Front: The Laboring of American Culture in the Twentieth Century* (London: Verso, 1998), p. xvii.

14. Daniel Bell, *The End of Ideology* (New York: Macmillan, 1965), p. 300.

15. Graham Barnfield, 'A Reversal of Fortune: *Culture and the Crisis*, Yesterday and Today', (December 2003). Available at *Working Papers on the Web*: http://www.extra.shu.ac.uk/wpw/thirties/thirties%20barnfinal.html.
16. Ibid.
17. Denning, *The Cultural Front*, p. xvi.
18. Gene Ruoff, 'The New Criticism: One Child of the 30s That Grew Up', in Warren French (ed.), *The Thirties: Fiction, Poetry, Drama* (Deland: Everett Edwards, 1967), p. 172.
19. Quoted in Christopher Wilk, *Modernism 1914–1939: Designing a New World* (London: V&A Publications, 2006), p. 13.
20. Erika Doss, 'The Art of Cultural Politics: From Regionalism to Abstract Expressionism', in Lary May (ed.), *Recasting America* (Chicago: University of Chicago Press, 1989), p. 201.
21. Christopher Brookeman, *American Culture and Society Since the 1930s* (London: Macmillan, 1984), p. 191.
22. Ibid., p. 199.
23. Morris Dickstein, 'Copland and American Populism in the 1950s', in Carol Oja and Judith Tick (eds), *Aaron Copland and his World* (Princeton: Princeton University Press, 2005), p. 91.
24. Brookeman, *American Culture and Society*, p. 41.
25. Quoted in Brookeman, *American Culture and Society*, p. 51.
26. Dwight MacDonald, *Against the American Grain* (London: Gollancz, 1963), p. 40.
27. Robert Warshow, 'The Legacy of the 30s', in *The Immediate Experience: Movies, Comics, Theater and other aspects of Popular Culture* (New York: Atheneum, 1962), p. 35. See also Brookeman, *American Culture and Society*, chapter 6.
28. Robert Cantwell, 'When We Were Good: Class and Culture in the Folk Revival', in Neil Rosenberg (ed.), *Transforming Tradition: Folk Music Revivals Examined* (Chicago: University of Illinois Press, 1993), pp. 40, 58.
29. Benjamin Filene, 'O Brother, What Next? Making Sense of the Folk Fad', *Southern Cultures* (Summer 2004), 60.
30. Cantwell, 'When We Were Good', p. 40.
31. Neil Rosenberg (ed.), *Transforming Tradition: Folk Music Revivals Examined* (Chicago: University of Illinois Press, 1993), p. 18.
32. Cantwell, 'When We Were Good', p. 54.
33. John Hersey, 'Introduction: Agee', in James Agee and Walker Evans, *Let Us Now Praise Famous Men* (Boston: Houghton-Mifflin, 1988), p. xxxiii.
34. Quoted in Jeanne Folansbee Quinn, 'Work of Art: Irony and Identification in *Let Us Now Praise Famous Men*', *Novel: A Forum on Fiction*, 35.3 (2001), 362.
35. Robert Brent Toplin, *History By Hollywood: The Use and Abuse of the American Past* (Urbana: University of Chicago Press, 1996), p. 130.
36. Ibid., p. 145.
37. Quoted in Lester Friedman, *Bonnie and Clyde* (London: BFI Film Classics, 2000), p. 8.
38. Robert Newman, quoted in Friedman, *Bonnie and Clyde*, p. 67.
39. Quoted in Lawrence Murray, 'Hollywood, Nihilism, and the Youth Culture of the Sixties: *Bonnie and Clyde* (1967)', in John O'Connor and Martin Jackson (eds), *American History/American Film: Interpreting the Hollywood Image* (New York: Ungar, 1979), p. 249.

40. A copy of the 1965 legislation is available on the NEA website at: http://www.nea.gov/about/Legislation/Legislation.pdf.

41. Quoted in Bonnie Nelson Schwartz, *Voices from the Federal Theater* (Madison: University of Wisconsin Press, 2003), p. xvii.

42. See: http://www.nea.gov/about/Legislation/Legislation.pdf.

43. See: http://www.nea.gov/about/Facts/AtAGlance.html.

44. Andrew Chancey, 'A Sense of Place: NEH Regional Centers', *Organization of American Historians Newsletter*, February 2001, available at: http://www.oah.org/pubs/nl/2001feb/chancey.html; Jerrold Hirsch, *Portrait of America: A Cultural History of the Federal Writers' Project* (Chapel Hill: University of North Carolina Press, 2003), p. 236. Neither project has yet been developed; Ferris's term as chairman of the NEH ended in November 2001 and President George W. Bush's nominee, Bruce Cole, has not pursued them.

45. Peter Bailey, *The Reluctant Film Art of Woody Allen* (Lexington: University Press of Kentucky, 2001), p. 145.

46. David Grimsted, 'The Purple Rose of Popular Culture Theory: An Exploration of Intellectual Kitsch', *American Quarterly* 42.4 (December 1991), 541–78.

47. Bailey, *The Reluctant Film Art*, p. 151.

48. Ibid., p. 151.

49. Ibid., p. 153.

50. Ibid., pp. 151, 156.

51. Grimsted, 'The Purple Rose', p. 565.

52. Christopher Bigsby, *Arthur Miller: A Critical Study* (Cambridge: Cambridge University Press, 2005), pp. 340, 344.

53. Arthur Miller, *Timebends: A Life* (London: Methuen, 1987), p. 71.

54. Susan Abbotson, *Student Companion to Arthur Miller* (Westport: Greenwood, 2000), p. 88.

55. Bigsby, *Arthur Miller*, p. 337.

56. Ibid., p. 330; Abbotson, *Student Companion to Arthur Miller*, p. 89.

57. Abbotson, Student Companion to Arthur Miller, p. 91.

58. Arthur Miller, 'The American Clock', in *Plays: Three* (London: Methuen, 1990), p. 5.

59. Abbotson, *Student Companion to Arthur Miller*, p. 89; Bigsby, *Arthur Miller*, p. 340.

60. Marty Jonas, 'Ambitious, deeply flawed: *Cradle Will Rock*' (January 2000), available at World Socialist website: www.wsws.org.

61. Sean Chadwell, 'Inventing that "Old Timey" Style: Southern Authenticity in *O Brother, Where Art Thou?*', *Journal of Popular Film and Television* 31.1 (2004), 7. See also Martin Harries, 'In the Coen Brothers' new film, the dark, utopian music of the American South', *Chronicle of Higher Education* 47.21 (2 February 2001), B14.

62. Lewis Erenberg, *The Greatest Fight of Our Generation: Louis vs. Schmeling* (New York: Oxford University Press, 2006), p. 160.

63. 'Rediscovering America's Cinderella Man', Film Production Notes, available online at: http://www.cinderellamanmovie.com/index.php.

64. 'The Cinderella Story of James Braddock', available online at: http://www.cinderellamanmovie.com/index.php.

65. David Walsh, 'A Story, not the story of the Depression Years: *Seabiscuit*, written

234 American Culture in the 1930s

and directed by Gary Ross' (August 2003), available at the World Socialist website: www.wsws.org/articles/2003/aug2003/seab-a07_prn.shtml.
66. Graham Barnfield, 'Cultural Depression: *Seabiscuit* and *Dogville* give differing views of 1930s America' (November 2003), available at: http://www.spiked-online.com/Articles/00000006DFB4.htm.
67. Ibid.
68. National Park Service at: http://www.nps.gov/fdrm/.
69. Robert Dallek, 'The Franklin D. Roosevelt Memorial, Washington D.C.', in William Leuchtenberg (ed.), *American Places: Encounters With History* (New York: Oxford University Press, 2000), pp. 73–4.
70. Ibid., p. 73.
71. Ibid., p. 76.
72. Sally Stein, 'The President's Two Bodies: Stagings and Restagings of the New Deal Body Politics', in Alejandro Anreus et al. (eds), *The Social and the Real: Political Art of the 1930s in the Western Hemisphere* (Philadelphia: Pennsylvania State University Press, 2006), p. 287.
73. Ibid., p. 286.
74. Dallek, 'The Franklin D. Roosevelt Memorial', p. 76.

Bibliography

General

Baskerville, Stephen and Ralph Willett (eds), *Nothing Else to Fear: New Perspectives on America in the Thirties* (Manchester: Manchester University Press, 1985).

Browder, Laura, *Rousing the Nation: Radical Culture in Depression America* (Amherst: University of Massachusetts Press, 1998).

Cooney, Terry A., *Balancing Acts: American Thought and Culture in the 1930s* (New York: Twayne, 1995)

Denning, Michael, *The Cultural Front: The Laboring of American Culture in the Twentieth Century* (London: Verso, 1998).

Levine, Lawrence, 'American Culture and the Great Depression', *Yale Review* 74 (January 1985), 196–223.

Levine, Lawrence, 'The Folklore of Industrial Society: Popular Culture and Its Audiences', *The American Historical Review* 97.5 (December 1992), 1369–99.

McDonald, Gail, *American Literature and Culture 1900–1960* (London: Blackwell, 2007).

McElvaine, Robert, *The Great Depression: America, 1929–1941* (New York: Times Books, 1984).

Mullen, Bill and Sherry Lee Linkon (eds), *Radical Revisions: Rereading 1930s Culture* (Urbana: University of Illinois Press, 1996).

Peeler, David, *Hope Among Us Yet: Social Criticism and Social Solace in Depression America* (Athens: University of Georgia Press, 1987).

Stott, William, *Documentary Expression and Thirties America* (Chicago: University of Chicago Press, 1973).

Susman, Warren, *Culture as History: The Transformation of American Society in the Twentieth Century* (New York: Pantheon, 1973).

Intellectual Context

Alexander, Charles, *Nationalism in American Thought, 1930–1945* (Chicago: Rand McNally, 1971).

Alexander, Charles, *Here the Country Lies: Nationalism and the Arts in Twentieth Century America* (Bloomington: Indiana University Press, 1980).

Barnfield, Graham, 'A Reversal of Fortune: *Culture and the Crisis*, Yesterday and

Today' (December 2003) available at *Working Papers on the Web*: http://www.
extra.shu.ac.uk/wpw/thirties/thirties%20barnfinal.html.

Brinkley, Alan, *Voices of Protest: Huey Long, Father Coughlin and the Great
Depression* (New York: Knopf, 1982).

Brinkley, Alan, *The End of Reform: New Deal Liberalism in Recession and War* (New
York: Vintage, 1996).

Brinkley, Alan and Davis Dyer (eds), *The American Presidency* (Boston: Houghton
Mifflin, 2004).

Buhle, Paul, *A Dreamer's Paradise Lost: Louis Fraina/Lewis Corey and the Decline of
Radicalism in the United States* (Atlantic Highlands: Humanity Books, 1995).

Burns, James MacGregor, *Roosevelt: The Lion and the Fox* (New York: Harcourt
Brace, 1956).

Conkin, Paul, *The New Deal* (Arlington: Harlan Davidson, [1967] 1992).

Cowley, Malcolm, *Exile's Return: A Literary Odyssey of the 1920s* (New York:
Penguin, [1934] 1994).

Fried, Albert (ed.), *Communism in America: A History in Documents* (New York:
Columbia University Press, 1997).

Hegeman, Susan, *Patterns for America: Modernism and the Concept of Culture*
(Princeton: Princeton University Press, 1999).

Hickman, Larry and Thomas Alexander (eds), *The Essential Dewey. Volume 1:
Pragmatism, Education, Democracy* (Bloomington: Indiana University Press,
1998).

Janeway, Michael, *The Fall of the House of Roosevelt: Brokers of Ideas and Power from
FDR to LBJ* (New York: Columbia University Press, 2004).

Jennings, Michael (ed.), *Walter Benjamin: Selected Writings. Volume 3 – 1935–1938*
(Cambridge, MA: Harvard University Press, 2002).

Kammen, Michael, *Mystic Chords of Memory: The Transformation of Tradition in
America* (New York: Knopf, 1991).

Kennedy, David, *Freedom from Fear: The American People in Depression and War,
1929–1945* (New York: Oxford University Press, 1999).

Kutlas, Judy, *The Long War: The Intellectual People's Front and Anti-Stalinism 1930–
1940* (Durham: Duke University Press, 1995).

Leikin, Steve, 'The Strange Career of Lawrence Dennis: Race and Far-Right Politics
in the Great Depression' (2007, unpublished conference paper provided by
author).

Miller, Perry, *The New England Mind: The Seventeenth Century* (Cambridge:
Harvard University Press, 1939).

Muresianu, John, *American Intellectuals and the World Crisis, 1938–1945* (New York:
Garland, 1988).

North, Joseph (ed.), *New Masses: An Anthology of the Rebel Thirties* (New York:
International, 1970).

Novack, George, 'American Intellectuals and the Crisis', *New International* 3.1
(February 1936) available at: http://www.marxists.org/archive/novack/1936/02/
x01.htm.

Parrish, Michael, *Anxious Decades: America in Prosperity and Depression, 1920–1941*
(New York: Norton, 1992).

Patterson, James, *America's Struggle Against Poverty 1900–1980* (Cambridge, MA:
Harvard University Press, 1981).

Pells, Richard, *Radical Visions and American Dreams: Culture and Social Thought in the Depression Years* (New York: Harper and Row, 1973).

Roosevelt, Eleanor, *This I Remember* (London: Hutchinson, 1950).

Rourke, Constance, *American Humor: A Study of the National Character* (New York: Harcourt Brace, [1931] 1959).

Rubin, Joan Shelley, *Constance Rourke and American Culture* (Chapel Hill: University of North Carolina Press, 1980).

Salzman, Jack (ed.), *Years of Protest* (Indianapolis: Bobbs-Merrill, 1970).

Shenton, James P., 'The Coughlin Movement and the New Deal', *Political Science Quarterly* 73.3 (September 1958), 352–73.

Steel, Ronald, *Walter Lippmann and the American Century* (New York: Transaction, 1999).

Stone, Albert E., 'Seward Collins and the *American Review*: Experiment in Pro-Fascism, 1933–37', *American Quarterly* 12.1 (Spring 1960), 3–19.

Tugwell, Rexford, *The Industrial Discipline and the Government Arts* (New York: Columbia University Press, 1933).

Zwagerman, Sean, 'Review: *American Humor*', *Journal of Popular Culture* 38.3 (2005), 600–1.

Literature and Drama

Aaron Daniel, *Writers on the Left: Episodes in American Literary Communism* (New York: Harcourt Brace, 1961).

Amer, Robert, ' "The Black, Memorable Year 1929": James Thurber and the Great Depression', *Studies in American Humor* 3.2–3 (1984), 237–52.

Awkward, Michael (ed.), *New Essays on Their Eyes Were Watching God* (Cambridge: Cambridge University Press, 1990).

Bogardus, Ralph and Fred Hobson, *Literature at the Barricades: The American Writer in the 1930s* (Tuscoloosa: University of Alabama Press, 1982).

Burbank, Rex, *Thornton Wilder* (Boston: Twayne, 1978).

Cardullo, Bert, 'Whose Town Is It, Anyway? A Reconsideration of Thornton Wilder's *Our Town*', *CLA Journal* 42.1 (September 1998), 71–86.

Conn, Peter, *Literature in America: An Illustrated History* (Cambridge: Cambridge University Press, 1989).

Filreis, Alan, *Modernism from Right to Left: Wallace Stevens, the Thirties and Literary Radicalism* (Cambridge: Cambridge University Press, 1994).

Foley, Barbara, *Radical Representations: Politics and Form in U.S. Proletarian Fiction, 1929–1941* (Durham: Duke University Press, 1993).

Folsom, Michael (ed.), *Mike Gold: A Literary Anthology* (New York: International Publishers, 1972).

French, Warren, *The Thirties: Fiction, Poetry, Drama* (Deland: Everett Edwards, 1967).

Harwell, Richard, *Gone With the Wind as Book and Film* (Columbia: University of South Carolina Press, 1983).

Hemenway, Robert, *Zora Neale Hurston: A Literary Biography* (London: Camden Press, 1986).

Himelstein, Morgan, *Drama Was a Weapon: The Left Wing Theatre in New York, 1929–1941* (New Brunswick, NJ: Rutgers University Press, 1963).

Horsley, Lee, *The Noir Thriller* (London: Palgrave, 2001).
Hunter, Carol, 'The Historical Context in John Joseph Mathews' *Sundown*', *Melus* 9.1 (Spring 1982), 61–72.
Hurston, Zora Neale, *Their Eyes Were Watching God* (London: Virago, [1937] 2003).
Hyman, Colette, *Staging Strikes: Workers' Theatre and the America Labor Movement* (Philadelphia: Temple University Press, 1997).
Jones, James P, 'Nancy Drew: WASP Super Girl of the 1930s', *Journal of Popular Culture* 6.4 (Spring 1973), 707–17.
King, Richard, *A Southern Renaissance: The Cultural Awakening of the American South, 1930–1955* (New York: Oxford University Press, 1980).
Ludington, Townsend, *John Dos Passos: A Twentieth Century Odyssey* (New York: Dutton, 1980).
Madden, David (ed.), *Nathanael West: The Cheaters and the Cheated* (Deland: Everett, 1973).
Madden, David, *Tough Guy Writers of the Thirties* (Carbondale: Southern Illinois University Press, 1968).
Malmgren, Carl, 'The Crime of the Sign: Dashiell Hammett's Detective Fiction', *Twentieth Century Literature* 45.3 (Fall 1999), 371–84.
Mintner, David, *A Cultural History of the Novel: Henry James to William Faulkner* (Cambridge: Cambridge University Press, 1994).
Nyman, Jopi, *Men Alone: Masculinity, Individualism, and Hard-Boiled Fiction* (Atlanta, Rodopi, 1997).
Rabinowitz, Paula, *Labor and Desire: Women's Revolutionary Fiction in Depression America* (Chapel Hill: University of North Carolina Press, 1991).
Rabkin, Gerald, *Drama as Commitment* (Bloomington: Indiana University Press, 1964).
Railton, Ben, 'What Else Could a Southern Gentleman Do?: Quentin Compson, Rhett Butler, and Miscegenation', *Southern Literary Journal* 35.2 (Spring 2003), 41–63.
Ruland, Richard and Malcolm Bradbury, *From Puritanism to Postmodernism: A History of American Literature* (London: Penguin, 1991).
Schulman, Robert, *The Power of Political Art: The 1930s Literary Left Reconsidered* (Chapel Hill: University of North Carolina Press, 2000).
Siebold, Thomas (ed.), *Readings on 'Our Town'* (San Diego: Greenhaven, 2000).
Singal, Daniel, *William Faulkner: The Making of a Modernist* (Chapel Hill: University of North Carolina Press, 1997).
Smith, Wendy, *Real Life Drama: The Group Theater and America, 1931–1940* (New York: Knopf, 1990).
Swados, Harvey (ed.), *The American Writer and the Great Depression* (Indianapolis: Bobbs-Merrill, 1966).
Wald, Alan, *Exiles From a Future Time: The Forging of the Mid-twentieth Century Literary Left* (Chapel Hill: University of North Carolina Press, 2002).
Wall, Cheryl (ed.), *Zora Neale Hurston's Their Eyes Were Watching God: A Case Book* (Oxford: Oxford University Press, 2000).
Wiget, Andrew, *Native American Literature* (Boston: Twayne, 1985).
Willett, Ralph, *Hard-Boiled Detective Fiction* (Halifax: British Association for American Studies, 1992).
Wyatt, David (ed.), *New Essays on the Grapes of Wrath* (Cambridge: Cambridge University Press, 1990).

Film and Photography

Alexander, William, *Film on the Left: American Documentary Film from 1931 to 1942* (Princeton: Princeton University Press, 1981).

Balio, Tino, *Grand Design: Hollywood as a Modern Business Enterprise, 1930–1939* (Berkeley: University of California Press, 1995).

Belton, John (ed.), *Movies and Mass Culture* (London: Athlone, 1996).

Bergman, Andrew, *We're in the Money: Depression America and its Films* (Chicago: Ivan Dee, 1971).

Black, Gregory, *Hollywood Censored: Morality Codes, Catholics, and the Movies* (Cambridge: Cambridge University Press, 1996).

Buhle, Paul and David Wagner, *Radical Hollywood: The Untold Story Behind America's Favorite Movies* (New York: New Press, 2002).

Cohan, Steven (ed.), *Hollywood Musicals: The Film Reader* (London: Routledge, 2002).

Cohen, Henry (ed.), *The Public Enemy* (Madison: University of Wisconsin Press, 1981).

Custen George, *Twentieth Century's Fox: Darryl F. Zanuck and the Culture of Hollywood* (New York: Basic Books, 1997).

Curry, Romana, 'Mae West as Censored Commodity: The Case of *Klondike Annie*', *Cinema Journal* 31.1 (Fall 1991), 57–84.

Dance, Robert and Bruce Roberston, *Ruth Harriet Louise and Hollywood Glamor Photography* (Berkeley: University of California Press, 2002).

Doherty, Thomas, *Pre-Code Hollywood: Sex, Immorality and Insurrection in American Cinema, 1930–1934* (New York: Columbia University Press, 1999).

Eckert, Charles, 'Shirley Temple and the House of Rockefeller', in *Stardom: Industry of Desire*, Christine Gledhill (ed.) (London: BFI, 1991), pp. 60–73.

Ellis, Jack and Betsy McLane, *A New History of Documentary Film* (London: Continuum, 2005).

Goldberg, Vicki, *Margaret Bourke-White: A Biography* (New York: Harper and Row, 1986).

Grant, Barry Keith and Jeanette Sloniowski (eds), *Documenting the Documentary* (Detroit: Wayne State University Press, 1998).

Hamilton, Marybeth, *'When I'm Bad, I'm Better': Mae West, Sex and American Entertainment* (New York: HarperCollins, 1993).

Henderson, Brian, *Five Screenplays By Preston Sturges* (Berkeley: University of California Press, 1985).

Hendrickson, Paul, *Looking for the Light: The Hidden Life and Art of Marion Post Wolcott* (New York: Knopf, 1989).

Heyman, Therese Thau (ed.), *Seeing Straight: the f/64 Revolution in Photography* (Oakland, CA: Oakland Museum, 1992).

Hine, Lewis, *The Empire State Building* (Munich: Prestel, 1998).

Hove, Arthur (ed.), *Gold Diggers of 1933* (Madison: University of Wisconsin Press, 1980).

Jacobs, Lea, *The Wages of Sin: Censorship and the Fallen Woman Film, 1928–1942* (Madison: University of Wisconsin Press, 1991).

Kendall, Elizabeth, *The Runaway Bride: Hollywood Romantic Comedies of the 1930s* (New York: Knopf, 1990).

Kobal, John, *Art of the Great Hollywood Portrait Photographers, 1925–1940* (New York: Knopf, 1980).

Kozol, Wendy, *LIFE's America: Family and Nation in Postwar Photojournalism* (Philadelphia: Temple University Press, 1994).

Levine, Lawrence, 'Hollywood's Washington: Film Images of National Politics During the Great Depression', in Lawrence Levine, *The Unpredictable Past: Explorations in American Cultural History* (New York: Oxford University Press, 1993), pp. 231–55.

Louvish, Simon, *Monkey Business: The Lives and Legends of the Marx Brothers* (London: Faber and Faber, 1999).

MacDonnell, Frances, 'The Emerald City was the New Deal: E. Y. Harburg and *The Wonderful Wizard of Oz*', *Journal of American Culture* 13.4 (1990), 71–5.

Maland, Charles, *Chaplin and American Culture: The Evolution of a Star Image* (Princeton: Princeton University Press, 1992).

Maltby, Richard, 'More Sinned Against than Sinning: The Fabrications of "Pre-Code Cinema"', *Senses of Cinema* 29 (November 2004) at: http://www.sensesofcinema.com/contents/03/29/pre_code_cinema.html.

Mason, Fran, *American Gangster Cinema: From 'Little Caesar' to 'Pulp Fiction'* (London: Palgrave Macmillan, 2002).

May, Lary, *The Big Tomorrow: Hollywood and the Politics of the American Way* (Chicago: University of Chicago Press, 2000).

McBride, Joseph, *Frank Capra: The Catastrophe of Success* (New York: Faber and Faber, 1992).

McEuen, Melissa, *Seeing America: Women Photographers Between the Wars* (Lexington: University Press of Kentucky, 2000).

Mellen, Joan, *Modern Times* (London: BFI, 2006).

Meltzer, Milton, *Dorothea Lange: A Photographer's Life* (New York: Farrar, Strauss, Giroux, 1978).

Mora, Gilles and John Hill, *Walker Evans: The Hungry Eye* (London: Thames and Hudson, 2004).

Moran, Kathleen and Michael Rogin, '"What's the Matter with Capra?": *Sullivan's Travels* and the Popular Front', *Representations* 71 (Summer 2000), 106–34.

Munby, Jonathan, *Public Enemies, Public Heroes: Screening the Gangster from Little Caesar to Touch of Evil* (Chicago: University of Chicago Press, 1999).

Neve, Brian, *Film and Politics in America: A Social Tradition* (London: Routledge, 1992).

O'Connor, John E. and Martin Jackson (eds), *American History/American Film: Interpreting the Hollywood Image* (New York: Ungar, 1976).

O'Connor, John E. (ed.), *I am a Fugitive from a Chain Gang* (Madison: University of Wisconsin Press, 1981).

Pricola, Jennifer, 'Age of Lost Innocence: Photographs of Childhood Realities and Adult Fears During the Depression' (2003), available at: http://www.xroads.virginia.edu/~MA03/pricola/FSA/index.html.

Rapf, Joanna, '"What Do They Know in Pittsburgh?": American Comic Film in the Great Depression', *Studies in American Humor* 3.2-3 (1984), 187–200.

Rathbone, Belinda, *Walker Evans: A Biography* (New York: Houghton Mifflin, 1995).

Roddick, Nick, *A New Deal in Entertainment: Warner Brothers in the 1930s* (London, BFI, 1983).

Ross, Steven, 'American Workers, American Movies: Historiography and Methodology', *International Labor and Working Class History* 59 (Spring 2001), 81–105.

Rubin, Martin, *Showstoppers: Busby Berkeley and the Tradition of Spectacle* (New York: Columbia University Press, 1993).

Rushdie, Salman, *The Wizard of Oz* (London: BFI, 1992).

Schickel, Richard, *The Disney Version: The Life, Times, Art and Commerce of Walt Disney* (London: Pavilion, 1986).

Shindler, Colin, *Hollywood in Crisis: Cinema and American Society, 1929–1939* (London: Routledge, 1996).

Sklar, Robert and Vito Zagarrio (eds), *Frank Capra: Authorship and the Studio System* (Philadelphia: Temple University Press, 1998).

Snead, James, *White Screens/Black Images: Hollywood from the Dark Side* (New York: Routledge, 1994).

Spaulding, Jonathan, *Ansel Adams and the American Landscape: A Biography* (Berkeley: University of California Press, 1998).

Sundell, Michael G., 'Berenice Abbott's Work in the 1930s', *Prospects* 5 (1980), 269–92.

Thorp, Margaret, *America at the Movies* (New Haven: Yale University Press, 1939).

Trachtenberg, Alan, *Reading American Photographs: Images as History, Mathew Brady to Walker Evans* (New York: Hill and Wang, 1990).

Walsh, Frank, 'The Films We Never Saw: American Movies View Organized Labor, 1934–1954', *Labor History* 27 (1986), 564–80.

Watts, Steven, *The Magic Kingdom: Walt Disney and the American Way of Life* (New York: Houghton Mifflin, 1997).

Wineapple, Brenda, 'Finding an Audience: *Sullivan's Travels*', *Journal of Popular Film and Television* 11 (Winter 1984), 152–7.

Yochelson, Bonnie, *Berenice Abbott: Changing New York* (New York: New Press, 1997).

Music and Radio

Allen, Ray and George Cunningham, 'Cultural Uplift and Double-Consciousness: African-American Responses to the 1935 Opera *Porgy and Bess*', *Music Quarterly* 88.3 (2005), 342–69.

Allen, Ray, 'An American Folk Opera? Triangulating Folkness, Blackness, and Americaness in Gershwin and Heyward's *Porgy and Bess*', *Journal of American Folklore* 117 (2005), 243–61.

Baker, Nancy Kovaleff, 'Abel Meeropol (a.k.a. Lewis Allan): Political Commentator and Social Conscience' *American Music* 20.1 (2002), 25–79.

Barnouw, Erik, *The Golden Web: A History of Broadcasting in the United States: Volume 2 – 1933 to 1953* (New York: Oxford University Press, 1968).

Block, Geoffrey, *Enchanted Evenings: The Broadway Musical from Show Boat to Sondheim* (Oxford: Oxford University Press, 1997).

Brown, Robert, *Manipulating the Ether: The Power of Broadcast Radio in Thirties America* (London: McFarland, 1998).

Callow, Simon, *Orson Welles: The Road to Xanadu* (London: Jonathan Cape, 1995).

Cantril, Hadley, *The Invasion from Mars: A Study in the Psychology of Panic* (Princeton: Princeton University Press, 1940).

Crawford, Richard, 'Where Did *Porgy and Bess* Come From?', *Journal of Interdisciplinary History* 36.4 (2006), 697–734.

Culbert, David, *News for Everyman: Radio and Foreign Affairs in the Thirties* (Westport: Greenwood, 1976).

Ely, Melvin, *The Adventures of Amos 'n' Andy: A Social History of an American Phenomenon* (New York: Free Press, 1991).

Erenberg, Lewis, *Swingin' the Dream: Big Band Jazz and the Rebirth of American Culture* (Chicago: University of Chicago Press, 1998).

Green, Stanley, *Broadway Musicals of the 1930s* (New York: Arlington, 1982).

Havig, Alan, *Fred Allen's Radio Comedy* (Philadelphia: Temple University Press, 1990).

Hilmes, Michele, *Only Connect: A Cultural History of Broadcasting in the United States* (Boston: Wadsworth, 2002).

Hilmes, Michele and Jason Loviglio (eds), *Radio Reader: Essays in the Cultural History of Radio* (London: Routledge, 2002).

Hilmes, Michele, *Radio Voices: American Broadcasting 1922–1952* (Minneapolis: University of Minnesota Press, 1997).

Horn, David, 'Who Loves You Porgy? The Debates Surrounding Gershwin's Musical', in *Approaches to the American Musical*, (ed.) Robert Lawson-Peebles (Exeter: University of Exeter Press, 1996), pp. 109–26.

Horowitz, Joseph, *Understanding Toscanini: How He Became an American Culture-God and Helped Create a New Audience for Old Music* (Minneapolis: University of Minnesota Press, 1988).

Hunter, John O., 'Marc Blitzstein's *The Cradle Will Rock* as a Document of America, 1937', *American Quarterly* 18.2 (1966), 227–33.

Klein, Joe, *Woody Guthrie: A Life* (New York: Random House, 1980).

Knapp, Raymond, *The American Musical and the Formation of National Identity* (Princeton: Princeton University Press, 2005).

Kostelanetz, Richard (ed.), *Aaron Copland: A Reader, Selected Writings 1923–1972* (London: Routledge, 2004).

Levy, Beth, ' "The White Hope of American Music"; or, How Roy Harris Became Western', *American Music* 19.2 (2001), 131–67.

Margolick, David, *Strange Fruit: Billy Holiday, Café Society, and an Early Cry for Civil Rights* (London: Canongate, 2001).

McBrien, William, *Cole Porter: The Definitive Biography* (London: HarperCollins, 1999).

McLeod, Elizabeth, *The Original Amos 'n' Andy: Freeman Gosden, Charles Correll and the 1928–1943 Radio Serial* (London: McFarland, 2005).

Miller, Edward, *Emergency Broadcasting and 1930s American Radio* (Philadelphia: Temple University Press, 2003).

Oja, Carol and Judith Ticks (eds), *Aaron Copland and His World* (Princeton: Princeton University Press, 2005).

Reuss, Richard, 'Woody Guthrie and his Folk Tradition', *Journal of American Folklore* 83 (1970), 273–303.

Reuss, Richard, 'Folk Music and Social Conscience: The Musical Odyssey of Charles Seeger', *Western Folklore* 38.4 (1979), 221–38.

Schuller, Gunther, *The Swing Era: The Development of Jazz, 1930 through 1945* (New York: Oxford University Press, 1989).

Stowe, David, *Swing Changes: Big Band Jazz in New Deal America* (Boston: Harvard University Press, 1994).

Tischler, Barbara, *An American Music: The Search for an American Musical Identity* (New York: Oxford University Press, 1986).

Young, William H. and Nancy Young, *Music of the Great Depression* (Westport: Greenwood, 2005).

Art and Design

Albrecht, Donald, *Designing Dreams: Modern Architecture in the Movies* (London: Thames and Hudson, 1986).

Anderson, Susan M., *Regionalism: The California View, Watercolors 1923–1945* (Santa Barbara: Museum of Art, 1988).

Anreus, Alejandro, Diana Linden and Jonathan Weinberg (eds), *The Social and the Real: Political Art of the 1930s in the Western Hemisphere* (Philadelphia: Pennsylvania State University Press, 2006).

Baigell, Matthew, *The American Scene: American Painting of the 1930s* (New York: Praeger, 1974).

Baigell, Matthew, *Thomas Hart Benton* (New York: Abrams, 1974).

Bayer, Patricia, *Art Deco Interiors: Decoration and Design Classics of the 1920s and 1930s* (London: Thames and Hudson, 1990).

Benton, Thomas Hart, *An Artist in America* (New York: McBride, 1937).

Bush, Donald, *The Streamlined Decade* (New York: Braziller, 1975).

Corn, Wanda, *Grant Wood: The Regionalist Vision* (New Haven: Yale University Press, 1983).

Corn, Wanda, *The Great American Thing: Modern Art and National Identity, 1915–1935* (Berkeley: University of California Press, 1999).

Dennis, James M., *Grant Wood: A Study in American Art and Culture* (New York: Viking Press, 1975).

Doss, Erika, 'New Deal Politics and Regionalist Art: Thomas Hart Benton's *A Social History of the State of Indiana*', *Prospects* 17 (1992), 353–78.

Doss, Erika, *Twentieth-Century American Art* (Oxford: Oxford University Press, 2002).

Douglas, George, *Skyscrapers: A Social History of the Very Tall Building in America* (New York: McFarland, 2004).

Duncan, Alastair, *American Art Deco* (London: Thames and Hudson, 1986).

Eldredge, Charles, *Georgia O'Keeffe: American and Modern* (New Haven: Yale University Press, 1991).

Grief, Martin, *Depression Modern: The Thirties Style in America* (New York: Universe, 1975).

Hanks, David and Hoy, Anne, *American Streamlined Design: The World of Tomorrow* (Paris: Flammarion, 2005).

Haskell, Barbara, *The American Century: Art and Culture, 1900–1950* (New York: Whitney Museum of Art, 1999).

Hemingway, Andrew, 'To "Personalize the Rainpipe": The Critical Mythology of Edward Hopper', *Prospects* 17 (1992), 329–404.

Hemingway, Andrew, *Artists on the Left: American Artists and the Communist Movement, 1926–1952* (New Haven: Yale University Press, 2002).

Hills, Patricia, *Social Concern and Urban Realism: American Painting of the 1930s* (Boston: Boston University Art Gallery, 1983).

Hoffmann, Donald, *Frank Lloyd Wright's Falling Water: The House and Its History* (New York: Dover, 1978).

Kaufman, Edgard (ed.), *The Rise of an American Architecture* (London: Pall Mall Press, 1970).

Kranzfelder, Ivo, *Edward Hopper 1882–1967: Vision of Reality* (Koln: Taschen, 1995).

Langa, Helen, *Radical Art: Printmaking and the Left in 1930s New York* (Berkeley: University of California Press, 2004).

Levin, Gail, *Edward Hopper: The Art and the Artist* (New York: Norton, 1980).

Levine, Neil, *The Architecture of Frank Lloyd Wright* (Princeton: Princeton University Press, 1996)

Lipman, Jonathan, *Frank Lloyd Wright and the Johnson Wax Buildings* (New York: Dover, 2003).

Marling, Karal Ann, 'Joe Jones: Regionalist, Communist, Capitalist', *Journal of Decorative and Propaganda Arts*, 4 (Spring 1987), 46–59.

Marquardt, Virginia, 'Art on the Political Front in America: From *The Liberator* to *Art Front*', *Art Journal* 52.1 (Spring 1993), 72–81.

Meikle, Jeffrey, *Twentieth-Century Limited: Industrial Design in America, 1925–1939* (Philadelphia: Temple University Press, 1979).

Meikle, Jeffrey, *Design in the USA* (Oxford: Oxford University Press, 2005).

Okrent, Daniel, *Great Fortune: The Epic of Rockefeller Center* (New York: Penguin, 2003).

Pulos, Arthur, *The American Design Adventure: 1940–1975* (Cambridge, MA: MIT Press, 1938).

Remington, Roger, *American Modernism: Graphic Design 1920 to 1960* (London: Laurence King, 2003).

Roth, Leland, *American Architecture: A History* (Oxford: Westview Press, 2001).

Schmied, Weiland, *Edward Hopper: Portraits of America* (Munich: Prestel, 1995).

Smith, Kathryn, *Frank Lloyd Wright: America's Master Architect* (New York: Abbeville, 1998).

Stewart, Rick, *Lone Star Regionalism: The Dallas Nine and Their Circle* (Austin: Texas Monthly Press, 1985).

Wagstaff, Sheena (ed.), *Edward Hopper* (London: Tate Publishing, 2004).

Wilk, Christopher (ed.), *Modernism 1914–1939: Designing a New World* (London: V&A Publications, 2006).

Wilkin, Karen, 'Stuart Davis in Philadelphia', *The New Criterion* (April 2005), 42–7.

New Deal Culture

Beckham, Sue Bridwell, *Depression Post Office Murals and Southern Culture: A Gentle Reconstruction* (Baton Rouge: Louisiana State University Press, 1989).

Bentley, Joanna, *Hallie Flanagan: A Life in the American Theatre* (New York: Knopf, 1988).

Bindas, Kenneth, *All of this Music Belongs to the Nation: The WPA's Federal Music Project and American Society* (Knoxville: University of Tennessee Press, 1995).

Blakey, George, *Creating a Hoosier Self-Portrait: The Federal Writers' Project in Indiana* (Bloomington: Indiana University Press, 2005).

Boger, Astrid, *People's Lives, Public Images: The New Deal Documentary Aesthetic* (Tubingen: Gunter Narr Verlag, 2001).

Bold, Christine, *The WPA Guides: Mapping America* (Jackson: University of Mississippi Press, 1999).

Bordelon, Pamela, *Go Gator and Muddy the Water: Writings by Zora Neale Hurston from the Federal Writers Project* (New York: Norton, 1999).

Bustard, Bruce, *A New Deal for the Arts* (Washington DC: University of Washington Press, 1997).

Cooper, Elizabeth, 'Dances About Spain: Censorship at the Federal Theatre Project', *Theatre Research International*, 29.3 (2004), 232–46.

Craig, Evelyn Quita, *Black Drama of the Federal Theater Era: Beyond the Formal Horizons* (Amherst: University of Massachusetts Press, 1980).

Craig, Lois, *The Federal Presence: Architecture, Politics and Symbols in United States Government Buildings* (Cambridge: MIT Press, 1978).

Curtis, James, *Mind's Eye, Mind's Truth: FSA Photography Reconsidered* (Philadelphia: Temple University Press, 1989).

Daniel, Peter, *Official Images: New Deal Photography* (Washington, DC: Smithsonian Institution Press, 1987).

Flanagan, Hallie, *Arena: The History of the Federal Theater* (New York: Blom, 1965).

Fox, Daniel, 'The Achievement of the Federal Writers' Project', *American Quarterly* 13.1 (Spring 1961), 3–19.

Fraden, Rena, *Blueprints for a Black Federal Theatre, 1933–1939* (Cambridge: Cambridge University Press, 1994).

Gibson, Lisanne, 'Managing the People: Art Programs in the American Depression', *Journal of Arts Management, Law and Society* 31.4 (Winter 2002), 279–91.

Harris, Jonathan, *Federal Art and National Culture: The Politics of Identity in New Deal America* (Cambridge: Cambridge University Press, 1995).

Hirsch, Jerrold, *Portrait of America: A Cultural History of the Federal Writers Project* (Chapel Hill: University of North Carolina Press, 2003).

Jones, Alfred Haworth, 'The Search for a Usable Past in the New Deal Era', *American Quarterly* 23.5 (December 1971), 710–24.

Kazacoff, George, *Dangerous Theater: The Federal Theater Project as a Forum for New Plays* (New York: Lang, 1989).

Linden, Diana, 'Ben Shahn's New Deal Murals: Jewish Identity in the American Scene', in *The Social and the Real: Political Art of the 1930s in the Western Hemisphere*, (eds) Alejandro Anreus et al. (Philadelphia: Pennsylvania State University Press, 2006), pp. 241–60.

Lorentz, Pare, *FDR's Moviemaker: Memoirs and Scripts* (Reno: University of Nevada Press, 1992).

MacCann, Richard Dyer, *The People's Films: A Political History of U.S. Government Motion Pictures* (New York: Hastings House, 1973).

Mangione, Jerre, *The Dream and the Deal: The Federal Writers' Project, 1935–1943* (Boston: Little, Brown, 1972).

Marling, Karal Ann, *Wall-to-Wall America: Post Office Murals in the Great Depression* (Minneapolis: University of Minnesota Press, 2000).

Mathews, Jane De Hart, *The Federal Theatre: Plays, Relief and Politics* (Princeton: Princeton University Press, 1967).

Mathews, Jane De Hart, 'Arts and the People: The New Deal Quest for a Cultural Democracy', *Journal of American History* (September 1975), 316–39.

McDonald, William, *Federal Relief Administration and the Arts* (Columbus: Ohio State University Press, 1969).

McKinzie, Richard, *The New Deal for Artists* (Princeton: Princeton University Press, 1973).

Melosh, Barbara, *Engendering Culture: Manhood and Womanhood in New Deal Public Art and Culture* (Washington DC: Smithsonian Institution Press, 1991).

Meltzer, Milton, *Violins and Shovels: The WPA Arts Projects* (New York: Delacorte, 1976).

Meyer, Richard, 'Profile: Paul Cadmus', *Art Journal* 57.3 (Fall 1998), 80–4.

Meyer, Richard, *Outlaw Representation: Censorship and Homosexuality in Twentieth-Century American Art* (New York: Oxford University Press, 2002).

Nadler, Paul, 'Liberty Censored: Black Living Newspapers of the Federal Theater Project', *African American Review* 29.4 (1995), 615–22.

O'Connor, Francis (ed.), *The New Deal Art Projects: An Anthology of Memoirs* (Washington, DC: Smithsonian Institution Press, 1972).

O'Connor, Francis (ed.), *Art for the Millions: Essays from the 1930s by Artists and Administrators of the WPA Federal Art Project* (Boston: New York Graphic Society, 1975).

O'Connor, John and Lorraine Brown, *Free, Adult, Uncensored: The Living History of the Federal Theater Project* (Washington, DC: New Republic Books, 1978).

Park, Marlene and Gerald Markowitz, *Democratic Vistas: Post Office and Public Art in the New Deal* (Philadelphia: Temple University Press, 1985).

Penkower, Monte, *The Federal Writers' Project: A Study in Government Patronage of the Arts* (Urbana: University of Illinois Press, 1977).

Schindler-Carter, Petra, *Vintage Snapshots: The Fabrication of a Nation in the WPA American Guide Series* (New York: Lang, 1999).

Schwartz, Bonnie Nelson, *Voices from the Federal Theater* (Madison: University of Wisconsin Press, 2003).

Snyder, Robert, *Pare Lorentz and the Documentary Film* (Norman: University of Oklahoma Press, 1968).

Sporn, Paul, *Against Itself: The Federal Theater and Writers' Projects in the Midwest* (Detroit: Wayne State University Press, 1995)

Stryker, Roy and Nancy Wood, *In This Proud Land: America, 1935–1943 as Seen in the FSA Photographs* (Greenwich: New York Graphic Society, 1973).

Szalay, Michael, *New Deal Modernism: Literature and the Invention of the Welfare State* (Durham: Duke University Press, 2000).

Weinberg, Jonathan, *Male Desire: The Homoerotic in American Art* (New York: Abrams, 2004), p. 73.

Witham, Barry, 'Censorship in the Federal Theatre', *Theater History Studies* 17 (June 1997), 3–15.

Witham, Barry, *The Federal Theatre Project: A Case Study* (Cambridge: Cambridge University Press, 2003).

Legacy of the 1930s

Abbotson, Susan, *Student Companion to Arthur Miller* (Westport: Greenwood, 2000).

Bailey, Peter, *The Reluctant Film Art of Woody Allen* (Lexington: University Press of Kentucky, 2001).

Barnfield, Graham, 'A Reversal of Fortune: *Culture and the Crisis*, Yesterday and Today' (December 2003). Available at *Working Papers on the Web*: http://www. extra.shu.ac.uk/wpw/thirties/thirties%20barnfinal.html.

Bell, Daniel Bell, *The End of Ideology* (New York: Macmillan, 1965).

Bigsby, Christopher, *The Cambridge History of American Theatre* (Cambridge: Cambridge University Press, 1999).

Bigsby, Christopher, *Arthur Miller: A Critical Study* (Cambridge: Cambridge University Press, 2005).

Black, Allida, 'Struggling with Icons: Memorializing Franklin and Eleanor Roosevelt', *The Public Historian* 21.1 (1999), 63–72.

Brookeman, Christopher, *American Culture and Society Since the 1930s* (London: Macmillan, 1984).

Chadwell, Sean, 'Inventing that "Old Timey" Style: Southern Authenticity in *O Brother, Where Art Thou?*', *Journal of Popular Film and Television* 32.1 (2004), 3–9.

Dallek, Robert, 'The Franklin D. Roosevelt Memorial, Washington D. C.', in *American Places: Encounters With History*, (ed.) William Leuchtenberg (New York: Oxford University Press, 2000), 70–7.

Doss, Erika, *Benton, Pollock and the Politics of Modernism: From Regionalism to Abstract Expressionism* (Chicago: University of Chicago Press, 1995).

Ekirsch, Arthur, *Ideologies and Utopias: The Impact of the New Deal Upon American Thought* (Chicago: Quadrangle, 1971).

Erenberg, Lewis, 'Things to Come: Swing Bands, Bebop and the Rise of a Postwar Jazz Scene', in *Recasting America: Culture and Politics in the Age of Cold War*, (ed.) Lary May (Chicago: University of Chicago Press, 1989), pp. 221–45.

Eyerman, Ron and Scott Barretta, 'From the 30s to the 60s: The Folk Music Revival in the United States', *Theory and Society* 25.4 (1996), 501–43.

Filene, Benjamin, 'O Brother, What Next? Making Sense of the Folk Fad', *Southern Cultures* 10.2 (Summer 2004), 50–69.

Friedman, Lester, *Bonnie and Clyde* (London: BFI Film Classics, 2000).

Grimsted, David, 'The Purple Rose of Popular Culture Theory: An Exploration of Intellectual Kitsch', *American Quarterly* 42.4 (December 1991), 541–78.

Kazin, Alfred, *On Native Grounds: An Interpretation of Modern American Prose Literature* (New York: Reynal and Hitchcock, 1942).

Leuchtenberg, William, *In the Shadow of FDR: From Harry Truman to George W. Bush* (Ithaca: Cornell University Press, 2001).

Lyons, Eugene, *The Red Decade: The Stalinist Penetration of America* (Indianapolis: Bobbs-Merrill, 1941).

Macdonald, Dwight, *Against the American Grain* (London: Gollancz, 1963), p. 40.

Miller, Arthur, *Timebends: A Life* (London: Methuen, 1987).

Orbanes, Philip, *Monopoly: the World's Most Famous Game, and How it Got That Way* (New York: DaCapo Press, 2006).

Rosenberg, Neil (ed.), *Transforming Tradition: Folk Music Revivals Examined* (Chicago: University of Illinois Press, 1993).

Rozell, Mark and William Pederson (eds), *FDR and the Modern Presidency: Leadership and Legacy* (Westport: Praeger, 1997).

Stein, Sally, 'The President's Two Bodies: Stagings and Restagings of the New Deal Body Politics', in *The Social and the Real: Political Art of the 1930s in the Western*

Hemisphere, (eds) Alejandro Anreus et al. (Philadelphia: Pennsylvania State University Press, 2006), 283–310.

Toplin, Robert Brent, *History By Hollywood: The Use and Abuse of the American Past* (Urbana: University of Chicago Press, 1996).

Warshow, Robert, 'The Legacy of the 30s', in *The Immediate Experience: Movies, Comics, Theater and other aspects of Popular Culture* (New York: Atheneum, 1962).

Wilson, Edmund, *The Shores of Light: A Literary Chronicle of the 1920s and 1930s* (London: Allen, 1952).

Audio-Visual and Internet Resources

'America in the 1930s' at: http://www.xroads.virginia.edu/~1930s/front.html. Includes material from newsreels, photographs, radio productions, films and hyper-text editions of cultural texts from the decade.

Gellert, Hugo, *Karl Marx's 'Capital' in Lithographs*. Hypertext edition online at: Graphic Witness: http://www.graphicwitness.org/contemp/marxtitle.htm.

Library of Congress, Manuscript Division, 'American Life Histories: Manuscripts from the Federal Writers' Project, 1936–1940'. Online access at: www.memory.loc.gov/ammem/wpaintro/wpahome.html.

McCain, Andrew, 'Audiohistory: An Experiential Model for Teaching 30s Era American Culture'. Includes an audio re-enactment of the Federal Theatre Project's *Triple A-Plowed Under*. Online at: http://www.xroads.virginia.edu/~MA04/mccain/audiohist/intro.htm.

Mercury Theatre on the Air at: http://www.mercurytheatre.info/. Includes mp3 download of Orson Welles's *War of the Worlds* broadcast.

Museum of the City of New York, Berenice Abbott's *Changing New York*. Online exhibition at: http://www.mcny.org/collections/abbott/abbott.htm.

New Deal Network, online at: http://www.newdeal.feri.org/index.htm. Includes photo gallery and document library.

RUSC.com operates (by subscription service) an archive 'old time radio', including many programmes from the 1930s such as *Amos 'n' Andy*.

Index